HENRY VII

BY

GLADYS TEMPERLEY

FELLOW OF NEWNHAM COLLEGE, CAMBRIDGE

WITH AN INTRODUCTION BY
JAMES T. SHOTWELL

ILLUSTRATED

GREENWOOD PRESS, PUBLISHERS
WESTPORT, CONNECTICUT

HENRY VII

1457—1509
From the Picture in the National Portrait Gallery, painted in 1505 by an unknown
Flemish artist

Originally published in 1914
by Houghton Mifflin Company, Boston and New York

First Greenwood Reprinting 1971

Library of Congress Catalogue Card Number 75-110871

SBN 8371-4550-3

Printed in the United States of America

CONTENTS

APPENDICES

CONTENTS

ILLUSTRATIONS

ILLUSTRATIONS

INTRODUCTION [1]

A HISTORY of England through the biographies of her kings naturally suggests something vastly different from the contents of these volumes. It brings up visions of the pageantry of courts and the pomp and circumstance of royalty. It recalls those well-worn classics of an earlier generation which fed our youth with the romance of the unreal part of reality. But there is little here of Miss Strickland or the mere gossip of courtly circles. There is romance still, but its charm is of another kind, the charm of discovery mainly; for the theme of these biographies is royalty at work rather than on display. This is a side of kingly life which seldom is mentioned in the courtly chronicle, and when told from the outside is too likely to come from unsympathetic hands, so that the monarch generally stands out in our histories as either a do-nothing king leading a life of vast self-indulgence, or as a meddler with a bent toward tyranny. Both pictures are false, as are all general categories in the portrayal of life, but of the two the former is most misleading. Kings have been more than masters of idleness. Few careers have been more strenuous than theirs. One can pick out the idle kings throughout the centuries; they are notorious in any monarchy. Whenever the king is weak the fact is attested before the whole world, either by the rise of a great vizier, a Richelieu or a Walpole, or by the vicious intrigues of the courtesan and the anarchy of state and government. A king is born to his title; but he must work to make the title real. The court of Louis XIV was the model to Europe for the display of idleness, and yet the king worked secretly, behind the scenes, like any impressario, rising early, so it was said, for the transaction of pressing business of state with his ministers, and then retiring for the formal ceremony of a royal *levée*, so that he might pass the day with the becoming semblance of a *roi fainéant*. The palace of his more magnificent successor Napoleon was merely a workshop furnished with imperial elegance. Of course he, as an adventurer, had to work for his living; but the cost of power has always been its constant exercise, and no legitimist who lays it by can rely upon the deeds of his ancestors to secure recognition for himself in the page of history.

The story of the kings at work is novel. The result is a new appreciation both of the kings and of the institution of royalty. Take for instance Henry VII. What a colorless figure he used to be in the older histories! His victory over the shrewd Richard III was a foregone conclusion to those who knew of Gloucester only through the plays of Shakespeare or the haunting juvenile stories of the princes murdered in the tower. His marriage with the Yorkist princess placed the crown easily within his reach, and once the kingdom was his, he developed a most unlovely character, jealous of his wife and miserly in money matters. His reign was presented as one of practical stagnation, like a quiet interval before the stir and movement of Henry VIII. Such was the view of Henry VII so long as royalty was judged by the superficial standards of the courtly or constitutional historian. A king who suppressed retainers and led the sober life of a hard-headed practical man, cut a poor figure, considering his achievements, in the story of England. More recently, however, historical research has gone beneath the surface and revealed the strong, if sober, character of the first of the Tudors. The unlovely elements are still there, but we realize now that the miserly hoarding was directed towards statesman-like ends, in accordance with the ideas of his time; that the transformation of England under his reign was one of the most vital changes in its whole history, and that the strong hand of the monarch kept the nation on the lines of a national policy which made possible the great age of Elizabeth. In short, historians are coming to recognize in this stern, unsympathetic and apparently timidly conservative king a telling force in the creation of modern England.

But, it will be objected, this is a false "interpretation" of history. An attempt to read the story of a nation's evolution through the biographies of its kings, is something we have long since given up. It belongs to the days of Carlyle's hero worship, and, farther back, to the philosophy of a Bossuet and the foolish talk of a James I on the divine kingship. This biographical survey is a strange enterprise in an era of democracy when history is written in terms of "the sovereign people," and the world of business arranges the fate of nations on an impersonal basis. Royalty seems to us a shadow or an ornament in a world where shadows and ornaments count for little. The occupant of a throne seems to us — in theory — almost a grotesque character, and in our happy confidence in the efficiency of republican institutions, those of us who have not married into the European nobility or have not been presented at court, are properly scornful of such an outworn symbol of tyranny as kings or queens. And as our histories always tend to reflect our major interests, we have been remaking the story of an undemocratic past to correspond with our outlook into the present. In the latter half of the nineteenth century when the mass of the nation was winning the victory for constitutional government, Stubbs supplied the story of that framework of courts and parliament which was the nation's heritage, and Freeman and Green traced the human story of the nation itself. In the opening of the twentieth century the new democracy has come to that self-consciousness which the middle class achieved a century or so before, and now it is looking back to the history of village laborers, of peasant insurrections, enclosures of common lands, and all the homely and intimate detail of daily life. The movement, just setting in, is of vast significance and magnificent possibilities. No one to whom the word "history" has any real meaning, whose imagination stirs at its suggestions of tales yet untold as well as at its achievements in its joint field of art and science, can fail to extend a welcome to the new histories of democracy, and the exploration of the economics and industries of the past. But it is easy, in our enthusiastic approval of the new arrivals, to lose our own perspective, and to imagine that the obscure paths of social movement which they trace in distant centuries were the only roads that lead to modern times. In short, the *Zeitgeist* is upon us; the spirit of our time distorts the view of any other.

There is something, after all, in heroes. Carlyle's gospel, preached to unheeding ears, had more truth in it than we like to admit. The strong man, or the man who holds the post of power, is more than a single unit in the great multiples of society. This is still the case in our democracies; we know it and are glad to recognize it to the full

in the laudation of our candidates for public office as well as in our
laws to curb the activity of unscrupulous "captains of industry."
Half the problems of democracy are due to the need of vigilance
against the possible agression of those "in power." It was in this
connection that Mr. Bryce, in an address delivered at Washington a
few years ago, uttered a significant warning to political theorists.[1]
Speaking from the full experience of a long life in public affairs, he
said that he had never known a country that was not really governed
by a little group of some half-dozen men, adding, though in guarded
phrase, that few people even in a democracy, had any idea of how
completely this small group of men were dominating the country.

If such is the case in a democracy and in a country of general
enlightenment, how much more has it been true of all the past. The
pomp of royalty is not something merely extraneous to society, but
the outward sign of its most definite and lasting seat of power. One
does not need to go back to anthropology, and follow the rich fields
of scholarship opened up by Dr. Frazer,[2] as he traces the kingship
back to its priestly and then its divine prototypes, in order to realize
the dominant rôle of royalty in the past. For the king has been warrior as well as priest, and has laid the basis for the national state by
conquest and the rule of the sword. So, the Conqueror re-made
England, and the Capetians welded together France. It would be
an absurd distortion of history which would eliminate these master
forces from its processes because their power is now transferred to
other hands. A history of the past with the kings suppressed would
be not less false and more grotesque than one in which the kings
alone receive the credit for the joint work of king and people. History must be written historically and not as a pamphlet to justify
the present by the past.

We are accustomed to think of the King of England as being
shorn of all authority. And recent events in the English Parliament
tend to impress this view still more upon us. But in the theoretical

---

[1] The presidential address of the American Association for Political Science, Christmas, 1908. This remark was not printed in the text of the speech
as printed in the *Proceedings*.

[2] Cf. *Lectures on the Early History of the Kinship*, and much of *The Golden
Bough*.

powers which are his still, one may catch the reflection even in this present age of the vast scope of his office in the centuries when the king ruled as well as reigned. It may be fitting to sum these up in the words of Mr. Gladstone, written to present to American readers some idea of the machinery of the British Constitution. After speaking of the functions of the ministry, Mr. Gladstone thus summarizes the position of the Crown in the nineteenth century:[1] —

"The sovereign in England is the symbol of the nation's unity, and the apex of the social structure; the maker (with advice) of the laws; the supreme governor of the Church; the fountain of justice; the sole source of honor; the person to whom all military, all naval, all civil service is rendered. The sovereign owns very large properties; receives and holds, in law, the entire revenue of the state; appoints and dismisses ministers; makes treaties; pardons crime, or abates its punishment; wages war, or concludes peace; summons and dissolves the Parliament; exercises these vast powers for the most part without any specified restraint of law; and yet enjoys, in regard to these and every other function, an absolute immunity from consequences. There is no provision in the law of the United Empire, or in the machinery of the Constitution, for calling the sovereign to account; and only in one solitary and improbable but perfectly defined case — that of his submitting to the jurisdiction of the Pope — is he deprived by statute of the throne. Setting aside that peculiar exception, the offspring of a necessity still freshly felt when it was made, the Constitution might seem to be founded on the belief of a real infallibility of its head. Less, at any rate, cannot be said than this. Regal right has, since the Revolution of 1688, been expressly founded upon contract; and the breach of that contract destroys the title to the allegiance of the subject. But no provision, other than the general rule of hereditary succession, is made to meet either this case or any other form of political miscarriage or misdeed. It seems as though the genius of the nation would not stain its lips by so much as the mere utterance of such a word; nor can we put this state of facts into language more justly than by saying that the Constitution would regard the default of the monarch

[1] In an article entitled "Kin beyond the Sea," in the *North American Review*, vol. cxxvii (1878), pp. 196.

with his heirs as the chaos of the state, and would simply trust to the inherent energies of the several orders of society for its legal reconstruction."

This is, in theory, the position of kingship as it stands at present in the British Constitution. The theory, of course, is nullified by the single fact that Parliament holds the power of the purse — the final sovereign power in any land. But the theory of the British Constitution is not like most other political theories; it is not a creation of theorists but the embodiment of history. Every power of royalty in this tremendous total was once exercised by English kings. The story of how those powers were won, used — and lost, is more than the incidental side of history; and, since democracy aspires less to destroy than to appropriate the attributes of sovereignty, it can find in the biographies of these kings, whose power it now assumes, a chapter of its own adoptive past!

Of the powers of the Crown of England, only a shadow is left. But the kingship itself is much more than a shadow. Such is the force of long tradition, the reverence for the past, the love of pageantry and — not least — the pride in a royal and imperial name, that the king still remains, in spite of all the age-long struggle against his claims, the living sign of the nation's unity. No bald words or abstract phrases such as love of country, liberty, equality, fraternity, can quite match, in a genuine British breast, the appeal to loyalty for the sovereign. Kipling has given expression to this feeling with especial force, and however much a lover of peace may object to its possibilities of insular belligerency, it must be reckoned with as a vital element in the maintenance not only of the Crown, but of the empire itself. For, whether it is the "Widow at Windsor" or the "Sailor King," the British soldier and sailor will give their lives as readily now for the exalted head of the empire, as when the monarch really ruled. It is not power but sentiment which holds the allegiance of the nation to-day; but the sentiment thrills with the sense of all the glory of England's past and with the common consciousness of a world-empire concentrating its attention upon the symbol of its own greatness.

J. T. SHOTWELL.

HENRY VII

HENRY VII

CHAPTER I

EARLY LIFE

HENRY TUDOR was born at Pembroke Castle on 28th January 1456–7. England was still torn by the last violent years of the Wars of the Roses, and Margaret, widow of Edmund Tudor, was living at Pembroke Castle under the protection of her brother-in-law, Jasper, Earl of Pembroke. There, three months after her husband's death, she gave birth to her son Henry, Earl of Richmond, afterwards Henry VII. A small room in the east end of a tower on the northern wall of the fortress, which in Leland's time contained a " chymmeney new made with the arms and badges of King Henry VII.," is still shown as Henry's birthplace.[1] The babe came of an illus-

[1] The exact date of Henry's birth is not beyond dispute owing to the contradictory statements made by Bernard André, Henry's biographer. He states that he was born on " Februarii kalend. decimo septimo " (16th January), on the feast of St. Agnes the Second (28th January): *Memorials of Henry VII.* (Rolls Ser.); André, *Vita*, p. 12. The latter date has been generally adopted, as André was probably more familiar with the saints' days than with the Roman calendar. Many years after, Henry's mother, writing " on the day of Seynt Anne's," referred to it as the day of his birth, but this difficulty has been overcome by the suggestion that she wrote " Seynt Anne's " inadvertently for " St. Agnes'." W. Busch, *England under the Tudors* (Eng. trans.), p. 220; *Letters and Papers of Richard III. and Henry VII.* (ed. Gairdner) (Rolls Ser.), i. 422–3.

trious race. His mother was of the House of
Plantagenet, by descent from John of Gaunt through
his union with Katherine Swynford, whose descendants the Beauforts had been declared legitimate by
Act of Parliament in the reign of Richard II. On
the death of her father, the Duke of Somerset, in
1444, she had inherited a share in the vast lands of
the Beauforts. She had married Edmund Tudor at
a very early age, and at the time of her son's birth
was not quite fourteen years old. Edmund, Earl
of Richmond, traced his descent, on his father's
side, back to Cadwallader and the ancient kings of
Britain, and through his mother Katherine, widow of
Henry V., was allied to the royal blood of France.
The young Earl of Richmond inherited, therefore, a
threefold claim to royal descent.[1]

Henry's first years were spent at Pembroke Castle
under his uncle's care. Before he was four years old
his mother had married, as her second husband,
Henry, Lord Stafford, a younger son of the Duke
of Buckingham. At the accession of Edward IV.,
Henry Tudor was attainted, the honour of Richmond
being granted to the king's brother George, Duke of
Clarence. The Earl of Pembroke was attainted at
the same time, but in spite of this the boy remained
for a while in safety at Pembroke Castle, which stood
for the House of Lancaster long after the rest of
England had submitted to Edward IV., and, on its
fall, was transferred to Harlech Castle. His education
was begun by Andreas Scotus, and Hasely, Dean of
Warwick. Owing to his delicacy he was taken about

---

[1] Henry's shield bore the arms of France and England quarterly,
within a border azure, charged alternately with fleurs-de-lys and
martlets or, his father having abandoned the old arms of Tudor.

from place to place for change of air, but Bernard
André later declared, in his courtly way, that the
boy showed himself remarkably quick and brilliant.[1]
This comparatively peaceful time was interrupted by
the capture of Harlech Castle by William, Lord
Herbert, in 1466.   Henry fell into the hands of the
victor, who was rewarded with the title of the Earl
of Pembroke and given the wardship of the young
Earl of Richmond.   He intended to marry the latter
to his daughter Maud, but a year later he was killed
at Banbury.   A brief gleam of Lancastrian success
followed.   Richmond was restored to the keeping of
the Earl of Pembroke, who was one of the first to
welcome Henry VI. at his restoration.   He presented
his young kinsman to the king, this being the occasion
of the frequently repeated though probably apocryphal
prophecy concerning the boy's future, which appears
in *Henry VI.* :—

> " His looks are full of peaceful majesty,
>   His head by nature framed to wear a crown,
>   His hand to wield a sceptre, and himself
>   Likely in time to bless a regal throne." [2]

According to Bernard André, the king advised
that the boy should be sent abroad to escape the
malice of his enemies.   The defeat of the Lancastrians
at the battle of Tewkesbury in 1471, followed by the
deaths of the Prince of Wales and of Henry VI.,
made the Lancastrian cause seem hopeless.   Even
Wales was no longer safe.   Earl Jasper, at the request
of the boy's mother, embarked with his nephew on
a vessel bound for France.   The ship was driven out

---

[1] André said he had heard this directly from Scotus.   *Vita,* p. 13.
[2] *Henry VI.,* Part III., Act iv., Sc. 6; *Vita,* p. 14.

of its course by storms, and the fugitives were landed on the coast of Brittany, which was then ruled by Duke Francis. He received them hospitably, policy suggesting that he had in his hands a possible means of buying the alliance of England against his threatening neighbour France. Bernard André, however, puts into the duke's mouth a speech which suggests that he was induced to help by the boy's appearance and " evident good qualities." The duke certainly made good his promises of protection, and Henry remained in safety in Brittany in spite of the untiring efforts of Edward IV. to obtain his surrender. At one time he was in very great danger. An embassy from Edward IV. persuaded Duke Francis that the king intended to marry the young earl to one of his own daughters. He surrendered Henry to the envoys, who had reached St. Malo, *en route* for England, when they were detained there by a force sent by the duke, which conveyed Henry into sanctuary and refused to give him up. He remained in Brittany more closely guarded until the death of Edward IV His mother remained in England, and in 1482, on the death of Henry Stafford, had married, as her third husband, Thomas, Lord Stanley, a prominent Yorkist and the steward of King Edward's household. He gained the favour of Richard III., and his wife enjoyed a position of security and was even prominent at Court.[1]

Meanwhile many Lancastrian exiles, driven from England by the tyranny of Richard III., began to gather round Richmond, who was released from restraint on the death of Edward IV. Even in

[1] She actually held the queen's train at the coronation of Richard III.

England a party was being formed in his favour.
The Duke of Buckingham, though mainly instru-
mental in gaining the throne for Richard III., had
retired in dissatisfaction from the Court. The cause
of his defection is uncertain, but it may well have
been disgust at the king's violence, working upon
thwarted ambition. Some very curious stories are
told of the way in which he was induced to give up
his design of winning the throne for himself for a
plan which involved the elevation of the exiled earl.
According to the chroniclers, Hall and Grafton,[1] the
duke discussed his plans fully with the Lancastrian
John Morton, Bishop of Ely, then a prisoner in the
duke's custody, who cleverly inflamed his discontent.
The story goes that the duke had quite forgotten
the superior claims of the Countess of Richmond and
her son, until, riding between Worcester and Bridg-
north, he met the former, and it flashed into his
mind that " she and her son, the Earl of Richmond,
be bothe bulwarcke and portecolice betwene me and
the gate to entre into the majestie royall and gettynge
of the crowne." The Countess of Richmond sounded
Buckingham with regard to her son's claims, and
mentioned the fact that a marriage between the latter
and one of the daughters of Edward IV. had been
proposed. Though the duke returned an evasive
answer at the time, he subsequently told Morton
that if Richmond bound himself to such a marriage,
he would be prepared to help him to the crown of
England as heir of the House of Lancaster. This
was a great triumph. By the advice of Morton,
whose influence seems to have settled many of the

---

[1] Their accounts are founded on the *Life of Richard III.* by
Sir Thomas More, pp. 88–91.

details of the conspiracy, Richard Bray (steward of
the household to the Countess of Richmond) was
summoned to Wales, and despatched thence with
orders to advise his mistress to gain the consent of
Elizabeth, the queen-dowager, widow of Edward IV.,
to the proposed alliance, and then to communicate
the plan to Richmond in Brittany.

Bray started on his mission but found that part
of the scheme was already accomplished, the
Countess of Richmond having approached Elizabeth
in the matter.[1] The queen-dowager was then in
sanctuary at Westminster with her daughter, surrounded by the king's guards. The disappearance
of her two sons was still a mystery and their tragic
fate unknown, but her position seemed hopeless.
Elizabeth was a fickle, wayward woman, ever ready
to dabble in conspiracy, and the countess's emissary
Lewis easily won her over to a plan which offered a
hope of Richard's overthrow. They were about to
send news of the scheme to Brittany when Bray
arrived with proofs that the Duke of Buckingham
was considering a similar plan. Two messengers,
Hugh Conway and Thomas Ramme, were sent to
Henry by different routes, with orders to acquaint
him with the conspiracy, supply him with funds, and
advise him to return as soon as possible and land in
Wales, " where he shoulde not doubte to fynde both
aide and comforte and frendes."

The messengers arrived in Brittany on the same

---

[1] On this point Polydor Vergil and Hall disagree. The account
in the text is derived from the former, who, as a contemporary,
is the best authority for the reign. Dr. Busch has made it clear
that the whole scheme originated with Margaret. Pol. Verg.,
Anglicæ Historiæ Libri (1555 edition), lib. xxvi., p. 550; Hall,
Chronicle (ed. 1548), p. 390 ; Busch, p. 321.

day, and the news they brought was the turning
point in the young earl's career. His ambition had
not yet turned in the direction of the English crown,
and it is quite possible that he was unaware of the
strength of his hereditary title.[1] He was in great
favour with the Duke of Brittany, and there were
rumours of negotiations for his marriage with the
duke's daughter and heiress Anne. Though the
duke was reluctant to defy Richard III. openly, he
constantly evaded his requests for the earl's surrender.
Richard's ambassador Hutton reached Brittany in
the summer of 1483, and in August the duke sent a
diplomatic answer, in which he mentioned that Louis
XI. of France was also trying to get hold of Richmond.

The project for Henry's marriage with Anne of Brittany, however, was abandoned when Henry heard of
the brilliant prospect open to him if he married Elizabeth of York. On the 24th of September, Buckingham wrote to Richmond announcing that the 18th of
October was the date fixed upon for a joint movement.
Richmond's landing in Wales was to coincide with
risings in all the southern counties from Kent to
Devon. Henry matured his plans, and succeeded
in obtaining help from Duke Francis, who seems to
have had great faith in the success of the conspiracy.
Unfortunately in England things were moving too
fast. Popular excitement, which may have been
due to the murder of the princes in the Tower becoming known about this date,[2] led to a premature

---

[1] He was apparently in ignorance of a fact, well known to
Buckingham, that the words in the Act of Henry IV. barring the
claim of the Beauforts to the throne were an interpolation not found
in the original Act of Richard II. *L. and P. Hen. VII.*, ii., Intro. xxx.
See below, p. 29.

[2] Buckingham was probably aware of it long before.

rising in Kent early in October, the news of which had reached Richard by the 11th of the month. Richard does not seem to have suspected Buckingham and was taken completely by surprise, but his measures were prompt and effective. On 15th October a proclamation was issued against Buckingham, and troops were immediately raised. Three days later, according to the plan, Richmond's adherents in the southern counties rose, and on the same day Buckingham raised his standard at Brecknock. But the disaffection of some of the Welsh leaders, a violent storm which, by making the Severn impassable, prevented a junction with Henry's Devonshire supporters, and the prompt action of the king sealed the fate of the rising. Many of the Welshmen deserted; Buckingham fled from his troops, but was betrayed to King Richard [1] and beheaded at Salisbury on November 2nd. With him perished the hopes of the rising.

Meanwhile Richmond, by the help of Duke Francis, had collected a fleet of fifteen ships and 5000 mercenaries [2] and embarked on 12th October. Dispersed by a storm, most of the ships were driven back upon the coast of Brittany. Only Richmond's ship and one other crossed the Channel. Finding the coast at Poole well guarded, he sailed westward to Plymouth. But Devon and Cornwall were in arms against him; he had to give up hope of landing, and set sail for Normandy. In spite of the failure of his enterprise, he obtained the passport he asked for

[1] Hall in his *Chronicle* (p. 395) tells a quaint story of the horrible fate that punished the traitor and all his children with madness, leprosy, deformity, and violent death.

[2] Hall gives the number as forty ships (*Chron.*, p. 395), but Polydor Vergil, the earlier authority, states that there were fifteen only. (*Hist. Ang.*, p. 553.)

from the young king Charles VIII., who also provided him with money. He stayed for a short time
in Normandy, passing thence to Brittany, which he
reached by 30th October. There he heard of the
failure of the rising and of Buckingham's fate, and
was joined by a crowd of refugees implicated in the
rising, among whom were the Marquis of Dorset, the
Bishops of Salisbury and Exeter, John, Lord Wells,
Sir Edward Courtenay, Sir Giles Daubeney, Sir John
Bourchier, Sir Richard Edgecombe, Sir Edward
Poynings, and many others, who later obtained the
reward of their devotion. Morton, who had escaped
from Buckingham's keeping to Flanders just before
the rising, was working with the aid of Christopher
Urswick in Henry's interests, " sending preuie letters
and cloked messengers " to stir up hostility to King
Richard. Sir Edward Woodvile, with his naval experience, had been a member of Henry's growing
court since July 1483. The Duke of Brittany still
remained his friend and protector, and upon his return
lent him 10,000 golden crowns. The scattered fleet
had escaped Richard's warships and returned again
to Brittany. Henry seems to have resolved upon a
further attempt without delay, and summoned a
council of the refugees to meet at Rennes. The
conspiracy this time was inaugurated with some
pomp and ceremony in Rennes Cathedral on Christmas Day, 1484. Henry was now the only leader of
the opposition to Richard. He took a solemn oath
in the cathedral that he would marry Elizabeth,
daughter of Edward IV., as soon as he obtained the
crown of England, while the assembled company
swore fealty to him and did homage " as though he
had bene that tyme the crowned kynge and anoynted

prince." The scheme was communicated to the duke,
who lent a large sum of money for arming and fitting
out ships, on the security of Henry's word as a prince
to repay it as soon as his scheme succeeded.[1]

In England the failure of the rising had brought
punishment. The Earl of Richmond and many of
his adherents were outlawed by the Parliament of
January 1484, but in consideration of the support
Lord Stanley had given to the king against his step-
son's adherents, Henry's mother was committed to
her husband's custody. Worst of all, King Richard
had won over the queen-dowager. She lacked the
courage to continue faithful to a design which had
received such a severe check, and was prevailed upon
by Richard, in spite of the grave reasons she had for
doubting him, to leave sanctuary, and trust herself
and her daughters to him, upon his taking an oath
before Parliament to protect them. Richard, with
Richmond's destined bride in his power, " thought
the erle's chiefe combe had ben clerely cut," and
troops were levied and arrangements made for the
defence of the coast against the threatened invasion
from Brittany. At the same time Richard was ill
at ease. As Vergil put it he was " continually pricked
and tortured by perpetual dread of the earl's return,"
and he redoubled his efforts to obtain his surrender.
An embassy was despatched to the Duke of Brittany,
promising him all the revenues of the honour of

---

[1] It is possible that this refers to the 10,000 crowns of gold which
had already been paid to Henry (Add. MSS., Brit. Mus., 19,398,
No. 16, f. 33), in which case Hall's narrative is in error in the order
of the events (*Chron.*, pp. 396–7). The duke's warrant for the delivery of the money is dated 22nd November, *L. and P. Hen. VII.*,
i. 54. Bernard André's account of this period (pp. 24, 25) confuses
Henry's first and second attempts on England.

Richmond, and of the estates of Richmond's adherents, in return for the earl's surrender. Owing to
the illness of the duke, who was already showing
signs of mental infirmity, the envoys were received
by Pierre Landois, an upstart favourite. He resolved
to give way to Richard's demands, not (as Polydor
Vergil is careful to point out) through any enmity to
Henry, but in the hope of gaining powerful support
against the bitterly hostile nobles of Brittany. Richmond, however, was warned in time. Nothing escaped
Morton in his exile in Flanders, and he sent Christopher Urswick to warn Henry and persuade him to
escape into France. The messenger found Richmond
at Vannes, and was at once sent on into France to
ask for passports for the earl and his followers. The
long-standing jealousy between France and Brittany
again served Henry's turn. As soon as the duke's
policy of favouring the exile had been abandoned by
Landois, who, with less faith in Henry's star, preferred the substantial bribe offered by the king
de facto to the problematical gratitude of an exiled
pretender, it was adopted by the French court. In
September 1484, Henry received a favourable answer.
It only remained, then, to choose the time and means
of escape. A number of Henry's followers, under the
leadership of the faithful Earl of Pembroke, rode
towards the borders of Brittany, announcing that
they were going to visit the invalid duke, and the
earl, acting on Henry's secret instructions, led them
over the border into France. Henry remained in
Vannes for a couple of days, and then started for
Anjou with five servants, suspicion being averted by
the fact that 500 Englishmen, who knew nothing of
his purpose, remained in Vannes. Five miles from

the town Henry turned into a wood, " and clothinge himselfe in the symple cote of his poor servaunte," followed one of his men in the garb of a page, and rode without drawing rein towards the frontier. He crossed it only just in time. The horsemen sent in pursuit by Landois were barely an hour behind him,[1] and the destinies of the Tudor dynasty hung by a slender thread. Henry made his way to the French king's court and received a promise of help. A payment of 3000 livres was made to him in November.

The position of the English exiles who remained in Vannes was very critical, but fortunately the duke recovered his health to some extent, and showed his friendship for Henry by giving Sir Edward Woodvile and Sir Edward Poynings permission and funds to convey them to rejoin their leader, who remained at the French court, accompanying the king and the regency to Paris.

There Richmond was joined by other English refugees who had fled from Richard's tyranny,[2] among them being Richard Fox, afterwards one of Henry's most trusted ministers. In addition the Earl of Oxford, the most powerful of all the Lancastrian nobles, who had been ten years a prisoner in the castle of Hammes near Calais, won over its captain, James Blount, to Henry's cause, and prevailed on him to set him at liberty and accompany him to join Richmond

[1] In the story of the flight, Hall's narrative is practically only a translation of Vergil's. Unfortunately no date is given, but it appears from the records of the deliberations of the Regency that the flight took place in September 1484. *Proces-Verbaux de séances du conseil de régence de roi Charles VIII.* (A. Bernier.)

[2] Hall gives a vivid account of the excesses to which Richard was driven by " the wilde worme of vengaunce waverynge in his hed." *Chron.*, p. 398.

in Paris. Oxford's adherence was specially welcome
to Henry, the earl being reliable as a strong Lancastrian, not a discontented Yorkist driven to him
by hatred of Richard. Hall, following Vergil, writes
of Henry's joy at the earl's arrival, " he was
ravyshed with an incredibile gladnes, . . . and be-
ganne to have a good hope of happy successe." [1]

About this time the queen-dowager prevailed on
her son, the Marquis of Dorset, to abandon Richmond's
cause, partly through despair of the earl's success,
and " partly onerate and vanquesshed with the faire
glosynge promises of Kyng Richard." Fortunately
for Henry, the deserter, who had stolen out of Paris
by night, was stopped and brought back. Negotiations as to the amount of support to be given by
France to Richmond's enterprise were still going on,
but were complicated and delayed by the disputes in
the French council between the Regent Anne and
the opposition party led by the Duke of Orleans.
Henry saw that further delay would dishearten his
followers, and determined to make another attempt
on England. It was at this time, probably, that he
wrote the letters to his supporters in England that
have been preserved, asking for their support of his
" rightful claim, due and lineal inheritance of the
Crown of England." He alludes to Richard as " that
homicide and unnatural tyrant," and speaks of himself
as their " poor, exiled friend." The letters were all
signed H. R. [2] He borrowed a small sum of money
from King Charles and from private friends, leaving the
treacherous Dorset and Sir Charles Bourchier at Paris
as hostages for its repayment, and left for Rouen,
where he began to collect a fleet to sail from Harfleur.

[1] Pol. Verg., 556; Hall, 405.   [2] Halliwell, *Letters*, i. 161.

But Henry had not come to the end of his difficulties. While at Harfleur he heard of news which
threatened the basis of his enterprise. In March
1485, King Richard had been left a widower, his
wife Anne having died "either of grief or by
poison," and a rumour spread rapidly that the king
intended to marry his niece, Elizabeth of York.[1] This
news reaching Henry, it was "no maruell," as the
chronicler quaintly puts it, "though it nypped hym
at the verie stomacke." Further disheartening delay
seemed inevitable. There was little chance of obtaining Yorkist support in England if there was no hope
of Richmond marrying the daughter of Edward IV.
It seemed madness to go further without trying to
enlist support in some other quarter. According to
Vergil, who has been followed by Hall, Henry entertained a plan for marrying the sister of Sir Walter
Herbert and so gaining his alliance and influence
in Wales, and actually sent messengers to the Earl
of Northumberland, who had married another of
Herbert's sisters.[2] The messengers, however, were
intercepted by Richard's spies.

[1] Elizabeth's attitude to this proposal, which is of some interest
in view of the fact that she afterwards became Henry's wife, has
been much discussed. According to Polydor Vergil (pp. 557-8) and
the chroniclers (Hall, p. 407), she was violently opposed to the proposal, and this seems to be the soundest view. Sir George Buck,
however, took the view that she was by no means reluctant (*Hist.
of Rich. III.*), founding his assertion on a letter written by her to
the Duke of Norfolk, which he saw, he expressly states, in her
own handwriting among the Arundel papers. The letter was never
seen, apparently, by any one else. Stow, Speed, Holinshed, and
Camden, Buck's contemporaries, are silent about it. For a full
discussion of the question, see Gairdner, *Richard III.*, pp. 202-4.

[2] Dr. Busch does not think this plan was ever seriously contemplated, but regards it as a ruse to win the Welsh alliance. There
seems to be no evidence on which to form a decision. Vergil's

Meanwhile, the king's plan of marrying Elizabeth had raised such an outcry in England that he publicly disowned it. In June he issued a proclamation in which Richmond and his adherents were described as "open murderers, advoutrers, and extortioners," their "captain, . . . Henry Tydder," being described as of bastard blood on both sides. Richmond was still looking between hope and fear at the English coasts when better news came over. A Welsh lawyer, John Morgan,[1] reported that Rhys ap Thomas and Sir John Savage were ready to take up his cause, and that money had been collected by Reginald Bray. Rhys ap Thomas was by birth, ability, and education the leading spirit in South Wales.[2] Wales, it appeared, would be on the side of the Tudor prince, and in Wales he was urged to land.

Any risk seemed preferable to further delay, and on August 1st Richmond sailed from Harfleur, having with him about 2000 men, including a French contingent supplied by King Charles, and commanded by Philibert de Shaunde, afterwards Earl of Bath.[3]

words are a little indefinite, but it may be that Henry would have married any woman for a crown. Busch, *op. cit.*, p. 19; Pol. Verg., p. 559; Hall, p. 410.

[1] Hall gives this name as Morgan Kidwelly, from which it has been inferred that Richard's Attorney-General betrayed him. Vergil, however, gives the name as John Morgan, and a Welsh biographer of considerable authority calls him John Morgan of Kidwelly, who later became a member of Henry's council. Obviously the latter was referred to. Hall, p. 410; Pol. Verg., p. 559; *Cambrian Register* (1795), p. 96.

[2]   "All the kingdom is the king's,
        Save where Rhys doth spread his wings."—*Welsh Ballad.*

[3] A long speech, said to have been delivered by Henry at the embarkation, is reported by André (pp. 25–28). It is full of Biblical allusions; Richmond compares himself to Moses and so forth. The authorship is obvious.

The little fleet was favoured by a following wind and
smooth seas, and after seven days' voyage reached
Milford Haven without opposition. The powerful
fleet got together by Richard lay inactive off Southampton. It had been prophesied that Richmond
would land at Milford, and the royal fleet guarded a
village of that name near Christchurch. Richmond
and his followers landed near the village of Dale.
The earl, we are told, knelt and kissed the ground,
and after beginning the psalm *Judica me Deus et
decerne causam meam*, he ordered his followers to
advance in the name of God and of St. George.[1] Just
after landing, Henry knighted certain of his followers,
exercising the attributes of the sovereignty he
claimed.[2] At sunrise he broke up his camp at
Dale and advanced to Haverfordwest, ten miles
away, where he was received with shouts of " King
Henry, King Henry ! Down with the bragging white
boar ! " There the bad, and as it subsequently
appeared untrue, news was brought him that John
Savage and other prominent Welshmen had made
up their minds to support King Richard ; but the
hopes of the adventurer's followers were revived by
a message of welcome from the town of Pembroke,
Henry's birthplace, which was prepared to support
its " natural and immediate lord." From Haverfordwest Richmond marched to Cardigan, where
he was joined by Richard Griffith and John Morgan
with their men, and then rapidly forward, taking the

---

[1] *Rutland Papers*, i. 7 ; Fabyan, *Chron.*, p. 672. Rhys ap Thomas,
who had sworn to King Richard that any pretender would have
" to make entrance over his bellie," is said to have kept the letter
of his oath by throwing himself on the ground and allowing Richmond to step over him.

[2] Harl. MSS., 75, fo. 31d.

places garrisoned against him without difficulty. He sent messengers to his mother, to her husband, Lord Stanley, and to the latter's brother, Sir Gilbert Talbot, announcing his intention of marching on London, and asking them to meet him with all the force they could muster. It was about this time, probably, that Henry wrote to his kinsman, John ap Meredith, the letter that has been preserved. The letter is headed " By the King," and is written throughout in terms of sovereignty. The earl speaks of his " loving and true subjects " and of his realm of England, denouncing the king *de facto* as " the odious tyrant Richard, late Duke of Gloucester, usurper of our said right," and commands Meredith to join him with all the force at his disposal, " as ye will avoid our grievous displeasure and answer it at your peril." Bold language this for a proscribed exile who had only just landed, and who had but a handful of followers to match with the forces of a kingdom, but its boldness was justified by success.

The attitude of the Stanleys was of the utmost importance—one had all Lancashire at his back, the other ruled North Wales ; but they preferred not committing themselves to either party until they saw how things were going. They were ready, it seemed, to betray Richard, in spite of the favour he had shown them, as soon as Henry's success appeared probable.[1] It soon appeared that Richmond had done well in setting up his standard in Wales. Welsh chieftains rallied to support the descendant of Welsh kings and fight under the red dragon of Cadwallader ; Welsh bards and minstrels roused local feeling in his

[1] Their timorous policy is explained by the fact that Stanley's son and heir, Lord Strange, was a hostage in Richard's hands.

favour, and Welsh prophecies were quoted to the effect
that a Welshman of the line of Cadwallader would
one day be King of England.[1] The invader marched
on to Shrewsbury, taking the long route through
Wales to gain as many adherents as possible,[2] and
from Shrewsbury advanced to Newport. The force
under his banner was growing daily, but still the
Stanleys hesitated. Sir William Stanley had a conference with Richmond at Stafford, but nothing
came of it. Stanley rejoined his troops, and Henry
marched on unchecked to Lichfield.

The news of Richmond's landing did not reach
King Richard, who was at Nottingham, until 11th
August, when he had already reached Shrewsbury.
The king appears to have underestimated the danger,
and though he summoned the Duke of Norfolk, the
Earls of Northumberland and Surrey, and the Stanleys
to join him at once, he did not move until he heard
of Henry's advance to Shrewsbury. Lord Stanley
excused himself on the plea of illness, and Richard
discovered from Lord Strange that he was meditating
treachery. Sir William Stanley, who had allowed
Henry to march through Wales unopposed, was
proclaimed a traitor. In August Richard mustered
a large army and set out for Leicester, which he
reached on 20th August. Henry was steadily advancing into the heart of England, and marching from

[1] As a ballad put it—

> " Richmond, sprung from British race,
> From out this land the boar shall chase."

[2] An interesting account of Henry's march through Wales is
given by a descendant of the Rhys family. It is, however, coloured
by partiality to Rhys. *Cambrian Register*, pp. 88–112. See also
Gairdner, *Richard III.*, pp. 274–280.

Lichfield to Tamworth was joined by Sir Walter
Hungerford, Sir Thomas Bourchier, and other de-
serters, who brought the force summoned by Richard
to the standard of his rival.   Lord Stanley's attitude
still made Henry very anxious.   He lingered in the
rear of the army " as a man disconsolate, musyng
and ymagenynge what was best to be done," and so
lost sight of his rearguard in the darkness, and fearing
to betray himself by asking his way stayed at a small
village all night.   He returned to his anxious army
at daybreak, rather characteristically explaining his
absence as caused, "not by mistake but by design, to
receive a message from secret allies."   A little later
he made another secret journey to Atherstone, where
he consulted the Stanleys, and received assurances of
Lord Stanley's support.

On Sunday, 21st August, Richard marched out of
Leicester, camped near the village of Market Bosworth, and on the following day pitched his battle in
the plain, his army being so large that his front was
extraordinarily long.   The vanguard was composed of
archers, under the Duke of Norfolk, and King Richard,
riding on a white charger, followed in command of the
main body, the flower of his army.   On 20th August
Henry's force had been encamped at Atherstone, near
Merevale Abbey; on the following day he marched to
White Moors, being then within three miles of the
royal army, and in the morning led out his men and
prepared for battle.[1]   The Stanleys still seemed to
hold the key of the situation.   The men under Lord
Stanley were drawn up midway between Richmond
and the king, with Sir William Stanley opposite.

[1] Plan of battle of Bosworth.   Hutton, *Battle of Bosworth
Field*, p. 1.

Henry appealed to Lord Stanley to come and help
him form his men, but was put off with an evasive
answer. Having hesitated so long, he had determined to be found on the winning side.

The chroniclers give an interesting description of
Richmond's appearance as he stood on a hill to
address his troops on the most critical day of his
adventurous life.[1] " He was of no great stature,"
we are told, " his countenance and aspecte was
chereful and couragious, his heare yelow lyke the
burnished golde, his eyes gray shynynge and quicke."
The orations said to have been delivered by the two
leaders have been handed down to us, but Henry's
appeal and the speech of the fiery Richard rest on
the same slender foundations. Henry's speech seems
to have contained the same bold claim to sovereignty
he had made on landing and continued ever since.
He asserted that Richard usurped his lawful patri-
mony and lineal inheritance, and hinted that the host
ranged against him, which appears to have been at
least twice as large as his own, contained soldiers " by
force compelled and not with goodwill assembled."
According to Hall he inveighed against " younder
tyraunt, Richard Duke of Gloucester . . . which is
both Tarquine and Nero," urged his men not to be
dismayed by the disparity of numbers, and bade
them advance like " trew men against traytors,
pitifull persones against murtherers, trew inheritors
against usurpers, ye skorges of God against tirauntes "
in the name of God and of St. George. Inspired by
some such stirring appeal Henry's men advanced to
the attack, their right wing being protected by marshy

[1] Hall, *Chron.*, pp. 416–18; Halliwell, *Letters of Kings of Eng.*, i.
164–9.

BATTLE of BOSWORTH, 22ND AUGUST. 1485

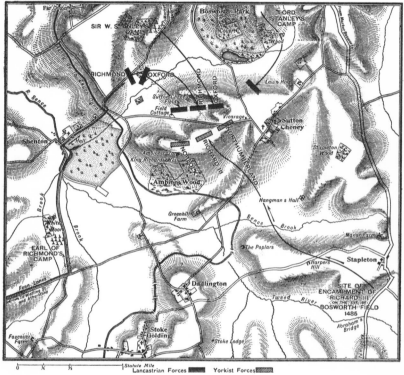

Adapted by permission from the plan by Sir James H. Ramsay, Bart.,
in *Lancaster and York*

ground, their left and rear by a little stream, while
the sun shone into the faces of the royal host. The
advance, though a bold move, was well managed.
The Earl of Oxford, with the archers, was in the
centre; the right and left wings were led by Sir Gilbert
Talbot and Sir John Savage; Henry, with the Earl of
Pembroke, led the main guard. His whole force did
not exceed 5000, though, strangely enough, he seems
to have been considerably stronger than Richard in
artillery, the new weapon of war against which the
chivalry of a feudal host was powerless.[1] As Richmond's men were moving to the attack and had just
passed the marsh, the royal army fell upon them.[2]
The Earl of Oxford, fearing to be surrounded by the
overwhelming force opposed to him, paused in the
attack; but, realising from the weakness of their
resistance that the royal troops were fighting half-
heartedly, pressed on again. At this critical moment
Stanley led his 3000 men over to join Richmond.
This seems to have decided the issue of the battle;
but a little later Henry was singled out for personal
combat by King Richard, who slew his standard-
bearer, and was fighting hand to hand with his rival,
when the Homeric contest was ended by Sir William
Stanley, whose men, " in their coats as red as blood,"
fell upon the king's lines. Richard, with the fierce
bold spirit of the Plantagenet race, refused to fly, and
died fighting desperately.

In a short time the battle of Bosworth Field was
over. Henry had gained a decisive victory. Though
the fight only lasted two hours, the loss was heavy,

[1] Gairdner, *Archæologia*, lv. 168–9.
[2] Hall's account of the battle is unreliable, Vergil's simpler story
is to be preferred.

especially on King Richard's side, those slain including the Duke of Norfolk, Lord Ferrers, Sir Richard
Ratcliffe, and Sir Robert Brackenbury. Lord Lovel
and the Staffords fled to sanctuary at Colchester, and
the Earls of Northumberland and Surrey were taken
prisoners. Henry only lost about 100 men, among
them being his standard-bearer, William Brandon.
This was the last of the thirteen battles of the Roses,
and of them all the most important.

Henry, after giving thanks for the victory " with
devoute and Godly orisons," stood on a mound, called
to this day " King Harry's Hill," to address his
victorious troops, bidding them care for the wounded
and bury the slain. He was hailed with shouts of
" King Henry!—King Henry!" The crown which
the dead king had worn into battle was found in a
hawthorn bush and brought to Lord Stanley, who
set it on Richmond's head.[1] Henry Tudor was
King of England.[2]

[1] André mentions Fox and Christopher Urswick as present in
the battle. *Vita*, pp. 33, 34.

[2] Richmond's persistent assumption of sovereignty appears even
in a contemporary ballad, which makes him say, on the eve of the
battle : " I trust in England to continue king " (*Ballad of Bosworth
Field*). Other ballads, *The Rose of England* and the *Song of the Lady
Bessy*, give vivid and dramatic details. *Percy MSS.* (ed. Hales and
Furnivall) ; Gairdner, *Richard III.*, pp. 345–362.

CHAPTER II

ENGLAND AT THE ACCESSION OF HENRY VII.— SETTLEMENT IN THE KINGDOM, 1485–1487

HENRY TUDOR had been hailed as King of England by the shouts of his victorious army, but he was still far from his goal. The difficulties that faced him dwarfed his early struggles. He had might not right behind him, and a claim that rested on force invited a later trial of strength, and involved associations of tyranny and subjection. He had been raised by the result of a successful conspiracy, by an unnatural union of York and Lancaster due to a common detestation of King Richard. It was on the maintenance of this union that Henry's hold on England depended during the first difficult months of his reign, but there was no guarantee that it would survive now that its chief object had been attained in Richard's overthrow. The vicissitudes of the long struggle between York and Lancaster had bred in the minds of the people a familiarity with violent changes which, while it had contributed to Henry's success, might as easily cause his fall. Loyalty to the Crown was almost extinguished, reverence for its wearer had vanished. The Crown had become the prize of private ambition. No great king had lifted it out of the arena of conflict, the wearers of it had frequently been overthrown and met with violent deaths. The country that had produced Warwick the King-maker had become accustomed to sudden changes in the titular sovereignty. The York and Lancaster quarrel had been the curse of England. There were no great principles at stake. The conflict had all the bitterness of a family feud, all the unscrupulousness of a quarrel over property, all the ruthlessness of a violent age, all the obstinacy of a struggle between evenly matched opponents, all the fanatic fierceness that fired the blood of the Angevin kings. Plantagenet had destroyed Plantagenet until the race was almost extinct, and the kings who had fought their bloodstained way to the throne had dealt out destruction with a savage hand. The nation was familiar with tyranny, usurpation, and regicide, with bitter feuds in the royal house, with wholesale slaughter in battle, with open executions, and with cold-blooded secret murders in royal palaces.

The whole country was exhausted and disorderly. The prospect of settled government, the only hope of the people, aroused no enthusiasm among the nobles, whose overgrown power was at the root of many of the evils that distracted the country. The Crown had been far too weak to keep in subjection men who were almost kings in their own castles, and in whose veins ran royal blood. Ever since the loss of the French possessions had removed an outlet for their tempestuous energy, England had been their battleground. Rebellion had become a habit, treason an occupation. The weakness of the government of Henry VI. removed the only check on anarchy, and England had been plunged into a struggle of unprecedented bitterness. Each great noble had his retinue, fed, lodged, and armed at his expense, clothed in his livery, and obeying his orders blindly. Six oxen were killed to provide one meal for the Earl of Warwick's household, and even the neighbouring taverns were supplied with his meat. More than four hundred and fifty persons dined and supped in one day at the table of the Duke of Buckingham. There are constant references in the *Paston Letters* and other collections to the prevalence of a custom so dangerous to the central government.[1] Again, the custom of placing the sons of the gentry in the households of the great nobles to be brought up extended the influence of the feudal nobility and added to the number of the families personally involved in quarrels between them.

Another part of the constitution from which some stability might have been hoped for had failed. Parliament, which had enjoyed a brief but promising time of development under the early Lancastrians, failed when the sheltering hand of a strong king was removed. The House of Commons fell under the influence of the great nobles, became a mere tool and echo of the Upper House, and slavishly reflected the vicissitudes of the Civil War, proscribing attainders as ordered and reversing them when required.[2]

The lower ranks of society, though not involved to

[1] An Italian observer wrote : " The titled nobility . . . were extremely profuse in their expenditure, and kept a very great retinue in their houses (which is a thing the English delight in beyond measure) ; and in this manner they made themselves a multitude of retainers and followers, with whom they afterwards molested the Court and their own countries ; and in the end themselves, for at last they were all beheaded."—*Italian Relation* (Camden Society), p. 39.

[2] " It claimed a cogency and infallibility which every change of policy belies."—Stubbs, *Const. Hist.*, iii. 252. The composition of the House of Commons was dependent upon the influence of the nobles over the local elections.

the same extent in the dynastic struggle, had not escaped the evils of civil war. Roughly speaking, North was fighting against South in the cause of the white and the red roses. Law and justice were paralysed, juries were overawed by open violence or unblushing bribery.[1] Writs of all kinds were bought and sold. Gangs of outlaws and desperadoes haunted the royal forests and exterminated the deer in the royal parks. Murder had become horribly frequent, and often went not only unpunished but unprosecuted, as the coroners often failed in their duty. The custom of sanctuary had become a crying abuse Sir Thomas More, drawing a picture of the state of England ten years after Henry's accession, thought that few sanctuary men were driven to that refuge by necessity. " Thievis bring thither their stolen goods and live theron . . . nightly they steal out, they robbe and steale and kill and come in again as though those places gave them not only a safeguard for the harm they have done but a license to do more." Further, he says, " rich men run thither with poor men's goods, there they build, there they spend and bid their creditors go whistle them." [2] Benefit of clergy had also been abused to such an extent that crime increased. The Italian writer said that " priests are the occasion of crimes," and pointed out the ease with which criminals could escape punishment by pleading benefit of clergy. " Yet notwithstanding all these evasions," he continued, " people are taken up every day by dozens, like birds in a covey, and especially in London, yet for all this they never cease to rob and murder in the streets. . . .

[1] e.g., *Paston Letters*, ed. Gairdner, i. 208, 215.
[2] *Utopia; Ital. Rel.*, p. 35.

There is no country in the world where there are so many thieves and robbers as England, insomuch that few venture to go alone in the country except in the middle of the day, and fewer still in the towns at night, and least of all in London." [1] Even in the walled towns, comparatively immune from the disturbances of the Civil War, there was poverty and decay, due to the interruption of trade and heavy taxation. The coasts were ill defended, piracy flourished unchecked. The Crown was heavily in debt, and many of the Crown jewels were in pawn. Ireland was almost independent of the English king, and was even a potential enemy of Henry VII., the dominant party among the Anglo-Irish lords being Yorkist in sympathy.

The influence of England in Europe was negligible. All the energies of the nation and of its kings had been sucked into the whirlpool of civil strife. England was even losing her foreign trade, and much of what remained was monopolised by privileged aliens. The conquests of Henry V. had gone, and with them the prestige of England which, exhausted and without allies, had sunk into a mean position. But, when considering the position of England in Europe in 1485, it must not be forgotten that the country enjoyed one great advantage. It was not, like France or Spain, only lately consolidated and united by the accident of dynastic succession. It had long been a separate nation, and the people were already becoming self-conscious and proud of their nationality. " These English," wrote an Italian observer, " are great lovers of them-

---

[1] *Ital. Rel.*, pp. 34, 36. The Italian visitor gives a very lively account of " the Islanders," of their love of good living and fine clothes, their hatred of foreigners and insular pride, their great wealth and avarice. *Ibid.*, pp. 20, 21, 23, 25, 28, 29, 72.

selves, and of everything belonging to them; they think
that there are no other men but themselves, and no
other world but England." [1] It was to this awakening
patriotism that Henry VII. later successfully appealed.

It was a formidable task to face, and Henry's right
to undertake it was open to very grave objections.
The principle which regulated the descent of the
Crown was by no means certain. It was clear enough
that the monarchy was hereditary, but whether it
could be transmitted through females was not so
clear. In addition there was the difficulty arising
from Parliamentary acknowledgment of variations
from the hereditary principle. In the confusion, both
parties could claim that they had right on their side.
If the Crown could be inherited like a private estate,
Henry VII. might claim it as nearest heir of Henry
VI., who had inherited a Parliamentary title from
Henry IV. If the throne of England descended like a
peerage and by law of strict inheritance confined to
the heirs male, it belonged to the Yorkist party, and
Edward, Earl of Warwick, should have been King of
England. Both claims, however, had been barred
by attainder. The Lancastrian usurpation had been
legalised by Act of Parliament and dignified by three
generations of kingship, but Henry VII. could only
show a flawed descent. He was neither heir general
nor heir male of Edward III.; his claim to inherit
from Henry IV. was through the half blood, and
therefore doubtful. He could claim that he was heir
general of John of Gaunt, but even that was open to
some dispute. The issue of John of Gaunt's union
with Katherine Swynford had been legitimised by
Act of Parliament, and research has shown that

[1] *Ital. Rel.*, p. 21.

the clause reserving the royal dignity contained in the later confirmation did not exist in the original Act of Richard II. It is doubtful whether such an interpolation, involving as it did an alteration in the nature of the Act it purported to confirm, was of binding force. Henry himself was probably unaware of the strength of his own claim,[1] and Richard III. had in many proclamations insisted on the bastardy of his ancestry. There was another difficulty. What claim Henry had he derived from his mother, and this recognition of the principle of descent through females involved the admission that the Yorkists descended from Lionel came before him. The fact that if Henry's title was good his mother's was better seems to have been completely and fortunately overlooked.[2]

As far as hereditary right went the Yorkists undoubtedly had the stronger position. They had been very popular in London and in the north, especially in the city of York,[3] but their prodigality and violence had brought reaction. The brilliant court of Edward IV. had little influence outside a narrow area, and the failure of his attempts at foreign invasion aroused memories of the splendid achievements of Henry V. The claims of both parties had been discredited by their failures. The Yorkists could claim "the divine right of hereditary succession," but their tyranny had alienated loyalty ; the Lancastrian rule had a Parliamentary basis but had failed to provide strong government. The whole difficult question of prin-

[1] *L. and P. Hen. VII.*, ii., Intro. xxx. Busch, *op. cit.*, p. 22.

[2] On the question of Henry's title see Stubbs, *Lect. on Med. and Mod. History*, 394–5.

[3] Davies, *York Records*, pp. 220–4. The corporation expressed their deep regret at the result of the battle of Bosworth.

ciple was admirably summarised by the Italian observer, who noticed that though the king theoretically succeeded by hereditary right, if the succession were disputed the question was often settled by force of arms. " And heretofore it has always been an understood thing that he who lost the day, lost the kingdom also." [1] Technicalities of title were of little importance at a time when every member of both the royal houses had been attainted at one time or another, and when ambition and violence had proved the most successful title to the throne.

In the absence of a clearly recognised and binding principle of succession, Henry's claim that he was the heir of the House of Lancaster was good enough to enlist the loyalty of those who had fought for the red rose. The vitality of the Lancastrian dynasty is noticeable. Its roots went deep into the soil ; it was hard to upset, and revived in the face of great odds. Was there really a popular appreciation of their " politic " rule ? Possibly ; there certainly was a revulsion from the tyranny of the House of York. The violence of the later stages of the dynastic struggle had strengthened Henry's position. The murders and executions that preceded and followed Richard's coronation paved the way for the Tudor by removing his competitors. The direct line of the House of Lancaster had been wiped out, and of the House of York there remained only Edward, Earl of Warwick, and the daughters of Edward IV. Henry had enlisted the support of many of the Yorkists alienated by the brutality of Richard III.,[2] and could

[1] *Ital. Rel.*, p. 46.
[2] On this point see Leadam, *Star Chamber Cases* (Selden Soc.), i. Intro. cliv.

count on its continuance. The young Earl of Warwick, who had a hereditary claim upon their loyalty,
was a feeble-minded boy, and Henry's promise to
marry Elizabeth of York presented an attractive
compromise. The Yorkists who helped Henry to
the throne hoped to see him reign by virtue of this
marriage. From this view Henry dissented. To
reign in right of a Yorkist wife was to " be but a
King at courtesy, and have rather a matrimonial than
a regal power." [1] Yorkist loyalty would be due to
the queen rather than the king, and would be uncertain and undependable at best. Henry meant, if
possible, to be crowned King of England in his own
right alone, and to make his marriage appear a
concession rather than a compromise.

From Henry's point of view the situation was
promising. The nation was weary of anarchy and
looked for a strong central government as the only
hope of peace. Defects of title would be ignored in
a king who would govern with a strong hand and
justly. The forces that had formerly acted as a
check on royal power were demoralised. The Church,
wrapped in a materialistic slumber, had ceased to be
the guardian of popular freedom; Parliament represented only popular apathy and lack of interest in
politics. There was no force in England that offered
hope of salvation to society except the Crown, and
no force that could resist it, if it took up the challenge.
Anarchy gave birth to despotism.

Everything depended on the character and ability
of the new king. He needed all his statecraft and
tenacity if he was to keep his seat on the uneasy
throne of the Plantagenets. One moment's slacken-

---

[1] Bacon, *Henry VII.* (ed. Spedding), p. 29.

ing of grip, the first appearance of weakness, and
Henry VII. would add another to the long list of
deposed or murdered kings. But the hour had produced the man. The new king had given proofs of
marked ability in the difficult years of exile. Something was due to his personal gifts, more perhaps to
the teaching of adversity. All the chroniclers agree
that Henry had the gift of winning friendship and
retaining loyalty. The Duke of Burgundy, we are
told, was won over to support him by his good looks
and fine bearing, his gravity in spite of his youth,
and his modesty and uprightness.[1] A similar reason
is given to explain the support he obtained from the
King of France. Even allowing for the bias of the
courtly narrator, it is clear that Henry was extraordinarily successful in inspiring his supporters with
faith in his ultimate success. He retained the friendship of France and Burgundy in the face of Richard's
tempting offers, and the failure of his first attempt
upon England was not followed by any notable seces-
sions from his cause. Though an exile in a foreign
court, dependent upon the bounty of a foreign prince,
he had escaped subservience and incurred no fettering
obligations. To patience in waiting he added boldness in action. He did not hesitate to land a handful
of men on the English coast, and take the style and
title of King of England. But to the qualities
common to all adventurers, Henry added gifts of a
very different calibre. Circumstances had made him
subtle, tactful, secretive, had given him judgment
and experience of men and their motives. Hall
speaks of him as having the "ingenious forcast of
the subtyl serpent." It needed no mean capacity to

[1] André, *Vita*, p. 17.

keep together his band of exiles, watch those who meditated treachery, negotiate the alliance with the queen-dowager, win over the Welsh chieftains and the wavering Stanleys.   Thus it was a man who had already learnt something of the statesmanship which afterwards distinguished him as the "politic king," who took up the task of kingship at the age of twenty-eight.

On the field of battle Henry knighted eleven of his followers, among whom were Gilbert Talbot and Rhys ap Thomas.   In the evening the conqueror marched with his victorious army into Leicester.   There too the body of the late king was shamefully brought, strapped on the back of a horse, "naked and despoyled to the skynne . . . and byspryncled with mire and bloude."   Bacon's statement that the king, "of his nobleness," ordered that his defeated rival should have honourable burial is supported by the words of André,[1] but the king's body seems to have been buried in the Grey Friars' church with little ceremony.   In later years the king had a tomb raised to Richard's memory.[2]

It was all important for Henry to have in his power the surviving members of the Yorkist royal family, the Princess Elizabeth and the Earl of Warwick, who had been confined by Richard in the castle of Sheriff's Hutton in Yorkshire.   While Henry was still at Leicester, Sir Richard Willoughby, armed with a royal warrant, obtained the surrender of the Earl of Warwick, who was at once conveyed to London and lodged in the Tower, where he was to spend the rest of his unhappy life.   In this "act of policy and power" Bacon finds Henry acting as a partizan rather than a king,

[1] André, *Vita*, p. 34; Bacon, p. 27.
[2] *Excerpta Historica* (Privy Purse Expenses), ed. Bentley, p. 105.

but the young earl, though without character or capacity, was dangerous as the heir of the Yorkist line and of their claim upon the people's loyalty.　At the same time the Princess Elizabeth, attended by a considerable retinue, was taken to join her mother in London.

After two days in Leicester Henry advanced towards the capital, marching by easy stages along roads lined with cheering spectators.　He reached London on Saturday, 27th August, being met at Hornsey by the mayor, sheriffs, and councillors in their scarlet robes, and by a great crowd of citizens, who pressed forward to kiss the hands " which had overcome so monstruous and cruell a tyrant." [1]　André, who greeted him with an ode of welcome, records his triumphant entry into the joyful city.　He rode " with greate pompe and triumphe " to St. Paul's,[2] where with prayers and a *Te Deum* he offered up his victorious standards, the standard of St. George, a banner bearing the red fiery dragon of Cadwallader, and a yellow banner emblazoned with a dun cow.[3]

The king took up his quarters at the Bishop of

---

[1] The date of the king's entry into London, given by Dr. Gairdner as 3rd September, has been corrected by Dr. Busch on the authority of the *City Chronicle* (MS. fo. 141, ed. Kingsford, p. 193).　He certainly entered London on a Saturday (André, *Vita*, p. 34), "which day . . . of the week he accounted and chose as a day prosperous unto him."　Bacon, p. 32.

[2] Bacon's suggestion that Henry entered the city in a closed chariot, perhaps based upon Speed's misreading of André's narrative, has been finally disposed of by Dr. Gairdner.　*Henry VII.*, p. 33 ; *Memorials*, Intro., p. xxv. ;　Busch, *op. cit.*, p. 322, *n.* 6.

[3] The significance of this banner has not been discovered.　Most of the king's standards were argent and vert, the Tudor colours ; one only bore the azure and gules of the Plantagenet kings.　This last, which bore a crowned lion, red roses encircled with rays of gold, and fleurs-de-lys, was the standard of Edward III., with the addition of the Tudor roses.—*Excerpta Historica*, pp. 57, 61.

London's palace, and summoned a council at which he renewed his promise to marry Elizabeth. According to Polydor Vergil a day was fixed for the marriage, but Henry did not abandon his intention of first being acknowledged as king in his own right.   Before he had been a week in the capital he surrounded himself with the trappings of his new dignity, royal robes of cloth of gold and ermine, rich plate and jewels.   " Playes, pastymes and pleasures were shewed in every part of the cytie."   On 3rd September the king paid a state visit to the city, a free gift of 1000 marks being voted to him.   On 15th September writs were issued for a Parliament to meet on 5th November " to discuss pressing and weighty measures for the government and defence of the kingdom and church of England." Henry, in the words of Bacon, "as a prudent and moderate prince, made this judgment that it was fit for him to haste to let his people see that he meant to govern by law, howsoever he came in by the sword."

During the weeks that followed the king secured his hold on the possessions as well as the dignity of royalty, rewarding his followers, taking over the Crown lands, appropriating the confiscated property of the late king's supporters, and getting the machinery of administration into his hands.   The first weeks of his reign are a fair specimen of the occupations of his whole laborious life and of his intimate knowledge of all the details of administration.   Grants of land and money were made to all the king's faithful supporters, from the Earl of Oxford down to simple yeomen who had done service " at the late victorious felde." [1]

---

[1] Among those who were rewarded were Sir Richard Edgecombe, the Stanleys, Hugh Conway, Christopher Urswick, and Rhys ap Thomas.

No one who is known to have served the king was
forgotten, and those who had suffered for the House
of Lancaster in the past were rewarded.   One William
Stoughton, for instance, who had " dispended his
youth in the service of Henry VI.," was made an
alms-knight of St. George's Chapel, Windsor.   Nearly
all these grants contained a clause stating that the
gift was made to the king's servant " in consideration
of his services against the king's rivalling enemy and
adversary, Richard, late Duke of Gloucester, the
usurper of the king's right and crown aforesaid."   Some
such description of the late king was always inserted,
in accordance with custom ; in fact the shorter form,
" King in dede but not in right," became a stereotyped
formula attached to any mention of Richard's name.

Changes were made in the administrative and
judicial offices.   The Bishop of Exeter became Keeper
of the Privy Seal,[1] and Thomas Lovell Chancellor of
the Exchequer.   New judges and law officers were
appointed.   Many important offices were bestowed
upon the king's suite.   John, Earl of Oxford, became
Constable of the Tower of London for life.[2]   Sir
William Berkeley became " master and operator of
the king's monies and keeper of the king's exchange " ;
Sir Richard Guildford, another faithful supporter,
became Master of the Ordnance and Keeper of the
Armoury in the Tower of London.   The king's activity

[1] He also obtained a grant of the temporalities of the Bishopric of
Salisbury, forfeited by the bishop's "many rebellions against the
king."

[2] He was also appointed " keeper of the lions, lionesses, and
leopards within the Tower," receiving for this office wages of 12d.
a day, and 6d. a day for the support of each of the animals in his
charge.—*Materials for History of Reign of Henry VII.*, ed. Campbell
(Rolls Ser.), i. 31.

also showed itself in the disposition of church patronage all over England, from the appointment of a new Dean of the Chapel Royal at Windsor to the confirmation of the election of a new Abbess of Wilton.[1]

All these acts of sovereignty were significant. By them Henry boldly asserted that his tenure of the Crown was independent of Parliamentary sanction. He even disposed of the estates of the rebels before they had been pronounced forfeited by Parliament,[2] and arranged for the collection of the customs before Parliament had granted them to him.[3]

The Patent Rolls of this year show how rapidly and firmly the once landless exile took up the duties of royalty, with quick eyes and brain restoring order and checking waste. The new arrangements made in these first weeks of the reign for the management of the Crown lands show his business-like methods and grasp of financial detail.[4] Land was leased out at improved rents, " overseers of works and repara- tions " were appointed in many royal castles and lordships. He saw that the royal castles were put into the hands of faithful servants, appointed keepers of parks and forests, bailiffs of royal towns, and so on. Provision for sport was not overlooked. The king appointed foresters and masters of the game, ser-

[1] On 25th September, less than a month after Henry reached the capital, he founded a chantry " for the soul of the king and his mother and of their noble progenitors."

[2] *Materials,* i. *passim.*

[3] Collectors of tonnage and searchers in the chief ports of the kingdom were appointed with instructions to confiscate all wool, skins, and leather that had not paid custom, gold and silver coins, bullion, jewellery and plate, as well as " letters and bulls pre- judicial to the king or his heirs." *Ibid.*

[4] Extraordinarily minute accounts were kept : " id. for divers things needful," is one of the entries. *Materials,* i. 230.

geants of the hart-hounds in Somerset and Dorset, a
"yeoman of the king's buckhounds," and a master of
"the king's dogs called harriers." [1]   There is evidence
of considerable reorganisation of the royal household.[2]   By the end of September the reins of government were fairly in the king's hands. Neither revenge
nor weakness disfigured the first months of the reign.
The past years of bloodthirsty violence were forgotten.

On 24th September a general pardon had been
issued, from which a few only of Richard's followers
were excepted.   Policy dictated the king's attitude ;
there was trouble threatening in the North.   Scotland
was just emerging from barbarism under her chivalrous and enlightened king, James IV., who shared
the traditional hostility to England.   The unsettled
conditions in England afforded him too tempting an
opportunity to be resisted.   On 25th September, the
sheriffs and gentlemen of the northern counties were
ordered to hold themselves in readiness to repel an
anticipated Scotch invasion.   The terms of the
pardon proclaimed in the city of York on 8th October
betrayed Henry's dread of the Scotch danger.   The

---

[1] *Materials*, i. *passim*.   A "master viner" at Windsor Castle
was appointed at 6d. a day, and the same man became keeper of
"the grete gardyne in Wyndesore."   *Ibid.*, p. 69.
[2] The clerk of the market of the king's household was appointed
to hold office for life.   Other men were appointed to provide, for
a period of six months, the beef and mutton, salt and fresh fish,
corn, capons and fowls for the use of the household, horsemeat
and litter for the king's stud, and so on.   Esquires of the king's
body were appointed for life at a salary of 50 marks yearly, and
other posts filled about the same time were "a grome of his mouth
in the cellar," and a keeper of beds within the castle of Windsor.
Benedict Frutze became one of the king's physicians.   One of the
gentleman ushers was given the office of keeping "paradise, hell and
purgatory" within Westminster Hall.   *Materials.*

proclamation stated that the men of the north "who have doone us nowe of late grete displeaser, being agenst us in the feld with the adversarye of us, enemy of nature and of all publique wele," were pardoned owing to their repenting their "defaultes" and being descendants of those who had fought and suffered for Henry the Sixth, and—here comes the real reason —"because they . . . be necessarye and according to there dutie most defend this land ayenst the Scottes." The king was prepared to forgive them "almaner riottes, murders, tresons, felonyes, insurreccions, conspiracies ayenst there liegaunces doone and committed" before the 22nd day of September. On 16th October a commission was issued to assemble men in the home and south-western counties. On 20th October the men of Norfolk and Suffolk were ordered to be ready at an hour's notice.[1] This exhibition of readiness to resist attack had the desired effect, and by 20th October the sheriffs of the northern counties were ordered to proclaim that the Scots, "understanding the king's politique and mighty purviaunce" had "withdrawen them silf and bee severally departed sore abasshed and rebuked." The northern gentlemen were thanked for their services and given leave to disperse. The danger was over for the time.

Henry had made up his mind to be crowned before Parliament met. He meant to meet the representatives of the people as a crowned and anointed king, who had no need to wait for their sanction and acceptance. He was busy preparing for his coronation when the "sweating sickness," hitherto unknown in England, appeared in London. The disease was very virulent. "It was so sore peynfull and sharp

[1] *Materials*, i. 89, 93–4; *Paston Letters*, iv. 325.

that the lyke was never harde of," but it ran its
course rapidly, and the patient who survived the first
twenty-four hours was almost certain to recover.   It
was extremely contagious and spread rapidly.   According to Hall, not one among a hundred escaped,
and it carried off, among other victims, two lord mayors
and six aldermen.   The king withdrew to his manor
of Guildford to be out of danger of contagion, but
before the end of October the sickness had disappeared.
Many have thought that the disease was brought to
the crowded streets of the capital by Henry's foreign
mercenaries.[1]   The visitation was popularly regarded
as an omen of " a stern rule and a troubled reign."

The preparations for the coronation were continued,
and the capital looked forward to a spectacle which
promised to be more brilliant than anything that
had ever been seen before.   On 19th October the office
of Lord High Steward of England had been put into
commission, and the elaborate preparations for the
ceremony were made under the direction of the Earl
of Oxford as Lord Chamberlain, Lord Stanley as
Lord High Constable, and the Earl of Nottingham
as Earl Marshal of England.   A sparing distribution of honours signalised the coronation.   On 27th
October, Jasper, Earl of Pembroke, was created Duke
of Bedford, Lord Stanley was made Earl of Derby,
and Sir Edward Courtenay was raised to the peerage as
Earl of Devon.   On the eve of the coronation the king
held a chapter of the Bath and created twelve new
knights.   On the 30th of October he set out from the
Tower to Westminster to be crowned.   The details
of the forgotten scene can be reconstructed after a

[1] It is curious how little is known of the fate of Henry's Breton
troops.

lapse of four centuries.[1] The king, still in the splendour of his youth, made a magnificent figure. Over a doublet of cloth of gold and satin in the Tudor colours of white and green the king wore a "long gowne of purpure velvet, furred with ermyns poudred, open at the side and purfiled with ermyns, laced with gold and with taselles of Venys gold, with a riche sarpe and garter." He rode a charger with trappings of cloth of gold, and a golden canopy was held above him, " riding opyn-heded," by four noble knights. Seven horsemen, in crimson and gold, riding bareheaded and leading a spare charger, followed the king. His henchmen and footmen wore liveries of white and green, and there was a long line of heralds and trumpeters in their gorgeous clothing. The red rose of Lancaster and the crowned portcullis of the House of Tudor appeared everywhere. A minute description of the order to be followed at the ceremony has been preserved among the Rutland papers.[2] The scene in the Abbey was full of colour and splendour. All the important posts at the ceremony were filled by the king's personal friends ; his sword was borne by the Earl of Derby, his crown by the Duke of Bedford, and his spurs by the Earl of Essex. He was supported on his right and left hand by the faithful Bishops of Exeter and Ely. The lost duchies

[1] See the Wardrobe Accounts printed in *Materials*, ii. 163–180, also the Privy Purse Expenses (*Excerpta Historica*).

[2] The " device," as it was called, probably drawn up between 27th and 30th October, was merely a draft submitted to the king for correction. The order of the queen's coronation is included, and the robes to be worn by her are described, a blank space being left for the insertion of the queen's name. Lord Lovell is set down as the bearer of the queen's sceptre. He was, of course, a fugitive exile long before the date of Elizabeth's crowning. *Rutland Papers* (Camden Soc.).

of Guienne and Normandy were not forgotten, and mantles and caps of estate were borne to represent them. This brilliant scene inaugurated the era of symbolic pageantry characteristic of the House of Tudor. But the Lady Margaret "wept marvellously," partly for joy and partly from dread of the future.[1]

On the following day the king created Philibert Shaunde—whom Hall describes as " lord Chandew of Brittany, his especiall frende "—Earl of Bath. At the same time Edward Stafford was restored to the rank of Duke of Buckingham, and remained throughout the reign one of the most brilliant figures of Henry's court.

According to contemporary writers the day of the coronation was marked by the formation of a royal bodyguard of fifty archers known as the Yeomen of the Guard.[2] There is evidence, however, that the king formed this bodyguard immediately upon his arrival in London or possibly during his exile abroad.[3] By surrounding his person with guards, in imitation of the practice of the court of France, the king em-

[1] Fisher, *Month's Mind of Lady Marg.* (Early Eng. Text. Soc.), p. 306. £1556, 18s. 10¾d. was spent in gorgeous raiment for the coronation. The Wardrobe Accounts take us behind the scenes, and show us the material the king relied upon for his effects. Twenty-one tailors, under " George, the kinges taillour," and fifteen skinners had been working for three weeks—sometimes by the light of lanterns and Paris candles—in a room securely bolted and barred " for suerty and keeping of the kinges stuff." For the details of the coronation see *Rutland Papers*, pp. 2–24 ; *Select Papers* (ed. Ives), pp. 93–119 ; Fabyan, *Chronicle*, pp. 681, 683 ; *Grey Friars Chron.*, p. 24 ; *Materials*, i. pp. 92, 97–9, 178–84; ii. pp. 1–29, 163–80.

[2] Stow, *Annales* (ed. 1615), p. 471 ; *Ital. Rel.*, pp. 39, 104, 105.

[3] In September a grant was made to a " yeoman of the king's guard " for his faithful service beyond the sea as well as on the king's " victorieux journeye." *Materials*, i. p. 8.

phasised the royal dignity.   Perhaps also " the crown upon his head had put perils into his thoughts." [1]   This bodyguard, increased by Henry and maintained until his death, became a permanent appanage of English royalty, and the nucleus of the standing army.[2]

Between the coronation and the opening of Parliament the king probably formed his council.   Its composition is significant.   Henry called to the council competent men of the middle class, upon whose gratitude and obedience he could rely, as a set-off against the great nobles with their traditions of aristocratic defiance.   The peers summoned to the council were men who, like the Duke of Bedford, the Earls of Oxford, Derby, and Devon, Lords Willoughby de Broke, Daubeney, Dynham, and Strange, were bound to the king by ties of blood or tried loyalty.   Prominent from the first among the members of the council were two great churchmen—John Morton, Bishop of Ely, who became Archbishop of Canterbury in the following year, and Richard Fox, Bishop of Exeter, " vigilant men and secret, and such as kept watch with him almost upon all men else." [3]   Other councillors who had shared the king's exile were Sir Richard Edgecombe, Sir Reginald Bray, who is described as " a very father of his country, a sage and grave person, and a fervent lover of justice," Sir Edward Poynings, and Sir Richard Guildford, both of whom had led risings against Richard III.   Chesney, Tunstall, and Lovell and Sir William Stanley were men of the same

---

[1] Bacon, p. 35.

[2] The yeomen of the guard were picked men upon whose devotion the king could rely.   They were often given posts of responsibility, —the keeperships of royal castles, surveyorships of ports, and so on. Their wages were fixed at 6d. a day.   See *Materials, passim.*

[3] Bacon, p. 40.

stamp.[1] The king occasionally summoned outsiders to the council to give their advice on special questions. This group of " occasional councillors," as Vergil calls them, included the Marquis of Dorset, the Earl of Shrewsbury, Thomas Earl of Ormonde, Richard ap Thomas, Morgan Kidwelly, Henry Marney, William Say, Master of the Horse, William Ody, Gilbert Talbot, William Udal, Thomas Troys, Richard Nanfan, formerly Governor of Calais, Robert Poyntz, James Hubert, Charles Somerset, Thomas Howard, Earl of Surrey, Henry Bourchier, Earl of Essex, William Blount, Lord Mohun, John Bourchier, John Fyneux, Peter Edgecombe, Hugh Conway, Thomas Tyrell, Henry Wyatt, Robert Throgmorton, Thomas Brandon, John Wingfield, Edmund Dudley, Edward Belknap, Richard Hemson, and others. Many of these men later played an important part in the events of the reign. Some of them were the founders of noble families, who served the State until the end of the Tudor dynasty.

With the exception of Morton and Fox, and possibly of Bray, the members of the king's council were Henry's servants and nothing more. They owed everything to Henry's gratitude, and echoed rather than advised their master. Vergil suggests that Henry chose them in order that cases referred to them might be decided without the bitterness of conflict, or as Hall paraphrases it, " without great bearing or expense in long sute." There is no evidence of any dispute between king and council throughout the reign. Henry could trust it to carry out his orders and reflect his

[1] To these names, all of which are given by Polydor Vergil, Hall adds that of Sir John Risley, which is placed by Polydor Vergil among the occasional councillors. Pol. Verg., *op. cit.*, pp. 566-67; Hall, *Chron.*, p. 424.

personality.   Lack of originality meant lack of opposition; the former the king supplied, the latter he
could not tolerate.   From this docility it came about
that the sphere of action of the council was greatly
extended during the reign.   It became the apt tool of
despotism.

On 7th November Parliament met.   Proceedings
began with an elaborate sermon by the Lord Chancellor,
Thomas Alcock, Bishop of Worcester.   Preaching on
the text, *Intende, prospere, procede et regna*, he alluded
to Agrippa who stilled sedition in Rome, reminded his
hearers of the mutual duties of subjects and king,
and spoke of Henry (who was present in person) as
" a second Joshua, a strenuous and invincible fighter
who was to bring in the golden age." [1]   On the same
day, following the usual custom, separate committees
were appointed to receive and try petitions from
England, Wales, and Scotland, and from Gascony and
the lands beyond the sea.   On Tuesday the Commons
elected Thomas Lovell as their speaker, a choice
very satisfactory to Henry, as Lovell had shared his
exile, fought on Bosworth Field, was a member of the
Council and Chancellor of the Exchequer.   The king
came down to the House on the following day, and
made a short speech in which he declared that his
right to the Crown and realm of England rested on
" just title of inheritance and upon the true judgment
of God as shown by the sword on the field of battle,
giving him victory over his enemy." [2]   At the same
time he promised that all his subjects of whatever

[1] *Rot. Parl.* vi. 267, *seq.*
[2] The king's will mentioned " the Crown which it hath pleased
God to give us with the victory of our enemy at our first field ";
Henry was aware that he had obtained his crown by conquest.

rank and condition should enjoy their lands and goods under his protection; with the significant exception of "all such persons as had offended his sovereign majesty." The nature of this exception soon appeared.

The Commons then granted tonnage and poundage at fixed rates,[1] with a subsidy on wool, wool-fells, and hides, to the king for life, "for the defence of the Realm and in especiall for the saufeguard and keeping of the See," an important proviso being added "that these Graunts be not taken in ensample to the Kinges of England in tyme to come." [2]

Parliament then passed to deal with another matter, which, though of vital importance, had not been mentioned in the writs of summons—the confirmation of the king's title. Henry was reluctant to appear to owe his crown to an Act of Parliament, and the importance of the matter had been studiously minimised. The vexed question that had involved two generations of Englishmen in intrigue and civil war was settled, as far as Parliament could settle it, by a simple act which stated "in covert and indifferent words," [3] "that the inheritance of the crowns of the realms of England and France, with all the pre-eminence and dignity royal to the same pertaining, be, rest, remain and abide in the most royal person of our now sovereign lord King Harry the Seventh, and in the heirs of his body lawfully coming perpetually with the grace of God so to endure and in none other." [4] The wording of the entail was a triumph for the king.

[1] The rates fixed were 3s. a ton on wine, and 12d. in the pound on other merchandise.

[2] *Rot. Parl.*, vi. 269. The Hanse merchants were exempted from the operation of the Act, also the Staple merchants on consideration of their paying a fixed sum to the garrison of Calais.

[3] Bacon, *op. cit.*, p. 36.   [4] *Rot. Parl.*, vi. 270.

He "would not endure any mention of the Lady Elizabeth," and succeeded in obtaining a limitation of the crown to his heirs without binding himself to marry the Yorkist princess.   He escaped conditioning his kingship with an obligation which would have hinted at a crown matrimonial.   An air of indifferent detachment, in which deep policy lurked, clothes the words in which Parliament recognised the pre-eminence of Henry's doubtful claim.

The duchies of Lancaster and Cornwall were formally confirmed to the Crown, and the honour of Richmond annexed to it.   An Act of Resumption restored to the Crown all lands belonging to Henry VI. on 2nd October 1455, gifts made since the beginning of the reign being excepted, and the rights of the king's mother and of Cecily Duchess of York being saved.   Vast estates were thus restored to the king. While making this generous provision, the Commons took the opportunity to draw attention to an old grievance, the abuse of purveyance for the royal household.   The king responded by initiating a measure of financial reform, which separated the money required for the expenses of the royal household and wardrobe from the revenues of the State.[1] Another Act reversed the attainders of the Lancastrians passed in the reign of Richard III., it being provided that they should not enter into possession of their property until the session was over.[2]   The Act was a pressing necessity, as many of the men returned to this Parliament had been attainted and were legally disqualified from sitting, and the judges had given the decision that they were not to serve

---

[1] See below, p. 280.

[2] The names recited in this bill extended to 94 lines of print.

in the House until their attainders had been reversed. The king himself was technically an outlaw, but the judges decided that the fact that he had taken upon himself the supreme authority purged him from the taint of outlawry, a decision which added to the growing theory of royal immunity.[1]

An Act of Attainder against the late king and his adherents followed, the preamble of which is vindictive enough, mentioning as it does the "unnatural, mischievous, and great perjuries, treasons, homicides, and murders in shedding of infants' blood, with many other wrongs, odious offences, and abominations against God and man, and in especial our said sovereign lord, committed and done by Richard, late Duke of Gloucester, calling and naming himself by usurpation King Richard the Thirde." By this Act Henry's reign was said by a legal fiction to begin on 21st August, the day before the battle of Bosworth, so as to bring within the net of treason all who had borne arms against him on that day. The attainted persons were therefore described in the Act as " traitourously conspiring the destruction of the king's royal person by assembling to themselves a great host on 21st August in the first year of the reign," a striking inversion of the real facts of the case. This expedient, though convenient at the moment, was a dangerous precedent to set. As the Monk of Croyland put it, " What security are our kings to have henceforth that in the day of battle they may not be deserted by their subjects ? " It has been described by one eminent historian as " a notorious lie and a blot upon

---

[1] All records, however, of the king's attainder were to be erased. The doctrine was that the Crown took away all defects and stops in the blood.

the statute-book." [1] Its immorality is beyond doubt, though the casuistry dear to Henry might build an argument on the proclamations made by the king on his landing. He had boldly called himself king while his fate was still in the balance. This claim, endorsed by his victory at Bosworth, he logically continued in prosperity. His views, however, it must be confessed, underwent great modification when ten years of kingship had given him sympathy for the position of the king *de facto*. The statute of 1495 is the best condemnation of Henry's earlier attitude to Richard's adherents. Among those whose property was declared forfeited to the Crown under this Act of Attainder were the late king, the Duke of Norfolk, the Earl of Surrey, and Lords Lovell, Ferrers, and Zouche, and about twenty knights and gentlemen. The Act did not pass without some opposition, fruitless, however, " for it was the king's pleasure."

A few days later, on 19th November, the king appeared in person in Parliament, and an oath " for the reform of divers crimes and enormities " was taken by certain knights and gentlemen of the royal household, then by the members of the House of Commons. On the motion of the Lord Chancellor the House of Lords, consisting of the Archbishop of York with twelve bishops, seventeen abbots and priors, two dukes, eight earls, one viscount, and seven barons took the oath, each with his left hand on his breast and his right on a copy of the gospels. By the terms of the oath they swore not to " receive, aid, or comfort murderers, felons, or outlaws, not to reteine any man by indenture or othe, not to give liverie, signe, or token contrary to law, or make, cause to be

[1] Dr. Gairdner in *L. and P. Hen. VII.*, ii., Intro. xxxi.

made, or assent to any maintenance, imbracerie, riotts, or unlawful assemblie, not to hinder the execution of royal writs, nor lett any known felon to bail or mainprise." [1]

The oath taken with such solemnity was unpalatable enough. The nobles bound themselves to abjure their cherished weapons of riot and rebellion. It struck at the source of their power, and threatened to reduce them to the despised level of the obedient small men. The king, however, had the driving power of a strong will, and the prestige of recent victory behind him. The "much runyng among the Lords," recorded in a contemporary letter,[2] ended in obedience.

On the 10th of December, the king being present to prorogue Parliament, a petition of the Commons was presented by the Speaker, asking the king to marry the Lady Elizabeth of York. At once the lords spiritual and temporal rose in their seats, standing before the throne, and, bowing their heads, made the same request. All reference to Henry's earlier promise to make Elizabeth his wife was tactfully omitted, and the king briefly replied that he was willing to proceed according to their desire and request. Then, after a short speech from the Chancellor, urging them to take care in putting down violence and disorder, especially to repress the vagabonds who were " running about the country spreading discords and lies under colour of begging," Parliament was prorogued until 23rd January.

This first session of Parliament had been an important one. Henry had clothed his conquest

---

[1] *Rot. Parl.*, vi., 278; see also *Rot. Parl.*, iv. 344, 422.
[2] *Plumpton Correspondence* (Camden Soc.).

with the forms of law. His adherents had been re-warded, and his enemies punished under strict legal forms. Violent usurpation and tyranny seemed to have given place to a dynasty wedded by choice and necessity, as well as by Lancastrian tradition, to a Parliamentary form of government. The session had had a reassuring effect upon the popular mind. The new king had shown strength of mind and purpose; it was clear that he meant to be obeyed. Contemporary writers were not blind to the promise of the new reign. " The king," wrote an Italian to the Pope in December, " shows himself very prudent and clement: all things appear disposed towards peace." [1]

The king spent the rest of the month in London making preparations for his marriage. In addition he had the task of paying the late king's debts as well as his own. Among the former he redeemed a " salt of gold, a coronall of gold," and other plate pledged by Richard. Other obligations were more pressing, and Henry had to apply to the city for a loan of 6000 marks. Part of the money was applied to the release of the Marquis of Dorset and Sir John Bourchier, who were still in Paris as sureties for the money advanced to Henry by the King of France. Debts due in respect of the pay of the Calais garrison, and for armour bought for the king during his exile in France, were paid about the same time.

Messengers had been sent to Rome to obtain bulls for the marriage, but on 18th January 1485–6, before the brief arrived, the long-delayed marriage was solemnised under a dispensation obtained from the Papal legate, James, Bishop of Imola. There is an

[1] *Cal. of State Papers* (Foreign Series), Venetian (ed. Brown), i. No. 506.

appearance of haste about this after the long delay.
Perhaps Henry, with his instinct for catching the
drift of public opinion, found his Yorkist supporters
chafing at the delay.[1] The marriage was received
with many signs of popular approval. As Hall said,
" By reason of this marriage, peace was thought to
discende oute of heaven into England." [2]

In one part of England the temper was anything
but peaceful. The North, the stronghold of the
Yorkist party, was restless and dissatisfied, and sedition flourished dangerously near the Scotch border.
In the county and city of York, the hostility to the
new king was pronounced. The corporation had
expressed its regret at the result of the battle of
Bosworth, and had boldly resisted the king when
their Recorder, one of the Yorkists exempted from
the general pardon, had been deprived of office. A
great agitation had been got up in his favour, which
the king seems to have been either unable or unwilling to resist. He was reluctant to alienate the
city, when trouble was threatening on the border.[3]
The state of feeling in York continued to give
ground for uneasiness. On 24th December the king
sent down a letter ordering a search to be made in

[1] The Papal bull confirming the action of the legate was dated
6th March, and another bull was issued on 27th March excom-
municating any one who rebelled against the king. Rymer, *Fœdera*,
xii. 294, 297–99.

[2] Upon Bacon's suggestion that the rejoicings were not liked by
Henry, and that he showed himself " no very indulgent husband,"
an imaginative structure was subsequently reared. See below, p. 386.

[3] After writing two letters to the city expressing his determination to uphold the man who had replaced the dispossessed Recorder,
suddenly within three days (30th November to 3rd December) the
king changed his mind and sent down a writ *de non molestando*.
Gentleman's Magazine (New Series), xxxv., 1851, pp. 164–70.

Emery Walker, Photo

ELIZABETH OF YORK
Queen Consort ot Henry VII
1466—1502
From the painting, by an unknown artist, in the National Portrait Gallery

every household in the city every night, beginning at
eight o'clock, for "vagabonds, idlers, beggars, and
suspect persons."[1]   A truce was made with Scotland
on 30th January 1485–6 which removed the most
pressing danger, but as soon as Henry was able to
leave London, after the dissolution of Parliament, he
determined to make a royal progress through the
disaffected districts.   He started early in March, with
all the great nobles of his court in his train, and
rode by way of Cambridge, where he was honourably received by both the town and the university, through Huntingdon and Stamford to Lincoln.
There he kept Easter Day devoutly, washing the
feet of twenty-nine poor men, and giving alms to
the poor, to the prisoners and lepers.   At Lincoln
he heard that Francis, Lord Lovell, and Humphrey
and Thomas Stafford had fled from Colchester, where
they had remained in sanctuary since the battle of
Bosworth, and that no one knew to what part of the
country they had gone.   Henry, however, "lytle
regardyng the tale," continued his progress, and
advanced, "without any bayting bycause they died
at Newark," to Nottingham, which he reached on
Tuesday, 11th April.[2]   Then he heard the news of
a rising in Yorkshire.   He hastily summoned the
men of Lincoln to his standard, ordering them to
come unarmed, evidently underrating the importance
of the rising, and advanced to Doncaster, where he
stayed over Sunday.   Just beyond Doncaster he was

---

[1] *Gentleman's Magazine* (New Series), xxxv., 1851, pp. 169–70.

[2] Sir Hugh Conway is said to have given the information to the
king, who "said it could not be so, and reasoned always to the
contrary with him," being much displeased that Conway did not
give the name of his informant.   *L. and P. Hen. VII.*, i. 234.

joined by the Earl of Northumberland, who brought
all the territorial influence of his great family to the
king's side. Henry reached Pontefract on Monday
and stayed there until Thursday, 20th April, and
daily large numbers of the local magnates, who had
hastily armed at the news of the revolt, joined him.
On his advance towards York, the king heard that
Lord Lovell was about to attack the city, and that a
simultaneous attack was to be made upon Worcester
by the Staffords, who had got together a large force.
It was a critical moment.   Henry was in great danger.
His men were not equipped for war, and he was close to
a city which had been the heart of the Yorkist cause,
and was still devoted to King Richard's memory.[1]
Henry, however, acted promptly.   The Duke of
Bedford was despatched at once with 3000 lightly
armed men to attack Lovell.   When he came upon
the insurgents he proclaimed that all who laid down
their arms and submitted would be pardoned.   The
proclamation took the heart from Lovell's host, and,
deserted by their leader, who fled in the night into
Lancashire, they laid down their arms and surrendered
to the duke.[2]   At the news of Lovell's failure,
Humphrey Stafford gave up the plan of attacking
Worcester, and fled with his brother to sanctuary
near Abingdon.   The Court of King's Bench, however,
decided that the right of sanctuary would not cover
men accused of high treason.   This important ruling,
which deprived traitors of their chief refuge against
the power of the Crown, led to the Staffords being

---

[1] *Gent. Mag.* (N. S.), xxxv. 481–83.   A plot to seize the king
just escaped success.

[2] Vergil and Hall credit the duke with the idea of this proclamation.   Pol. Verg., p. 569 ; Hall, p. 427.

taken out of sanctuary, and removed to the Tower.
Humphrey Stafford was executed at Tyburn. His
younger brother Thomas was pardoned, as it was
decided that he had been led into the rebellion by his
brother. Lovell remained in hiding, and early in the
following year fled to Burgundy.

Henry advanced in triumph to York, which he
reached on 22nd April. Five miles out of the city
the mayor and aldermen rode forth to meet him,
and a great crowd of citizens welcomed him with
shouts of " King Henry—King Henry ! Our Lorde
preserve that swete and well faverde face." There
were many pageants in honour of his arrival, the
" King Solomon " of one of them addressing the
king as " most prudent prince of provid provision,
sovereign in sapience," and so on. Another displayed
a royal rich red rose, and a rich white rose crowned
coming out of a cloud with the other flowers " lowting
low." The city was gorgeously adorned with tapestries,
and from the windows hailed down " comfetts as it
had been haylstones." [1] The king's generosity in
announcing that he would not expect the customary
present of money from the city owing to its poverty
led to a lavish present of provisions being enthusiastically voted.[2] After a *Te Deum* in York Minster,
the king withdrew to his lodging in the archbishop's
palace. From York Henry moved through Doncaster,
Nottingham, and Birmingham to Worcester, where
he spent Whitsuntide, being received with the usual
shows and pageants. One orator, having compared
him to Noah, Jason, Julius Cæsar, Abraham, Isaac,
Jacob, David, and Scipio, welcomed him as the

[1] Leland, *Collectanea*, iv. 185; *Gent. Mag.* (N. S.), xxxv. 481–85;
Surtees Soc. Public., vol. 85, pp. 53–7.   [2] *Ibid.*

lineal descendant of Cadwallader, " the very Britain
king " !   After visiting Hereford and Gloucester, the
king proceeded to Bristol, then the second or third
city of the kingdom.   As he rode through the city a
woman threw down wheat from her window, crying,
" Welcome and good luck ! "   Again he was received
with pageants, but the orators on this occasion spoke
in a less heroic and more practical strain than usual,
bewailing the decay of Bristol, which they thought
was due specially to the decline of the navy and the
decay of the cloth trade.   The king showed his
sympathy with their complaints and gave audience
to the mayor and aldermen, encouraging them to
build new ships to make up for their heavy losses
during the last five years.   On the following day
Henry left for London, leaving behind him golden
opinions, the mayor saying that " they harde not this
hundred yeres of noo king so good a comfort." [1]   On
the 5th of June the king came by water from Sheen
to the capital and, being welcomed home by the mayor,
had a *Te Deum* sung in the Abbey.

About this time he received an embassy from
Scotland, and after their departure the king left
London.   He was at Sheen on 12th August,[2] and
afterwards went westwards to hunt in the New
Forest.   In September Henry was in Winchester, and
there, on the 20th of the month, his son and heir was
born.[3]   This important event was celebrated by *Te
Deums* and processions, and by lighting bonfires in the
streets.   The babe was christened on the following

[1] Leland, *Collectanea*, iv. 185–200.
[2] *Paston Letters*, iii. 329.
[3] André, *Vita*, p. 41 ; Leland, *Collect.*, iv. 204 ; Pol. Verg., p. 569 ;
Hall, p. 428.

Sunday with great pomp, receiving the name of Arthur in honour of the mythical Celtic ancestor of the House of Tudor.[1]   Winchester Cathedral was hung with arras, the prince being borne to the font under a crimson canopy by the Lady Cecily, the queen's eldest sister. The infant wore a mantle of crimson cloth of gold, trimmed with ermine, with a long train borne by Sir John Chesney and the Marchioness of Dorset.[2]   When the queen had recovered from an attack of ague (to which she was always subject) the court moved to Greenwich and remained there over Christmas.   The king's position was infinitely stronger after the birth of an heir, who fused the claims of the rival royal houses.   The new dynasty had its hand on the future.

But it was only on the surface that there was peace. The leaders of the Yorkist party were discontented; the union of the roses had brought them no profit, the chief offices of state and the king's confidence had been bestowed upon Lancastrians, and the delay in the queen's coronation aggravated their dissatisfaction. The country was full of strange rumours that fed the hopes of the Yorkists.   The claims of the im-prisoned Earl of Warwick were a topic of discussion as early as November 1486,[3] and a sinister rumour spread that the king was to be another King Richard, and that he proposed to murder the boy.   Another report was that one of the sons of Edward IV. was still living.   "Thus," says Bacon, "was fuel pre-pared for the spark that afterwards kindled such a fire and combustion."

It was at Oxford that the spark of sedition was lit.

[1] Leland, *Collectanea*, iv. 204–6.
[2] The king is not mentioned as being present.
[3] *Plumpton Corresp.*, p. 54.

The rumour that the young Duke of York still lived
bred in the "fantasticall ymagination" of a priest
named Richard Symons the idea of making one of his
pupils personate him. This pupil was Lambert Simnel,
"one of gentle nature and pregnant wit," and though
of poor parentage "not without extraordinary dignity
and grace of aspect." [1] The later report that the young
Earl of Warwick had escaped, and the rejoicings with
which this rumour was received, led Simon to change
the boy's rôle to that of the Earl of Warwick. He succeeded in instilling into the boy sufficient knowledge
of "princely behaviour, civil manners, and fruitful
literature" to deceive the important Yorkists, to
whom he was afterwards presented, who were perhaps
not inclined to scrutinise too closely the pretensions
of a pretender who served their purpose. The priest
showed great skill in the place he chose for the first
appearance of his protégé. The leading men in
Ireland were devotedly Yorkist,[2] and the nobles, with
Celtic enthusiasm, instantly accepted the boy on his
arrival in January 1486-7 as the young Earl of Warwick. This "feigned fable and ymagined juggling"
was passed from one to another and accepted as truth.
The Earl of Kildare, who was Lord Deputy and the
most powerful man in Ireland, espoused the boy's
cause and lodged him in his castle. His brother, the
Chancellor, joined, and men, arms, and money poured
in.[3] Messengers were sent to the Yorkist party in
England, and to the Dowager-Duchess of Burgundy
to enlist her sympathy.

[1] He was probably the son of an organ-builder (*Carew Papers*, 472),
though his father is elsewhere described as a carpenter, a baker, and
a tailor, *Rot. Parl.*, vi. 397; André, *Vita*, 49.
[2] See below, p. 291.   [3] *Carew Papers* (Misc.), 388, 472-4.

The court of the dowager-duchess had long been a refuge of fugitive Yorkists.[1] As the sister of Edward IV., she was consumed with hatred of the House of Lancaster. " Inflamed with malyce diabolicall she invented and practised all mischiefes, displeasures, and dammages that she could devyse against the Kyng of England." [2] She had "the spirit of a man and the malice of a woman," says Bacon. Wealthy and childless, she was ready to devote the whole of her very considerable ability to an attempt to overthrow Henry VII., " against whom she bare a mortal hatred." In her " fury and frantike mood " she promised to help the conspirators.

The affair had reached this point when news that a pretender had been set up against him in Ireland reached the king. Henry was then at Sheen, where on 2nd February 1486-7 he held a council to decide on the necessary measures of precaution.[3] The murmuring and discontent in England had already led to a few rebels being proclaimed, among others Sir Henry Bodrugan, who had been stirring up sedition in Devon and Cornwall.[4] On the news of Lovell's escape, Henry decided to issue a general pardon for all offences, even for high treason, to all who submitted. There could be no greater proof of the king's uneasiness. His throne was undermined by a conspiracy he was not strong enough to punish. He tried, therefore, to detach some of its supporters by this offer of a pardon. As a second measure of precaution the captive earl was to be led through London to expose

---

[1] The latest arrival was Lord Lovell, who had fled there in January.

[2] Hall, *Chron.* p. 430.   [3] Leland, *Collectanea,* iv. 208.

[4] *L. and P.,* ii. 369 ; *Paston Letters,* iii. 329.

the imposture of the claimant in Ireland. A third measure, an unexpected and mysterious one, was decided upon at this council. It was directed against the queen-dowager. Her jointure lands were confiscated, a pension of 400 marks only being allowed her, and she was assigned apartments in the abbey of Bermondsey.[1] No cause was publicly assigned for these proceedings. The vague expression, " for various considerations," used in the Act certainly shrouds a mystery. Various suggestions of the cause of the queen's disgrace have been put forward. Vergil states that it was the punishment of the queen's treachery to Henry in surrendering her daughters to King Richard. His authority, though constantly first-rate on matters of fact, is not always to be followed on the question of the king's motives. This betrayal had been long since condoned. The queen-dowager's estates had been restored by Henry's first Parliament, and she had since enjoyed the king's favour. Hatred of the House of York, the motive suggested by Bacon and those who followed him, may also be dismissed. Henry was too cautious a man to attack a prominent Yorkist at this inopportune moment without other motive than blind hatred of a family to which he had shown honour in the person of his queen.[2] It is more reasonable to connect her disgrace with the conspiracy then on foot, and to suppose that she may have been implicated in it to some extent. She was certainly an indiscreet,

[1] *Materials*, ii. 148–9, 265, 302 ; *Privy Purse Expenses of Eliz. of York*, ed. Nicolas, Intro. lxxvii.–lxxix.

[2] This hypothetical hatred, too, did not prevent Henry from granting the queen-dowager's forfeited lands to the queen. The grant was confirmed by Henry's second Parliament. *Rot. Parl.*, vi. 386.

MARGARET OF YORK
From the picture in the possession of the Society of Antiquaries

capricious woman. No evidence, however, survives
to connect her with the plot, and the question cannot
be decided. A balancing of probabilities remains.
No legal proceedings were taken against her, but the
fact that no reason was assigned for her retirement
and the forfeiture of her property hints at a desire
to hide the fact that those near the king's person were
implicated in the plot, and perhaps to spare the queen
consort the disgrace.[1]

At this moment the conspirators gained over a
very important convert, John de la Pole, Earl of
Lincoln. He had been chosen as his heir by Richard
III., and though he had been received into favour
by Henry, was ill content with the loss of his brilliant
prospects. Thwarted ambition made him join the
plot. For some time he wore the mask of loyalty,
and was actually present at the Council held at Sheen,
but a little later he, with Sir Thomas Broughton and
others of less note, fled to join Lovell at the court of
his aunt, the Duchess Margaret.

The king returned to London, and on the Sunday
following the Earl of Warwick was taken from the
Tower along the principal streets of the city to St.
Paul's, where many of the nobles suspected of complicity in Simnel's conspiracy were given an opportunity of talking to him. After Lincoln's escape,
the king ordered that strict watch should be kept
along the east coast to prevent the escape of other
traitors, and to guard against invasion from Flanders.
Commissions of array were issued on 7th April and

---

[1] Vergil's account of the queen-dowager as spending the rest
of her life in misery seems to be slightly overdrawn. Three years
later her annuity was increased (Pat. 5 *Hen. VII.*, m. 20) and she
afterwards appeared at court. Leland, *Collectanea*, iv. 249.

the beacons were set in order.[1]   Leaving London in
the second week in Lent the king made a tour through
the eastern counties that were nearest to the
threatened danger.   He rode through Essex to Bury
St. Edmunds in Suffolk, and thence to Norwich, where
he kept Easter.[2]   There he heard that the Marquis
of Dorset was coming to him to explain and excuse
" certeyne thynges he was suspected to have done
lightely while he was in France."   Henry thought it
best, however, to be on the safe side, and ordered the
Earl of Oxford to conduct him to the Tower.   On
Easter Monday the king made a pilgrimage to the
famous shrine at Walsingham, and then leaving the
eastern counties rode by way of Cambridge, Huntingdon, and Northampton to Coventry, which he reached
on 22nd April.   On the following day he kept the
Feast of St. George with great ceremony.   The Papal
bulls " touching the king's and the queen's right "
were read, and those who resisted Henry were cursed
with bell, book, and candle.

Meanwhile in Flanders the conspirators were ready
for action.   Lincoln and Lovell appear to have decided
that it would be wise to support the Irish rebellion.
Lincoln's attitude in taking up the cause of a boy
whom he must have known to be a pretender, has been
explained by the theory that he meant to use Simnel
as a catspaw, and if the revolt succeeded to remove
him to make way for a new Plantagenet.[3]   Two

---

[1] On 4th March Thomas Brandon was put in command of an
armed force " about to proceed to sea against the king's enemies
there cruising."   *Materials*, ii. 104, 106.

[2] Both Polydor Vergil (p. 572) and Hall (p. 433) give Christmas
instead of Easter, an obvious mistake.   See *Collectanea*, iv. 209.
The corrected draft for Vergil's history preserved in the Vatican
Library gives the right date.   *Hist. Soc. Trans.*, Ser. II., vol. xvi. 1–17.

[3] Polydor Vergil, *op. cit.*, p. 572.

thousand German mercenaries had been got together by the help of the duchess, and early in May the whole force sailed for Ireland under the command of one Martin Swart, landing on 5th May. Practically the whole country, with the important exception of Waterford, which remained loyal to Henry, had espoused the cause of the pretender, and on 24th May Lambert Simnel was crowned King of England in Dublin Cathedral under the title of Edward VI. He was afterwards taken in procession through the streets of Dublin and received with great enthusiasm. The bishops and nobles took an oath of allegiance to him. Writs were issued for a Parliament in the name of the crowned adventurer, and new coin, struck in June, bore the name of Edward VI. Confident of success, Simnel and his supporters were eager to try their fortune in England. In June the pretender, " with a great multitude of beggerly Irishmen allmost all naked and unarmed savynge skaynes and mantelles," under Lord Thomas Fitzgerald, sailed for England. They landed on the coast of Lancashire —near Furness Fells—on 4th June, hoping to join forces with Sir Thomas Broughton.

The king was at Kenilworth when he heard—from a loyal Irishman, the lord of Howth—that Lincoln and Lovell had landed in Ireland.[1] He at once sent some of his nobles to raise troops in their own counties, thinking " he should be well enough able to scatter the Irish as a flight of birds, and rattle away this swarm of bees with their king." [2] At Kenilworth he was joined by the queen, the Countess of Richmond, and the Earl of Ormond,

---

[1] *Original Letters* (ed. Ellis), i. (1), 18.
[2] Bacon, *op. cit.*, p. 55; *Materials*, ii. 135.

and there the landing in Lancashire was reported to
him by one of the horsemen he had sent to watch
the western coast.   The Duke of Bedford and the
Earl of Oxford were given command of the royal
forces.   Very stringent proclamations were made to
secure good order among the troops.   Sacrilege and
violence were forbidden on pain of death, there was
to be no forcible levy of provisions, no fighting or
quarrelling in the host, no shouting or blowing of
horns after the watch was set, and so on.   At the
same time no one was to be molested on the pretext
of any offence formerly committed against the king.[1]
From Kenilworth Henry returned to Coventry, where
he was joined by a large force under the Earl of
Devon.   Thence he marched to Leicester and Loughborough, where the " stokkes and prisones were
reasonabley filled " with offenders against the proclamations.   Meanwhile Lincoln had led his men into
Yorkshire and " passed softely on his journey without
the spoilyng or hurtyng of any man."   He did not
meet with the increase of strength he had hoped for,
and continued his advance towards Newark.   Henry
had marched to Nottingham, where he was joined by
a large force " inow to have beten all the king's
enemies."   Thursday and Friday nights were enlivened by " a great skrye or false alarm which caused
many cowards to flee."   On Saturday morning, 16th
June, the king rose early and, after hearing two
Masses, led his host to cut off the foe on the road to
Newark.   Before nine o'clock he had reached Stoke, a
village a mile out of the town, where he met the rebel
army.   The battle was fiercely contested ; the German
veterans under their experienced leader and the half

----

[1] Leland, *Collectanea*, iv. 210–12.

savage, rudely armed Irishmen, fought desperately. For three hours the issue of the fight was doubtful, but rebel valour was no match for the royal artillery and the victory lay with the king.[1]

The desperate nature of the struggle appears from the fact that nearly all the rebel leaders—Lincoln, Lord Thomas Fitzgerald, Sir Thomas Broughton, and Martin Schwartz—with about four thousand of the rank and file, perished. Lovell disappeared after the battle and his fate is a mystery.[2] The loss on the king's side was not nearly so heavy. His victory was signalised by the creation of thirteen knights banneret and fifty-two other knights, among them being Sir John Paston of the *Paston Letters*. Lambert Simnel and the priest, Richard Symons, were both captured during the battle. The latter passed from the page of history into lifelong captivity, but his tool was treated by Henry with contemptuous lenience. The boy who had been crowned with great pomp as Edward VI. of England became a scullion in the king's kitchen and afterwards one of the royal falconers. It was novel treatment for a defeated pretender. Henry's scornful clemency was judicious, and the presence of Simnel in the royal household kept alive a " continual spectacle " and galling reminder of the fate of un-

[1] It appears that only the vanguard of the king's army had come into action. *Rot. Parl.*, vi. 397; *Carew Papers*, 189 ; Harl. MS., 541, fo. 218 *b*.

[2] Vergil says that he was killed in battle, another authority that he fled and was drowned while trying to cross the Trent, a third story is that he lived a long time in concealment in a secret room at Minster Lovell, where he died. See André, *Vita*, pp. 49–52 ; Leland, *Collectanea*, iv. 209–13 ; Pol. Verg., pp. 574–5, for accounts of the battle. Lovell's attainder was " ignorauntly lefte oute and omitted " in the Parliament that followed. He was not attainted until 1495. *Rot. Parl.*, vi. 502.

successful imposture. Once again, many years later, the boy is heard of, when he appeared as cup-bearer to a party of Irish lords. The king, with one of his occasional flashes of ironic humour, sent a message that " their new king, Lambarte Simnel, brought them wine to drink and drank to them all." All shrank from the cup except the loyal lord of Howth.[1]

A report of the king's defeat had been carried to London, and so great was the panic that the Lieu-tenant of the Tower offered the keys of his prison to the Earl of Surrey, who, however, chivalrously refused to accept his liberty from any but the king himself. Henry appreciated his fine spirit, released him soon after the rebellion, and later sent him north against the Earl of Northumberland. Surrey repaid the king's confidence by his subsequent devotion to his cause.[2] There had been disorderly scenes in the capital, the sanctuary men committing many out-rages.[3] This brought into prominence a great abuse, and in a letter dated July 5, Henry appealed to the Pope to limit the right of sanctuary. His letter quoted the appalling fate of a man who had scoffed at Papal edicts and immediately fell dead, " his face and his whole body became blacker than soot." He also asked for a bull of excommunication against the Irish prelates who had supported the pretender.[4]

Henry's uneasy mind seems to have been bent on discovering the truth about the late rebellion. He knew that the ground was mined beneath him. A few months of apparent respite had been followed by

[1] See below, p. 297.   [2] *L. and P. Hen. VII.*, ii., Intro. lv.
[3] *L. and P. Hen. VII.*, i. 94–6 ; *Cal. of Venetian Papers* (ed Brown), No. 519 ; *City Chron.* (ed. Kingsford), p. 194.
[4] The bull was issued by the Pope on 6th August following. Rymer, xii. 332–4.

a plot which grew so swiftly and dangerously that it had forced him to fight for his crown on the field of battle. The death of the Earl of Lincoln, from whom he hoped to have discovered the details of the conspiracy, left him in the dark. After three days at Lincoln, he set out on a progress through Yorkshire, making searching inquiries and sending out spies in an attempt " to purge his land of all sedicious seede and double-hearted fruit." Many executions followed, those less deeply involved being punished by heavy fines. After visiting York, he continued his progress or judicial circuit northwards as far as Newcastle. He reached Newcastle in August, and remained there for a time, despatching an embassy into Scotland. He returned south in the autumn, again visiting York and receiving a French embassy at Leicester.[1] On 4th November he entered London in triumph, and rode through the city to St. Paul's to give thanks for his victory. His wife and mother, "being secretly in a house by Bishopsgate," watched the king pass in triumph and then retired to Greenwich.

On 9th November 1487 the king met his second Parliament, which had been summoned by writs issued on 1st September. Proceedings began with a speech from Morton, now Archbishop of Canterbury and Lord Chancellor, on the text, *Declina a malo, et fac bonum, inquire pacem et prosequere eam.* On the following Monday the king confirmed the election of John Mordaunt as Speaker.

The Act of Attainder against those implicated in the rebellion was a long one. The preamble recited the treachery of John, Earl of Lincoln, dating its

---

[1] See below, p. 73.

commencement from 19th March 1485-6. Twenty-
eight other persons, of whom the most important
were Sir Henry Bodrugan, Sir Thomas Broughton,
Thomas and James Harington, and John Beaumont,
were attainted of high treason and their lands and
goods forfeited.[1] The legislation of this Parliament,
which included the famous Star Chamber Act, will
be considered below.[2] Early in the session Parliament had granted the king two fifteenths and tenths,
and a subsidy from aliens resident in England.[3] The
object of the grant was stated to be " the hasty and
necessarie defence of this youre Realme " ; foreign
difficulties had arisen.

Before the end of the year the long-delayed coronation of the queen took place. Henry's position was
now so secure that the coronation would not appear
to be a necessity forced upon him by Yorkist discontent. As an act of grace there was no reason
for further delay, and the date was fixed for 25th
November. Henry's young and lovely queen was
the central figure in a succession of brilliant scenes.
On Friday the queen came from Greenwich by water,
followed by the mayor and liverymen in gaily decorated barges, the one attracting most notice being
the " Bacheler's barge " with its great red dragon
" spowting flamys of fyer into Temmys." Elizabeth
landed at the Tower, where she was welcomed by the
king in a way that was " right joyous and comfortable

[1] *Rot. Parl.*, vi. 397–400. The Duke of Suffolk was specially
exempted from the operation of the Act against his son. The first
Act of this Parliament confirmed the letters patent granting the
queen-dowager's forfeited lands to the queen, the second Act gave
the queen right of action in her own name.

[2] See Chapter VII.

[3] See below, p. 274.

to behold." There is a contemporary word picture of the young queen being borne through the streets of the city in a litter covered with cloth of gold, reclining on " pillowes of Downe covered with like Clothe of golde," royally apparelled in robes of white and gold, furred with ermine, " fastened with a great lace curiously wrought of golde and silke and riche knoppes of gold at the end tasselled . . . her faire yelow hair hanging down pleyne behynd her bak with a caul of pipes over it," and a circlet of gold, richly garnished with precious stones, on her head. Singing children, arrayed like angels and virgins, greeted her as she passed on her way to be crowned in Westminster Abbey. A banquet in Westminster Hall followed the ceremony, and the gorgeous attire of the nobles is enthusiastically described by the herald. Two of the queen's ladies, we are told, " went under the table, wher they satt on ether side the queene's fete al the diner time." The king and his mother " sat priveley " on a stage built outside one of the windows of the Hall to watch the proceedings. At the end the queen departed " with Godd's blessing and to the rejoysing of many a true Englishe mannes hert." The " great besynesse " of Parliament put a stop to further celebrations.[1]

[1] *Select Papers* (ed. John Ives), pp. 120–156; *City Chron.*, p. 194; Hall, p. 438.

CHAPTER III

HENRY was now to be faced with difficulties from outside, hitherto fortunately absent. England for a long time had played no important part in foreign affairs, prestige had gone with the French conquests, and the Wars of the Roses had absorbed all the fighting strength of the country. The nice balance of affairs in Europe, however, and the activity of national rivalries gave Henry an opportunity of proving the recovered strength of his country, and regaining the influence that waits on power. The theory of the universal rule of Pope and Emperor over the whole of Christendom was exploded, and escaping from the bonds of Papacy and Empire, the separate states of Europe pursued their individual ambitions. Many of them had just fused their elements into unity, rulers and kings were fired by dynastic ambitions. At no time did personality count for more in diplomacy. The personal characters of the kings who ruled the striving powers influenced the whole course of history. It was an age when the whims of the ruler were of more account in negotiation than the wishes of a people, when marriage alliances and dynastic considerations overruled international hatreds and the traditions of history. This or that ambitious prince set himself to modify the map of

70

Europe.   Territorial ambitions were extraordinarily
keen.

It was an atmosphere which suited Henry admirably, and in which he proved himself no mean
match for his dexterous opponents—Ferdinand, King
of Spain, and Maximilian, King of the Romans.
Ferdinand of Aragon was undoubtedly one of the
ablest men of the time.   He had great ambitions and
took a wide and general view of the course of European
politics, using his unmatched diplomatic skill to play
upon international rivalries for his own purposes.   He
was constitutionally inclined to crooked methods and
was incurably suspicious.   In his ambitions he was
ably seconded by his wife, Isabella of Castile, who
showed the curious union of a narrow and rigid piety
with considerable statesmanship.

Maximilian was the stormy petrel of Europe.   He
was a man of restless ambition, always bent on sacrificing substance for shadow, the prosaic reality of
authority in Germany for glittering dreams of universal rule.   Though not personally base, he was
utterly unreliable; he was volatile and mercurial,
incurably hopeful and incessantly active; he took
up giants' tasks only to throw them down like a
light-hearted child.[1] To the steady, cautious, tenacious Henry, with whom fate frequently threw him
into contact, he makes the most extraordinary contrast, and this perhaps embittered the undercurrent

---

[1] In the words of the late Bishop of Oxford's brilliant sketch,
he was " the most delightfully unprincipled hero of the age of transition; always in every feast and every fray, always wanting money
and selling himself for promises, and never getting the money and
never keeping his engagements; a good deal of the rake, and a good
deal of the knight-errant."   Stubbs, *Lectures on Medieval and Modern
History*, p. 387.

of mutual hostility. Maximilian was typical of an age which is the blurred boundary line between modern and medieval Europe. " Just as from him the Austrian monarchy begins, so with him the Holy Empire in its old meaning ends." [1] He was the heir of the Empire, and the founder of the mighty house of Hapsburg.

[Forces in Europe were very evenly balanced, and several foreign princes showed considerable anxiety to secure Henry's friendship. Other foreign powers were marking time, waiting to see whether Henry was strong enough to keep the crown he had won. France had from the first shown her friendly intentions, and within a few days of Bosworth field a truce for one year between England and France had been signed. | At the moment Brittany focussed the eyes of Europe. French ambition was awake. The terrible struggle with England and the foresight of Louis XI. had called a nation out of chaos. The borders of France had been extended and the great vassals subdued. Brittany alone held out, and upon Brittany, Anne of France, the capable, energetic regent, had set covetous eyes. A pretext for interference was the shelter given by Duke Francis to the Duke of Orleans, the discredited leader of the French opposition. A French invasion was threatened, and it was clear that Brittany alone could not hope to resist her formidable neighbour. The old duke, casting about for an ally, baited his hook with the hand of his elder daughter and heiress, Anne. Already the bait had attracted the needy and adventurous Maximilian. At the moment he was hopelessly involved ; he had only just forced the reluctant Flemish states to recognise him as ruler

[1] Bryce, *Holy Roman Empire.*

of Burgundy in the right of his young son Philip, and
in the spring of 1486 he had been elected to the lofty
claims and empty honours of the King of the Romans.
In March 1486, he, however, concluded a treaty in
which he guaranteed the independence of the duchy
in exchange for the hand of its heiress, while his son
Philip was to marry her younger sister. Two other
suitors for the duke's young heiress were also in the field
—the Duke of Orleans, and Lord D'Albret, a powerful
Gascon noble. They were included in this league.[1]

In 1487 a French army invaded Brittany and besieged Nantes. The town held out stoutly, and in
August the French were compelled to raise the siege
and make a treaty of peace. Maximilian as usual
had done little to help, owing to renewed difficulties
in Flanders, where resistance to him was encouraged
by France ; but his alliance, though a thing of
little practical value to Brittany, had made France
anxious to find a makeweight, and in September an
embassy was despatched into England, which met
the king at Leicester on his return after his stay in
the north. The ambassadors explained that their
king was making war against the Duke of Brittany
on account of the help given by him to the rebel
Duke of Orleans. They pointed out the danger
of neighbouring princes being allowed to succour
each other's rebels—an obvious truth of which Henry
had just had ample evidence—and asked Henry to
join France in the war, or at least to preserve a strict
neutrality. As to the question of the annexation of
Brittany, the ambassadors tactfully " bare aloof from
it as from a rock."

[1] Of Anne's three suitors one was a widower, another was already
married, and a third was old enough to be her father.

Henry's position was rather delicate ; he owed a debt of gratitude to both France and Brittany, and his personal history had emancipated him from the century-old tradition of hostility to the former.   One of the first acts of his reign had been the arrangement of a truce with his " most derest cousyn Charles of France," on 12th October 1485, replaced on 17th January 1485–6 by a three years' treaty, negotiated by Oliver King, which ensured freedom of intercourse.[1]   The natural bent of the king's mind was peaceful.   " A fame of war he liked well," says Bacon, " but not an achievement." He preferred the arts of diplomacy, in which he was conscious that he excelled.   Further, his position in England made the preservation of peace more than desirable.   The nation craved for rest, the old martial spirit of the country was suffering an eclipse after two generations of civil war.   Time was healing the smarting sore of the loss of the French conquests, and the traditional hatred of the old enemy France had been merged in the bitterness of civil strife.   Thus many things seemed to force the king's hand, and to point to a favourable reception of the proposals of the French ambassadors.   But, on the other hand, it was difficult to ignore the tradition of alliance with Brittany, and the claims her sovereign had on his gratitude.   The treaty signed on 22nd July 1487, a long and detailed document, which provided for peace and complete commercial intercourse during the lives of the duke and King Henry, and for one year afterwards, bore a much more permanent air than the French treaty.[2]   Moreover, it was obvious that the alleged cause of the attack

[1] Rymer, xii. 277, 278, 281 ; *Materials*, i. 192, 199, 602 ; Brown, *Venetian Col.*, i. No. 506.   [2] Rymer, xii. 303–12.

on Brittany was but a cloak for French ambition.
Though the old hostility to France slumbered it was
not dead, and no English king, however enlightened,
could afford to ignore it and acquiesce in the disappearance of Brittany, and a menacing addition to
the power of France.

After a long consultation in search of a conclusion
"that coulde satysfye or pleas hys doubtfull mynde
and gentle harte, lothe to offende anye of them, of
whom he had receaved eyther benefite or friendship," [1]
Henry found a loophole of escape from a difficult
position in the suggestion that he might promise to
remain neutral, and thus perhaps exercise considerable
influence without offending either party.[2] His almoner,
Christopher Urswick, who knew something of both
countries, was sent to France in May. His offer was
accepted in France but rejected in Brittany, where,
owing to the duke's illness, he was received by the
Duke of Orleans. The latter " made an answer in
somewhat high terms," refused the offer of mediation,
and appealed to the king, "for his safety and reputation," not to allow Brittany to be swallowed up
by France, and " his continuell enemyes to be next to
the gate of his realme." The embassy left the duchy
without accomplishing much, and the French again
laid siege to Nantes.[3] Henry continued his efforts
to mediate, and sent a second embassy, consisting of
the Abbot of Abingdon, Sir Richard Edgecombe, and
Christopher Urswick, through Brittany into France.

Meanwhile the king was employed in preparing a

---

[1] Hall, *Chron.*, p. 437.
[2] Brittany and Maximilian had their ambassadors still with
Henry at Windsor in May. *Paston Letters*, iii. 344.
[3] Hall, *op. cit.*, p. 438.

fleet under Sir Charles Somerset, in which many
Spanish vessels were included, and for which supplies
had been voted by Parliament, to proceed against
" the king's enemies then congregating on the sea." [1]
The object presumably was to give weight to his
self-suggested position as mediator, but at this
moment his carefully guarded neutrality was im-
perilled by the hasty action of some of his subjects.
The anti-French and warlike feeling ran high in the
council, and Lord Woodville, the queen's uncle and
governor of the Isle of Wight, suggested that he
should be allowed to take a force over to the assistance
of the duke. " The kinge," we are told, " woulde
in nowise geve the brydle to hys hote, hasty and wilde
desire," [2] but, in spite of his express prohibition,
Woodville raised a force of 400 men in the Isle of
Wight, and secretly embarked at Southampton in
a Breton ship. He captured a French merchantman
on the way across the Channel, and placed himself as
a " valyaunt captaine and bolde champion " in the
service of the duke. There was naturally a great
outcry in France at Henry's apparent treachery, and
feeling reached such a pitch that Christopher Urswick
was in personal danger.[3] Lord Woodville's indiscre-
tion therefore drove Henry from his neutral position
and made it necessary for him to conciliate France.
He offered the most ample apology for Woodville's
exploit, and on 14th July 1488 accepted his ambas-

[1] Pat., 4th May, 3 Hen. VII., Part II., m. 3, *d.* ; *ibid.*, 16th June,
3 Hen. VII., Part I., m. 6, *d. ; L. and P. Hen. VII.*, ii. App. 369–70.

[2] Hall, p. 439.

[3] Bacon's suggestion that the king did not really dislike an
enterprise he publicly disavowed is not supported by the evidence.
Woodville's action seriously hampered the king's negotiations.
Paston Letters, v. 367 ; Pol. Verg., p. 578 ; Hall, p. 440.

sador's action in renewing the treaty with France
until January 1491-2.[1] Thus Henry was forced
against his will to commit himself to France.[2] The
ambassadors returned by way of Brittany, where they
made another fruitless effort to bring about a settlement, hostilities being suspended from the 1st to
the 26th of June. Before the end of the month,
however, events took place abroad which roused
English feeling by threatening the immediate ab-
sorption of the duchy. On 28th July[3] the French
troops utterly defeated the Bretons at the battle of
St. Aubin. Woodville and most of his Englishmen
fell, the Duke of Orleans was taken prisoner, and on
31st August Duke Francis was forced to sign a most
disadvantageous treaty, by which he surrendered
several important towns as pledges and agreed not
to give his daughter in marriage without the consent
of " his sovereign lord the King of France." He
promised to expel the foreign troops and not to
harbour the enemies of France.

Nine days later he died, leaving his daughter Anne,
then aged twelve, as heiress of the distracted duchy.[4]
The French at once claimed the wardship, but their
claim was resisted, the Marshal de Rieux acting as
the young duchess's guardian. War therefore began
again in Brittany. It was obvious that the end of
it all would be the conquest of Brittany unless the

---

[1] Rymer, xii. 344.

[2] Bacon (pp. 73-4) suggests that Henry made the double mistake
of under-estimating the strength of France and over-estimating that
of Brittany, and considers that his neutral position was a failure.

[3] Hall says Monday, 27th July, but a contemporary letter
written the day after the battle gives the 28th as the date. Morice,
Hist. de Bretagne, iii. 594 ; Busch, p. 44, *n.* 1.

[4] His younger daughter died soon after this.

young duchess could find help outside.   It was useless
to expect assistance from Maximilian.   He had been
a captive in the hands of the rebel Flemings from
February until May, when he was released under
humiliating conditions which outraged the feeling
of Europe.   To avenge his treatment he was now
engaged with his father's assistance in a war of
retaliation.   Henry of England had just committed
himself to a French treaty, the Duke of Orleans was
a prisoner.   The duchess's fortunes were at a low
ebb, when the whole situation was changed by the
entrance of another power into the struggle.

This power was Spain, which was then first beginning to rise to the position of one of the great
powers of Europe.   Under the strong rule of Ferdinand the recently united kingdoms of Aragon and
Castile had been consolidated and their turbulent
nobility reduced to obedience.   The monarchy was
established upon a sound financial basis, and
strengthened by the monarchical tendencies of the
Inquisition, which began its reign of terror in 1481.
It is a tribute to Henry's sagacity that he realised
the potential strength of the Spanish monarchy, and
made immediate efforts to win its alliance.   He was
both conscious of the comparative unimportance of
his country in Europe, and personally anxious to
secure his dynasty by an alliance with one of the
royal houses of Europe.   There was no bitter legacy
of mutual hatred and rivalry between England and
Spain, and there was the link of friendly commercial
intercourse.   To Spain therefore the king turned in
the hope of finding an ally who would neutralise the
effect of the French successes in Brittany.   In March
1488 an embassy, consisting of Christopher Urswick,

Savage, and Aynsworth, set out for Spain with powers to conclude a treaty of peace and commerce. The reception of the embassy was extremely encouraging, and shortly after they arrived in Spain we hear for the first time of the marriage project which was to absorb many years of diplomacy.

The suggestion of a marriage between the infant Prince of Wales and Ferdinand's youngest daughter Katherine probably originated with Henry. It is first mentioned in the commission given to de Puebla, the Spanish ambassador, on 30th April 1488, but Henry's envoys must have received verbal instructions to make such a proposal, as de Puebla speaks of them as having been the first to solicit the marriage, and Henry was obviously very keen on it. Thus opened the long diplomatic duel between Henry and Ferdinand, in which both parties used the sordid weapons of cunning and chicanery and spent themselves in mercenary hagglings over marriage portion and dowry. The preliminary negotiations offered delusive hopes of a speedy settlement of the question. The principle of a matrimonial alliance was accepted, and a Spanish envoy was sent to England on 30th April 1488 to discuss details. " *Te Deum Laudamus!* " exclaimed Henry, hearing that the envoy had power to conclude a treaty and a marriage alliance ; but he soon discovered that he would have to pay a formidable price for the alliance. The course of these early negotiations brings out the inferiority of Henry's position. The Spanish ambassadors allowed themselves a sinister hint as to the instability of Henry's throne. " Bearing in mind what happens every day to the Kings of England, it is surprising that Ferdinand and Isabella should dare to give their daughter at all." [1] De Puebla's vivid account preserves the bargaining between the commissioners as to the amount of the dowry.   Henry tried in vain to induce the Spanish merchants in London to become security for the payment, and Ferdinand to provide her with her trousseau and jewels.   Henry's anxiety for the conclusion of the treaty appeared from the practical sacrifices he was willing to make for it, though reluctant to let his inferior position appear.   He showed special favour to the ambassadors, said the most flattering things of Ferdinand and Isabella, " every time he pronounced their names taking the measure of his bonnet," and granted licenses to Spaniards at the request of his " beloved Doctor de Puebla." [2] The ambassadors, on Henry's suggestion, made a journey to see the baby Prince of Wales and discovered in him " such excellent qualities as are quite incredible." Beyond these courtesies, however, the king was unwilling to go.   The draft of the treaty and alliance drawn up on the 8th of July, which provided that the princess was to receive a dowry of 200,000 gold scudos and be endowed with one-third of the revenues of Wales, Cornwall, and Chester, contained no promise of Henry's to make war on France at the bidding of Spain.   The special envoy left for Spain to obtain his master's ratification, which was of course withheld, and an embassy from England to settle the details of the alliance followed.

Ferdinand was bent upon recovering the two provinces of Rousillon and Cerdagne ceded to France in 1462, and Henry was to be his cat's-paw in this attempt.   The critical situation in Brittany opened up a prospect of succeeding in this aim, without

---

[1] Bergenroth, *Cal. of Spanish Papers*, i. No. 21.   [2] *Ibid.*

diverting his forces from the Moorish war in Granada. The Spanish plenipotentiaries stipulated that Henry should promise to join Spain in a war against France, and not to make peace without the inclusion of Spain. Spain in return promised to include England in any peace she made. These terms were so obviously unfavourable to England that Henry's agents hesitated to agree to them, and were not daunted by hints that the Spanish alliance was much more important to the King of England than the latter's was to Spain. Their national pride seems to have been roused to protest against embodying in writing an arrangement so derogatory to their sovereign's dignity. " It was not permissible, just, or honest," they said ; " the King of England had received many services from the King of France." They suggested, however, that their master might be willing to agree to these terms, if they were made the subject of a verbal agreement and not set down in writing. " Such things were more justifiable and honest when done than when written," they said.[1] This sophistry alarmed the Spaniards, and the English agents had to reassure them by taking a solemn oath before the crucifix that it was Henry's intention to conclude the alliance and marriage, and then make war upon France for the recovery of Rousillon and Cerdagne, " according to the King of Spain's bidding." Then followed weary months of negotiation, when disputes about the princess's dowry, trousseau, and travelling expenses were used by each power to veil attempts to get the other committed to its own view. In fact the interests of the would-be allies were practically conflicting. Ferdinand wished to push the

---

[1] Bergenroth, *Cal. Span. Papers*, p. 9.

peaceful Henry into war for the recovery of his lost
provinces; Henry hoped to gain the prestige of the
Spanish alliance without venturing on a war with
France, or, if he found that impossible, to bind down
Ferdinand to give Brittany some substantial help.

In October, when negotiations in Spain were still
in progress and there seemed little hope of an alliance,
Henry made overtures to the Duchess Anne, the basis
of the proposal being that the duchess should marry
the Duke of Buckingham. It may be that the suggestion alarmed Ferdinand, at all events it was
obvious that the limits of Henry's concessions had
been reached, and the Spanish offers were slightly
modified. To counterbalance the claim of the King
of Spain to retreat from the war as soon as his two
provinces were restored, the English were offered a
similar right of withdrawal on the cession of Guienne
and Normandy. But this modification brought no
real equality in the terms; France might possibly
restore Rousillon and Cerdagne to Spain, the state
to which they originally belonged, but the cession of
Normandy and Guienne to her old enemy involved
a surrender of French pride to which nothing short
of absolute conquest would drive her. These altered
instructions were sent to de Puebla on the 17th
of December. At the same time he was ordered to
dissuade Henry from the Brittany marriage scheme,
and to point out that it would alienate two of the
duchess's most powerful supporters, Orleans and
D'Albret. The king seems to have thought that the
Spanish alliance was worth the price he had to pay
for it, but he did not disguise his irritation from
de Puebla. He spoke of his obligations to the King
of France, and of the many friends he was losing by

not acting in concert with France, but expressed his
intention of sacrificing them in order to come to an
understanding with Spain. The overtures to the
duchess were abandoned. On the 11th of December
Thomas Savage and Richard Nanfan were despatched
to Spain, with power to conclude a marriage alliance.
Ambassadors from Maximilian, offering to make a
treaty with Henry on any terms provided he promised
to help the duchess with a powerful army, had
been in England some time. On the same 11th of
December another embassy left England to try and
bring about the better understanding with Maximilian
which Ferdinand had advised. In the first year
of his reign (2nd January 1485–6 [1]) the treaty of
Edward IV. with Burgundy had been renewed for a
year, but the depredations of Flemish pirates continued to be a source of complaint,[2] and the shelter
and assistance given to Yorkist conspirators by the
Dowager-Duchess of Burgundy gave Henry just
ground for hostility, which he only abandoned under
pressure from Ferdinand.[3] The embassy despatched
to Maximilian in December concluded a defensive
alliance on 14th February 1488–9.[4] The embassy
which left England for Spain on 11th of December
was directed to go on to Portugal to revive the
ancient treaty made by Richard II. in 1387, and
bestow the Order of the Garter upon the king. Little

[1] Rymer, xii. 320–1.
[2] See the complaints in January 1488, *Materials*, ii. 233–4, when
reprisals were authorised. See also *Cely Papers* (Camden Soc.).
[3] In July 1481 he was expressing to the Spanish ambassador,
de Puebla, his refusal to make any treaty with Maximilian.
[4] Rymer, xii. 360. On the same date (11th December), Henry
despatched five separate embassies, including one to Philip, Duke
of Burgundy.

came of this at the moment beyond the confirmation, on 18th August 1489, of the treaty, but it initiated the policy of playing off Portugal against Spain, which Henry in later and stronger days pursued with some success.

On the same 11th of December Christopher Urswick, at the head of another embassy, was despatched to Charles VIII. to ask him to desist from the war in Brittany and to make another offer of English mediation. He was instructed to warn him that if he persisted in his designs, Henry was going to send troops to support Brittany, which had formerly been a subject and vassal of England and had always been friendly to England, "which message," we are told, King Charles "dissimuled as little to regarde as the byting of a flee."

The ambassadors, Sir Richard Edgecombe and Henry Ainsworth, sent into Brittany on 11th of December, took advantage of the duchess's necessities to drive a very hard bargain. Henry had hoped at first to save the duchy by negotiation; but, though driven by self-interest to take up arms in her defence, he was not the man to champion the duchess without receiving the market value of his services. He promised to send a force of 6000 men from Portsmouth in February to protect the duchy until the following feast of All Saints, but required and obtained the surrender of two towns with their castles as securities for the repayment of the expenses he had incurred. Further, the duchess agreed, after the expiration of the Anglo-French truce, to help Henry, if called upon, to recover Normandy, Gascony, or even the crown of France. No treaty was to be made by Anne without Henry's

approval except treaties with Maximilian or Ferdinand,
and the duchess was to swear not to marry without
Henry's consent.[1] These terms were agreed to on
10th February 1489, and four days later the treaty
with Maximilian was signed. Thus the foundations
of a great anti-French coalition were laid. It was a
recognition of the value of the balance of power and
an attempt to maintain it by a league of European
powers against any nation that threatened to disturb
the *status quo*, which anticipated the principle underlying diplomacy from the sixteenth century until the
present day.

The king had spent the summer and autumn
hunting in comparative tranquillity which was disturbed by the unexpected turn of events in Brittany.
In November a Great Council had been summoned
to consider measures for securing the safety of the
duchy, and Henry began to push on preparations for
war. In December 1488 commissions of array were
issued for troops to be sent to the assistance of
Brittany, and all through this month and in January
musters were being taken.[2] Men were being impressed in London to make bows and arrows for the
king's service, and Henry announced to the Papal
collector, Gigli, in January his intention of defending
the " orphan duchess " with all his might.[3]

On 13th January Parliament met. Henry found
that there was a strong feeling in favour of supporting
Brittany, and that the deep-seated hostility to France

[1] The drafting of this treaty is a good example of Henry's foresight. His men were to be sent over and back in ships provided
by the duchess and at her expense, and the provisions as to the
delivery of the pledge towns were very elaborate. Rymer, xii.
362–9.

[2] *Materials*, ii. 384–7, 395.   [3] Brown, *Venet. Cal.*, i. No. 550.

could be profitably played upon. Bacon manufactures a speech for Morton which speaks of the
vanished greatness of England, of the once dependent
confederates, Burgundy and Brittany, already partly
lost, of the danger that the island would be " confined
in effect within the salt waters," a prospect galling
enough to the minds of those who hankered after the
lost conquests of Henry V. As the peroration of
the speech expressed it, " You know well how the
kingdoms about you grow more and more in greatness, and the times are stirring and therefore not fit
to find the king with an empty purse."

On 3rd February Parliament granted the king a
subsidy of £75,000 towards the £100,000 required to
provide an army of 10,000 men for a year, " ayenst
the auntient enymies of this Realme and for the
defence of the same," and authorised a similar levy
for the two following years if the war still continued.
This was an enormous grant, nearly three times as
large as a fifteenth and a tenth, and forty-one days
were spent in deliberations before the Commons could
screw themselves up to the vote. The exceptional
nature of the grant was emphasised. It was not to
be taken as a precedent, as it had been made owing
to the great necessity of the time in order to accelerate
the payment. The money was to be raised by a levy
of one-tenth on all incomes and a tax of 8d. on every
ten marks of personalty. After a long discussion it
was agreed that the balance of the £100,000 was to
be contributed by the clergy.[1]

---

[1] *Rot. Parl.*, vi. 420–4. No sign of the " much alacrity and for-
wardness " mentioned by Bacon (p. 82) appears. Hall and Vergil
mention the grant without comment. Pol. Verg., *op. cit.*, p. 579; Hall,
Chron., p. 442; Wilkins, *Concilia*, iii. 625–6; *Materials*, ii. 424–5, 452.

On 27th February Parliament was prorogued until
October 14th.   Henry continued his preparations
for the assistance of Brittany, collecting a force
to sail in the spring.   Some of his subjects, not
willing to wait, went on at once to Brittany,
throwing themselves into Morlaix, which was being
besieged.[1]

Henry's lack of enthusiasm for the war was justified
by a sudden revelation of the smouldering disaffection
which menaced the safety of his throne.   " The harsh
and bitter fruit " of the subsidy had still to be
gathered, and " on a sudden, the people grew into a
great mutiny."   Disturbances in the city of York[2]
were followed by resistance to the levy of the subsidy
in the counties of York and Durham.   The people
" greatly grudged and murmured," and declared that
they would not pay one penny of the huge sum now
required of them.   Their resistance was stiffened by
the adherence of discontented Yorkists.   The royal
collectors complained to the Earl of Northumberland,[3]
who wrote to the king asking for directions.   Henry's
spirit always rose in an emergency, and he never
showed less weakness than when confronted by the
" base multitude."   Northumberland was ordered by
the king to proceed at once to raise the money by
distress or otherwise, " and by compulsion to enforce
suche to payment as whyned moost at it." [4]   Opposition to the levy could not be overcome, and, led by
one John a Chambre, " a simple fellow," the people

---

[1] See *Paston Letters*, v. 355.

[2] *Gent. Mag.* (N. S.) vol. xxxvi., 1851, gives a full account of the
disturbances.

[3] He was one of Richard's supporters who had been made Warden
of the Scotch Marches and Sheriff of Northumberland in 1488.

[4] Hall, p. 443.

broke into open rebellion. Northumberland's attitude
showed weakness; a fight took place between the
malcontents and the earl's men near Thirsk, and the
earl and many of his followers were killed. The rebellion under the leadership of Sir John Egremont, who
had Yorkist leanings, spread and called for the king's
presence. The terms of a curious proclamation have
been preserved bidding the men of the north assemble
to " geynstonde such persons as is aboutward for
to dystroy owre sufferyn Lorde the Kynge and the
Commouns of England, for suche unlawfull poyntes
as Seynt Thomas of Cauntybery dyed for." Henry
sent the Earl of Surrey northwards in command of
troops. On 30th April he wrote from the castle
of Hertford ordering artillery to be sent forward
against his " unnatural subgietes in the north partes
. . . whose sedicious purpose we with Gode's mighte
entende breefly to subdue in owre persone." [1] On
10th May gunners, smiths, and carpenters were being
impressed and the king's tents repaired,[2] and on
22nd May he went northwards himself.

The rebels attacked York on 20th May, but " having
no leaders and little credit," [3] lost courage as Surrey
advanced. " Their hartes were in their heeles and
their stomackes coulde as any stone." They dispersed in all directions, but did not escape Henry's
summary vengeance. John a Chambre was hanged
at York on a high gibbet " lyke an archetraytoure,"
and his accomplices were executed " on lower gibbets
round about their master." Sir John Egremont succeeded in escaping and made his way to Flanders.
Sir Richard Tunstall was left in the north to see to

[1] Leland, *Collect.*, iv. 246.   [2] *Materials*, ii. 447–8.
[3] Report of Papal Envoy, 9th May, Brown, *Venet. Cal.*, No. 553.

the collection of the subsidy, and the Earl of Surrey was given the late earl's office of Warden of the Scotch Marches.

Leaving everything quiet Henry returned south-wards, spending Whitsuntide at Nottingham and then returning to hunt in Windsor Forest.[1] The king had apparently triumphed, but of the large grant made in February only about £27,000 was collected. Apparently resistance was encountered all over England, though there was no other open disturbance.

Of the adventures of the important embassy which left London for Spain on the 11th December we know a good deal, thanks to the narrative of the Richmond herald. He has given a detailed account of their stormy voyage from Southampton, which took nearly a month, in two Spanish ships; of their journey through Spain to Medina, which they reached on the 14th March ; and of the details of the Queen of Spain's rich dresses (one worth 200,000 gold crowns on the herald's estimation), of the mumbled speech of the bishop, " who was old and had lost all his teeth," of the court balls and joustings and bull-fights, of the appearance of " notre princesse d'Angleterre," attended by fourteen maidens, and of the bull-fight at which the " princess of Wales " assisted sitting on her mother's knee,[2] but of the actual negotiations we know little. They ended in the treaty of Medina del Campo, which was ratified on 28th March 1488–9 by Ferdinand and Isabella. General provisions securing mutual protection and free commercial inter-

[1] Leland, *Collect.*, iv. 246. André's account (pp. 47–9) contains verses on the death of the earl. He places it *before* the Lambert Simnel conspiracy.

[2] *Memorials* (Rolls Ser.), pp. 157–84.

course were followed by an agreement, which provided
for the marriage of Arthur and the Infanta when they
reached a suitable age, the dowry of the latter being
fixed at 200,000 crowns (4s. 2d.), half of which was
to be paid on her arrival in England and half of it
two years later.   The terms of the alliance with regard
to the French war were laid down.   No hostile steps
were to be taken until after 19th January 1490, when
the truce between France and England expired.   One
of the clauses provided that as Henry had concluded
a truce with France until 19th of January, he should
not call upon Spain to make war with France during
this truce, but that both parties should be free to
make a new truce with France, on 19th January 1490,
or within a year afterwards, unless at that date
England was at war with France.   At first sight it
appeared that Henry held the key of the situation.
The apparent fairness of this provision, however, was
more than counterbalanced by the clause making the
cession of Rousillon and Cerdagne or of Normandy
and Guienne the conditions for the withdrawal of
Spain and England from the war, the former being
a probable, the latter almost an impossible con-
tingency.   It was a case of diamond cut diamond.
Henry appeared to the Spaniards as already at war
with France, but as he did not consider himself a
belligerent, he secured for himself the freedom of
choice in the time for making war, which Ferdinand
hoped to deprive him of.   Thus the practical effect
of the clause was slight.[1]   It was open to France to

[1] The exact value of this clause and of the sophistical interpreta-
tions of it open to both Ferdinand and Henry have been discussed
at length by Dr. Busch and Dr. Gairdner.   Busch, *Henry VII.*,
pp. 330, 435–8.   To put it briefly, Ferdinand wished to be able to

buy off Spain at the price of a comparatively small
cession, leading England to maintain single-handed
the huge task of a war of conquest or make what
terms she could.   In spite of this, Henry could look
upon the treaty as a great victory for his diplomacy.
The title of his dynasty was recognised by a treaty
which provided for a marriage between a Tudor prince
and a princess of the Spanish royal house, and
England's weak and isolated position was improved
by the prestige of such an alliance even on rather
unequal terms.   No proof, however, has been found
that the English envoys, Thomas Savage and Richard
Nanfan, had authority to accept these terms, and the
treaty as yet bound no one.   It had not been ratified
by Henry, who delayed in the hope that something
might turn up to improve his position and modify
the bargain.   He demanded that the princess should
be sent over to England, and that half her marriage
portion should be paid within four years, obviously
raising difficulties to gain time.[1]   Thereupon the
signatures of Ferdinand and Isabella were cut off
from the copy of the treaty.

Henry seems to have considered that he could
give considerable help to Brittany, in accordance
with his treaty with the duchess, without violating
the truce with France.   In April 1489, 6000 Englishmen under Lord Willoughby de Broke and Sir John
Chesney landed in Brittany, occupied Guingamp and

postpone his entrance into the war until 1490, and to gain by this
clause the power of making Henry go to war at his bidding, which
the King of England had refused to promise publicly though ready
to swear to privately. See *Eng. Hist. Review*, viii. 353.

[1] According to Dr. Busch, public opinion in England did not
incline to the war with France, but Henry was pushed into it by
his eagerness for the Spanish alliance.

Moncoutour, which were evacuated by the French, and besieged Concarneau. The troops were well-disciplined and were joined by many of the Breton nobles, the duchess in Rennes being guided by the advice of Sir Richard Edgecombe.[1] So far Henry's measures were prospering, but a quarrel between the young duchess and her guardian, the Marshal de Rieux, introduced fresh complications into the situation. De Rieux wished her to marry the powerful Gascon noble, D'Albret, and in May sent an embassy to Henry suggesting that if he helped to bring about the marriage D'Albret would assist the English in a war to recover Guienne. The lady, however, refused to accept her suitor, who was old enough to be her father. Henry did not interfere in the way De Rieux hoped, but he alienated the duchess and her party by continuing to negotiate through De Rieux instead of with Anne directly.

In Burgundy, however, he was giving her valuable help by co-operating with her ally Maximilian in accordance with the treaty of the 14th February. The rebellious Flemings, assisted by France, were still holding the combined forces of Maximilian and the Empire in check. The French, under the command of Lord D'Esquerdes, were engaged in the siege of Dixmude, and their operations appeared to threaten Calais.[2] Lord Morley was sent with 1000 men, ostensibly to protect the fortress. He soon took the offensive, and on the night of 10th June secretly entered Flanders, with a force of about 2000 men from the

---

[1] See letter of Henry VII. dated Hertford, 22nd April. *Paston Letters*, iii. 357.

[2] In the autumn before there had been rumours of a French plot to take the city. Brown, *Ven. Cal.*, No. 535.

garrisons of Calais, Hammes and Guisnes under the command of Lord Daubeney, in addition to some 600 Germans. They relieved Dixmude on 13th June, after a hotly contested action, in which Lord Morley fell—the news of his death leading to a great massacre of French and Flemings—drove the French out of Ostend, burning part of the town, and took the guns and the rest of the spoil to Niuport. According to Hall " the field was profitable to the Englishmen, for they that went forth in clothe came home in sylke, and they that went out on foote came home on greate horses." Lord Daubeney retired to Calais, leaving a small garrison with many sick and wounded at Niuport. There they were attacked by Lord D'Esquerdes and very hard pressed. The French had actually entered the town when a ship arrived from Calais with eighty archers, to whom the women of the town " cryed with lamentable and loude voyces, ' Helpe, Englishmen ! ' and themselves helped so valiantly by cutting the throats of the Frenchmen whom the Englishmen struck down, that the French were driven out." [1]   Lord d'Esquerdes, foiled this time in his attempt on Calais, " which he so sore longed for that he would commonly saye that he would gladly lye vii yeres in hell, so that Caleys were in the possession of the Frenchmen," withdrew. Operations continued in Brittany during the months that followed with no very obvious advantage on either side. In July, however, France gained a great diplomatic triumph by separating Maximilian from the allies. Of all the self-seeking princes of the time he seems to have been the most selfish and faithless, and treaty obligations never bound him long against his own

[1] Hall, *Chron.*, p. 446.

interests.[1]   His necessities at this time, however, were
very pressing, and the situation in Flanders was in-
tolerable, as long as the rebels could look to France
for help.   Charles offered to use his influence to
settle the Flemish difficulty; the Duchess Anne was
to have all her fortresses restored, on condition that
she turned the English out of the country, and
promised not to allow them to get a footing there
again.   On this basis the treaty of Frankfort was
drawn up on 22nd July 1489, but the duchess
hesitated to ratify it.

Meanwhile the English troops which had reached
Brittany in April had been carrying on the war,
capturing the town of Concarneau in September.   The
Spaniards were making a simultaneous attack on
Fontarabia, and the coalition seemed to have some
chance of success, but the inopportune desertion of
Maximilian and the dissensions in Brittany neutralised
Henry's efforts.   The young duchess, believing a
rumour that De Rieux had been won over by Henry
and had agreed to abduct her and force her into
a marriage with the hateful D'Albret, mistrusted
Henry's attempts to reconcile her with her guardian.
In November she accepted the treaty of Frankfort.
Henry was in a difficult position.   One of his allies
had deserted him, his other ally, Spain, had done
practically nothing, and was even then receiving
French embassies to discuss a settlement involving the
cession of the two provinces.   De Rieux and D'Albret,
however, played Henry's game by refusing to acknow-
ledge the treaty.   They continued hostilities, and

---

[1] Dr. Stubbs writes of " his absurd dishonesty, which did more
harm to himself than any one else."   *Lect. on Med. and Mod.
History*, p. 387.

Charles found that the treaty was worthless unless he could persuade Henry of England to become a party to it. Henry therefore held the key of the position. The English were in possession of many important fortresses in Brittany, and without his acquiescence the treaty of Frankfort could not be carried out. Further, though for the last year French and English had been fighting in Brittany and Flanders, the Anglo-French truce did not expire until January 1490, and the feeling of the time apparently decided that though " their subjects' swords have clashed, it is nothing into the public peace of the crowns." The strength of the English position was apparent when, at the end of 1489, Charles sent embassies to England to try and detach Henry from Spain and conclude a treaty with him. One embassy had been received and dismissed in the autumn, but the operations of the English army in Brittany drove Charles to make another attempt,[1] and a second embassy came to England about Christmas and after prolonged negotiations was equally ineffective. According to Bacon—but of this no confirmation has been found—Henry refused to treat unless his title to the crown of France was recognised, and the French ambassadors hotly retorted that their king's sword would maintain his sceptre. There was evidently some strong feeling aroused by the course of the fruitless negotiations, and one of the Frenchmen revenged himself in a bitter Latin epigram. It may be that Henry touched upon the old claim that made the title of King of France part of his style.[2]

[1] Berg., *Spanish Cal.*, i. No. 41.

[2] We have the Spanish ambassador's evidence that Henry received the suggestion of a perpetual peace by demanding the restitution of Normandy and Guienne. Berg., *Spanish Cal.*, No. 41.

Meanwhile the prorogued Parliament reassembled
on 14th October 1489. It was allowed to consider
the French proposals, in order that its opposition
might strengthen the king's hand in negotiation
and, possibly in the hope of a settlement, was again
prorogued until 24th January 1489–90. Some renewal of the truce must have taken place, though
no record of it has been found, for the French ambassadors were still in England after the date when
it was due to expire, and were accompanied on their
return to France by an English embassy. At Calais
they were met by a Papal envoy, Lionel, Bishop of
Concordia, who had been despatched by the Pope to
try and effect a settlement between France and
England in view of the danger to Christendom
threatened by the advance of the Turks.[1] He had
had some success in his negotiations at Paris and was
on his way to England. Henry, however, would not
commit himself beyond a general statement that " he
would be glad and joyous to live in peace and mutual
amity with all Christendom." [2]   As the Pope's agent
reported, " The Bishop of Concordia laboured greatly
for peace with the English and achieved nothing." [3]
Henry continued his warlike preparations. Ferdinand
made an attack on Rousillon, which diverted some
of the French troops, and tried to win over the
Duchess Anne by a proposal—later disowned—that
she should marry the infante Don Juan.

Between January and May the improvement in
Henry's diplomatic position becomes clear. The
operations of his troops had been successful, and
France, Spain, and the duchess were all bidding for

---

[1] See below, p. 228.
[2] Brown, *Ven. Cal.*, i. No. 593.   [3] *Ibid.*

his friendship.   The Spaniards showed signs of great
alarm at the mission of the Legate ; hostility to Spain,
not zeal for peace, seemed to them the motive.[1]   In
February the attitude of the duchess had changed.
She sent an embassy to assure Henry of her submission and ask for his continued help, and promised
not to marry without his consent.

On the 27th of January 1489–90 the prorogued
Parliament met, and while remitting the uncollected
arrears of the former subsidy voted a new war grant
of a tenth and a fifteenth (about £32,000).[2]   On
27th February Parliament was dissolved.

The hope of a general settlement had not yet been
abandoned and a congress was held in the summer.
Envoys of England, France, Brittany, the Emperor and
Maximilian met at Boulogne and Calais.   The Bishop
of Concordia made another attempt to reconcile the
powers and restore peace to Christendom.   As a preliminary a seven months' truce between France and
Brittany was agreed upon.   The internal dissensions
in the duchy had been settled by a reconciliation
between Anne and De Rieux, and the prospect of a
settlement seemed favourable.   The difficulty which
wrecked the congress, however, was the fact that
French and English troops were in occupation of
some of the chief towns of Brittany, and, owing to
mutual distrust, the envoys demanded hard terms as
the price of their surrender.   Thus Henry's envoys
asked that the duchess should repay the expenses
incurred by the English in her defence before they

[1] Berg., *Spanish Cal.*, No. 41.

[2] A sum of £6000 was deducted for remissions to " poor towns,
cities, and boroughs " wasted desolate or impoverished, Lincoln,
New Shoreham, and Great Yarmouth being specially excepted.
Rot. Parl., vi. 438–9.

gave up the towns. The French seem to have refused
to surrender theirs until the king's claim to the duchy
had been considered, and finally in August negotiations were abandoned. The internal condition of
Brittany was desperate. French, English, and Spanish
troops, though acting independently and rarely in
concert,[2] were overrunning the duchy. In June,
Henry sent fresh troops under Lord Daubeney and
fitted out a fleet under Lord Willoughby de Broke.
Meanwhile the coasts were prepared to repel invasion,
beacons were set in order, and men were pressed for
the garrison of Calais.[3] The English garrison of
Morlaix, which had been added to the towns held
by Henry as security, had to crush a revolt of the
miserable peasants, who refused to pay a hearth-
tax imposed by the duchess. But, in spite of the
smouldering disaffection among the peasants, a better
understanding between Maximilian and Henry made
the maintenance of the independence of the duchy
much more hopeful. Maximilian had by French
help succeeded in beating down the resistance of the
Flemings to his rule. Having gained all he wanted
by the French alliance, he suddenly declared that
the treaty of Frankfort had been violated by continued occupation of the Breton strongholds by
French troops, and repudiated the treaty. For once
Maximilian's treachery was an advantage to Henry;

[1] Meanwhile there was little co-operation between the English
and Spanish troops in Brittany. Ferdinand had been angered by
the Pope's attempt to reconcile Charles and Henry, and was now
secretly treating for a separate alliance with France and offering
the infanta Joan as wife to Charles.

[2] Letter of Henry VII., dated 15th August 1490, from Eltham.
L. and P. Hen. VII., i. 97.

[3] Pat., May–July, 5 Hen. VII., m. 21, *d*; Pat., 8 July, 5 Hen. VII.,
m. 22, *d*; *L. and P. Hen. VII.*, ii. App. 371.

on 11th September 1490 a treaty between Maximilian
and Henry was signed, the object of which was the protection of Brittany against France.   On Christmas Day
Maximilian was invested at Neustadt with the Order
of the Garter as a special pledge of Henry's friendship.

About the same time there is evidence that Henry
was extending the sphere of his diplomatic activity.
A Portuguese embassy was in England discussing a
marriage between the cousin of the King of Portugal
and the elder sister of Henry's queen.   Nothing
seems to have come of it.[1]   In July of the same year
a treaty with the Duke of Milan was signed, though
the project for his marriage with the queen's sister
Cecily, perhaps never seriously considered, seems to
have fallen through.   Less than a week after the
important treaty with Maximilian, Henry at last
confirmed the treaty of Medina de Campo.   His
long delay had been useless.   There had been no
change in the general situation, as he had hoped
there might be, which would enable him to make
better terms.   He was forced to ratify the treaty
in order to keep the coalition alive.   He still
hoped, however, that the treaty might be modified,
and additional clauses were sent to Spain, which, as
they were an improvement from Henry's point of
view, were not accepted.[2]   The secret negotiations
for a marriage between the Duchess Anne and the
Spanish prince had fallen through, and, outwardly at
least, in the autumn of 1490 Spain, Maximilian, and

---

[1] Brown, *Ven. Cal.*, No. 603.

[2] One clause annulled the provision allowing the King of Spain
to make peace if Rousillon and Cerdagne were restored, and forbade
either ally to make peace without the consent of the other.   The
other provided that the Princess Katherine was to be sent to
England as soon as she was twelve years old.

England were allied against France in defence of
Brittany. At the end of the year Maximilian felt
himself strong enough to defy France by a proxy
marriage with Anne, attended with a curious ceremonial described by Hall as " a new invencion and
tricke." [1] Anne was then publicly proclaimed Queen
of the Romans and the coalition seemed to be secure.
The marriage, however, hampered the duchess instead
of helping her. It alienated D'Albret, who, in spite
of his rejection by the duchess, had not lost hope of
becoming her husband, and drove him into alliance
with the French. He surrendered Nantes to France
in April 1491. Further, Charles, exasperated by
Anne's defiance, again invaded the duchy. The
coalition proved a broken reed. Maximilian gave no
help, and indeed was in no position to do anything.
The year before, as if he had not already enough on
his hands, he had become a candidate for the throne
of Hungary, and was now absorbed in a war against
his successful competitor the King of Bohemia.

Spain was gathering together all her forces for a
great attack on Granada, and actually in the winter
of 1490–1 withdrew all her troops from Brittany with
the exception of a small garrison in Redon. This
was a contravention of the treaty of Medina, and
practically left Henry alone of the coalition to defend
the duchy. In April he sent more troops into Brittany.[2] In May he received an urgent appeal from
Anne for further help, as the Spaniards were secretly
dealing with France and again offering a Spanish
marriage to the young king. The French were in
possession of Nantes, Charles VIII. had come of age

[1] Hall, p. 449; Pol. Verg., p. 581.
[2] L. and P. Hen. VII., ii. App. pp. 371–2.

and was reconciled to the Orleanist party, and the French attack threatened to be unusually vigorous. In the face of this danger Henry made great exertions.[1] All through the spring he seems to have feared a French invasion; men had been raised and a fleet fitted out. Money was necessary, and the king, unwilling to " aggravate the common people . . . whome his mynde was ever to kepe in favoure," summoned a Great Council, and obtained its assent to the raising of benevolences, after the manner of Edward IV. Thus the " benevolent mynde of the riche sorte " was searched out by the appointment of commissioners, it being published abroad that " by their open gifts he [the king] would measure and searche their benevolent hartes and loving myndes towarde hym, so that he that gave mooste shoulde be judged to be mooste lovinge frende, and he that gave litel to be estemed accordynge to his gifte." Troops were sent into Brittany, but the situation had become desperate; it was obvious that half measures would not save the duchy. In October Henry called Parliament together and made a spirited appeal to them, announcing his intention of taking the field in person, to make war upon France, not as before in defence of Brittany but to recover the ancient rights of England. " The French king troubles the Christian world, that which he hath is not his own, yet he seeketh more. Let us by the favour of Almighty God, try our right for the crown of France itself, remembering that there hath been a French king prisoner in England and a King of England crowned in France." These are the words put by Bacon into

[1] Pat., 5th May, 6 Hen. VII., m. 9, d; L. and P. Hen. VII., ii. App. pp. 371–2.

the king's mouth.[1] This appeal to national ambition and the war spirit met with a good response. Two fifteenths and two tenths were granted for the war, in which it was the king's purpose " to hazard his most noble person." Meanwhile he attempted to bind Ferdinand in some more effective way. Spanish co-operation had hitherto been of little value, and in November, finding his first effort had not succeeded, Henry attempted a second modification of the terms of the treaty of Medina de Campo by drawing up supplementary treaties. The first bound Spain and England to declare war upon France before 15th April 1492, and to begin hostilities before 15th of June at the latest; the second stipulated that the Princess Katherine should be sent to England to marry Prince Arthur as soon as he was fourteen, and that her dowry of 200,000 crowns should then be paid.

Less than a fortnight later the cause which Henry had striven for by diplomacy, by treaties, and by force of arms—the independence of Brittany—had gone for ever. The young duchess, weary of looking to her allies for the help that never came, saw her duchy being devastated alike by the arms of friend and foe. In the summer the French troops advanced, took Redon from the Spaniards, Concarneau from the English, and besieged Anne in Rennes. Her position was desperate. She had pawned all her jewels, she was living in the midst of a disorderly and mutinous garrison of English, German, and Spanish troops. Henry had provided the means of flight and advised her to escape to the English ships

---

[1] Bacon, *op. cit.*, 116, and 116, *n.* 1; *Rot. Parl.*, vi. 440; Stubbs, *Lec. on Med. and Mod. Hist.*, p. 422. Polydor Vergil alludes to some speech of the kind.

and make her way to join Maximilian, but with characteristic courage and determination she refused to abandon her capital. She also rejected Charles's offer to find her a suitable husband. Charles then bought over the mutinous garrison, entered Rennes in triumph, and asked for Anne's hand. In her extremity, finding that the vaunted league of three kings was worthless as a defence, she came to terms. She repudiated her betrothal and proxy marriage to Maximilian; Charles on his side renounced Maximilian's daughter, whom he had formally married years before, when she was only three years old. Papal dispensations were obtained, and on the 6th of December Charles VIII. married Anne of Brittany and her duchy became part of the kingdom of France.

The coalition had failed. To two of the allies, involved in wars of more vital consequence, the defence of Brittany was a secondary consideration. Brittany, however, had been Henry's objective, and with the loss of its independence all his trouble had been thrown away. It appeared at once that Spain and Maximilian were not prepared to undertake a war of revenge upon France. In the heat of his first disappointment Maximilian talked loudly of an attack upon Brittany, and promised to send 10,000 men to serve with the English for two years, but in the spring of 1492 the war in Hungary absorbed all his resources. Spain had just won a great triumph which made her comparatively indifferent to the check received in Brittany. In January 1491-2 the long efforts of the Spaniards were crowned by the fall of Granada, an event which was received in London with great rejoicings.

Henry alone of the allies seems to have been

serious in his intention of making war on France, and he was probably swayed to some extent by the war spirit aroused in England by the French success.[1] It is clear that he felt very bitter against France at this time. A letter written to the Pope on 8th December 1491[2] breathes hostility against France. Henry writes of her insatiable coveting of the dominions of others, her fostering of rebellion in Ireland, her violent thirst for annexation, and her insolent lawlessness. The king spoke of war as a hateful necessity forced upon him to whom the slaughter of men and the shedding of Christian blood was abhorrent.[3] A few weeks later he wrote to Milan of the French, "who are so on the watch to increase their power by any villany . . . that they may annihilate all neighbouring sovereigns to their own advantage," and announced his intention to make war and "to carry our banners against them in person."[4]

Henry's actions reflected the strength of his hostile feelings. He made great preparations, assembled a large force at Portsmouth,[5] three breweries being

[1] Bacon says that Henry did but "traffic with the war to make his return in money," and that he had no intention of making war in earnest (*Hen. VII.*, p. 119). This is probably an overstatement of the truth. Henry may have been a reluctant warrior, but he made his preparations in good earnest.

[2] It is quite possible that he had already heard of Anne's marriage, which took place on the 6th. The *Cely Papers* prove that communication between England and Brittany was rapid.

[3] This warlike letter is signed "your devoted and most obedient son, Henry, by the grace of God King of England and France and Lord of Ireland," an unusually elaborate signature from Henry to the Pope. There is an interesting despatch (dated March 1492) from Henry's ambassador, John de Giglis, describing the Pope's reception of this letter. *Report on MSS. of Lord Middleton* (Hist. MSS. Com. 1911), pp. 260–263, and App. 612.

[4] Brown, *Ven. Cal.*, No. 617.

[5] Rymer, xii. 463, 477–480; *Paston Letters*, iii. 375; *Plumpton Correspondence* (Camden Soc.), 102–103.

built near the town, and appointed John, Earl of
Oxford, and the Duke of Bedford as leaders. He
spared no efforts to rouse his nominal allies, of
whom " one had power and not will, and the other
had will and not power." [1]   An embassy was sent to
Maximilian, which found him as usual utterly un-
prepared, urging him to co-operate. He summoned
the Duke of Milan to take part in the war and made
an appeal to the Pope. He further tried to make
capital out of the disaffection in Brittany, where many
of the nobles were discontented at the union with
France, by entering into negotiations for the surrender
of Brest, but the plot was found out and came to
nothing. Parliament made regulations for the conduct
of the war and the payment of troops, and additional
ships were provided.   A force sailed from Portsmouth
in June, but beyond ravaging the coasts of Brittany
and Normandy and carrying off booty little was done.
In the autumn an English fleet of twelve ships under
Sir Edward Poynings was sent to co-operate with
Maximilian's troops in the siege of Sluys, which had
been holding out ever since the Flemish rebellion had
been put down. It had been the headquarters of
pirates who did great damage to the merchandise of
nations trading with Antwerp, and the English cloth
trade had suffered considerably. On 13th October
the town surrendered, the two forts being handed
over to Sir Edward Poynings. The fate of Sluys was
of considerable commercial and political importance,
as it heralded the end of the Flemish civil war. It
proved to Europe that England, under the leadership
of her able king, was emerging from the period of
failure and weakness.

[1] Bacon, *op. cit.*, p. 120.

Though the fleet was thus profitably employed, Henry's army was delaying in England until late in the year. The spring and summer went by without the invasion of France taking place. In May there was a great tournament at the palace of Sheen, " to warm the blood of the nobility and gallants against the war." In August a French attack seems to have been feared, and the southern counties were armed to repel an expected invasion.[1] The explanation of the delay was that Henry was still trying to induce his allies to give him some real assistance in an invasion that would be undertaken in their joint interests. He had lost the towns he had held as securities for the repayment of his expenses,[2] and was disinclined to incur further costs without some assurance of support from his allies. Nothing came of his attempts. Even the Spaniards, though set free by the fall of Granada, sent no help. Henry at last saw that it was a choice between making war upon France single-handed or acquiescence in the loss of all that he had been fighting for, and he reluctantly decided on war. The long-continued threats of war were at last turned into earnest. Henry resolved upon an invasion of France, for since he had accumulated men and money for the purpose, to abandon the project would be unpopular at home and would involve a loss of prestige abroad. The young Prince of Wales was appointed regent, and given power over Church and State in his father's absence.[3] On 2nd October the king sailed from Dover for France in *The Swan*, landing at Calais at 11 o'clock. His army of about 25,000 foot and 1600

[1] Rymer, 482 ; *L. and P. Hen. VII.*, ii. App. p. 373.
[2] The date of the fall of Morlaix is not certain.
[3] Rymer, xii. 487-8.

horse had been transported by a fleet of Venetian merchant ships on the same day.[1]   At Calais the army heard, what the king already knew, that no help could be expected from Maximilian, who excused himself on the plea of poverty, " for," says Hall, " he could neither have money nor men of the drunken Fleminges, nor yet of the crakyng Brabanders, so ungrat people were they to their lorde."

On the 18th October, however, Henry advanced to besiege Boulogne.   The town was strongly fortified, and the reduction of it at that late season of the year would have been a big undertaking. Maximilian " laye style lyke a dormouse, nothynge doynge," and Henry therefore was inclined to welcome proposals for peace laid before him by Lord d'Esquerdes on behalf of Charles VIII.[2]   The King of France was just then inflamed with the ambitious plan of invading Italy in support of his claim to the kingdom of Naples.   An English invasion and the presence of an English army, which might lead to a revolt of the discontented nobles of Brittany, would be fatal to this scheme.   Charles VIII. therefore, following his father's lead, offered a substantial sum in return for the withdrawal of the English army. Henry was similarly inclined for peace.   He must have seen clearly enough that he had been the cat's-paw of his wily allies, that he was fighting Ferdinand's battles, Maximilian's battles, not England's battles by any means, and not even Brittany's battles, since

[1] Dr. Gairdner, following Polydor Vergil and Hall, gives 6th October as the date.   The correct date, 2nd October, is found in the Privy Purse Expenses (*Excerpta Historica*, 91–2).   See Busch, *op. cit.*, p. 333.

[2] Overtures had been made even before he sailed from England and were discussed while he was at Calais, " where the calm winds of peace began to blow."

the independence of the duchy was lost beyond
recovery. The spirited appeal by which he had
obtained a Parliamentary grant and aroused something like a war fever in England, was, as the king
well knew, a century out of date. The conquests
that England had failed to keep were not readily to
be won back. France was consolidated and growing
stronger every year, and England had been weakened
by fifty years of civil war. A war of ambition was a
formidable undertaking for the first Tudor king, and
the sinister rumour of a new Yorkist plot had just
reached him. Henry's sound, dull common-sense kept
his mind free from quixotic schemes. It was the path
of safety, not the road to glory, that allured him.
His imagination was never fired with the ambition of
carving out the career of an Alexander or a Henry V.
It is clear, however, that he had an adequate if
not an aggressive feeling for the maintenance of the
national honour, and the terms suggested for the
treaty gave him a chance of withdrawing without
dishonour from a war into which he had reluctantly
entered.[1] Moreover, he could congratulate himself on
being the only one of the great powers that had not
deserted his allies and been false to his engagements,
a signal distinction at a time when diplomatic double-
dealing was more than usually fashionable. Charles's
overtures gave him a chance of repaying his treacherous
allies in their own coin, and he decided to make peace.

The king attempted to throw the glamour of
popularity over his sound but inglorious decision to
abandon the war. His captains drew up a petition
speaking in feeling terms of the " great and outrageous

---

[1] Money, as usual, was a powerful motive with Henry. Further
expense involved heavy taxation and grave political danger.

cold of the winter season," of the difficulty of pro-
visioning the camp when cut off from England by
" the great rage and tempest of winds and weather ";
the allies, they said, were treacherous, the town was
strong, Sir John Savage had already fallen, and so on.
The treaty of Etaples therefore was signed on 3rd
November 1492. By it Charles VIII. agreed to pay
725,000 gold crowns in yearly instalments of 50,000
francs.[1] Each party promised not to help the other's
enemies ; Henry undertook not to assist Maximilian
and Charles promised not to harbour Henry's rebels.

On 4th November the camp before Boulogne heard
the peace proclaimed. The news of peace, we are
told, was " bitter, soure and dolourous " to the
English, " they were in great fumes, angry and evil
content, that the occasion of so glorious a victory to
them manifestly was . . . refused, putte by and
shamefully slacked." The king was thought to have
betrayed his people, to have imposed heavy taxation
for the sake of a sham war. But Henry's policy,
though it failed to win popular approval, was obviously
the right one. Peace with honour, or at all events
without dishonour, was desirable for England, as well
as an absolute necessity to the founder of the Tudor
dynasty, which was shortly to be faced, as the king
perhaps already knew, by another dangerous conspiracy. The king, much wiser than his people, saw
that he could never hope to reconquer Normandy
and Guienne, and he had already found that the

---

[1] This money was paid every year. Popular opinion in England
regarded it as a tribute paid to buy off the old claim to the crown
of France. Henry's diplomacy had in this respect appeased the
national vanity. As the " écu d'or " was worth about ten or eleven
shillings the indemnity amounted to about £370,000, or over three
and a half millions of modern money.

expenses of foreign war led inevitably to tumults in England.

With the withdrawal of his army from Boulogne Henry's first and last appearance as leader of an English army, bent upon foreign conquest, was at an end. He never again took up arms outside Britain, and his policy became studiously insular.

A month later (January 1492–3), Charles and Ferdinand also came to terms. The two border counties of Rousillon and Cerdagne were restored to Spain, which had thus gained its point without any very great exertion. At the same time, as if to show the value of the treaty of alliance with Spain, upon which Henry set so much store, Ferdinand promised to help Charles against all his enemies, and in particular against his " old enemies " the English, as well as against Maximilian, and the chances of the Anglo-Spanish match apparently vanished in a clause by which the kings of France and of Spain bound themselves not to entertain any proposal of a marriage alliance with Henry or Maximilian. Of all the powers engaged Ferdinand had come out of the affair the most successfully. He had scored all along the line. While the bulk of his forces had been engaged in a successful struggle with the Moors, a few men and the exercise of his unmatched skill as a diplomatist had won for him the coveted provinces and an alliance with the King of France. Even the ally he had overreached and made use of had not been lost, and Henry still counted Ferdinand his friend and ally.

Maximilian, as might have been expected, felt Henry's desertion keenly.[1] All his splendid schemes

---

[1] In justice to Maximilian it should be noticed that his inactivity had not been due to want of will to co-operate with Henry. At the

had come to nothing, both his allies had deserted him, his daughter had lost her royal husband, and he had lost the heiress of Brittany.   Though France had been the instrument of his humiliation he soon came to terms with Charles, but appears to have pursued Henry henceforth with bitter hatred.   Frankfort might be set off against Etaples, but Maximilian was slow to forgive his ready pupil in the art of repudiating binding obligations.

The net results of Henry's first achievements as a diplomatist had been moderate rather than brilliant. He had made good his footing among the great powers of Europe, but the treacherous friendship of Ferdinand was more than counterbalanced by the embittered hostility of Maximilian.   He had gained a large sum of money, but the old enemy France had advanced her borders and faced England across the Channel.   He had great hopes of the Spanish alliance, but so far he had served Spain and obtained no reward.

As far as the relations of England and France are concerned, the treaty of Etaples, which remained in force all through the reign, marks the point at which medievalism gave way to modernism.   With it ended the last attempt of an English king to push his claims to the throne of France.   Henceforth the medieval ambition drops into the background, and anti-French feeling ceases to be the pivot of English policy.   Wars of conquest are replaced by years of peace and friendly commercial rivalry.

moment when Henry was negotiating the peace, Maximilian was straining every nerve to raise men, and a month later 4000 Germans would have joined the camp before Boulogne.

CHAPTER IV

BAD news had hastened the king's departure from France. He had been warned that another con-
spiracy was on foot. Like the attempt of Lambert Simnel it was the work of disaffected Yorkists, and like that, too, it was an attempt to overthrow Henry by producing a pretender who claimed the throne as heir of the Yorkist line. The second conspiracy, however, was much more formidable than the first. It was the most dangerous plot that Henry ever had to face; it handicapped him at critical moments, and its shadow lies over many years of his reign.

The Perkin Warbeck plot first saw the light in Ireland in 1491. There the Yorkist malcontents had been emboldened by impunity. Bad harvests had brought famine; blood feuds and anarchy flourished. Henry had not dared to punish Kildare, the all-powerful Lord Deputy, for his share in Lambert Simnel's rising, and the oath of allegiance he had reluctantly taken did not prevent him from disobeying the king's summons to England and meditating further treachery. The hopes of the Yorkist party gathered round the young Earl of Warwick, and his name was the focus of conspiracy at home and abroad. In December 1489, the Abbot of Abingdon had been concerned in a plot to set him free, and executed for his share in it. Rumours of his escape were constantly

pierre varbeck naïf de Tournaÿ suppose pour Richard
Duc d'Jorck peind fils d'Edouard iv. hoy d'Angleterre l'an 149
J'ai perdu à londres sur la fin de l'an 1499

Emery Walker, Photo

PERKIN WARBECK
From the National Portrait Gallery photograph of a 16th century drawing by a
French or Flemish artist, preserved in the library of the town of Arras

started. A letter written in September 1491 by John
Taylor, a Yorkist exile,[1] to one John Hayes, who,
though formerly a servant to the late Duke of Clarence,
had been given an official position by Henry,[2] contains
the earliest mention of the plot. According to this
letter, the King of France had been brought into the
conspiracy, and had decided to support the claims
of the Earl of Warwick " in thre parties out of the
Royalme." [3] This letter makes it obvious that a
plot for advancing the claims of the imprisoned
earl was already on foot. It only remained for the
Yorkist conspirators, assured of French support, to
find a suitable person to pose as the imprisoned
earl. The plot thus gaining ground in England
and France had reached maturity in Ireland.
The Anglo-Irish lords were pondering the details
of the conspiracy when, with dramatic opportune-
ness, their attention was directed to a handsome,
graceful lad of about seventeen,[4] who, gorgeously
dressed in silk apparel, made a brave figure in the
streets of Cork. In him they found the figure-head
of whom they were in search, and they approached
him with the suggestion that he should declare
himself to be the Earl of Warwick. This boy was
Perkin Warbeck. According to his public confession,
the details of which are corroborated by contemporary

[1] Taylor had been a surveyor of customs under Edward IV.
and Richard III. He had been pardoned by Henry in June 1489,
but was still a malcontent and was living in France. He is
very prominent in all the early stages of the Perkin Warbeck
affair.

[2] *Rot. Parl.*, vi. 504 ; *Materials*, i. 20, 189, 198, 201, 211, 237, 296,
309, 400, 445, 459 ; ii. 89, 93–4, 454.

[3] See *Rot. Parl.*, vi. 454.

[4] He was aged twenty-three in 1497. Brown, *Ven. Cal.*, No. 760.

records and letters,[1] he was the son of John Warbeck
or Osbeck,[2] a boatman and collector of customs in
Tournay, and he was born in 1474 or 1475. His
childhood had been eventful. He had lived with his
successive masters in Antwerp and Middleburg, and
in about 1489 he had travelled to Portugal in the
service of the wife of Sir Edward Brampton, a well-
known Yorkist. He afterwards entered the service
of Pregent Meno, a merchant of Brittany, who brought
him to Ireland in the autumn of 1491. Here, as we
have seen, he was approached by the Yorkist conspirators. Warbeck, however, refused to personate
the Earl of Warwick, swearing before the mayor
" that he was not the son of Clarence or one of his
race," and denied upon oath a subsequent suggestion
that he was a bastard son of Richard III. This would
have been a curious claim to the throne in any case,
and Richard's son was known to be in Henry's hands.
The conspirators, however, seem to have determined
to cast the youth for the chief rôle in their production,
and offered him another part, that of Richard, Duke
of York, the younger of the princes murdered in the
Tower. By promising him powerful supporters, they
ultimately prevailed upon him. " And so," says
Perkin in his confession, " agaynst my will made
me to lerne Inglisshe and taught me what I shuld
doo and say." [3]

So far the conspiracy had not been joined by men

---

[1] *Registers of Tournay*, printed by Dr. Gairdner, *Perkin Warbeck*,
pp. 334–335; *Archæologia*, xxvii., 1838, pp. 156–158, 199–200.

[2] Warbeck is probably the correct form of the name. Gairdner,
op. cit., p. 334. Henry VII. in his letter to Waterford (Halliwell,
Letters, i. 177) writes Osbeck, and that form appears also in the
confession. See Appendix II. below.

[3] Hall, pp. 488–9 ; *City Chron.*, pp. 219–221.

of the first importance. Its leaders were Hubert
Burgh and John Walter, citizens of Cork, and John
Taylor, who had returned from his French exile, but
the conspirators counted upon the support of the
Earl of Kildare. In a letter written in 1493,[1] Kildare
stoutly denied that he had helped " the French lad,"
but this denial came at a time when Henry had
proved himself strong enough to punish treachery,
and cannot be accepted in face of the evidence of
his complicity.

Warbeck certainly remained in Ireland in the
winter of 1491–2, learning English and being coached
up in the part he was to play. He obtained the
active support of the Earl of Desmond, who wrote
letters in his own name and in that of " King Eduartis
son " to James IV. of Scotland,[2] who was then
meditating hostilities and hoped to help himself by
hindering Henry. A little later another of Henry's
royal neighbours joined the conspiracy. Charles VIII.
sent envoys inviting Warbeck to France. He accepted the invitation, " thinking to be exalted into
heaven when he was called to the acquaintaunce and
familiarite of kynges and princes," [3] and was present
at the court of Charles VIII. when Henry invaded
France. He was treated as a royal prince and was
joined by various Yorkist rebels. His stay in France
was brief; the intrigues of Taylor and Hayes came to
light, and while the peace negotiations were going on
Henry learnt of the new conspiracy. One of the
clauses of the treaty of Etaples bound Charles VIII.
not to harbour or support rebels or traitors against
Henry VII. Perkin, obliged to leave France, made his

---

[1] *L. and P. Hen. VII.*, ii. 55.   [2] *Ibid.*, pp. 326–7.
[3] Hall, p. 463.

way to the safe haven for all Yorkist traitors, the
court of Margaret of Burgundy. She received him
gladly, and openly acknowledged him as her nephew,
" the whyte Rose, prynce of England."   In this policy
she was supported by the counsel of the young Archduke Philip and by Maximilian, who was burning to
be revenged upon Henry for the treaty of Etaples.
Thus, within a few months of his first appearance,
Perkin Warbeck had been acknowledged by crowned
heads as well as by Yorkist leaders as a prince of
the House of York.   It is a curious point as to how
far Warbeck's powerful supporters believed in the
genuineness of their claimant.   Their readiness to
profess belief in his identity with the Yorkist prince
sprang from their interest in maintaining the imposture.   To set up a pretender who might shake the
king's throne was their object, and the impostor could
easily be replaced by the true prince if the conspiracy
succeeded.   Some of Warbeck's adherents may have
been genuinely convinced.   The fate of the two young
sons of Edward IV. was still a mystery, and no
conclusive proof of their death had been made public.[1]
Stories of their escape from the Tower were constantly being circulated, and Perkin's age and appearance corresponded closely enough to deceive people
remote from the court.   Thus the Yorkist conspirators
could count upon a certain number of genuinely
convinced supporters, and those who pulled the
strings of the puppet behind the scenes naturally
made loud professions of their belief in his claims.
One by one all the crowned heads in Europe (with

---

[1] One writer has suggested that Henry VII. murdered the princes,
but his arguments have been shattered by Dr. Gairdner. *Eng. Hist.
Rev.*, vi. pp. 250-83, 444-64, 806-15.

the possible exception of Ferdinand and Isabella)[1] acknowledged the youth as the Duke of York, and, what is more, they treated him with the honour due to his high rank. Some, like Maximilian, who, long years after Perkin's confession had been made public, spoke of him as the Duke of York, may have been genuinely convinced, others, like the Duchess Margaret, were convinced as a matter of policy.[2] Anyway it was galling enough to Henry.

From the duchess, "that fierce Juno" who pursued Henry with a "woman's undying hatred," Perkin probably received the training in the part of a Yorkist prince,[3] the story of which has been told often and with many exaggerations. In February 1492–3 Perkin was writing letters to Yorkists in England under the title of "The Merchant of the Ruby," and in these negotiations it is probable that some of the Hanse merchants acted as the pretender's agents.[4]

Henry was alive to the danger. He sent an embassy in July 1493 to remonstrate with Maximilian and Philip on the conduct of the dowager-duchess,[5] and on the 20th of the month he wrote to Sir Gilbert Talbot, ordering him to summon men to resist any attempt made by Margaret on behalf of Perkin.[6] From this important letter it appears that Henry was already in possession of the main facts as to Perkin's

---

[1] See Berg., *Spanish Cal.*, Pref. lxxxiii.

[2] Perkin later asserted that the duchess knew from the beginning that he was not the Duke of York. Berg., *Spanish Cal.*, p. 185.

[3] She had last seen her brother's court in 1480.

[4] *Archæologia*, xxvii.

[5] Rymer, xii. 544; *L. and P. Hen. VII.*, ii. 374; Ellis, 2nd Ser., i. 167 *seq.*

[6] Printed by Gairdner, *Perkin Warbeck*, pp. 275–6; Ellis, *Letters*, 1st Ser., i. 19–21; Halliwell, *Letters of Kings of Eng.*, i. 172–3.

birth, early career, and stay in Ireland. The king
mentions " the great malice that the Lady Margaret
of Burgaigne beareth continually against us . . . by
the untrue contriving eftsoons of another feigned lad
called Perkin Warbeck, born at Tournay in Picardy,"
and alludes to the duchess's method of getting
together supporters for the pretender by promising
" to certain alien captains of estrange nations, to
have duchies, counties, and baronies within the
realm of England." [1] The king's ambassadors, however, could not obtain any satisfactory reply to
these remonstrances. They were assured of the
friendship of Philip and Maximilian, but were told
that the duchess was an independent sovereign
within her dowry lands and that her conduct there
could not be interfered with.[2] Henry retaliated by
an original move which illustrates his despotic bent.
The interests of the English wool merchants were
sacrificed to the necessities of the Tudor dynasty.
On 18th September proclamations were issued forbidding all commercial intercourse with Flanders.
All Flemings were ordered to leave the country and
their goods were seized ; the Merchant Adventurers
were recalled from Antwerp and their mart was
transferred to Calais.[3] A similar prohibition of trade
with England was issued in Flanders, but not until
some months later (May 1494). The political consequences unfortunately did not justify Henry's action.
Merchants on both sides suffered loss by the dislo-

[1] He possibly obtained the information as to the pretender's
birth and family from his late master, Pregent Meno, who in April
1495 obtained a grant of £300, being later naturalised and made
governor of an Irish castle. *L. and P. Hen. VII.*, ii. 375.

[2] Pol. Verg., 592.

[3] *L. and P. Hen. VII.*, ii. 374 ; Hall, 467. *City Chron.*, p. 200.

cation of trade without the pressure upon Philip and
Maximilian being sufficient to make them dismiss
Warbeck from the Netherlands ; and in London the
privileges of the Hanse merchants, who as foreigners
were still engaged in the trade with Burgundy forbidden to Englishmen, led to a dangerous riot and
attack on the Steelyard (15th October 1493).[1]
There appeared to be no immediate danger to Henry
from Perkin Warbeck's pretensions.   Both Margaret
and Maximilian lacked the means required to provide
an invading fleet for their protégé, and he remained
under Margaret's protection, corresponding with
various English traitors until the late autumn of 1493.

   The relations between England and Spain at the
moment were friendly but not cordial.   In the treaties
of Etaples and Barcelona both Henry and Ferdinand
had ignored their mutual obligations under the treaty
of Medina de Campo.   The much discussed marriage
alliance seemed to have been abandoned.   Henry,
however, had not given up hope.   In March 1493,
months after the treaty between France and Spain,
he proposed a modification of the treaty of Medina,
but the Spaniards having gained Rousillon and
Cerdagne had no further use for the English alliance.
Ferdinand was too cautious to make an unnecessary
enemy, but the Barcelona treaty bound him not to
make a marriage alliance with England.   For the
moment the friendship of France was worth more
than that of England.   No answer was made to
Henry's overtures until nearly two years had gone
by, when, as will be seen, the aggressive attitude of
France made Henry's alliance again valuable to Spain.

   [1] *City Chron.*, p. 198; Hall, 468 ; Fabyan, *Chronicle* (ed. Ellis),
684.

Henry, however, had nothing to complain of in the
Spanish attitude to Perkin Warbeck. Perkin wrote
from Flanders to Queen Isabella of Castile asking for
her help and mentioning the support he had received
from France, Burgundy, Denmark, Scotland, the
King of the Romans, and the Archduke Philip.[1]
The Spanish monarchs were much too cautious to
take up Perkin's cause, and they obviously doubted
the truth of his pretensions. His letter, which gave
a very unconvincing account of his early life, being
conspicuous for its omission of all important names
and dates,[2] and for a mistake as to the age of the
prince he claimed to be, was endorsed " from Richard,
who calls himself the King of England."

In November 1493 Warbeck left the Netherlands
and moved into Austria, in the hope of gaining more
substantial help than the promises the duchess had
been lavish with. He was well received by Maximilian, was treated as a royal prince, and took his
place among the royalties who attended the funeral
of the Emperor Frederick III.[3] The fact that Perkin
was being received in Vienna as a royal prince was
an insult rather than a pressing danger, and Henry
was powerless to interfere. In the summer of 1494
Perkin Warbeck accompanied his latest patron to
Antwerp, and Maximilian went a step further. He
acknowledged the pretender as rightful King of
England, gave him a bodyguard of twenty archers
bearing the badge of the white rose, and allowed him

---

[1] *Archæologia*, xxvii. 199.

[2] The letter, dated 25th August 1493, is printed by Madden,
Archæologia, xxvii. 156. It mentions the " proud and wicked
tyranny of the usurper Henry of Richmond."

[3] *Archæologia*, xxvii. 2–7.

to decorate his house in Antwerp with the arms of England, inscribed with the legend, " The arms of Richard Prince of Wales and Duke of York," [1] an assumption which roused some travelling Englishmen to fury. This insult provoked Henry into remonstrance, and the Garter King at Arms was despatched to assure Maximilian and the duchess that Henry had proofs of their protégé's low origin, and to proclaim publicly the facts of Perkin's birth.

Meanwhile the relations between England and France were cordial. Payments of the pension due were punctually made, and Charles VIII. adopted a very correct attitude in the matter of the pretender. He kept Henry informed of his actions in Flanders, offered to help him with men and ships if the threatened attack was made, and forbade any help being given to the pretender in France.[2] In view of Charles's preoccupation with his ambitious schemes in Italy nothing could have been more generous than his offers. Henry replied in the same cordial spirit. The Richmond herald was sent into Italy with carefully drawn instructions (10th Aug. 1493) thanking Charles for his offer but making light of the pretensions of the "*garçon*," who, he said, was known to every one of rank and position in England to be but the son of a boatman of Tournay. He spoke guardedly of Charles's claim to Naples and suggested mediation. Henry also notified his brother that England was " more peaceful and obedient than it had been within the memory of man," and announced his

---

[1] Busch, *op. cit.*, p. 93, quoting Molinet, *Chroniques*, v. 15 *seq.*

[2] *Archæologia.* xxvii. 201-4 ; *L. and P. Henry VII.*, ii. 292-7 ; Rymer, *Fœdera*, xii. 526, 550, 569, 575, 623, 630.

intention of bringing the " wild Irish into peace and order." [1]

In England Henry was taking what steps he could to neutralise Warbeck's powerfully patronised pretensions. In November, Prince Henry, the king's second son, who was born on 22nd June 1491, was created Duke of York, the pretender's title. The occasion was celebrated by banquets and tournaments, the prize, a ruby ring, being presented by the Princess Margaret. The young prince, then aged four, rode upon a courser to Westminster. After these brilliant scenes, which gave "greate gladnesse to all the common people," [2] the king struck sudden blows at the Yorkist conspirators in England. There is evidence that he had for a long time been aware of the treasonable negotiations between his subjects and the pretender. [3] His spies had been busy in Flanders. Towards the end of the year he obtained the detailed information he wanted by buying over Sir Robert Clifford, one of Perkin's most enthusiastic supporters, who had declared that he knew the young man by his face to be the son of King Edward. His enthusiasm, however, was not proof against the offer of a pardon and the promise of reward—he obtained a grant of £500 in the following January [4]—and at the end of the year he came back to England to betray his former associates. [5] Already in November William

[1] *L. and P. Hen. VII.*, ii. 295; *Arch.*, xxvii. 200–204. Richmond also had secret instructions to point out that the help given by Maximilian to the pretender was an endeavour to set an enemy of France on the throne of England.

[2] Full details are given in Cott. MS., Jul. B., xii. f. 91, printed in *L. and P. Hen. VII.*, i. 388–402.

[3] *Rot. Parl.*, vi. 504 ; *Stat.*, ii. 632.

[4] *Excerpta Historica* (ed. Bentley), 100.

[5] *L. and P. Hen. VII.*, ii. 374 ; Bacon, *Henry VII.*, 152 ; Pol. Verg., 593.

Worsely, Dean of St. Paul's, Robert Ratcliff, John
Ratcliff, Lord FitzWalter, Sir Simon Montford, Sir
Thomas Thwaites, William Daubeney, the Provincial
of the Dominicans, and the Prior of Langley and
several others had been arrested before the mayor
in the Guildhall and condemned. The churchmen
escaped the death penalty ; the others were either
beheaded on Tower Hill or hanged at Tyburn, with
the exception of Lord FitzWalter. He was imprisoned
in the Tower but, attempting to escape, was executed
the following year. Two others, Cressyner and Astwood, were pardoned at the foot of the gallows in
consideration of their youth. All the rebels were subsequently attainted by Act of Parliament in 1495.[1]

A confession dated 14th March 1495-6, made by
one Bernard de Vignolles, implicates several men
(Dr. Hussey, Archdeacon of London, among others)
who were not punished, and it is therefore doubtful
how much weight can be given to it in details ; at
the same time it throws a flood of light upon the
nature of the intrigues by which Henry was surrounded. There is an extraordinary story of how
the conspirators, wishing to kill " the king and his
children, his mother, and those near his person,"
visited an astrologer in Rome, and how, the first man
failing, they obtained from a second a box of oint-
ment to spread along and across some door or passage
through which the king would walk, which would
bring about his murder by those who loved him best.[2]

The conspiracy was to claim a much more
exalted victim. The information given by Clifford

---

[1] *City Chron.*, 203 ; Pol. Verg., 592 ; *Rot. Parl.*, vi. 504-7 ; *Stat.*,
ii. 632-3.

[2] See Brit. Mus. Add. MSS., 5485, f. 230 ; *L. and P. Hen. VII.*,
ii. 318-23 ; *Arch.*, xxvii. 205-9.

implicated Sir William Stanley, whose help at
the critical moment had given Henry victory
at Bosworth Field. He enjoyed a full measure of
Henry's confidence, held high office at court, and his
brother was the king's stepfather. When one of
those nearest him fell into treason, the king's hardly
given confidence must have been shaken. Unfortunately the evidence of Stanley's share in the conspiracy
is slight, but he seems to have promised Clifford
to help the pretender with men and money.[1] Facts
which came to light many years later (1521) throw
light upon Henry's characteristic conduct and his
" convenient diligence for inveigling." It appears
that Henry knew of Sir William Stanley's treason
two or three years before he laid it to his charge,
" and covertly watched him, keeping it secret and
always gathered upon him more and more." [2] Stanley
was tried before the Court of King's Bench sitting in
Westminster Hall at the end of January, and was
beheaded on 16th February 1493–4. The whole of
his vast wealth fell to the king.[3]

The deadly character of the plot that was checked
for a time by these executions appears from certain
documents executed by the pretender in December
and January. Perkin Warbeck's pretensions had
reached the pitch of disposing of the towns and
castles of England and of the succession to the throne.
He actually acknowledged Maximilian, in return for

[1] See *Eng. Hist. Rev.*, xiv. 529–34, where Mr. Archbold prints a
report of Stanley's trial, from which it appears that Clifford was
Stanley's go-between with Warbeck from 1493 onwards.

[2] *L. and P. Hen. VIII.* (ed. Brewer), iii. 1, 490.

[3] According to Polydor Vergil he confessed his crime. Pol. Verg.,
593; *City Chron.*, pp. 203–5. André's statements are incorrect,
Vita, 69. Henry paid the expenses of Stanley's funeral, and made
grants to his servants. *Excerpta Hist.*, 101, 102.

his generous renunciation of an apocryphal claim to
the English crown, as his heir in the throne of England, if he died without male issue. He promised
to the Duchess Margaret, in whose mind the loss of
the English lands granted her by Edward IV. and
confiscated by Henry VII. still rankled, the town and
castle of Scarborough as well as the manor of Hunsdon
and the arrears of dowry for which she had long been
clamouring.[1] But the execution of Stanley and the
others was fatal to these preposterous schemes. The
back of the conspiracy was broken, and the danger
of a foreign invasion combined with a Yorkist revolt
passed away. Henceforth the conspirators in England " were as sand without lime."

The aggressive policy of Charles VIII. indirectly
strengthened the position of Perkin Warbeck. In
the autumn of 1494, Europe viewed with alarm the
young king's invasion of Italy in support of his claim
to the throne of Naples. By the end of February
Naples had fallen. His magnificent march through
Italy was unopposed. All Europe was alarmed.
Ferdinand of Spain, lately the ally of France, became
active in bringing together her enemies. A revival
of the coalition against France took place, the Pope,
Spain, Maximilian, Milan and Venice binding themselves together for mutual defence in the Holy League
of 31st March 1495. In view of the French danger,
the attitude of Spain changed ; the English alliance
was once more important, and an effort was made to
detach Henry from France. A long delayed answer
to Henry's overtures was sent early in 1495, declaring
that, since the former treaties were invalid for lack

---

[1] Documents in Archives of Antwerp, quoted by Dr. Gairdner,
Perkin Warbeck, pp. 290-2.

of Henry's signature, Spain had been obliged to make peace with France.   Henry had already shown that Italy was not outside the range of his foreign policy, and his interest in Italian affairs was noticed by the Milanese envoy.   "He is most thoroughly acquainted with the affairs of Italy and receives especial information of every event. . . . The merchants, most especially the Florentines, never cease giving the King of England advices."   He had obtained the nominal but practically useless alliance of the Duke of Milan in the Brittany affair,[1] and had even thought of a marriage between him and the queen's sister.   In 1493 he had approached another of the Italian princes, sending the Order of the Garter to Alfonzo, then Duke of Calabria, who became King of Naples in 1494, on the eve of the French invasion.   Henry had been on very friendly terms with Charles of France, but even he was beginning to show uneasiness about his designs in Italy.   He was reluctant to see an independent and friendly kingdom swallowed up by the advancing French monarchy, but his offer to mediate, conveyed by the Richmond herald, had come to nothing.   In 1495 the herald was again despatched to inquire into affairs in Italy, assure Charles that Henry had the love and obedience of his subjects as fully as any of his predecessors, and allude to the futility of the claims of the " *garçon*."   To the powers, however, the alliance between France and England seemed unimpaired, so that any attack on the latter would weaken the force opposed to the coalition. Maximilian, therefore, at last roused himself to a determined effort to set a pretender on the throne of England and replace a friend of the King of France

[1] 27th July 1490. See above, p. 99.

by a creature of his own.   As an Italian diplomatist
put it, " If the Duke of York obtained the crown,
the King of the Romans and the League might avail
themselves of England against the King of France
as if the island were their own." [1]   Henry's policy
had made "the island" count in European politics,
and the powers were anxious to replace him by a man
of straw, or at all events to stir up trouble for him
at home, that would prevent him from interfering
abroad.   Thus behind the pretender was the whole
weight of the Holy League.

In May the preparations were completed.   An
embassy from Scotland had promised Perkin the
support of James IV., the duchess appealed to the
Pope on behalf of her nephew and took the oppor-
tunity of vilifying Henry's ancestry and describing
him as an usurper of the throne by force of arms.
The adventurer sailed from Flanders at the end of
June with troops provided by the needy but hopeful
Maximilian at great inconvenience.[2]   On 3rd of July
Warbeck and his fleet of fourteen ships appeared off
Deal.   Five or six hundred of his men landed ;
Perkin, suspecting a snare, remained afloat.   Finding
they " cowde haue no comfort of the cuntre " they
withdrew towards their ships, but were attacked by
the country people under the Mayor of Sandwich,
and beaten off before the king's troops arrived.[3]

[1] Brown, *Ven. Cal.*, Nos. 651, 677.

[2] *Ibid.*, No. 648.   The exact strength of Perkin's force is uncertain.   The *City Chronicle* gives the number as 1400 (p. 205).
The Venetian ambassadors wrote of 1500, " and mariners besides."
The report that Perkin had 10,000 men with him as well as a Scotch
fleet and troops was an exaggerated story spread by the Milanese
ambassador.   Brown, *Ven. Cal.*, No. 642.   It is doubtful whether
the Scotch sent any help.   [3] *City Chron.*, 206–7.

Two of his followers were slain, others drowned, and
169 were captured. His great army of " valiant
captains of all nations, some bankrupts, some false
English sanctuary men, some thieves, robbers, and
vagabonds," had not inspired confidence among the
Kentish peasants. Warbeck did not act on the suggestion of the villagers " that he should return to his
father and mother, who lived in France and were well
known there," but sailed away to Ireland, deserting
his beaten followers. The Sheriff of Kent led 159 of
them to London, " railed in ropes, like horses drawing
in a cart." Some were imprisoned in the Tower and
others in Newgate. The king was in no mood to be
merciful; the prisoners were arraigned and condemned.
One hundred and fifty were hanged in Kent, Essex,
Sussex, and Norfolk " by the sea side," the foreign
leaders were beheaded in London and their heads
set upon London Bridge.[1]

The long threatened expedition, the climax of so
many ambitious schemes, had been a miserable failure.
The effect of the fiasco in Europe was to strengthen
Henry's position and to discredit the claims of the
pretender. Ferdinand and Isabella, who had never
believed in Warbeck, wrote in August to their ambassador making light of his pretensions. " As for
the affair of him who calls himself the Duke of York
we hold it for a jest." [2] Henry's improved position
appears from Ferdinand's anxiety for him to become
a member of the league against France, as he had
shown some intention of doing. For this a recon-

---

[1] *City Chron.*, pp. 206–7 ; Pol. Verg. 595–6 ; Hall, 472 ; *Paston
Lett.*, iii. 386, 387 ; *Excerpta Hist.*, 101 ; Berg., *Spanish Cal.*, pp. 58–60.
André's account (p. 66) is brief and inaccurate.

[2] Berg., *Spanish Cal.*, Nos. 99, 103.

ciliation with Maximilian was necessary. This unpalatable suggestion was pressed upon Henry with
the old offer of the Spanish marriage, and in August
their ambassador was instructed to sound him on the
question of joining the Holy League. A new alliance
between England and Spain was proposed, the King
of Spain declaring that the treaty of Medina was
invalid because the King of England had not sworn
to it. This description, which audaciously made
waste-paper of the treaty the Spaniards themselves
had spoken of as " concluded," showed great lack of
consideration for Henry's feelings. Henry, however,
faithful as ever to his Spanish dream, " spoke always
in most bland words," and professed himself willing
to be reconciled to Maximilian " in spite of his ingratitude." [1] The King of Spain at the same time
warned Henry against French treachery, promised
assistance against Perkin, and expressed his intention
of persuading Maximilian and the King of Scots to
have nothing to do with the pretender.[2] Maximilian,
however, who in his sanguine way had rejoiced in
vain over a report that Warbeck's invasion of England
had been successful,[3] still seems to have believed in
his claims. In September 1495 he wrote to the
Pope appealing to him to support " Richard, Duke of
York, the born son of Edward, the lawful and late
deceased king," and his " excellent title to the kingdom of England." [4] Reconciliation with Henry
seemed quite out of the question, but Maximilian's
attitude was not popular with the other European

---

[1] Berg., *Spanish Cal.*, No. 103.
[2] *Ibid.*, Nos. 92–99, 103, 107.
[3] Brown, *Ven. Cal.*, No. 649.
[4] *Ibid.*, iv. 1042.

powers.   In England, too, the King of the Romans
" was held in no account." [1]

Perkin's expedition had sailed westward after the
failure of the attempt in Kent, bound for Ireland,
where the conspiracy had first seen the light.   The
years that had gone by since Warbeck had last been
in Ireland had seen a great change there.   As Henry
had informed his brother Charles, he had reduced the
wild Irish to submission.   His lordship of Ireland had
become a reality ; Kildare had been deprived of the
office of lord deputy, and was in disgrace.   Sir Edward
Poynings had crushed others of Perkin Warbeck's
former adherents and was in command of a disciplined
English force. [2]

The pretender reached Ireland at the end of July
in command of a fleet of eleven ships, some of which
were probably Scotch,[3] and boldly attacked Waterford,
the only town which had been consistently loyal to
Henry VII.   The siege lasted for eleven days.   Poynings led a force to relieve the town, and on 3rd
August Warbeck was obliged to raise the siege with
the loss of three of his ships.[4]   For several months,
from August to November, when he reappeared in
Scotland, we have no record of his doings.   Part of
the gap may be filled by importing a story from the
Lambeth MS.,[5] part of which is, no doubt wrongly,
assigned to the year 1497.[6]   According to this story,

---

[1] Brown, *Ven. Cal.*, No. 655.   [2] See below, pp. 297–300.

[3] One of the three captured by the English was called "*le
Kekeoute.*"   *L. and P. Hen. VII.*, ii. 299.

[4] *Carew Papers*, 472 ; Hattcliffe's report, *L. and P. Hen. VII.*,
ii. 297–318, 375 ; *Excerpta Hist.*, 100–103.

[5] *Carew Papers* (Misc.), 472.

[6] Dr. Gairdner discusses this point fully in *Perkin Warbeck,*
pp. 321–326.

Warbeck on raising the siege of Waterford made his
way to Cork, where he was received by his friend,
John Walters, then mayor. Ships from Waterford
followed in pursuit. Finding his cause in Ireland
hopeless for the time, Warbeck decided to try his luck
in Scotland. Here part of another narrative, that
of Zurita the Spanish historian, may be dovetailed
into the story, and we can trace the adventurer sailing
for Scotland, but being driven back and wrecked
upon the Irish coast. He crossed the mountains in
disguise to a small Irish port and, finding another
ship at last, made his way to Scotland.[1]

It is not quite clear to what extent the King of
Scotland had pledged himself to Perkin. As we have
seen, the adventurer applied to him almost at the
beginning of his chequered career. It is probable
that the story he told appealed to the romantic strain
in the Stuart character, while policy suggested that a
pretender to the English throne might be a useful
weapon. There is no proof that James gave help to
Warbeck before 1495,[2] when he is found negotiating
with the Duchess of Burgundy and her court of
disaffected Yorkists. In the spring of 1495 a Scotch
invasion of England was contemplated. James certainly made preparations to send ships and men to
assist Perkin's invasion of England, and votes of
money are recorded for the " passage in Ingland in
fortifieing and supleing of the prince of Ingland,
Richard, Duke of York." [3] At all events, Warbeck

---

[1] *Ibid.* Polydor Vergil and Hall are wrong in saying that Perkin
Warbeck returned to Flanders and thence went to Scotland.
Pol. Verg., p. 596 ; Hall, p. 472.

[2] Tytler, *Hist. of Scot.*, iii. 475 *n.*

[3] Gairdner, *Perkin Warbeck,* p. 300, quoting Aberdeen council
registers.

having failed in Ireland felt sure of a welcome in
Scotland, and late in November[1] he appeared at
Stirling, where he was given a royal reception.[2]
Great preparations had been made; hangings had
been brought from Edinburgh, and his royal host
presented the wanderer and his attendants with a
supply of garments suitable to his supposed rank.
There are notes of the " expenses made upon Prince
Richard of England his servitors," including the
purchase, for £28, of fourteen ells of white damask to
be the prince's "spousing gown," and seven ells of
velvet (£21) to be a " grete coite of the new fassoune
to the Prince with sleiffis." He received a handsome
yearly allowance, and even his offertory at Church
festivals was not forgotten. Later, at Perth, James
presented the Duke of York to his nobles; orders
were sent out to the sheriffs to assemble troops, and
early in 1496 arms and artillery were being made.[3]
These warlike preparations, however, were followed,
as often happened in Perkin's career, by a long delay.
It was probably about this time that James found a
bride for the adventurer in the person of his kins-
woman, Lady Katherine Gordon.[4] This lady lives
again after long years in the graceful and poetic
words of the letter ascribed to Perkin, which has been
unearthed among the Spanish archives. " Your

---

[1] The date was either November 20 or November 27. See *L.
and P. Hen. VII.*, ii. 327, 329. Gairdner, *op. cit.*, p. 301.

[2] Polydor Vergil, followed by Hall, reports a speech made by
Perkin to James IV. Though the whole speech was an effort of
the historian's imagination, it gives a useful reflection of contemporary rumours about the adventurer. Pol. Verg., p. 596 ;
Hall, p. 473 ; see Busch, p. 345.

[3] *L. and P. Hen. VII.*, ii. 330.

[4] Pol. Verg., p. 756.

face," he wrote, " bright and serene, gives splendour
to the cloudy sky, your eyes, brilliant as the stars,
make all pain to be forgotten and turn despair into
delight. All look at your neck which outshines
pearls, all look at your fine forehead, your purple
light of youth, your fair hair. . . . Love is not an
earthly thing, it is heaven-born. . . . Farewell, my
soul and my consolation, you, the brightest ornament
of Scotland, farewell, farewell." [1] Henceforward
Lady Katherine followed the adventurer, " whom she
ever fondly loved," through good and evil fortune,
to the end. The end of the year found Perkin still in
Scotland appearing in public as a royal prince, but still
unable to translate his shadowy royalty into reality.

Meanwhile, in England, Henry continued his preparations for resisting a Scotch invasion. His agents
kept him informed of what went on in Scotland. The
northern counties were armed, and in January and
February ships were manned and sent off against
Scotland. [2]

In view of the crisis, writs for a new Parliament,
the first since 1492, had been issued. It met on 14th
October 1495. The first statute passed was designed
to strengthen the king's hands at the critical moment.
It enacted that no one who supported the king *de
facto* should be liable to impeachment or attainder,
but excluded from the benefit of the Act any person
who should desert Henry in the future. Of course,
the Act was open to the obvious objection that it
would be repealed at once by any usurper who succeeded in dethroning Henry. But though it could

[1] Berg., *Span. Cal.*, No. 119.
[2] *L. and P. Hen. VII.*, ii. 376 ; Rymer, xii. 647 ; *Excerpta Hist.*,
pp. 110, 111.

not protect the king's faithful adherents from the consequences that would follow his defeat, it may have encouraged wavering Yorkists, who were genuinely unable to swallow the ambiguities of the Tudor title, to give their support to the man to whom Parliament declared allegiance was due. Henry realised that he was faced with the most dangerous combination that had threatened him since the beginning of his troubled reign, and he feared serious Yorkist defections in the northern counties on the arrival of the " Duke of York " and his Scotch army. Though war was imminent Henry abstained from asking for a money grant. He was empowered to collect the arrears of the last benevolence, received a grant of one tenth from Convocation, and was confirmed in his possession of the lands forfeited by the Yorkist conspirators who had been executed in 1495.[1]

But, while preparing for war, Henry did not give up hope of peace. He sent two embassies to Scotland, in June and August 1496, to propose a marriage between the Princess Margaret and James of Scotland. There is no record of the proceedings of the ambassadors, but James was obviously disinclined to discuss the matter and continued his preparations, which were duly reported to Henry by his spies. Henry had long ago elaborated an underground policy in Scotland, and spies kept him well informed of the movements of his foes. Scotch nobles, including the Earl of Angus and Lord Bothwell, were among his agents. Lord Bothwell had already taken Henry's pay for his share in an unsuccessful plot to kidnap

---

[1] *Rot. Parl.*, vi. 458–508 ; *Stat.*, ii. 568–635. For the other legislation of this Parliament, see below, p. 255.

the young king, and had been for some time in
England, but he had contrived to establish himself
in James's confidence and return to Scotland.   His
long reports to Henry are extraordinarily treacherous.
He seems to have been destitute of the elementary
instincts of patriotism, and hastened to betray his
country's secrets for gold.   He kept close watch upon
the king, reporting to Henry that the date of the
invasion was fixed for September, revealed the king's
want of money, the discontent of the people, and
even details of the artillery at Edinburgh.   Further,
he attempted to win over the king's brother, and
his letters contain hints of a plan of abducting and
carrying him off into England.   He wrote that it
would be best now in this " long night within his
tent to enterprise the matter ; for he has no watch
but the king's appointed to be about him." [1]

By this time the opinion of Europe was inclining
against the adventurer.   If Henry was to enter the
League he must be freed from the embarrassment of
Perkin's performances.   Ferdinand was again very
anxious to win Henry's friendship, and his attitude
was becoming markedly cordial.   The Anglo-Spanish
marriage, long a project in the air, became the subject
of serious negotiation.   In the summer of 1496 a new
effort was being made by the Spanish ambassadors
to induce Henry to enter the League and promise to
invade France in person, and, in return, they showed
themselves unusually amenable when discussing the
everlasting question of the marriage portion, and
genuinely anxious to heal the quarrel between England
and Scotland.   It was now the turn of Spain to de-
claim against the delay in the conclusion of the

[1] Ellis, *Letters I.* (1), 23.

English alliance, a specially awkward feature of it
being that English merchants were carrying on a trade
between France and Spain which was debarred to
the subjects of both belligerents.[1]

Henry's position in diplomacy at this moment was
undoubtedly strong. As de Puebla pointed out to
him, " the House of England now sees what never
before has been seen, that is to say that the whole
Christian world unites and allies itself with it." The
strength of Henry's position was chiefly due to the
caution which had governed his relations with France,
and the diplomatic instinct with which he extracted
gain from a complicated situation, profiting by the
fact that he seemed to hold the balance in Europe.
France and Spain were vying with each other in
repudiating Perkin, and trying to make peace between
Scotland and England. Early in 1496 Henry was
negotiating for a personal meeting with Charles,
reminding him of his offer of help, though he affected
to make light of the Scotch danger, and offering to
mediate between him and the Holy League. A marriage between Prince Arthur and the daughter of
the Duke of Bourbon had been proposed by Charles,
but Henry's answer was cold, and he hinted that
Charles's aggressions in Italy might cost him the
English alliance. A parade of friendship with France
served Henry's purpose in driving the members of the
League, especially Spain, to make still higher bids for
his alliance, while his negotiations with the League
alarmed Charles into proving how valuable his friendship could be to England. In the beginning of the
year he had sent Henry a paper describing Warbeck as
the son of a barber and offering to send his parents

[1] Berg., *Spanish Cal.*, pp. 106, 107.

into England.[1] A French embassy under Concres-
sault went to Scotland with Henry's knowledge,
armed with instructions to offer 100,000 crowns for
the surrender of Warbeck,[2] and to propose that James
should marry a French princess. Henry in the same
way was trying to induce Charles VIII. to surrender
James's cousin, the Duke of Albany, who was the
leader of the rebels and a refugee in France—perhaps
in the hope of playing off a Scotch pretender against
the English one.[3]

Maximilian's attitude was the great difficulty in
the way of Henry's entrance into the League. An
ambassador sent by Henry reported that Maximilian
was surrounded by adherents of " him of York," and
was communicating with Warbeck and the King of
Scotland.[4] Spanish influence was strong with Maximilian, and would be stronger when the proposed
marriage between the Archduke Philip and the Infanta
Juana came off;[5] but when this influence was used to
try and get him to come to terms with Henry he
showed great reluctance. To the Spanish ambassadors
who pressed him to acquiesce in Henry's inclusion
in the League, he at last give a grudging assent,
" although he could expect neither benefit nor
favour from the King of England ";[6] but when Lord
Egremont arrived as Henry's ambassador at Nord-

[1] Berg., *Spanish Cal.*, i. p. 92. This offer being reported to Spain,
brought a bid of the same kind from Ferdinand.

[2] The same brilliant idea entered into the Spanish negotiations
without success.

[3] *Cott. MSS*. D., vi. 26a ; *L. and P. Hen. VII.*, ii. 292-296; *Arch.*,
xxvii. 203.

[4] Berg., *Spanish Cal.*, i. 110.

[5] Juana sailed for Flanders in August 1496. *Ibid.*, i. 119.

[6] Brown, *Ven. Cal.*, p. 225.

lingen in January 1495-6 to meet the envoys of the
League, Maximilian proposed terms which were almost
insulting. He insisted that Henry should at once
make war upon France, and offered to negotiate a
ten years' truce and peace between him and " the
Duke of York." Ambassadors from other members
of the Holy League, Naples, Venice, and Milan, who
were present, followed the Spanish lead and strongly
urged Maximilian to omit the irritating clauses dealing
with the Duke of York. The Spanish ambassador
also pointed out, that as they knew Henry to be
" a very sage king and to be well advised," he would
not join a defensive league under an obligation to
attack France immediately, which did not bind other
members. Maximilian was persuaded to dismiss
Egremont with a present of a gold cup and 100
florins, and with an answer which acquiesced in the
inclusion of England in the League and omitted all
mention of the " Duke of York."

This seemed satisfactory, and Henry responded
by sending Christopher Urswick as his ambassador
to Maximilian. He arrived at the end of April 1496,
but found that the King of the Romans was again
wavering. He talked much of his obligations to maintain the cause of the " Duke of York," from whom he
had recently, in February, received letters stating that
he hoped for success owing to disturbances imminent
in England. He had a suspicion that Henry did not
mean to break with the King of France, but simply
wished to join the League in order to prevent them
supporting Warbeck. Though he personally wished
to dismiss Henry's envoy, he consulted the ambassadors of the other powers included in the League as
to whether he ought " to dissemble and dismiss

him with fair words," and they advised him to
admit Henry on his own terms, if he refused to
join under the obligation to begin the attack on
France. The Venetian ambassador was particularly
pressing, as he had received private assurances from
Urswick that the English king was only prevented
from attacking the French, " England's greatest and
oldest enemies," through fear of alienating their ally
the King of Scotland—" who although the poorest
king in Christendom, could put into the field for a
period of three weeks an army of 30,000 men, his
subjects being bound to serve him for that length of
time at their own expense." [1] Urswick adopted a
very firm attitude, indeed Maximilian hinted that he
had been suborned by France and had prejudiced
Henry against him.   He refused to pledge his master
to an offensive war against France, and hinted that
he might even find it impossible to send troops to join
in a defensive war, owing to being hampered by the
hostility of the Kings of Scotland and Denmark and
by the " Duke of York " and Irish rebels.   " The
king," he said, " is compelled to be much on the watch
against the youth who says he is son of King Edward
and went lately to Scotland, whose king received him
with many promises."   He made no secret of Henry's
distrust of Maximilian arising from their former relations, and of his fear that the latter would do little or
nothing against France. The pressure of his allies made
Maximilian dismiss Urswick in a friendly manner—
the intentions of the confederates being explained in
a " suitable and very flowery discourse," with the
promise that when Henry had joined the League

[1] Brown, *Ven. Cal.*, p. 241.

they would use their influence to arrange his differences with the supporters of the " Duke of York." [1]

To Spain the mutual antipathy between Henry and Maximilian was most unwelcome. Spain's jealousy of France made her the life and soul of the Holy League, and her ambassadors were indefatigable in trying to free Henry from the embarrassments which prevented him from joining the League. They showed themselves ready to assent to Henry's scheme for a marriage between his daughter Margaret and the King of Scotland, and had a great part in arranging a commercial treaty between Henry and the Archduke Philip (February 1495–6), which contained satisfactory clauses forbidding the harbouring of rebels.[2] Further, full powers for concluding the marriage treaty were issued in January 1495–6.[3]

Thus stood affairs in June, the confederates pressing for Henry's inclusion on his own terms, as a guarantee that if he would not attack France, he would at all events not help her. The march of events made the matter very urgent. Charles, who had been obliged to withdraw most of his troops from Italy at the end of 1495, was preparing another expedition in the summer of 1496, and the League wanted Henry's alliance on any terms. The Pope pressed him to take up arms against France in defence of the Holy See, " to send succour without delay, and not permit the Church to be trampled on." [4] The proclamation by the Pope of a crusade in England (half the profits of which were to go to the king) was held out as an

[1] Brown, *Ven. Cal.*, p. 241, Nos. 674–7, 690, 693, 698–703, 706.
[2] Rymer, *Fœdera*, xii. 579–81.
[3] Berg., *Spanish Cal.*, Nos. 123, 127 ; Rymer, *Fœdera*, xii. 661–3.
[4] Berg., *Spanish Cal.*, p. 108.

inducement, a singular attempt to apply Spanish
methods to England.[1] It is obvious from the tone
of the Spanish negotiations that Henry was drifting
away from France.   In June 1496 he promised to
make a demonstration against France by reviewing
his troops and arming his navy, and in July it was
reported that many of his subjects were inclined for
war.   The king, however, announced that he would
not promise to make war on France while affairs in
Scotland were still unsettled.[2]   The members of the
League were much alarmed at hearing a report that
Henry had sent ambassadors to France to arrange his
difficulties, but ultimately, on 18th July, the king was
formally admitted into the Holy League on his own
terms, his accession being published in Rome on that
date.[3] A printed copy, adorned with the portraits
of the allies, was circulated, there were processions,
bell-ringings, and bonfires.   The document embodying Henry's admission to the League was confirmed
by him at Windsor on 23rd September 1496, and, by
a solemn procession at St. Paul's on 1st of November,
he gave a public demonstration of his joy at entering
the League.   On the same day he received the sword
and cap of maintenance sent by the Pope, and a few
days later a second Spanish marriage treaty was
signed.[4] Chance and Henry's skill had combined to
give England a splendid position in Europe, and on
the action of her king hung the destinies of France.

His new allies, Spain, Italy, the Papacy and the
Empire, had been making continued efforts to bring

[1] *Ibid.*, p. 121.   [2] *Ibid.*, pp. 101, 103, 105.

[3] The negotiations were carried through at Rome by Henry's
secretary, Robert Sherbourne.   Brown, *Ven. Cal.*, Nos. 691, 713–4,
717–23 ; Rymer, *Fœdera*, xii. 638–42.

[4] Brown, *Ven. Cal.*, No. 725.   See below, p. 204.

about an understanding between Henry and James of Scotland. Ferdinand's ambassadors advised James to withdraw his support of Perkin—whom they always allude to as " him of York," or " him who calls himself the Duke of York "—make peace with Henry, and join the Holy League. At the same time, " for the purpose of deluding the King of Scots as long as possible with hopes," the Scotch ambassadors in Spain were beguiled with a favourable reception of their suggestion that a Spanish princess should be given to James in marriage.[1] The Pope added his persuasions, but James would do no more than give a vague promise to keep peace, a promise which he broke almost at once. Deaf to the remonstrances of foreign powers, blind to the dissatisfaction of his subjects, he was bent upon invading England.

On the 2nd of September Perkin signed an agreement by which he promised on " recovering " the kingdom of England to surrender Berwick and seven " sheriff-doms," together with an indemnity of 100,000 marks. Later in the month the King of Scots crossed the border with Perkin Warbeck and about 1500 men, but, though dignified by the name of an invasion, it was little more than a border raid on a large scale. Bold words were not wanting. An arrogantly worded proclamation was issued in the name of " King Richard of England," which spoke of the usurpation, murders, and exactions of " one Henry Tydder in this our realm," set a price of £1000 upon the king's head and made many large promises.[2] But Perkin's strength lay in words rather than deeds, and he and

[1] Berg., *Spanish Cal.*, No. 137.
[2] This proclamation has already been printed in Spedding's edition of Bacon's works. *Henry VII.*, 252–5.

his royal host, though " makyng greate boste and brag," did very little in England.   His men passed over the border and then gave themselves up to plundering and ravaging the countryside, burning towns and villages and killing women and children. If they intended in this way, as Hall suggests, " to apalle and daunte the hartes of the poore commons so that for very feare they should be enforced and compelled to submit them selfes to this newe found Mawmet," they were singularly unsuccessful.   The men of Northumberland failed to rally round the gorgeous gold-embroidered standard of the Duke of York, and the adventurer's outburst of pity and indignation at the brutal treatment of his " owne naturall subjects and vassals " came too late.   His " ridiculous mercy and foolish compassion " provoked James to suggest that Perkin was distressing himself unnecessarily over his subjects, not one of whom had taken up his cause.   The raid was the most hopeless failure.   The Scots apparently only advanced four miles beyond the border, and retired after a few days in a panic, as it appeared that the country was rising against them, and the approach of an English force under the Nevills was rumoured.[1] On the 21st of September Perkin was back in Scotland. He had struck his blow and failed.   The invasion had come and gone without the great revolt of disaffected Yorkists in the neighbouring counties which Henry had half feared in spite of his bold words.[2]   It proved,

[1] *City Chron.*, p. 210 ; *L. and P. Hen. VII.*, ii. 330 ; Pol. Verg., 598 ; Hall, 475.

[2] By November rumours had reached Venice that a great battle had been fought in which 15,000 men were killed.   Brown, *Ven. Cal.*, No. 727.   Similar rumours were again prevalent in March of the following year.   *Ibid.*, No. 735.

if proof were needed, that the new dynasty had taken
root in the English soil, and that even the north had
learnt loyalty to the Tudor.[1]

The failure of the expedition closed the most
successful period of Warbeck's career.   James IV. had
hoped for much, his bitter disappointment made him
consider the possibility of getting rid of his 'guest.
According to the chroniclers he " every day more
and more neglected and lesse phantesied and gave
credite to him," and though he may have continued
to believe in the " Duke of York's " claim (and his
words support this view, as he spoke of him as " the
Duke of York " long after his execution) he was
learning that those claims would meet with little
support in England and could not be profitably ex-
ploited in the interests of Scotland.   But James was
too chivalrous to follow the dictates of policy, and
Perkin remained in the country as his guest for some
time longer.   Henry did not proceed at once to the
retaliatory measures urged upon him by his spy Bothwell.[2]   The calmer counsels of the Spanish ambassadors
prevailed for a time, de Puebla's efforts being seconded
by those of Don Pedro de Ayala, who arrived in
Scotland as ambassador from Ferdinand and Isabella.
He was an extremely able diplomatist, and the strong
influence he soon acquired over James was used to
prevent him from making a further attack on England.   In London de Puebla was trying to persuade
Henry not to undertake a punitive expedition, " he

[1] A proclamation issued by Henry shortly after the invasion
laid emphasis on the total failure of the Scotch raid and on the
fact that it was a breach of a truce which had still four years to
run.   Bain, *Cal. of Documents relating to Scotland*, iv. App. i. 415.

[2] In his letters to the king he enlarged upon James's poverty and
the discontent of the people.

knew by experience how quickly a kingdom might be won and lost. Great as his power perhaps is, the result of the war is doubtful." [1] Neither of the ambassadors had an easy task. In January and February Henry was levying troops for the defence of the border and was preparing a fleet to send against Scotland. But the Spanish ambassador in Scotland played his cards very cleverly. In the main he furthered Henry's interests, which the Spanish sovereigns regarded for the time as identical with their own. [2] For a time he continued the old policy of deluding James with the hope of a Spanish bride. Henry felt some distrust of Ayala, [3] but was reassured by his falling in with the proposal that his daughter Margaret should be substituted for a Spanish princess. The idea of this marriage, which ultimately led to the union of the crowns, first appears in the diplomatic correspondence of June 1495, and it was renewed before and after the border raid. [4] Don Pedro had so far succeeded that a personal meeting between Henry and James was discussed. The offers made on behalf of James by the Earl of Angus and Lord Hume, however, did not satisfy Henry, and in June 1497 his patience gave way, and Lord Daubeney was placed in command of an army and ordered to invade Scotland. But at this moment events in England saved James, and Daubeney had to be recalled.

In order to obtain money for the invasion of Scotland without delay, the king had called together

[1] Berg., *Spanish Cal.*, i. p. 140.   [2] *Ibid.*, i. pp. 115, 116.
[3] Ayala had adopted Charles of France's ingenious plan, and was secretly negotiating for Warbeck's surrender to Spain. *Ibid.*, pp. 91, 97, 105, 112, 124, 135. In Oct. 1496 Perkin had been writing to try and gain support in Spain. *Ibid.*, p. 130; Arch., xxvii. 182.
[4] Rymer, xii. 529-531, 538, 540, 572, 636; Bain, *Calendar*, No. 1622.

a Great Council instead of summoning Parliament. This Council, which included besides the lords, judges and law officers, both burgesses and merchants— " the head wisemen of every city and good town of this our land "—from all parts of England, met on 24th October at Westminster,[1] and voted the king £120,000 for a war against Scotland. This expedient of a Council, which was born of haste, not policy, brought about a rather curious situation. The grant by Council did not legally warrant the collection of taxes, but seems to have been regarded as a kind of guarantee on the strength of which the king might borrow money which would be repaid when Parliament met. The Council broke up on the 5th of November, and the king at once took steps to obtain the money. On the 1st of December a number of privy seals were issued, addressed to individual rich men, asking them for a loan for the invasion of Scotland. All the privy seals were issued in the same form, beginning with the announcement that " for the revenging of the great cruelty and dishonour that the King of Scots hath done unto us, our realm and subjects of the same " . . . " two armies royall " were being prepared " by sea and land," and ending, " And because as we hear ye be a man of good substance, we desire and pray you to make loan unto us of the sum of £——, whereof ye shall be undoubtedly and assuredly repaid." [2] Like the unpopular forced loans of Richard III., the loan was collected by commissioners appointed for the purpose.[3] From the city of London he had already

[1] *City Chron.*, p. 211.

[2] *Cotton MS.*, Titus B, v. fol. 145, printed Bacon, *Henry VII.*, ed. Spedding, p. 174.

[3] In addition individual members of the Council lent large sums, and suggested that the king should raise £40,000 more by way of a loan.

asked for a loan of £10,000 and obtained £4000. The whole sum raised by way of loan amounted to £57,388, 10s. 2d.[1] With the money thus obtained Henry pushed on his preparations for war, but a Parliamentary grant was needed for the repayment of the loan. Parliament met on 16th January 1496–7. Proceedings began by a speech from Morton about the dangers that menaced the kingdom, illustrated after the prevailing fashion by elaborate parallels from the history of Rome. A very large grant was made, two fifteenths and tenths payable in May and November, and a subsidy in addition equal to two fifteenths and tenths. From these heavy imposts only those who possessed less than twenty shillings' rent from land or twenty marks' worth of personal property were exempted.[2] A large grant was also obtained from Convocation.

In March Parliament was dissolved, but Henry was fated " to fight for his money," [3] and had to face serious opposition. The attempt to collect the taxes in Cornwall produced a great uproar, the people, " lamentyng, yellyng, and crying, maliciously said the kyng's counsayle was the cause of this polling and shauing." Cornwall was a poor and barren county; the distant menace from Scotland seemed a slight pretext for the king's large demands. The angry people found leaders in Michael Joseph, a Bodmin blacksmith, " a notable talking fellow and no less desirous to be talked of," and a lawyer named Thomas Flammock, who encouraged the rioters by telling them the law was on their side, and that the

---

[1] *Excerpta Hist.*, pp. 110–113.
[2] *Rot. Parl.*, vi. 513–519 ; Stat., ii. 642–647 ; *City Chron.*, p. 212.
[3] Bacon, *Henry VII.*, p. 175.

king was being led astray by evil counsellors, who would destroy both him and the country. Archbishop Morton and Sir Reginald Bray, " the king's screens in this envy," were the scapegoats against whom the popular clamour was directed. The Cornishmen armed themselves with bows and arrows, bills and staves, and the host advanced eastwards through Devon into Somerset. At Wells they were encouraged by the accession of James Touchet, Lord Audley, whom a private grievance had made disloyal.[1] He led them on to Bristol; the city refused to open its gates to the rebels, and they continued their march eastwards through Winchester and Salisbury. Kent, which had played a conspicuous part in many rebellions, was their objective, but they were disappointed to find that the county did not rise at their approach. The men of Kent had proved their loyalty to Henry recently on Perkin's attempted invasion, and the Cornishmen found " the freest people of England " assembled under the Earl of Kent and other nobles to resist them. As usual, the first check led to many desertions from the rebel host, but the bulk of the insurgents, a body about 15,000 strong, encamped at Farnham near Guildford on 12th of June. So far the king had not moved; an undisciplined rout of peasants armed only with rude weapons, and apparently not stiffened by the accession of discontented Yorkists or other gentry, had marched all through the southern counties, and their camp now threatened the capital itself.

Henry's inactivity seems strange. Bacon, following Hall and Vergil, explains it as due to deep design on the king's part, the rebels being allowed to advance

[1] *Rep. of Deputy Keeper*, xxxvii. App. iii. 723.

in order to draw them far from their base and support.
Bacon also suggests that the king's inaction was due
to the fact that he was " attempered by fears and
less in love with dangers by the continued fruition of
a crown." The obvious explanation is probably the
true one—the king did not move before because he
could not. The rebellion took him completely by
surprise, all his attention had been directed to the
preparations for an invasion of Scotland. Since
February troops had been mustering, and large sums
of money had been sent to York, Durham, Newcastle,
and Berwick.[1] The rising of the Cornishmen came
like a bolt from the blue. Daubeney was recalled
and ordered to lead his men southwards against the
rebels, while the defence of the borders was entrusted
to the muster of the northern counties under the
command of the Earl of Surrey. Henry was faced
with a very grave situation—" a dangerous triplicity
to a monarchy, to have the arms of a foreigner, the
discontents of subjects, and the title of a pretender
to meet." [2]

The city of London was at first panic-stricken at
the imminent danger, but Daubeney's return brought
confidence. On Tuesday, 13th June, he, with eight
to ten thousand men, marched out to Hounslow Heath
and met some of the rebels in a skirmish near Guildford. On the same day the king left Woodstock and
advanced towards the capital, reaching Kingston
on the 16th. On Thursday, 15th June, Daubeney
had advanced to St. George's-in-the-Fields and there
received messages from some of the rebels, offering
to betray their leaders in return for a pardon. On

---

[1] *L. and P. Hen. VII.*, ii. 376 ; *Excerpta Hist.*, 110, 111. See
Rymer, *Fœd.*, xii. 647.   [2] Bacon, *Henry VII.*, p. 178.

Friday he joined forces with the king and returned
to St. George's, Henry going to Lambeth.   The
Cornishmen reached Blackheath the same day and
encamped there, but between them and the capital
lay a force of 25,000 men.   Friday night they spent
in "greate agony and variaunce," some being disposed to submit themselves to the king's mercy, "but
the Smyth was of the contrary mynde."   Henry also
passed the night "in the ffeilde, abrewyng and
comfortyng of his people." [1]   At six o'clock on the
following morning (Saturday, 17th June), a combined
attack upon flank and rear of the rebels was led by
Sir Humphrey Stanley and the Earl of Oxford, while
Lord Daubeney engaged the main body.   The rebels
made a desperate resistance, but finding themselves
surrounded at last surrendered.   According to Polydor
Vergil and Hall 2000 of them were slain. [2]   The loss
on the king's side was certainly slight, most of those
who fell being slain by the yard-long arrows of the
Cornishmen.   Henry, who commanded the rear-guard,
was never engaged.   The king rode into London after
the battle, being received at London Bridge by the
mayor and aldermen.   After returning thanks at St.
Paul's for his victory, he went to his lodging in the
Tower.   On the following Monday the rebel leaders,
Audley, Flammock, and Joseph, were examined before
Henry and the council in the Tower, and arraigned
and condemned at Westminster a week later.   The
next day, Tuesday, June 27th, Joseph and Flammock
were drawn through the city and hanged at Tyburn,

[1] *City Chron.*, p. 214.
[2] For the whole rebellion, see Pol. Verg., pp. 599–602; Hall, pp.
476–80; *City Chron.*, pp. 213–15; *Rot. Parl.*, vi. 544–5. Hall includes
in his account (p. 477) incidents which happened in the rising of the
following year.

the smith showing high courage and hoping " for a
name perpetual and a fame permanent and immortal." [1]
On Wednesday Lord Audley was led from Newgate
through the streets, wearing a torn paper coat adorned
with the arms of his house reversed, to Tower Hill,
where he was beheaded. The heads of the three
leaders were set up on London Bridge and their
quarters on the city gates. But this was the only
vengeance that Henry took ; the rest of the rebels he
spared. [2] According to Bacon, the king's clemency on
this occasion, as distinguished from the severity with
which Perkin's attempt in Kent was punished, showed
his discrimination " between people that did rebel
upon wantonness and them that did rebel upon
want." [3] The danger thus overcome is reflected in
the letters of the Venetian envoy with some extraordinary comments. According to him an army of
20,000 men was said to have taken up arms *in the
north* and marched on London " because a tax had
been laid on the priests contrary to custom." The
king was reported to have collected all his property
" in a tower near the coast " that he might escape if
necessary. [4]

Meanwhile there had been a change in the position in Scotland. Ayala, who since October 1496
had been negotiating to obtain the surrender of
Perkin Warbeck to Spain, worked upon the pretender by allusions to an approaching and inevitable reconciliation between the Kings of England
and Scotland, and suggested that he should sail to

[1] Hall, p. 479.
[2] *City Chron.*, p. 215. Many of them bought their ransom from
their captors at sums varying from 12d. upwards.
[3] Bacon, *op. cit.*, p. 183.   [4] Brown, *Ven. Cal.*, No. 743.

Ireland, whence he could be taken by Spanish fishing-boats to safe refuge in Spain. Ferdinand and Isabella set great hopes on this scheme, and strict precautions were taken to prevent Henry from hearing about it, de Puebla, then ambassador in London, being kept in the dark. Ayala probably succeeded in winning over the adventurer, but James was not disposed to surrender his protégé.[1] The Cornish rising raised hopes that Warbeck would find in England the support he had hitherto looked for there in vain. James proposed to co-operate with the rebels by invading England on the north while Perkin was trying his fortune in Cornwall.[2] Early in July, there-fore, Warbeck sailed from Scotland, with his wife and child, in a ship victualled and provided by James,[3] escorted by two other vessels, one of them being a Breton merchant ship, which was perhaps impressed by James for this service.

There was some delay before James carried out his part of the plan. Shortly after Perkin sailed James received an embassy from Henry, who after the Cornish rebellion gave up the idea of a war of re-venge in Scotland, as it meant further taxation. On 4th July, Fox, Bishop of Durham, had been sent north

[1] Berg., *Spanish Cal.*, pp. 61, 85, 91, 97, 105, 115–20, 124, 135 ; Busch, *op. cit.*, p. 346, quoting Zurita, v. 103*b*, 110*a*.

[2] On this point there has been some discussion, but the evidence appears to support the view that James did not abandon his sup-port of Perkin when he left Scotland. Gairdner, *L. and P. Hen. VII.*, ii. pref. lvii. pp. 185–7 ; Busch, p. 347.

[3] *Ibid.*, ii. 331–3. Some of the details of the equipment have been preserved. We read of the purchase of $3\frac{1}{2}$ ells of " rowane tawnee to ye Duches of York to be her ane seegown," *L. and P. Hen. VII.*, ii. 331–4. See also Ellis, i. (i.) p. 32. Busch (p. 346) makes it clear that Perkin had not made another expedition between September 1496 and July 1497.

to try and obtain the surrender of Perkin and persuade James to send an embassy into England to ask
for peace, " to save the dignity of the stronger power."
The ambassador was instructed to make every
possible effort to arrange a peace.   Even the demand
for Perkin's surrender was to be dropped if it stood
in the way of a settlement.[1]   James of Scotland, however, was not inclined to treat.   His unopposed and
unpunished raid encouraged him.   Henry, with his
kingdom ablaze with revolt, seemed powerless, and
the opportunity too good to lose.   In August, therefore,
James again crossed the border, and, after wasting
and burning the country side, besieged the castle of
Norham-on-Tweed.[2]   Henry, however, while making
overtures for peace, had not abandoned his preparations for war.   In July all the Scotch were ordered
to leave England, and on July 1st, £12,000 had been
sent northwards for the expenses of the war.   Norham,
strongly fortified and garrisoned by the Bishop of
Durham, " a wise man and one that could see through
the present to the future," made a stout resistance to
the Scotch assault.   The Earl of Surrey advanced from
Yorkshire with 20,000 men, and a fleet put to sea under
Lord Willoughby de Broke.   At the news of Surrey's
advance James raised the siege of Norham and retreated over the border, with Surrey in pursuit.   The
English leader destroyed several border forts and
took the castle of Ayton.   The Scotch army, which
lay a mile off, made no attempt to save the castle,
but James offered to decide the whole question by
single combat with Surrey, the castle of Berwick to
be the victor's prize.   The earl refused this quixotic

---

[1] Rymer, xii. 676; *L. and P. Hen. VII.*, 104–111; Bain, *Calendar*,
iv. 1635.   [2] *L. and P. Hen. VII.*, ii. 333.

offer, and thanking him " harteley of the honoure that
he offered him . . . to admit so poore an earle to
fight with him body to body," but explaining that
Berwick was the king's and not his to pledge at his
will, prepared for battle. James, " not performyng
his great crakes and boastes," retreated by night.
Difficulty in obtaining supplies forced Surrey to withdraw his troops from that " tempestious, unfertile,
and barayne region," where they had been " dayly
and nightly vexed with continual wynde and un-
measurable reyne." [1]

James's great scheme had fallen to the ground and
nothing had been heard of Perkin. It was a favourable moment for the renewal of negotiations, and
Ayala fostered the peaceful tendencies by every means
in his power. Henry, who was also strongly urged to
peace by Spain, and who " did not love the barren
wars in Scotland though he made his profit of the
noise of them," sent a plenipotentiary. The chief
difficulty which had wrecked the earlier negotiations,
James's reluctance to surrender Perkin at the King
of England's bidding, had been removed by the
adventurer's departure from Scotland. Other points
in dispute, such as the compensation for losses inflicted
on both sides, were waived, and on 30th September
a seven years' treaty was signed at Ayton.[2] Ultimately, after negotiations skilfully conducted by
Ayala as mediator,[3] the term of peace was prolonged
to the lifetimes of the two sovereigns.[4] It was
publicly proclaimed in London on the 6th December.[5]

[1] Pol. Verg., pp. 602–3 ; Hall, pp. 480–2 ; L. and P. Hen. VII.,
ii. 332–4.

[2] See Rymer, xii. 673–8 ; Bain, Calendar, iv. No. 1636.

[3] Berg., Spanish Cal., p. 145.   [4] Rymer, xii. 678–80.

[5] City Chron., p. 222.

The importance of this arrangement is happily crystallised by Bacon. " Ayala's embassy," he says, " set the truce between England and Scotland, the truce drew on the peace, the peace the marriage, and the marriage the union of the kingdoms." [1]

Warbeck himself wrecked his last chance of success by abandoning James's plan of sailing direct to Cornwall and landing there. In spite of the failure of the rising, and in spite of, or perhaps because of, the king's clemency, disaffection was rife in Cornwall. " The king's lenity had rather emboldened than reclaimed them, insomuch as they stuck not to say to their neighbours and countrymen that the king did well to pardon them, for that he knew he should leave few subjects in England if he had hanged all that were of their mind." [2] On the face of it James's scheme was a possible if not a likely one—invasions on the north and south to combine with treachery within. The adventurer, however, abandoned this plan and sailed away to Ireland, allured by the promise of help given to him by Sir James Ormond, then in arms against Henry.[3] On 25th July he landed in Cork, where he was well received by one of his earliest supporters, John Walter. He stayed there some time, but found that there was little chance of winning further support. Fate seemed to be fighting against the adventurer. Sir James Ormond had been killed on the 17th of July, and his former powerful friends held aloof. The temper of Ireland had completely changed. Kildare had just been re-appointed Lord Deputy, and was bent on proving his loyalty. Desmond and the Munster chieftains had been par-

---

[1] Bacon, *op. cit.*, p. 185.   [2] *Ibid.*, p. 189.
[3] *L. and P. Hen. VII.*, ii. pref. xlix.

doned,[1] the south of Ireland was submissive and loyal to the Tudor. The faithful city of Waterford at once sent off news to Henry that Perkin had re-appeared in Cork, and Kildare and Desmond made an attempt to capture him, but Walter arranged his escape by sea to Kinsale. There the adventurer found and rejected a last chance of escape. In Kinsale harbour there were three Spanish ships, either those provided by Ayala to convey the fugitive to Spain or merchant ships hired by Walter. But with characteristic hopefulness he decided to try his fortune once more in England, and, encouraged by letters from the Cornish malcontents, determined to land in Cornwall. He put to sea at the end of August or the beginning of September, but the ship in which he sailed was overtaken by an English vessel and boarded, and the surrender of the pretender was demanded. The offer of a reward of 1000 marks, however, did not induce the captain to betray the fugitive, who lay in the hold of the ship hidden in a cask of wine.[2] He landed at Whitsand Bay near the Land's End with about 120 men.

This little company soon grew into thousands; Cornwall was seething with disaffection, and Perkin proclaimed himself as King Richard IV., and advanced to Bodmin at the head of 3000 men. Thence he marched to Exeter and appeared before the city on September 7th. Though without artillery he made a bold attempt to storm the city, setting fire to the gates, but was beaten off with the loss of 200 men, and marched to Taunton, which he reached on September 20th. Here the adventurer's courage began

[1] Ware, *Annales*, p. 59 (ed. 1658).
[2] Halliwell, *Letters*, i. 174–180 ; Smith, *Waterford*, p. 135 ; *Carew Papers*, p. 468 ; Pol. Verg., p. 604 ; Hall, p. 483.

to fail. " He put small trust and lesse confidence in
the remnant of his army . . . because the mooste part
of his souldioures wer harnessed on the right arme
and naked all the body and neuer exercised in
warre nor marciall feates, but only with the spade and
shovell." [1] Moreover the royal army was advancing
to meet him under the command of Lord Daubeney,
Lord Broke, and Sir Rhys ap Thomas, Henry, with
his usual caution, keeping part of his troops in reserve
under his own command.   But these precautions
soon appeared to be needless.   At the rumoured
approach of the royal forces Warbeck's courage failed,
and at midnight on 21st September he stole secretly
away with sixty mounted men, who had been his
captains, leaving his host leaderless to face the king.

Perkin with three of his followers reached sanctuary
at Beaulieu, the others were probably captured.   The
rebels at Taunton, finding themselves deserted, threw
down their arms at the king's approach and submitted themselves to his mercy, " holdyng up their
handes in askyng mercy, offering and promising him
faythe, loyaltie, and obeysaunce."   The ringleaders
only were taken, the rest were allowed to disperse,
being later punished by the infliction of heavy fines.
Meanwhile Perkin, after a week in sanctuary, saw
that his last chance had gone, and being brought to
the " verie poynte and prycke of extremytie," and
being assured of pardon, surrendered to the royal
troops, who were surrounding the sanctuary.   He was
brought before the king at Taunton on 5th October
and made a full confession. [2]   Henry took him to

---

[1] Hall, *Chronicle*, p. 484.

[2] Pol. Verg., pp. 604–5; *City Chron.*, pp. 217–21; Hall, pp. 483–6;
Excerpta Hist., pp. 113, 114 ; Halliwell, *Letters*, i. 175–8.

Exeter, and there Lady Katherine Gordon, who had
been found by the royal troops at St. Michael's
Mount in Cornwall, was brought in to the king.
Perkin was forced to repeat before her the whole story
of his imposture, and she was then honourably escorted
to Sheen, where she became a member of the queen's
household.

From Exeter Perkin wrote a sad letter to his
mother.[1] He explained that he had submitted himself to the king and begged for a pardon, laying stress
on the fact that he was not by birth Henry's subject.
He had not as yet received a favourable reply, " nor
had any hope of receiving one, wherefore his hearte was
very sorrowful." While at Exeter Henry appointed commissioners to inflict fines upon Warbeck's adherents,
and they proceeded, we are told, with such severity as
" to obscure the king's mercy in sparing of blood
with the bleeding of so much treasure." A very
searching procedure seems to have been adopted, and
as late as 1500 arrears of fines were being collected.
Once again the king made rebellion profitable.[2]

After settling the disturbed west, the king turned
towards London, taking Perkin in his train, " not
withoute a great concourse of people metynge hym
oute of every quarter to see this Perkyn, as he was a
Monstre, because he, beinge an alien of no abilitee by
his poore parents . . . durst once invade so noble a
realme." The king reached Westminster on 27th of
November, and Perkin was obliged to repeat his confession before the mayor and aldermen. This confession, which is now regarded as practically true in

---

[1] Printed by Gairdner, *Perkin Warbeck*, pp. 329–30.
[2] Rymer, xii. 696–8 ; *L. and P. Hen. VII.*, ii. 335–7 ; Pol. Verg.,
p. 606.

all its details,[1] gives a full account of the pretender's
birth and early adventures. His proceedings after he
reached Ireland, and his adventures in Flanders and
Scotland, are dismissed in a few words. Warbeck's
connection with the Duchess of Burgundy is utterly
ignored ; the explanation probably is that the object
of the confession was to make public details of the
pretender's birth hitherto unknown to the people.
The king's object was to discredit him once and for
all as a Yorkist prince, and there was no special object
in loading the confession with the Duchess's intrigues [2]
and Perkin's well-known later adventures.   On the
following day Warbeck was conveyed on horseback
through London, being greeted with " many a curse
and wonderyng inowth," and was then brought back
to Westminster, where he was given a lodging.[3]   He
remained there for some months, being treated with
remarkable lenience and allowed a certain amount of
liberty.   His wife remained under the queen's protection in safety and honour many years ; " the name
of the White Rose, which had been given to her
husband's false title, was continued in common speech
to her true beauty." [4]   Henry's treatment of her is
an instance of his generosity to those who opposed
him.

Perkin Warbeck's career, however, was over ; Henry
had at last respite from the canker which had poisoned
so many years of his reign.   Though he lived to cause
the king anxiety once more, he was never again the
centre of his diplomacy, or the chief danger in his

[1] See Busch, p. 335 ; also Appendix ii., p. 419, below.
[2] The relations between England and Burgundy had much improved.   [3] *City Chron.*, p. 221.
[4] Bacon, p. 193.   She married twice after Perkin's death.

path. In Bacon's vivid phrase, Henry was now " cured of those privy stitches which he had long had about his heart." The year that had seen the Scotch ravaging the borders, the Cornishmen marching on London, and the pretender raising his standard in the West, ended in the king's triumph and the defeat of an impostor whose claims had been backed by traitors at home and enemies abroad.

CHAPTER V

COMMERCE AND INDUSTRY

ONE of Bacon's epigrammatic sentences brings out the aim which gave unity and coherence to the commercial and industrial policy of Henry VII. " He bowed the ancient policy of this realm from consideration of plenty to consideration of power." The policy Henry adopted had been tried before tentatively and experimentally ; he gave it permanence and made it a success. An increasingly conscious subordination of each legislative act to the general scheme replaced empirical legislation. His reign saw the inauguration of the policy known in later years as the Mercantile System, which aimed at the regulation of commerce and industry with a view to increasing the national power. The system not only harmonised admirably with the general character of the king's government, but it gained inspiration and success from the approval of his people. Henry's standpoint faithfully represented the view of the best Englishmen of the day. For a hundred years England had been growing more and more into a commercial nation. Foreign trade had become the centre of ambitious hopes that a generation or two earlier would have spent themselves on schemes of conquest. England was beginning to become conscious of her commercial destiny, and a spirit of keen international rivalry gave flavour to the trade policy of her kings. The king

who guided the nation's destinies at this critical
moment was a man who, innately shrewd, far-sighted,
and a lover of peace, found a congenial sphere for
the exercise of his talents in these bloodless victories
of trade.

The guiding principles of the Mercantile System
were the accumulation of treasure, the encouragement
of native shipping, the maintenance of an adequate
food supply, and the provision of employment for
the support of an effective population.   Though it
would be an exaggeration to claim that Henry grasped
the system as a logical conception—and, indeed, its
full development belongs to a later era—the tenacity
with which he kept its main features before him, at
a time when economic generalisations were unknown,
is a proof of extraordinary ability.   In the early part
of the reign we find exceptions, waverings, apparent
retrogressions, the guiding idea obscured by the
necessities of an uneasy throne, but before Henry
died the Mercantile System was firmly rooted in
England, where it flourished until the dawn of free
trade.   As the pioneer of the commercial policy
under which England won and kept her colonial
empire, Henry VII. appears in one of his most interesting and significant aspects.

The king's position, above the arena of commercial
competition, gave him a general view of the whole
field of trade and industry.   A speech supplied by
Bacon for Morton, warning Parliament to manage
industry and foreign trade so that " the kingdom's
stock of treasure may be sure to be kept from being
diminished," touches on the guiding aim of most sixteenth century statesmen.[1]   Henry did not neglect

---

[1] Bacon, *op. cit.*, p. 81.

KING HENRY VII
From a picture in the possession of the Society of Antiquaries

this point,[1] but he had much wider views. His attempts to regulate the flow of the precious metals were a small part of his plan and perhaps the least successful. The way in which he dealt with the export and import trade of the kingdom proves a larger spirit and a wider survey. Much of his legislation is designed in a consciously protective spirit. He hoped to gain for England a larger share in the commerce of Europe, and find the sinews of war that came from flourishing trade; to restrict alien competition and provide profitable employment for his subjects. It is this desire that makes the spirit though not the letter of his legislation harmonise with the theories of modern protectionists, who look back beyond free trade to the era of the Mercantile System inaugurated by Henry. " England for the English " is a motto which would have enlisted Henry's sympathy.[2]

The encouragement of English shipping has been mentioned as one of the essential features of the Mercantile System. Henry was king of an island kingdom with awakening ambitions, and the necessity of having a large merchant fleet which in time of war could supplement the small royal navy and in time of peace would give profitable employment to his subjects, did not escape him. A great effort was necessary. The state of affairs when Henry came to the throne seemed almost hopeless. The merchant fleet, like everything else, had decayed, and foreign ships carried the sea-borne trade of England. The

[1] See below, p. 190.

[2] The reign brings into relief the keen contrast between the standpoint of the protectionist jealous for national prosperity; and that of the free-trader looking forward to an ideal of cosmopolitan brotherhood.

Navigation Laws, which made a determined attempt to secure the carrying trade for English ships, are an illustration of the operation of the principle of Power *versus* Plenty. A deliberate sacrifice of the latter to the former was made early in the reign by the passing of Navigation Acts which, at all events at first, must have diminished the volume of trade. The preamble of the first Navigation Act [1] drew attention in striking language to the " grete mynyshyng and decaye that hath ben now of late tyme of the Navie within this realme of England and ydelnesse of the mariners within the same by the whiche this noble Realme within short processe of tyme withoute reformaccion be had therin shall not be of habilite and power to defend itself." The Act forbade the importation of wine or woad from Guienne or Gascony except in English, Irish, or Welsh ships, manned by English, Irish, or Welsh sailors. This Act was temporary only,[2] its experimental character being due to the king's appreciation of the fact that the merchant fleet of England was not yet large enough to carry her sea-borne trade. It was not renewed until 1490, but in the interval Henry had succeeded in obtaining a share of the carrying trade in Italian wine.[3] By 1490 restored peace and order and the king's fostering care had led to such a development of English shipping that it became feasible to pass a second Navigation Act. The new law included a very important provision to the effect that no foreign ship should be freighted in an English port while an English ship

[1] 1 Hen. VII., cap. 8.

[2] *Stat.*, ii. 502. Edward IV. had made a similar attempt to restrict the carrying trade to English ships, but had been forced to abandon it. Henry's effort was crowned with success.

[3] See below, p. 178.

remained unladen.[1] Henry's commercial relations
with Burgundy, Venice, and Spain were influenced
by the same aim of encouraging English shipping, and
his policy was strikingly successful. By the end of
the reign the English merchant navy was flourishing,
and its energies, outgrowing their former sphere, were
finding an outlet in voyages of discovery in search of
new markets.[2]

The two most important branches of England's
trade with the Continent were the export of raw
wool and of manufactured cloth. The former was
the oldest and still the most important. The state
of the trade at Henry's accession is illustrated by
the *Cely Papers*,[3] which reveal the insecurity of the
roads and of the sea, the dislocation of trade by
constant wars, and the smuggling of wool to Flanders
without going through Calais, the chief market for
English wool, where the subsidy was collected.
In 1484 certain " banished Englishmen " turned
pirates were robbing Spanish ships, and French,
Flemish, and Danish pirates were roving the Channel.
The English merchants retaliated by capturing a
ship or two themselves, whenever they got the
chance. Henry's accession brought peace and strong
government, and for a time the wool and cloth
trade flourished. Antwerp, then the centre of the
commercial world, was the mart for English cloth ;
Burgundy was also the chief buyer of English wool.
All through the reign, therefore, Henry's relations with
Flanders remained the vital point of his commercial

[1] 4 Hen. VII., cap. 10 ; *Stat.*, ii. 534–5.

[2] See below, pp. 317-24.

[3] *Cely Papers* (Royal Hist. Soc.). Wool was brought from the
pastures by pack-horses over rude roads to one of the Cinque Ports,
and then shipped to Calais, the gate of trade with Flanders.

policy.[1] The king had two main objects in view—
to widen the market for English cloth, and keep the
trade in the hands of English merchants. Smuggling
was diminished by an Act of 1487, which handed over
to the fellowship of the Staple, the oldest organisation of English merchants, which had become a
powerful corporation controlling all the details of the
trade, the customs upon wool and leather, in return
for the maintenance by them of the Calais defences.[2]

Unfortunately the peaceful development of the
wool and cloth trade was early checked by dynastic
complications. The personal hostility between Henry
and Maximilian, the intrigues of Perkin Warbeck and
Suffolk, Henry's anxiety to marry Margaret, all deeply
affected the course of the wool trade. In September
1493 Henry took the extreme step of forbidding all
commercial intercourse between his subjects and
those of Maximilian. All Flemings were ordered to
leave England, and the mart for English cloth was
removed from Antwerp to Calais. Six months later
Maximilian retaliated by a decree forbidding any
importation of English cloth, and forbidding English
merchants to trade in the Netherlands.[3] For three
years this state of affairs continued. There is some
evidence to show that the effect was more severely
felt in the Netherlands than in England, owing to
the fact that the want of English wool starved the
Flemish cloth manufacture, while the Flemish market
was no longer all important to the English cloth trade

[1] The special importance of the cloth trade may have impressed
itself on Henry's mind during his exile abroad. Cunningham,
Growth of English Industry and Commerce.

[2] *Rot. Parl.*, vi. 394-7.

[3] *L. and P. Hen. VII.*, ii. 374 ; Pol. Verg., p. 592 ; *City Chron.*,
p. 200.

since Henry's policy had opened new markets for it
in Germany.[1] Henry has been charged with deliberately sacrificing the welfare of his subjects for
his own personal advantage, but in his view,
dynastic considerations were all-important instead of
unimportant to his people. The Tudor dynasty had
given them peace and prosperity, and anything that
threatened the safety of the king's throne threatened
the safety of the subject's trade. Contemporary
evidence supports the view that the loss inflicted upon
English trade was infinitesimal compared with the
damage in the Netherlands. Criticism, however,
may be justly directed to the king's methods in the
matter. His attempt to forge a political weapon
from his restraint of commerce was a signal failure.
Maximilian got on so badly with his rebellious Flemish
subjects that care for their interests was not likely to
make him vary his policy, and there is no evidence
that Henry's action weighed with Maximilian at all.

Much relief was felt when a change in the political
situation made a renewal of friendly relations possible.
The commercial provisions of the treaty between
Henry and Maximilian, signed on February 24, 1495-6,
provided for free commercial intercourse between
England and Burgundy. The duties imposed upon
English and Flemish merchants were not to exceed the
rates customary during the last fifty years; piracy was
to be put down, and the fisheries were to be free.[2]

[1] See below, p. 173.

[2] Rymer, xii. 578–591; Berg., *Spanish Cal.*, pp. 85, 95, 103;
Brown, *Venet. Cal.*, Nos. 684, 690. The name usually given to this
treaty is the "Intercursus Magnus," but Dr. Busch has pointed out
(p. 357) that there is no contemporary evidence for this name, which
appears first in Bacon's *Life of Henry VII.* (p. 173), from which it
has been copied by later writers.

The treaty was not, as might have been expected, generally popular in England. In London there was no enthusiasm over it; jealousy of the Flemish traders was deep rooted, and the Mayor was reluctant to affix the seal of the city.[1] Only a few months, however, had gone by after this settlement before fresh difficulties arose. A new duty was imposed on English cloth which Henry complained of as contrary to the treaty. Retaliation followed immediately. The English mart was again removed to Calais, and this pressure led to the withdrawal of the new duty in July 1497. The English merchants returned to Antwerp, where they received a popular ovation.[2] The remaining difficulties were discussed at conferences at Bruges in 1498 and at Calais in the following year, and a treaty of 18th May 1499 settled the outstanding questions.[3] The assistance of the Staple merchants was obtained in the drafting of the treaty, and the gain to England was considerable. The price of English wool sold by the Staple merchants at Calais was slightly reduced in favour of Flemish purchasers, and in return duties on English cloth were removed, though its sale retail in the Netherlands was forbidden. The articles which allowed the English merchants to export gold from the Netherlands were regarded as specially advantageous.

This settlement, however, like those that went before it, was disturbed by the appearance of fresh political difficulties about the end of 1504. The cause of them remains obscure, but it seems more than probable that

[1] *City Chron.*, p. 209.
[2] *L. and P. Hen. VII.*, i. 329, ii. 69-72 ; Berg., *Spanish Cal.*, pp. 112, 133, 189, 196-8 ; Rymer. xii. 648, 654-7 ; Hall, p. 483.
[3] Berg., *Spanish Cal.*, pp. 196, 198, 209 ; Rymer xii. 713-20.

Philip, resenting a rumour that Henry was sending money to the rebellious Duke of Gueldres in the hope of buying the surrender of his rebel the Duke of Suffolk— a nice complication of dynastic interests—had again imposed heavy duties on English cloth. Though this is a surmise rather than a certainty, the fact of renewed trade difficulties is clear. After the failure of negotiations for the removal of the duties conducted by the Spanish envoy Manuel, Henry retaliated by transferring the English cloth market for the third time from Antwerp to Calais (15th January 1505), and followed this up by imposing a duty on English cloth exported from Calais to the Low Countries.[1] Philip raised the duty on English cloth to correspond, and finally imports were again forbidden on both sides. Once again there was a bad effect on the trade in Flanders without injuring English merchants to the same extent. André's flattering language, which suggests that the removal of the market to Calais was an advantage to England, cannot be relied upon, but the Venetian and Spanish papers support André's view. The silence of the English chroniclers also proves that trade in England cannot have been much affected.[2] The stoppage of trade was keenly felt in the Netherlands, and Philip, who had been obliged to withdraw the prohibition of the importation of English cloth, sent one envoy after another to England to try and improve the situation. Henry stood firm, supported by national feeling, and the whole course of the dispute is a proof, if proof be needed, of the

[1] *L. and P. Hen. VII.*, ii. 379; Berg., *Spanish Cal.*, pp. 266, 286; Brown, *Ven. Cal.*, Nos. 846, 860; Busch., *op. cit.*, pp. 185, 368.
[2] André, *Annales*, pp. 83, 84; Berg., pp. 368–9; Brown, *Ven. Cal.*, Nos. 846, 849, 860; *L. and P. Hen. VII.*, ii. 379.

great advances made by English trade since the beginning of the reign. The dispute lasted until 1506, when shipwreck left Philip in England at Henry's mercy.[1]

Under the provisions of the treaty signed in London on 30th April 1506, the tolls fixed in 1496 were to be continued, and were not to be arbitrarily raised above the rates which, in the view of those who drafted the treaty, " had been customary since the beginning of the world." English merchants, however, were to be exempted from certain local tolls, and retail sale of English cloth was to be permitted all through the Netherlands except in Flanders.[2] The obvious unfairness of these arrangements made the treaty of little practical value. For once Henry had overreached himself. It was one of the mistakes that mars the policy of Henry's later years, when his diplomacy loses the practical reasonableness before so characteristic of it. It was hopeless to expect Philip's subjects to acquiesce in a treaty which placed them at such a glaring disadvantage. Philip himself declined to ratify it, and on his death in September 1506 the commercial difficulty was still unsettled. The Regent Margaret at once suggested a return to the arrangements of the treaty of 1496.[3] Henry frankly expressed his keen disappointment, but as he was very anxious to remain on friendly terms with Margaret, he adopted a much less uncompromising attitude than in his negotiations with Maximilian and Philip. He drew up a draft scheme which became the basis for the final settlement of commercial relations. The treaty signed in June 1507 restored

[1] See below, p. 344.
[2] Rymer, xiii. 132–142; *L. and P. Hen. VII.*, i. 289–293, ii. 365.
[3] *L. and P. Hen. VII.*, i. 327–337.

the arrangements of 1496, the exemptions from local tolls allowed to English merchants in 1506, however, being allowed to stand. The arrangements of 1506 about the retail sale of English cloth were abandoned. This satisfactory settlement endured till the end of the reign.

Henry's policy with regard to the Hansard merchants was a reflection of popular feeling in England. The Hansard merchants had captured a great part of the trade between England and North Germany during the period when England was crippled by civil war, and Edward IV. had repaid them for their political and financial support by a charter granting them extraordinary privileges. Thus, at the accession of Henry VII., a body of alien merchants were settled in the country, trading in English goods on better terms than Englishmen themselves. Owing to the prevalent jealousy and suspicion of alien merchants, the favoured position of the Hansard merchants was as unpopular as it was anomalous.[1] Nothing proves more clearly the feebleness of the central government and the decay of English commerce than the position of the men of the Steelyard. The fact that English merchants had no corresponding privileges in the towns of the Hanse League made the arrangement a glaring humiliation and injustice.

Henry VII. set himself to vindicate the position of his own subjects and to restrain the privileges of the Hansards. Even in the stormiest years of his reign he pursued this policy, though many years elapsed

---

[1] The preamble of the Act of Henry's first Parliament raising the rates of the duties paid by the alien merchants is a vivid summary of the Englishman's jealousy. See 1 Hen. VII., cap. 3; *Stat.*, ii. 501–2.

before he met with much success. Caution and moderation were very necessary at first, in view of the great power of the Hansards. When Henry's first Parliament granted him tonnage and poundage for life, the Hanse merchants were exempted as before from the higher rates imposed on aliens. They paid exactly the same as the native merchants, and their special privileges were confirmed by charter in March 1486.[1] Signs of a change, however, soon appeared. A statute of Richard III. restricting exports was revived, Hansards were forbidden to export any cloth except fully dressed cloth, complaints of piracies committed by their ships were brought forward, and their privilege of trading in " their own commodities " was interpreted as meaning products of the Hanse towns only. At least one of their vessels was captured by Henry's ships, attacks on individual merchants were made, and the whole body was even threatened with expulsion from England. Henry's proposal that a Diet should be held to discuss the complaints and claims of English merchants, ignored at first, was acceded to in the face of the growing storm. The Diet met at Antwerp in June 1491, and came to an agreement under which English merchants gained the right to trade with Dantzig.[2] This slight gain was all that Henry's envoys won, and English merchants were still in a very inferior position in the North German trade.

In another direction, however, the king's quiet campaign against the Hansards had met with marked success. Much of the valuable trade with

---

[1] *Rot. Parl.*, vi. pp. 270, 407; Busch, *op. cit.*, p. 73.

[2] The town was important as a point of contact with the trade from the Far East. Rymer, xii. 441–2 ; Busch, *op. cit.*, pp. 333–5.

Iceland had been monopolised by the Hansards under licence from the King of Denmark, but some daring English merchants—men of Scarborough and Bristol—had carried on an unauthorised and contraband trade without the permission of the King of Denmark. The exclusiveness of the Hanse merchants had made them very unpopular in Denmark and Scandinavia, and Henry used their unpopularity to gain a regular footing for English merchants. In August 1489 he sent an embassy to Denmark, and on January in the following year a commercial treaty was drawn up admitting English merchants to trade with Denmark and Iceland on very favourable terms, and allowing them to incorporate themselves.[1]

These slight advantages obtained by Henry's diplomacy were not sufficient to disarm national jealousy of the Hansards, and it became acute when, during the cessation of commercial intercourse between England and Flanders, the Hanse merchants employed themselves in the trade forbidden to British subjects, gaining not a little advantage from their position. Bitter feeling led to a riot in London on 15th October 1493.[2] The Merchant Adventurers and other London citizens attacked the Steelyard, and were only repelled with the help of a force sent by the Mayor. Henry profited by this display of national resentment to extort from the Hansards a sum of £20,000, to be held by him as a pledge that they would not take part in the forbidden trade with the Netherlands.

[1] Rymer, xii. 373–7, 381–7. The fact that Henry had been able to form a combination, which threatened the interests of the Hansards elsewhere, gave his envoys a stronger position in the Antwerp Diet.

[2] See below, Hall, p. 468; Fabyan, p. 684; *Grey Friars Chron.*, p. 25.

A severe blow had been dealt at their privileged position. The unpopularity of their colony in London continued, and the governing bodies of the Hanse towns remonstrated with their merchants in London on their alleged dishonesty, extravagance, and dissolute behaviour. In spite of the efforts of the Hansards to gain redress, Henry continued hostile, but as he knew that English shipping was insufficient to carry on the whole trade (even if he were strong enough to wrest it from their hands), he stopped short of provoking an absolute breach with the powerful confederacy of towns. He made no secret of his unfavourable attitude, and treated the representatives of the Hansards with studied discourtesy. In 1497 the conference repeatedly asked for by the Hansards was appointed to meet at Antwerp, but the English envoys complained that the Hansard representatives had not authority to represent the whole confederacy, and left Antwerp before the hastily despatched envoys had returned with their fuller powers.[1]

Meanwhile, Henry was making a further attack on the Hansard monopoly of the North German trade. The agreement permitting English merchants to trade with Dantzig had proved a dead-letter owing to the hostility of the Dantzig merchants. He opened negotiations with the town of Riga, and in November 1498 an agreement was reached by which English merchants were allowed to trade in Riga on very favourable terms.[2] Henry hoped that he had thus obtained a point of entry into the profitable trade with the Far East, but the Hansards resented this arrangement, and at a diet held at Bruges in the summer of 1499, the feeling on both sides was so strong that there

---

[1] Rymer, xii. 651-2.   [2] *Ibid.*, 700-4.

seemed little prospect of an agreement being reached. The Hansards were bent on obtaining some redress of their grievances. What they had suffered in England ought to be recorded " with a pen of iron on a hard flint stone that it might never be forgotten." Henry's envoys told them loftily that the king would not hear of any alteration of the existing law, and that they had better trust themselves to his mercy. Henry's attempt to separate Riga from the League failed. The town submitted under pressure, and surrendered its separate arrangement with England.[1] Henry's anxiety to gain a share of the Baltic trade proved that English trade was growing fast enough to make the Hansard monopoly felt as a restriction, but his failure showed that English merchants, even when strongly supported by their sovereign, were not yet powerful enough to break through the fetters imposed by a powerful and well-organised league. Henry, however, has to his credit two attempts to gain new markets—or more strictly to recover old markets—for his subjects; he was a pioneer on the path ultimately thrown open to British traders.

After 1500 there is a distinct change in the character of the king's relations with the Hansard towns. His former freedom of action was fettered by the political complication of Suffolk's intrigues, and under the pressure of circumstances he made a serious mistake. Suffolk had taken refuge in one of the Imperial towns Henry had tried and failed to induce Maximilian to have him proclaimed as a traitor, and he decided to approach the Hansards, all powerful

---

[1] The submission of Riga was announced in the summer of 1500. Busch, *op. cit.*, pp. 154, 155.

in the towns of Germany, and negotiate through them for his surrender. This is the explanation of the Act of 1504 which removed all the disabilities under which the Hansards suffered, " saving only the freedom and privileges of the town of London." [1] It was a total reversal of Henry's policy. His willingness to sacrifice important trade interests to a very doubtful diplomatic advantage is another instance of the curious deterioration of policy visible in the king's later years. Fortunately, this reactionary measure never took effect. When Suffolk left Aix in April 1504, the attempt to bribe the Hansard towns became useless. Henry repudiated his obligations with cynical aplomb and resumed his former attitude of hostility. In an ambiguous saving clause of the Act of 1504, he found the way of escape he desired. The increased privileges of the Hansards were declared to be an infringement of the rights of the city of London, and customs were again imposed at the higher rates.

In 1504, when commercial intercourse with Burgundy was again forbidden, the Hansards in London were asked to hand over another large sum to the king as security that they would not engage in the forbidden trade. The original pledge of £20,000 still remained in the king's hands, and in July 1508, about the date when its restoration fell due, Henry declared it forfeited owing to the export of cloth to Burgundy during the prohibited period. Thus, all through the reign, with one brief interruption, Henry had consistently pursued his policy of hostility to the alien merchants. He had shorn them of many

---

[1] 19 Hen. VII., cap. 23 ; *Stat.*, ii. 664–5 ; Fabyan, *Chron.*, 688.

of their privileges, and left the field open for the competition of his own subjects, to their great gain.[1]

The position in the Mediterranean was closely analogous to the state of affairs in the Baltic and North Sea. At Henry's accession the lion's share of the trade with England had been grasped by Italian merchants—the men of Venice being the largest traders—and was carried in Venetian galleys. English merchants chafed jealously against their monopoly, but as the Italian merchants did not occupy a specially privileged position in England like the Hansards, the situation was not nearly so acute. Besides, the trade was specially profitable to both countries. English wool was the raw material upon which the Italian weaving industry depended, and the Venetian galleys brought to England the Italian wines, silks, cloth of gold, fine cloth, and other luxuries Englishmen were beginning to find it difficult to do without. Thus the Italian trade brought England into contact with the centre of European civilisation.[2]

The legislation of Henry's first Parliament left the position of the Venetian merchants who had settled in England unaltered, except that an Act was passed imposing upon those merchants who had become naturalised in England customs dues and taxes on the same scale as they had paid before naturalisation.[3] Early in Henry's reign English merchants tried to gain part of the carrying trade in Italian wine by offering much cheaper rates of freight. This attempt was checked by a decree of

[1] Brown, *Ven. Cal.*, Nos. 728–30, 736–41, 754, 764.
[2] *Ibid.*, Nos. 498–500, 502–5, 507–10, 512, 515, 517.
[3] 1 Hen. VII., cap. 2 ; *Stat.*, ii. 501–2 ; *Rot. Parl.*, vi. 289.

the Venetian Senate (14th November 1488), which imposed an additional duty on wine carried in foreign ships, thus not only equalising matters, but even penalising British ships.[1] It looked as though Englishmen would be driven out of the trade altogether when Henry took the matter up. The case did not call for the extreme caution that had marked his dealings with the Hansards. The king grasped the fact that Italy could not, even if she would, give up the English trade. He struck swiftly and surely ; the year 1490 saw the treaty with Venice's great trade rival Florence and the second Navigation Act,[2] both of which deeply affected Venetian traders. The treaty with Florence (15th April 1490) made the Florentine port of Pisa the staple for the sale of English wool, and provided that English ships alone were to be engaged in the trade. The treaty also provided that the English merchants in Pisa might form themselves into a company,[3] this being the first attempt to start " a regular factory of English merchants in the Mediterranean." [4]

For a time the Senate ignored both this treaty and the menacing Navigation Acts, and maintained the extra duty on wine brought in foreign ships.[5] Countervailing duties were imposed in England in 1492, and in spite of protests from Venice were continued for several years. Henry's firm attitude, and the economic dependence of Italy on English wool, at last resulted in the Signory giving way, taking off

[1] Brown, *Ven. Cal.*, No. 544.   [2] See above, p. 164.
[3] Rymer, xii. 389–93.
[4] Cunningham, i. 493–4. Florence was very favourably situated from the English point of view, owing to her trade with Egypt and Constantinople.
[5] Brown, *Ven. Cal.*, Nos. 561, 562.

the duties on wine and leaving English ships free to capture what they could of the carrying trade.[1] Even then the king did not have the Act of 1494 repealed, though he issued a proclamation allowing some deductions. It is noticeable that even at the height of the dispute the friendly relations between England and Venice were undisturbed, and as time went on they became more intimate. Venice set a high value on Henry's friendship, and was deeply anxious for his entry into the Holy League. After 1496 the Signory kept a permanent representative in England, whose letters are a valuable source of information. Venetian merchants enjoyed the king's favour and protection ; once or twice they were given assistance to repair damaged ships, and on one occasion a Venetian captain had the honour of dining at the king's table. Venice received signal proofs of Henry's friendship in later years. In 1506 a royal proclamation exempted the Venetians from the Act of 1490, which forbade the purchase of English wool by foreign merchants until six months after the shearing.[2] In March of the following year the Venetian merchants were given a new ten years' charter for trade with England, but at the same time they were forbidden to engage in the trade between England and the Netherlands.[3] This latter order is a proof of the recovery and steady growth of English shipping ; the Navigation Acts had gained for native shippers an ever growing share of the carrying trade. By his

[1] 7 Hen. VII., cap. 7 ; *Stat.*, ii. 553 ; *Rot. Parl.*, vi. 457 ; Brown, *Ven. Cal.*, Nos. 606, 609, 627, 795, 832.

[2] This was to give the English cloth manufacturers the advantage of time and choice, 4 Hen. VII., cap. 11 ; *Stat.*, ii. 535.

[3] The Venetian galleys had been in the habit of proceeding to Flemish ports after visiting England.

refusal to join the League of Cambrai Henry gave the last and greatest proof of his friendship for the threatened Republic.[1]

Henry's commercial relations with France were fairly simple. At his accession he signed a treaty (17th January 1486) which removed all the fresh burdens that had been placed upon the trade between England and France since the accession of Edward IV.[2] Commercial relations, disturbed by the war, were resumed immediately afterwards, but both parties had something to complain of. Henry had passed his second Navigation Act in 1490, but on the other hand English merchants complained of fresh duties imposed during the war and still exacted. Henry also made strong representations on the subject of the piracies committed by the seamen of Brittany and Normandy. Nothing was done, however, until Charles's attempt to conquer Naples gave Henry a chance of exacting a high price for English neutrality. He made good use of his opportunity. Charles signed a decree at Naples in April 1495, which annulled the new duties and restored to English merchants the privileges they had formerly enjoyed.[3] The very favourable character of this settlement from the English point of view can be seen from the bitter tone of the remonstrances made by the French merchants. From this date until the end of the reign they complained constantly but in vain of the restrictions under which they struggled, and of the extraordinary privileges allowed to English merchants in France. Charles's ambition had saddled his subjects with an

---

[1] Brown, *Ven. Cal.*, Nos. 639, 659, 673, 736, 739, 782, 798, 832, 887, 893, 931, 939, 940. See below, p. 367.

[2] Rymer, xii. 281–2.   [3] Busch, *op. cit.*, pp. 351, 358.

unfavourable treaty, and Henry had won another commercial victory, the results of which endured till the end of the reign.

Commercial relations between England and Spain played a comparatively unimportant part in the endless negotiations between the two powers. Henry won a considerable advantage at the outset by a misunderstanding. The Treaty of Medina del Campo had settled that the duties paid by Spanish merchants should be those customary thirty years before. This meant the surrender of concessions made to Spanish merchants in England since that date, and though the difficulty was obviously due to an oversight on the part of the Spanish agents, Henry clung to his advantage, and duties were exacted on the higher scale. The unfairness of this arrangement was constantly brought forward by the Spaniards during the prolonged marriage negotiations, and they also objected to English ships being employed, during the war between France and Spain, in trade between the ports of the two hostile powers. Thus trade afforded a subject for mutual recriminations if the ordinary topics of the dowry and the marriage portion palled. The Spaniards demanded securities from English ships clearing from their ports that they would not run into French ports, and threatened that duties on the same scale as those imposed on Spanish merchants in England would be levied from English merchants in Spain. The English Navigation Acts were also a subject of complaint.[1] None of these questions had been settled by the marriage treaty of 1496, and they

[1] Berg., *Spanish Cal.*, Nos. 39, 42–44, 47, 50, 61–63, 65–69, 74–76, 86–88.

continued to be a source of friction until 1499, when by the Treaty of 10th July both powers agreed to treat each other's subjects like their own, " with full preservation of the local laws, rights, and customs." The interpretation of this last clause involved a renewed dispute. Henry continued to enforce his Navigation Laws against Spain in spite of remonstrances.[1] Concessions were made to England by a treaty of 23rd June 1503, but many questions were still outstanding at the end of the reign.

The protective principles that gave unity to the king's commercial governed his industrial policy. Most of the industrial legislation of the reign was framed with a view to encouraging the native artificer at the expense of his foreign competitors. Many of the industrial enactments of Henry's Parliaments were not original, but followed legislation of Edward IV. What was new and interesting about Henry's policy was that it was the outcome of a definite principle and part of a well-considered plan. His legislation was not experimental like that of Edward IV., but was designed for permanence and met with some success. The most obvious illustration of this policy is found in the king's treatment of the wool trade and of the cloth industry.

The cloth trade was still comparatively small, and, from the Treasury point of view, financially unimportant. Yet whenever the interests of the two trades conflicted, as they often did, Henry postponed the interests of the wool trade, which, though profitable to the king personally, had led to great depopulation in the rural districts, to the interests of the industry that promised to give employment to an effective population.

[1] Berg., *Spanish Cal.*, Nos. 106–8, 114, 119, 123, 254.

The customs on wool amounted to fully one-third of the king's total revenue from customs, but in spite of this a very heavy duty, amounting in some cases to 70 per cent., was placed upon wool exported from England.[1] This almost prohibitive duty was imposed, as an Italian observer points out, to prevent the exportation of undressed wool and to stimulate the woollen cloth industry,[2] which was already flourishing in the eastern counties, especially in Norfolk and in the West Riding of Yorkshire. Two later Acts checked an anticipated decay in Norfolk by diminishing the restrictions on the taking of apprentices;[3] and according to tradition, though there is no clear evidence on the point, Henry secretly encouraged the immigration of alien workmen into Yorkshire to teach their methods to the native workmen.[4] Another statute (1489–90), which revived an earlier Act of Edward IV., had given English cloth-workers the exclusive right of buying in advance what they required of the unshorn crop of English wool. Foreigners were prevented from buying until some months after shearing, so that they could only take what the native manufacturers had left.[5] In order to prevent the later processes of manufacture from being monopolised by aliens, a statute of Edward was re-enacted and extended (1487). It forbade the export of " unrowed and unshorn cloth," whereby " outlandissh nacions with the same drapry arne sette on labour and occupacion to their greate

[1] The whole revenue from customs on wool was appropriated to the defence of Calais. *Stat.*, ii. 667–9.

[2] *Italian Relation* (Camden Soc.), p. 50. The duty on exported cloth was never higher than 9 per cent. of its value.

[3] 11 Hen. VII., cap. 11 ; 12 Hen. VII., cap. 1 ; *Stat.*, ii. 577, 636.

[4] Anderson, *Commerce*, i. 526 ; Busch, *op. cit.*, p. 385.

[5] 4 Hen. VII., cap. 11 ; *Stat.*, ii. 535–6.

enriching, and the kynges true liegemen . . . for lake of such occupacion dailly fall in greate number to ydelnes and povertie." [1]

In his endeavour to foster the English cloth industry Henry came into conflict with long-established monopolies, and the monopolists had to give way. His attacks on the Hansard merchants had greatly strengthened the position of their rivals, the Merchant Adventurers. The latter were specially strong in London, and there they had adopted an exclusive attitude which roused much jealousy in the provinces. They attempted to keep the whole of the Flemish trade in their hands, and passed a decree which required an entrance fee of £20 from every merchant trading with the Netherlands. This attempt to confine the trade to the wealthier merchants was quite at variance with the spirit of Henry's policy. He refused to allow the interests of an industry, which was of great importance from the national point of view, to be subordinated to the greed of a group of wealthy men. An Act of Parliament passed in 1497 declared trade with the Netherlands free, reducing the entrance fee to ten marks. [2] The selfish spirit of monopoly checked, the Merchant Adventurers continued to prosper, gaining strength as the restrictions on the Hansards increased. Having once got the upper hand of them, Henry made use of their powerful organisation to enforce throughout the kingdom royal regulations of the cloth trade. In the later years of the reign the Merchant Adventurers received many marks of royal favour. Thus, in

---

[1] 3 Hen. VII., cap. 12 ; *Stat.*, ii. 520–1. Foreign merchants complained that the unskilled English shearmen spoilt the cloth.

[2] 12 Hen. VII., cap. 6 ; *Stat.*, ii. 638–9 ; Busch, *op. cit.*, p. 244.

1499, the company obtained permission to use its own coat of arms, and in the following year its charter was confirmed. In 1505 there was a general reorganisation of the whole company by Act of Parliament. A governing body, composed of an elected governor and twenty-four assistants, was set up, and given power to settle the affairs of the trade and decide disputes between members, subject always to the king's authority.[1] By giving additional executive powers to a body which he had reduced to submission and dependence, Henry increased the control of the Crown over one of the most important trades in the country.

Henry's protective measures were not, however, framed in a spirit of rigid exclusiveness, and, where national interests were not involved, the interests of the consumer were considered. An example of this is his treatment of the silk trade. Though there was great jealousy of the Italian silk merchants, and the importation of certain manufactured silk goods was forbidden by Act of Parliament in 1485, Henry did not consider the native industry sufficiently advanced to supply the needs of the country, and in 1504 all silk goods except those mentioned in the Act—" corses, gyrdelles, rybandes, laces, calle sylke or coleyn sylke "—were to be imported free.[2]

Henry's attempts to deal with the agricultural problem were spirited but unsuccessful. The circumstances that produced the flourishing cloth trade had brought agriculture into difficulties. Owing to a variety of causes, of which the Black Death, the

---

[1] The meeting-place of the governing body was first Calais and afterwards Antwerp. Busch, *op. cit.*, p. 245.

[2] 1 Hen. VII., cap. 9 ; 19 Hen. VII., cap. 21 ; *Stat.*, ii. 506, 664.

decline of the monasteries, and the disorders of the civil wars are the most important, there had been almost complete stagnation in agricultural methods. What a man's father and grandfather had done, that he continued to do, often less thoroughly. This equilibrium gave way in the reign of Henry VII. The high price of wool, and the increased demand for it, led to the conversion of much arable land into pasture. Small holdings were thrown together, great flocks of sheep were kept, and there was a diminished demand for labour. The state of affairs is familiar to us through the indignant eloquence of contemporaries. " Where there hath been many houses and churches to the honour of God, now you shall find nothing but shepcotes and stables to the ruin of men." [1] " The husbandmen thrust out of their own, or else by covin and fraud, or by violent oppression, put beside it, or by wrong and injury so wearied that they sell all, . . . the noblemen and gentlemen, yea, and certain abbots, holy men no doubt, that leave no ground for tillage, they enclose all into pasture, they throw down houses, they pluck down towns and leave nothing standing, but only the church to be made a sheep house." [2]

The situation presented elements of grave political danger. The depopulation of the countryside, the number of men thrown out of employment, the widespread distress, all threatened the king's dearest aims. Henry made several attempts to stem the tide of revolution by legislative interference ; [3] but natural forces were too strong for him. As the great profits to be obtained from wool-growing were realised,

---

[1] Starkey, *Description of England.*   [2] More, *Utopia*, 32.
[3] 4 Hen. VII., caps. 16, 19; *Stat.*, ii. 540–42.

more and more land was laid down to pasture. A pressing social problem remained unsolved as a legacy for the next reign.[1] Fortunately, however, there was no great rise in the price of corn during the reign. Improved farming led to a greater production of corn from the diminished area under the plough,[2] and little corn was exported. On the rare occasions when prices rose owing to a bad harvest, as in 1491, the export of corn was forbidden,[3] the needs of the whole nation being preferred to the profit of the corn growers. The king also attempted to encourage the breeding of horses and cattle by legislation. The export of horses was forbidden,[4] and the licenses necessary for the exportation of cattle and sheep were very sparingly issued,[5] in order to prevent continental breeds being improved by mixture with the English stock. At the same time the fishing industry was regulated and protected.[6]

The same conflict between the old order and the new that embittered the agricultural difficulty was at work in the organisation of industry. The expanding

[1] Several cases which illustrate the enclosure movement may be found in *Star Chamber Cases* (Selden Soc. and Somers Rec. Soc.).

[2] The enclosure movement was not entirely due to sheep-farming. Some enclosures took place from a desire to escape the conservative methods of strip tenancy, and adopt improved methods on a consolidated holding. Cunningham (*Royal Hist. Soc. Trans.*, 1910); Busch, *op. cit.*, p. 386.

[3] *L. and P. Hen. VII.*, ii. 372 ; "*Victualia*" are usually mentioned in the commercial treaties of the reign among the articles which ought to be freely exported and imported. *E.g.*, Rymer, xii. 582 ; Busch, *op. cit.*, p. 387.

[4] 11 Hen. VII., cap. 13 ; *Stat.*, ii. p. 578.

[5] Edward IV. had issued these licenses frequently. The Duchess Margaret was deprived by Henry of her license to have 1000 oxen and 2000 rams exported to her every year.

[6] The fishing industry was the school of English mariners, and its interests were carefully considered by the king.

manufactures were outgrowing the craft gild regulations and rebelling against restrictions that
seemed ineffective as well as oppressive. The appearance of new ideas about competitive prices
jarred harshly with the medieval view of a fair
price. Gild regulations were not framed to harmonise
new ideas and old methods, and the effort to escape
from them caused the migration of woollen and linen
manufacturers into rural districts, which explains
the constant complaints of the decay of the towns.
Many of the older towns were in a very bad state,
with streets deserted and houses falling into ruins.
Remissions of taxation had to be constantly made to
the towns that were unable to sustain the burden
of the old assessment.[1] It was Henry's settled
policy to bring the gilds under his control. In nearly
every case State interference was exerted in the
interests of the community against a class of privileged monopolists. A series of Acts was passed controlling the craft gilds in particular cases. Thus
Parliament defined the weight and quality of cloth,
arranged the details of apprenticeship and inspection
by gild officials, and settled disputes between rival
gilds.[2] But the most important step of all (and one
which has attracted but little notice) was taken in
1504, when the gilds were brought under the control
of the courts. The Act declared that no gild regulation should be binding until it had been approved
by the Chancellor, the Treasurer, the chief justices

---

[1] Certain reductions were made every time a subsidy was granted.
York, Lincoln, and Great Yarmouth were much impoverished.

[2] 12 Hen. VII., cap. 4; 11 Hen. VII., cap. 11; 19 Hen. VII.,
cap. 17 ; *Stat.*, ii. 577–8, 637, 662. In 1501 complaints of a scarcity
of bread, which was thought to be due to the action of the bakers'
gild, led to the interference of Government.

of the King's Bench and Common Pleas, or the judges on circuit.[1] It was a measure which secured greater uniformity of trade regulations, broke down local jealousies, and most important of all perhaps, from Henry's point of view, rendered the king's control of industry effective.[2]

Henry's dealings with the capital are another illustration of his anxiety to break down local exclusiveness and advance towards the still distant ideal of free trade within the kingdom. In 1487 an Act of Parliament annulled an ordinance of the City of London which actually forbade London merchants to frequent markets outside the city.[3] At the same time the old privileges of the city which forbade foreigners to buy and sell retail except through citizens were confirmed.[4] Henry shared to the full the contemporary jealousy of the alien trader.

The importance to a statesman of the sixteenth century, when the credit system was in its infancy, of being able to lay his hand at any moment on a considerable hoard of treasure, can hardly be exaggerated. Henry VII. was not the only king in Europe who hoarded bullion, but he was the only one who made a considerable success of it. The possession of accumulated treasure strengthened him against rebellion and invasion, and his reputation for wealth won him consideration and deference in Europe. Taxes, fines, and benevolences replenished his hoard, and " golden showers poured down upon

---

[1] 19 Hen. VII., cap. 7 ; *Stat.*, ii. 652.

[2] A former Act of Henry VI., which had given the municipal authorities control over the gilds, had been almost a dead letter. 15 Hen. VI., cap. 6.

[3] 3 Henry VII., cap. 10 ; *Stat.*, ii. 518–519.

[4] Busch, *op. cit.*, p. 244.

the king's treasury." In addition he attempted to
prevent gold coin and bullion from leaving the
country. In 1487 he revived the law of Edward
IV. which forbade alien merchants or merchants
from Ireland or Guernsey to carry gold out of the
kingdom, and ordered that they should buy other
commodities with the money obtained from the sale of
their goods.[1] This Act, originally limited to seven
years, was made permanent by Henry VII. Three
years later alien merchants were forbidden to take
more than ten crowns out of the country,[2] and in
1504 it was enacted that not more than 6s. 8d.
should be exported by any merchant to Ireland.[3]
Henry tried to increase the supply of the precious
metals in another way by giving special rights and
privileges to the Southampton Metal Staple.[4] On
the whole these measures were very successful. A
long period of peace stopped the drain of gold to the
Continent, and Henry's considerable subsidies to his
allies were balanced by the payment of pensions.

The currency was in a chaotic condition during
the early years of the reign. Debased, clipped, and
foreign coins were in circulation, and there was much
counterfeit money.[5] André spoke of Henry's reform of the currency as one of his twelve herculean
labours, and he certainly had some success in a
difficult business.[6] Stern measures were taken to

[1] 17 Edw. IV., cap. 1; 3 Hen. VII., cap. 9; *Stat.*, ii. 452, 517. Henry
wisely gave up the attempt to make each merchant bring home
a certain amount of bullion for each cargo he exported.

[2] 4 Hen. VII., cap. 23; *Stat.*, ii. 546.

[3] 19 Hen. VII., cap. 5; *Stat.*, ii. 650–51.

[4] *L. and P. Hen. VII.*, ii. 373; *Pat. 6 Hen. VII.*, pt. i., m. 8, 7 *d*;
Report on MSS. of Lord Middleton (Hist. MSS. Com. 1911), p. 266,
and App. pp. 614–17.

[5] See the complaints recorded in the *Cely Papers* (Camden Soc.),
p. 159.   [6] André, *Annales*, p. 81.

COINAGE OF HENRY VII

| 1 | Gold—sovereign | 3 | Silver—groat |
| 2 | Silver—groat | 4. | Perkin Warbeck groat |

repress the activity of the counterfeit coiners, and the forging of foreign as well as of English coin was made high treason. Special efforts were made to prevent the circulation of the bad Irish coinage.[1] Finally an Act of 1504 dealt with the whole question in a statesmanlike way. The first step to a general reform of the coinage was made by abandoning the old principle that light or clipped coin was to be accepted at its face value. The new law enacted that gold coins were only to be accepted when of full weight. Clipped coins were to be refused, and new coins were to be stamped with a circle round the edge to prevent clipping.[2] The reform of the silver coinage did not go so far, and light (though not clipped) silver coins were to be accepted if they bore the royal stamp. A proclamation of the following year made the clipping of coin punishable by death, and a false coiner was hanged at Tyburn as a warning.[3] Modern coinage may be said to begin in this reign, the sovereign being issued for the first time in 1490, and the shilling in 1504. The new coinage has been described as " the best specimen of metallic portraiture coined in England since the time of Constantine." [4]

The king's reforming hand dealt also with the standard weights and measures, which were in a state of confusion equal to that of the coinage. Several

---

[1] 3 Hen. VII., cap. 9; 4 Hen. VII., cap. 18, cap. 23; *Stat.*, ii. 518, 541–2, 546. Much was also done by way of proclamation and Orders in Council. *L. and P. Hen. VII.*, ii. 372, 376, 377, 379.

[2] 19 Hen. VII., cap. 5; *Stat.*, ii. 650.

[3] *L. and P. Hen. VII.*, ii. 379; *City Chron.*, pp. 259–61.

[4] Traill, *Soc. England*, ii. 685. The early coinage of Henry VII. has the seated figure of the king robed and crowned on the obverse and the Tudor rose on the reverse; the later coinage has the king's portrait in profile.

statutes were passed which, like many others before
them, declared one standard to be obligatory throughout the kingdom; but, unlike the earlier efforts, they
were followed up by practical attempts to make the
standard measures known. Metal copies of them
were provided for distribution by the members of
Parliament to their boroughs, and in many ports
King's Beams were set up. Owing to the increased
power of the central government the laws of
Henry VII. were carried into effect, and the use
of the authorised measures was enforced.[1]

Henry shared the general dislike of usury, which
was regarded as a striking instance of an attempt to
sacrifice public welfare to private gain. To lend
money for interest was looked upon as a heinous
offence, an unchristian attempt to obtain profit where
no profit was due, by speculating in a "breed of
barren metal." Quite early in the reign, in 1487, an
Act was passed to restrain the "dampnable bargayns
groundyt in usurye, colorde by the name of newe Cheve-
saunce, contrarie to the lawe of naturell justis, to the
comon hurt of this land." Usurious bargains, that
is, all bargains in which a percentage was allowed
for the use of money, were declared void, offenders
being subject to a penalty of £100, "reservyng to
the Church the correcion of their soules according to
the lawes of the same." The Chancellor was given
jurisdiction in cities and boroughs, and justices of
the peace in the counties. A later Act dealt with
the same subject, and also forbade loans being
secured upon land by way of a rent-charge.[2]

---

[1] 7 Hen. VII., cap. 3 ; 11 Hen. VII., cap. 4 ; 12 Hen. VII., cap. 5 ;
Stat., ii. 551–2, 570–3, 637–8. Many delinquents who used false
measures were brought before the Star Chamber. See *Star Chamber
Cases* (Selden Soc.), i. 69–71.

[2] 3 Hen. VII., cap. 6 ; 11 Hen. VII., cap. 8 ; *Stat.*, ii. 514–5, 574.

In the reign of Henry VII. we may see the beginning of the paternal government both by legislation and ordinance characteristic of the Tudor dynasty. There are many examples of Parliamentary regulation of prices, the theory in most cases being that the retail traders were making unfairly large profits ; [1] the articles affected ranged from hats and caps to long-bows, the price of these latter being limited to check the threatened supersession of the characteristic weapon of England by the cross-bow.[1] Parliament had long ago undertaken the responsibility of regulating wages, and in 1495 a comprehensive measure fixing the maximum rates and ordering the payment of lower rates wherever they were prevalent was passed. Subsequent legislation affords evidence that the State was gradually extending its sphere of action. Acts of Parliament were passed regulating many of the details of employment, how many hours a day workmen were to work, how long they were to spend on their meals, and so on. A workman who left his job before he finished it was to go to prison for a month and pay a fine of £1, and holidays were not to be paid for.[2] Legislation also regulated apprenticeship, forbidding cards and dice except at Christmas, and so forth. Examples of the active control of Parliament over the conditions of industry might be multiplied indefinitely. Parliament stepped in to prevent manufacturers singeing their fustians, to arrange the details of the leather trade, to prescribe

---

[1] 4 Hen. VII., cap. 8, cap. 9 ; 3 Hen. VII., cap. 13 ; 19 Hen. VII., cap. 4 ; *Stat.*, ii. 521, 533–4, 649.

[2] 11 Hen. VII., cap. 2, cap. 22 ; 12 Hen. VII., cap. 3 ; *Stat.*, ii. 569, 585–6, 637. The Act of 1497 cancelled the clauses fixing maximum rates, perhaps, as Dr. Busch suggests (p. 265), because wages had remained so stationary that the clauses were no longer necessary.

the way in which feather beds should be stuffed, to compel all butchers, except those of Berwick and Carlisle, to do their butchering out of doors.[1] This minute supervision of social conditions was extended over much wider ground later in the reign, when the Crown devised machinery for controlling the craft gilds. It is not too much to say that by the end of the reign the influence of Henry the Seventh's personality touched the lives of his subjects at almost every point.

Changes in the standard of comfort have made it difficult to estimate the social conditions of labour in the reign. In some respects the labourer was very well off. Working eight hours a day—the ordinary length of a working day in the fifteenth century—he could earn two or three shillings a day ; house rent and fuel were cheap, and the average cost of necessaries was about one-twelfth of their cost to-day. There were many opportunities for amusement, and many compulsory holidays ;[2] rural sports and pastimes flourished, and nearly every parish had gilds or fraternities which gave dramatic performances. Movement from place to place, however, was difficult, and roads and bridges were much neglected, suffering from the decline in monastic activity. England was ravaged by plague several times during the reign. There were two outbreaks of the new and mysterious sweating sickness in 1485 and 1508, which, beginning in London, spread over the rest of England. In 1499–1500 an epidemic of the more familiar

---

[1] 1 Hen. VII., cap. 5; 4 Hen. VII., cap. 3; 11 Hen. VII., cap. 27; 19 Hen. VII., cap. 19; *Stat.*, ii. 502–4, 527–8, 591, 663–4.

[2] The gilds made stringent rules forbidding working on Church festivals.

plague wrought great havoc in London, and there
were less serious outbreaks in 1487, 1503, and 1504.[1]
The chief hardships came from the clashing of new
ideas and old habits.   The old tie between lord and
man had not yet lost the personal character that
made the master feel responsible for the welfare of
his dependants, but the new relations between
capital and labour were giving a changed colour to
society in the flourishing industrial districts.   In
agriculture and industry historic methods were being
abandoned.

The Crown drew to itself more and more power.
The strange thing is that this great extension of State
control was almost uniformly beneficent in effect, as
it was in intention.   We cannot point to a single one
of Henry's commercial statutes that was designed to
forward any selfish interests of the king or his
advisers.   The underlying principle of all the industrial and agrarian legislation was to provide for the
maintenance of the effective population upon which
all national ambitions depended.   Idleness, " the
cause and root of all evil," the parent of poverty and
crime, was the bugbear of the Tudor statesmen.   On
the other hand, the king's aim was not the modern
one of alleviating the lot of the worker.   He showed
no altruistic desire to add to his people's happiness.
Disorder and violence, the symptoms of economic
disease, were kept in check, but the root of the disease
lay beyond the king's reach and could be touched by
Time alone.   Henry's aim was to make his kingdom
strong and powerful, and the happiness of the mass
of the people found no place in this robust ideal.

[1] In 1497 there was an outbreak of a " wonderful sickness called
the Spaynysh pokkes." *City Chronicle,* 217.

CHAPTER VI

FOREIGN AFFAIRS, 1497–1503—MARRIAGE ALLIANCES

THE failure of Perkin Warbeck's attempt removed a thread which had been bound up in the tangled web of European diplomacy for many years. For the future foreign affairs were simpler and infinitely easier for the king. The position he had won for himself by tireless effort in the face of a dangerous conspiracy, supported at one time or another by nearly all the royal houses of Europe, could easily be maintained and improved now that the pretender was defeated and his supporters discredited. The dramatic interest lessens. There is no longer the atmosphere of suspense, the straining of every faculty to win from a reluctant Europe some recognition of the power and influence of the upstart king of a weak and divided nation. Already, by years of toil and anxiety, the Tudor dynasty was rooted in England, and England had been given a place in European politics.

Henry's strength and prosperity was beginning to attract the attention of foreign observers, and had been the subject of some comment in this critical year of his fortunes. The states of Venice and Milan both realised the value of Henry's friendship. An ambassador from Venice, Andrea Trivisano, was despatched in the summer of 1497 to assure Henry of the love the Signory bore him, congratulate him

on his " very great successes," and express their joy
at his joining the Holy League.   He was instructed
"to make great demonstrations of love on behalf of
the Republic " to the queen, Morton, and Prince
Arthur.   Further, he was ordered to send news of
England.   News indeed he sent, but not of the most
reliable, when on his journey,[1] but as soon as he
reached England and the court his tone changed.
He wrote that Henry's rule was " to be considered
much strengthened and perpetual" by the suppression
of the disturbances.   " The kingdom of England,"
he wrote, " has never for many years been so obedient
to its sovereign as it is at present to his Majesty the
king."   More detailed information to the same effect
was sent by the Milanese envoy.   He reported that
Henry was " admirably well informed and thoroughly
acquainted with the affairs of Italy."   Even the
courtiers knew so much about Italian affairs that he
fancied himself at Rome.   One sentence as to the
state of affairs in England towards the end of this
year is worth quoting.   " The kingdom is perfectly
stable by reason first of the king's wisdom, whereof
every one stands in awe ; and secondly, on account
of the king's wealth, for I am informed that he has
upwards of six millions of gold, and it is said that
he puts by annually five hundred thousand ducats."
He went on to speak of Henry's diplomatic skill,
that, for instance, he had kept the French ambassadors
who wished to visit Scotland in England, entertained
them magnificently, and sent them home laden with
presents, but without seeing Scotland.   The envoy
commented on the assistance Papal protection had
been to Henry ; the rebellious Cornishmen had felt the

[1] See above, p. 151.

efficacy of Papal censures. "All who eat grain garnered since the rebellion or drink beer brewed with this year's crops, die as if they had taken poison, and hence it is publicly reported that the king is under the protection of God eternal." [1]   The Spanish ambassador, de Ayala, wrote a few months later to the same effect. He reported that Henry's crown was undisputed, and that he was complete master in England, observing with some insight that he showed a desire to " govern England after the French fashion."   The settled policy by which Henry made himself the first of a line of despots did not escape shrewd observers.   The troubles he had passed through, however, had already left their mark upon the king.   " The king," wrote Ayala, " looks old for his years but young for the sorrowful life he has led."

The summer of 1497 saw also the departure of the Cabot expedition.[2]   This setting out of British merchants for unknown seas in this year of invasion and tumult emphasises the point at which the strife between medieval and modern influences, which pervades the whole reign, began to incline in favour of the latter.   Henceforward England begins to look westward with her spreading commerce, and draw away from the medieval background of " privy conspiracy and rebellion."

After 1497—the turning-point of the reign in so many spheres—foreign politics become comparatively simple and stable.   Diplomacy was to be dominated for many years by the attempts of the kings of France and Spain to win the alliance of England with a view to advancing or checking French designs in Italy.   It is a premature sketch of the system of

[1] Brown, *Ven. Cal.*, No. 751.   [2] See below, p. 320.

the " balance of power " later elaborated by Wolsey.
The outcome—after many waverings—was the completion of the alliance between England and Spain
which lasted for forty years and brought such weighty
results.

But while the ultimate issue is simple, the negotiations which led up to it were as complex as ever, and
the lack of dramatic interest is heightened by the
maze of trivialities, and the wearisome discussions of
foregone conclusions preserved in the State papers.[1]
Already in 1496 the principle of a marriage alliance
between England and Spain had been accepted on
both sides, but many years were still to be spent
bickering over the princess's marriage portion, the
extent of the English lands which were to form her
dowry, and even over her trousseau and jewels.

In negotiations of this kind Ferdinand and Henry
were very fairly matched. In both, as they grew
older, a habit of dealing carefully with money degenerated into stinginess; both seemed to have revelled
in an atmosphere of squalid haggling fitter for the
counter of a pawnbroker than for the antechambers
of great kings. The spirit of vulgarity pervading
these negotiations was personified in de Puebla, the
Spanish ambassador, who lived in England permanently from 1494 to 1509. A mean, spiteful, avaricious man, begging, whining, and backbiting, without
a shred of personal pride or official dignity, he
brought his high office into disrepute, and was a butt
for the sneers of the English court. One of his
fellow-countrymen reported him to be " avaricious
and a notorious usurer, an enemy of truth, full of
lies and a calumniator of all honest men, vainglorious

[1] Berg., *Spanish Cal.*, vol. i. pp. 159–472 ; Brown, *Ven. Cal.*, vol. i.

and ostentatious. It is generally said at court that
de Puebla comes a-begging. He is often glad of
the bad success of his masters." This unpleasant
picture was not a bit overdrawn. The ambassador
of Spain lived squalidly in a "vile and miserable
inn of bad repute," hanging round the court to save
himself the expense of meals, though he made large
sums by taking bribes from Spanish merchants to
push their interests with the English king. All the
time, in spite of his deformity, he was flattering himself with the hope that his master would allow him
to accept the English bishopric offered him by Henry,
or the "honourable marriage" with a wealthy
English bride arranged for him by the same patron.
It seems strange that the power and dignity of Spain
lay so long in these unworthy hands, but Henry seems
to have had some kind of affection for him, and to
have treated him with singular confidence. His pen
describes the ambassador as "industrious, vigilant,
and true and adroit in all negotiations entrusted to
him," and he gave him many marks of favour.

The strong personal influence exerted by all the
Tudors brought de Puebla early under Henry's sway,
and a keen Spanish observer saw that his popularity
with the king was due to his pliancy.[1] His absurd
vanity made him the dupe of Henry's flatteries. His
letters to Ferdinand echoed the king's opinions and
championed his point of view. He even concealed
important news from his master. The Spanish merchants complained bitterly of de Puebla's neglect of
their interests, and asserted that he deliberately lost
the opportunity of wringing commercial concessions
from Henry at a time when he was "in such difficulties that he would not have refused the half of

[1] Berg., *Spanish Cal.*, pp. 162–3.

his revenues if de Puebla had asked it." His despatches read like those of a confidential minister of
the English king rather than of a Spanish ambassador.
Ferdinand and Isabella were not deceived. As early
as 1498 they suspected that " de Puebla was entirely in the interest of King Henry." One of their
envoys, Londoño, wrote, " He is in such subjection
that he dares not say a word but what he thinks
will please the king. . . . He is a great partisan of
the King of England." But it was convenient for
Ferdinand and Isabella to have an agent who repeated all the gossip of the English court, and they
guarded against de Puebla's over great submission to
Henry by putting delicate negotiations in charge of
an ambassador of a much higher stamp, who became
the mark for de Puebla's jealous railings. He had not
even the wit to conceal his jealousy of Ayala. Bitter
recriminations against him fill his letters. He in-
sinuated that Henry would be glad if Ayala left the
country, " although he had written to the contrary," [1]
and proudly boasted about his own great influence
over Henry and the " wonders " he performed in spite
of " superhuman difficulties." Distrusted and despised
by both Spaniards and English, he yet remained in
England in nominal control of all the negotiations
between the two countries for many years.[2]

Towards the end of 1496 a peaceful tendency had

---

[1] Londoño's report of Ayala is very different. He was on good
terms with the king and the whole court, and was the only man in
the kingdom who really knew anything about Scotland, " all others
flying into a passion as soon as the name of Scotland is pronounced "
(*ibid.*, p. 161). He reported that de Puebla was the cause of the
disgraceful scenes between the two ambassadors.

[2] See Berg., *Spanish Cal.*, passim, especially pp. 109, 112, 120, 135,
146, 147, 148, 152, 155, 158, 189, 191, 195–7, 228, 232, 250, 277, 281,
294; Busch, *op. cit.*, pp. 135, 351–2.

become visible in Europe.   The shadow of French
ascendancy in Italy passed away after the successes
won by the Spanish infantry in the kingdom of
Naples.   Now that the danger was over the Holy
League was ready for peace, and Spanish successes
in the Pyrenees made France anxious to treat.   On
27th February 1496–7 a truce between France and
Spain was made, in which the other members of the
League were included shortly afterwards.[1]   Henry
was prepared to go further than this.   Peaceful relations with France were profitable as well as pleasant.
In May 1497 a commercial treaty strengthened the
bond between the two countries.   Henry's diplomacy
had put England into a very favourable position.
His entrance into the Holy League had brought him
invaluable help in the most anxious year of his reign.
He had gained the prestige of an alliance blessed by
the Pope, but his obligations under it had been merely
nominal, and he remained a defensive member of an
offensive league.   One power alone stood in the way
of a general pacification.   Maximilian remained
obstinately hostile to France, and on the sudden
death of Charles VIII. of France (7th April 1498),
he prepared for war.   The League, however, made
no move ; he dared not attack France without an
ally, and he was forced to swallow his hatred of
Henry and make overtures for his alliance.   He
worked hard to revive England's grudge against her
old enemy, suggested the recovery of the lost provinces, and promised " to perform wonders in the war
against France."   Henry was not to be drawn.   He
had seen too much of the contrast between the

---

[1] Berg., *Spanish Cal.*, pp. 118, 127–8, 142 ; Busch, p. 128, note 2,
giving references to Zurita.

promises and performances of the King of the Romans.
He did not conceal the fact that he was not over-con-
fident in the "constancy, veracity, and perseverance"
of his would-be ally, and he answered with ironical
politeness that he "should like to see the King of
the Romans at war with France, but only by way of
witnessing his wonderful feats, and not in order to
take part himself in the enterprise." [1]   The prospect,
however, of seeing Brittany again independent was
alluring, and Henry sent spies into the province to
see whether the revival of national spirit in Brittany
would lead to an attempt at separation.   His hopes
were disappointed.   The new King of France lost no
time in securing his hold upon Brittany by divorcing
his own wife and marrying the widow of Charles VIII.
Amicable relations between England and France were
not disturbed.   A solemn dirge or obsequy was sung
in St. Paul's Cathedral for the dead King of France.
De Puebla tried to make Henry break with France,
but in vain.   He reported to his master that owing
to the tribute paid by the King of France to Henry,
and the pensions given by him to English nobles,
Henry valued his friendship more than the whole of
the Indies; the new King of France had shown
every wish to please Henry, had undertaken all the
obligations of his predecessor, the pensions and so on.
On 14th July the treaty of Etaples was confirmed by
Henry's agents in Paris, and the clause relating to
rebels was made more binding than ever. [2]   The
thunders of the Papal chair were invoked on either of

[1] Berg., *Spanish Cal.*, i. p. 157.
[2] *City Chron.*, 223; Berg., *Spanish Cal.*, 151; *Excerpta Historica*,
118; Rymer, xii. 681–95, 706–7, 710–12, 736–8, 762–5; Busch, *op. cit.*,
p. 129.

the parties who should break a treaty which seemed
to bring the vision of universal peace in sight.   The
example set by Henry was speedily followed in
Europe.   On 2nd August the Archduke Philip made
peace with France and renounced his father's claim
to the duchy of Burgundy.   His peaceful attitude,
very popular in Flanders, was distasteful to Maximilian, who was carrying on hostilities in a desultory
way.   A few days later, Ferdinand of Aragon, who
had been the brains of the Holy League, also came
to terms with France, a treaty being signed at
Marcoussis on 5th August.   Thus the whole of
Europe, with the exception of Maximilian, had given
guarantees for the maintenance of peace, and even
he at last recognised the impossibility of the position,
withdrew his troops and made peace with France, in
which he was followed by Venice.   Thus the Holy
League broke up.[1]

Meanwhile the Anglo-Spanish negotiations were
revealing a much firmer attitude on Henry's part in
spite of the Perkin Warbeck complication.   By the
treaty of 1st October 1496 it had been provided
that the marriage between Arthur and Katherine
should take place when the prince had completed his
fourteenth year, that Katherine's marriage portion
was to consist of 200,000 crowns (4s. 2d.), half to be
paid within ten days of the marriage and the remainder within two years.   The last quarter might
be paid in plate and jewels.   The dower of the
Princess of Wales was to consist of one-third of the
revenues of Wales, Cornwall, and Chester, and was
to be increased to the usual amount when she became

---

[1] Even the Duchess Margaret wrote to Henry asking for pardon
and promising obedience.   Berg., *Spanish Cal.*, p. 196.

Queen of England.   Her rights of succession in
Castile and Aragon were saved, and a separate
document signed by Henry VII. assured the succession to the throne of England to Arthur's children
if he should die in Henry's lifetime.[1]   This treaty did
not completely satisfy Ferdinand.   It contained none
of the commercial concessions he hoped for and did
not bind Henry to an offensive and defensive alliance
with Spain.   The efforts of Spanish diplomatists
were concentrated upon obtaining some modification of the treaty.   Ferdinand first tried to induce
Henry to break with France by using the old
lure of the speedy settlement of the marriage.   But
this charm no longer worked.   Henry, well aware
that the marriage had now been definitely decided on
by the Spanish court, became less eager for its immediate because he felt sure of its ultimate fulfilment.
He realised the strength of his position, and even
the critical events of the year 1497 did not weaken
his attitude.   It is from the other side that the
flattering expressions come.   Isabella writes of Henry
as " a prince of great virtue, firmness and constancy,"
and hopes for a more intimate friendship with him
after the marriage.

Ferdinand seemed bent on giving every proof
of his friendly feelings.   He wrote that the absence
of harmony between Henry and the archduke
weighed on his mind; he welcomed the announcement of his intention to enter the Holy League,
forwarded evidence about the claims of the Duke of
York, and ordered de Ayala to use all his influence
to reconcile Henry and James of Scotland.   Henry
was assured that by the marriage of the Infanta

[1] *Ibid.*, pp. 129, 130.

Juana to the Archduke Philip he would have henceforth a daughter in Flanders.[1] Isabella wrote later
that she " confided in Henry as she would in a
brother." [1] Henry's firm attitude led to further
concessions. War with France, the original object
of the treaty, which had been strongly urged upon
Henry at first, was dropped when it appeared that
he would not bind himself. The treaty was too
valuable to Ferdinand to be jeopardised by obstinacy,
and in January 1497 Ferdinand and Isabella ratified
it.[2] A month later the arrival at Southampton
of the Princess Margaret of Austria—she was on
her way to Spain to join her husband and was driven
in by bad weather—gave Henry an opportunity of
showing his friendship. She received a very cordial
letter from him. " The arrival of his own daughter
could not give him more joy," he wrote. He placed
at her disposal his person, his realm, and all that
were to be found in it. They were not to spare
him and his realms, for they would render him a
very great service by accepting everything from
him.[3]

But these fair words did not augur any concession,
and it was not until July, the month of Perkin
Warbeck's adventure, that Henry at last ratified
the marriage treaty.[4] The betrothal of Arthur and
Katherine took place a month later by proxy at
Woodstock, where the court was established for
the early autumn.[5] The Spanish alliance was of
immense practical value during this year of difficulty,

[1] Berg., *Spanish Cal.*, p. 124.
[2] *Ibid.*, Nos. 167, 168.   [3] *Ibid.*, No. 173.
[4] Rymer, xii. 658–66 ; Berg., pp. 129–130.
[5] *Ibid.*, Nos. 167–8, and p. 132.

especially in the Scotch negotiations.[1]   Henry received cordial assurances of Spanish support at the time of Warbeck's landing in Cornwall.   Ferdinand and Isabella offered to despatch a fleet, and hailed the defeat of the adventurer and the " great victory of their beloved brother, Henry," with expressions of apparently sincere delight, announcing that " they had always known that he [Warbeck] was an impostor." [2]   On 4th February 1497–8, the treaty was ratified for the second time by Ferdinand and Isabella,[3] and in July, after a dispensation had been obtained from the Pope, Arthur and Katherine were married by proxy with great solemnity, de Puebla representing the princess.[4]   Henry expressed his joy at this event with a vigour that meant a great deal from a man of his unenthusiastic temperament.   He swore " on his royal faith " that he and the queen were more satisfied with this marriage than with any great dominions they might have gained with the daughter of another prince.   On another occasion Henry laid his hand on his heart and swore " by the faith of his heart," that if any one of his " best beloved subjects said anything against the King or Queen of Spain he would not esteem him any longer."   He and the queen had a playful dispute about the letters they received from their Spanish " brother and sister."   Henry professed to want to carry them about with him all the time, but the queen did not wish to give hers up.[5]   Henry and the Prince of

---

[1] See above, pp. 144–5.   Henry showed his gratitude by writing a very graceful letter to the Queen of Spain.   " He loved them so much," he wrote, " that it is impossible to imagine a greater and more sincere affection."   Berg., *Spanish Cal.*, p. 146.

[2] Berg., *Spanish Cal.*, i. p. 147.   [3] *Ibid.*, No. 189.

[4] *Ibid.*, pp. 148, 160, 168, 185, 190, 209–10.   [5] *Ibid.*, p. 190.

Wales both wrote personal letters to Spain, and the
king sent with his a curious gift—twenty-four
" blessed rings," one dozen of them being gold and
one dozen silver. Several young Spanish noblemen
came over to England to enter the Prince of Wales's
service, while an Englishman was recommended for
the service of the Princess Katherine.[1]

In the midst of these rejoicings Henry had an unpleasant reminder of the dangers he had passed
through. On June 9, 1498, Perkin Warbeck escaped
from court. He fled towards the coast, but, finding
the roads watched, took refuge in the monastery at
Sheen. The prior interceded with the king. Perkin's
life was spared, but the king, " that had an high
stomach and could not hate any that he despised,
bid take him forth and set the knave in the stocks."
After being thus publicly humiliated, and repeating
to the crowd the confession formerly made to the
mayor and corporation, he was taken to the Tower,
and there lodged in close confinement, " so that he
saw neither sun nor moon." [2] The rigour of his imprisonment had such an effect on his health that de
Puebla, who was present a few months later at an
interview between Henry and the Flemish ambassador, at which Perkin appeared, thought that his days
were numbered.

In July Henry received another Spanish envoy—
Londoño—with marked cordiality. " The king," we
are told, " made a remarkably fine speech in French,"
and Morton made a Latin oration. Henry offered
to serve Spain with his person and with his army.
" He said it with words which manifested great love

---

[1] Berg., *Spanish Cal.*, Nos. 229, 233.
[2] *Ibid.*, pp. 152, 156, 185–6 ; *City Chron.*, p. 223 ; Hall, 488–9.

and affection." [1]   De Puebla reported Henry's wish that the Princess Katherine should talk French to the Archduchess Margaret so that she might be able to speak the language fluently when she came to England, " as the English ladies could not speak Latin, much less Spanish." The princess was also advised to accustom herself to drink wine. " The water of England is not drinkable," wrote de Puebla, " and even if it were the climate would not allow the drinking of it."

On 10th July a supplementary treaty of alliance between England and Spain was signed. The articles dealing with commerce and the harbouring of rebels had been slightly altered, and Ferdinand and Isabella complained that de Puebla had shown himself very neglectful of their interests, and that he had exceeded the powers given to him ; they expressed their anger and astonishment, and ordered him to follow their instructions "without transgressing a single word for the future." He was to consult Ayala in all things, and regard him as joint ambassador at the court. [2]

But at this moment, in ominous contrast to the general atmosphere of success and self-congratulation, the darker thread that was never long absent from the tangled skein of Henry's life reappeared.

The name and claims of the young Earl of Warwick, who had been dragging out his miserable life in the Tower, sprang into sudden prominence through the appearance of another impostor. An Augustinian friar, one Patrick, persuaded Ralph Wilford, a boy of

---

[1] Berg., *Spanish Cal.*, i. pp. 154–6.

[2] The treaty, however, was confirmed by Ferdinand and Isabella on 20th January 1500. Rymer, xii. 741–7 ; Berg., *Spanish Cal.*, pp. 210–12.

mean birth who was a favourite pupil, to personate
the imprisoned earl, promising " that he would easily
make him King of England." Though this plot was
hatched in Kent, which had a reputation for supporting " phantastical fantasyes," it failed ignomini-
ously. The king's spies got wind of it. The friar's
miserable dupe was hanged on Shrove Tuesday (12th
February 1498–9), but Patrick, owing to the benefit
of clergy, escaped with perpetual imprisonment.[1]

The plot, a slight thing in itself, had weighty
results. The reappearance of the spectre of conspiracy had shaken Henry's growing confidence. His
Celtic blood inclined him to belief in prevalent super-
stitions. In March 1499 he consulted a priest who
was reputed to be a seer, and who had foretold the
deaths of Edward IV. and Richard III. Henry asked
him in what manner his end would come, and the
answer that his life would be in great danger all
through the year, and that the kingdom harboured
political plots, seems to have made a deep impression
on the king. Ayala reported that these two weeks
had aged him so that he looked twenty years older.
He was growing very devout, and had heard a sermon
every day during Lent.[2] Though the court was gay
with rejoicings over the birth of another prince,
though ambassadors from France had just brought
loving messages and presents from Louis XII., and
though the long dispute with Flanders had just been
settled by the treaty of May 1499,[3] the king himself
was ill at ease.

---

[1] *City Chron.*, p. 225. The boy's body was left hanging on the
gallows until the following Saturday night as a warning to the
people.

[2] Berg., *Spanish Cal.*, i., No. 239.   [3] See above, p. 168.

Another cause of alarm was the flight of Edmund
de la Pole, Earl of Suffolk, a nephew of Edward IV.,
who in spite of his brother's rebellion [1] had been restored by Henry to a portion of the family estates.
He had glittered in court tournaments, and won something of Henry's favour, but the king's generosity
failed to win allegiance. In the summer of 1499,
Suffolk, offended at being indicted for a manslaughter,
fled to Calais and thence to St. Omer. Henry feared
that he would put himself under the archduke's protection, and actually sent envoys to ask him to return.
He assented and returned to court. Henry's patience
seemed inexhaustible. [2]

But some little time elapsed before the danger that
seemed to be weighing on the king's spirits came to
a head. If Henry really believed, as he appears to
have done, that a great plot was being matured, he
may have regarded the Spanish marriage as a bulwark against the threatened danger. Arrangements
for it were pushed on, and a second proxy marriage
between Katherine and Arthur took place at Bewdley,
Prince Arthur's Herefordshire seat, on Whit Sunday,
19th May 1499. [3] The prince, " in a loud and clear
voice," expressed his joy in contracting this marriage " not only in obedience to the Pope and to
King Henry, but also from his deep and sincere love

---

[1] John, Earl of Lincoln, had been slain at Stoke 1487. His father,
John, Duke of Suffolk, died in 1491, and was succeeded by his son
Edmund, who in consequence of his comparative poverty was
restored to the rank of Earl, not Duke of Suffolk.

[2] *Rot. Parl.*, vi. 474–7, 546 ; *L. and P. Hen. VII.*, Intro. xxxix.,
i. 129–134, 392, 394–8, ii. 377 ; *City Chron.*, p. 201 ; Brown, *Ven. Cal.*,
Nos. 795–6. Gairdner and Busch have corrected Polydor Vergil's
errors. See Busch, p. 363, and the note by Dr. Gairdner, p. 441, as
to the order of these events.   [3] Berg., *Spanish Cal.*, pp. 209–10.

for the princess his wife," and thereupon his lord
chamberlain joined the hands of Prince Arthur and
de Puebla, who again stood proxy for Katherine.

Before the end of the year England was ringing
with the news of another desperate Yorkist plot.
The very name of the Earl of Warwick seemed to
have power to throw the black shadow of conspiracy
and dethronement across the king's path, and it was
this constant anxiety, working on a mind darkened
by superstitious terrors and the recent sinister revelations of underground conspiracy, which explains,
though it cannot justify, the judicial murder which
stains the king's reputation. The king's long patience
gave way at last, and the mere rumour of a plot
between Warbeck and Warwick sealed the fate of
both. No one, reading the brief account of the conspiracy that survives, can doubt that the earl was
condemned on trumped-up evidence. His dangerous
name outweighed his youth and innocence.

The evidence given at the Guildhall, probably by
one Robert Cleymound, who seems to have turned
informer,[1] was to the effect that the Earl of Warwick,
with Astwood, a former adherent of Warbeck's, and
Cleymound, while in the Tower, on the 2nd of August
" confederated and agreed that the earl should assume
the royal dignity and elect himself king, and falsely
and traitorously depose, deprive, and slay the king."
Subsidiary evidence was given to the effect that the
earl had plotted to seize the Tower and carry away
the jewels from the king's treasury, issue a public proclamation promising 12d. a day to any one who joined

---

[1] In spite of his share in the plot Cleymound was afterwards
pardoned. Busch, *op. cit.*, i. 120.

him, set fire to the gunpowder stored within the
Tower, and then escape beyond the seas in the confusion and bide his time to dethrone the king. A
certain Thomas Ward, clerk, was alleged to have
been won over to the plot by Robert Cleymound,
who showed him a wooden image as a token from
Warwick. Cleymound also declared that he had received a cloak and a velvet jacket from the earl.
It has been suggested that these objects, which seem
to be very clumsily dragged into the story, were
meant to be exhibited as tangible proofs of a guilt
that apparently rested only on the evidence of an
informer, but the jury found the proof sufficient, and
sent the earl for trial by his peers. The character
of some further evidence, which attempted to impli-
cate Warwick in a treasonable league with Perkin
Warbeck, throws still more doubt upon the earl's
guilt. It was alleged that Warwick had conspired
on August 2nd " to set him (Peter Warbeck) at large
and create and constitute him, the said Peter, to be
King and Governor of England." This obviously conflicts with the assertion that on the same August 2nd
Warwick concocted a plan to make himself king.
The informer did not prove that Warwick and Warbeck ever saw each other ; the story was that the
earl knocked upon the floor of his chamber in the
Tower and said to Warbeck, who was confined in the
cell below, " Perkin, be of good cheer and comfort."
Cleymound, who from his freedom of access to both
prisoners seems to have been a warder in the Tower,
promised to hand Perkin on the following day a
letter from an adherent, " one James, a clerk of
Flanders." According to the informer's story, the
earl, two days later, made a hole in the floor of his

chamber by which he could communicate with Perkin, but the only purpose for which he undertook the considerable feat of overcoming the massive masonry of the Tower—in the course of a single day, be it remembered—was " to comfort the said Perkin in his treason by saying to him, ' How goes it with you ? Be of good cheer.' " [1]

This lame story, with a few other adornments, the suggestion that Perkin had accused his fellow-conspirators to the king and council, and so on, bears on the face of it the secret motive of the whole business—to involve the last heir of the House of York and the impostor who had played the part of the White Rose in a common ruin.

On 21st November the Earl of Warwick, then aged twenty-one, was brought to trial before the Lord High Steward, the Earl of Oxford, who presided over a court formed of the Duke of Buckingham, the Earls of Northumberland, Kent, Surrey, and Essex, sixteen barons, and the Prior of St. John of Jerusalem. He pleaded guilty and was condemned to death as a traitor. Perkin Warbeck, John Walter *alias* Attwater, formerly Mayor of Cork, and his son, and James Taylor had been condemned to death previously, but the sentence was only carried out on Warbeck and Attwater. On the scaffold at Tyburn Perkin confessed his guilt, and after telling the story of his imposture to the assembled multitude, he " took his dethe meekly." His head was cut off after death and set upon London Bridge. The meteoric career of the White Rose was over. In Bacon's words, " It was one of the longest plays of the kind that hath been in memory, and might

[1] Baga de Secretis, *Thirty-seventh Report of Deputy Keeper.*

perhaps have had another end if he had not met
with a king both wise, stout, and fortunate."

The romantic career of the adventurer is full of
contrasts. Gay and self-confident, he had played his
rôle so long that he had almost come to believe in
it himself. His personal charm had won him love
and loyalty, he had fraternised with princes and
borne himself royally in pageant and banquet. But
his princely and gallant bearing deserted him in
danger. Twice at least, in a critical hour, he failed
those who trusted and followed him, and fled to
shameful safety. The lack of personal courage was
fatal. He had matched himself against a crowned
adventurer whose early career had been as difficult
and almost as romantic as his own, whose calculating
brain and iron nerve were never more at his service
than when rebellion and invasion threatened the
crown he had won on the battlefield.

On the following Thursday (28th November),[1] between two and three o'clock in the afternoon, Warwick was executed on Tower Hill. The king paid
the expenses of the funeral, and the earl's body was
taken by water to Bisham Abbey in Berkshire, and
buried there with his ancestors.[2] Thus did the
" winding ivy of a false Plantagenet kill the true
tree itself."

An attempt has been made to defend Warwick's
execution on the score of policy. It is alleged that

[1] The *City Chron.*, p. 228, gives the date incorrectly as 29th
November.

[2] Of the eight other conspirators indicted, four were condemned
to death, but only two were executed. For the plot see *City Chron.*,
pp. 226–8 ; Hall, 491 ; Pol. Verg., 609 ; Baga de Secretis, *Thirty-
seventh Report of Deputy Keeper*, 216–8 ; *Plumpton Corresp.*, 141–2 ;
Berg., *Spanish Cal.*, p. 213 ; *Excerpta Historica*, p. 123 ; Busch,
op. cit., 349–50.

Henry was induced to get rid of Warwick by the
urgent representations of the Spanish ambassador, who
dwelt on his master's reluctance to allow his daughter
to marry the heir to a throne constantly threatened by
the survival of a prince of another royal house.[1]
According to this view Warwick was sacrificed by
Henry as the price of the Spanish marriage.

But what is the evidence for this view ? There is
not a shred. There is no trace of or allusion to a
communication of the kind. The whole story seems
to have been evolved from the exulting words of de
Puebla " that not a doubtful drop of royal blood
remained in England," from Katherine's lamentation
many years later over the marriage that had begun
in blood, and from the coincidence in point of time
between the execution and the marriage. But these
are slender foundations on which to build a theory
inherently improbable. It does not even square with
the general view that Henry was an unscrupulous
politician who would commit any crime for gain, a
view that calls for proof that the marriage depended
in some way upon Warwick's removal. Of such a
connection there is no trace. The marriage had long
been decided upon by the Spanish court, the delay
came from Henry's side, and there is no evidence of
any pressure being put upon him. If policy dictated
the crime at all, a more plausible explanation would
be that Henry felt that his throne was insecure as
long as Warwick lived. He had tried generosity to
his captive foes and found it a failure. Extraordinary

[1] Hall, p. 491 ; Gairdner, *Henry VII.*, p. 174 ; *L. and P. Hen. VII.*,
i. 113.   See Busch criticising this theory, p. 354.   Bacon's hint
(p. 179), that Henry found in the alleged Spanish representations a
pretext for, rather than a motive of, the execution, is another
variation.

patience, considering the traditions of threatened dynasties, marked Henry's treatment of conspiracy. But even this is an insufficient explanation of the sudden cruelty that claimed a life spared in much more dangerous crises. The execution of Warwick was not an exhibition of inhuman calculation but of human weakness. Henry's temper was altering. " Age was fatal to the Tudor despots " ; his naturally calm and judicial spirit was being warped by constant threats, and by the suspicions of premature old age. It was no monster chuckling over the profit of premeditated murder, but a terror-stricken man driven to a sudden act of cruelty by anxiety and overstrain, who signed the warrant for Warwick's execution. Panic, not policy, drove the king on to crime.

The Anglo-Spanish negotiations of the year 1500 are more than usually wearisome. The arrival of Princess Katherine in England was expected. Prince Arthur had written in October 1499 expressing his anxiety to see his bride, and the king was spending enormous sums in preparing for her reception. But several things delayed her departure. Ferdinand made the sudden discovery, on comparing the earlier with the later marriage treaty, that the latter was less favourable to Spain instead of much more favourable, as de Puebla had often assured him it was. He declared that many of the conditions had been altered to suit Henry's views, and hoped that they might still be modified in spite of the number of times the treaty had been ratified on both sides.[1]

---

[1] The fact that the careful Ferdinand never made the discovery before seems almost incredible, but it rests on good authority. It may have been a manœuvre to keep de Puebla properly submissive by putting him in the wrong. Berg., *Spanish Cal.*, Nos. 236–7, 248, 250–2, 254, 266.

De Puebla, too, sent reports that made Ferdinand uneasy. Perhaps with a view of emphasising his heroic
achievements he reported that the feeling in England
was hostile to the Spanish match, and that he and
the Bishop of London had had infinite difficulty in
getting the council to agree to the treaty of alliance.
Members of the council objected to the omission of
the words " King of France " from the king's style
in letters from Ferdinand and Isabella, and vied
with one another in pointing out difficulties in the
treaty until Henry called them to order and told
them to stop disputing about words. The suspicious
Ferdinand took alarm, and his fears were increased
by the rumour that Henry was seriously considering
a match between the Prince of Wales and a French
princess. On Friday, 8th May, Henry and the queen
left England suddenly for Calais. No one knew of
their intention until a day or two before they started,
and there was much speculation in diplomatic circles
as to the motive of the visit. A French ambassador
came to Calais to pay his respects to the king and
bring an instalment of the tribute, and on Friday in
Whit week Henry had an interview with the Archduke Philip at a church in the fields. " The interview,
which was splendid and solemn, was very cordial. . . .
The archduke said that he loved Henry and regarded
him as his protector." [1] Henry, much flattered, made
a suitable reply. The king stayed a month in Calais
before returning. The meeting with the archduke
made Ferdinand suspect some manœuvre of Maximilian's with a view of substituting the Princess
Margaret of Austria for the Princess Katherine as a
bride for the Prince of Wales. Therefore, while he

[1] Berg., *Spanish Cal.*, No. 268.

concealed his suspicions in letters to de Puebla, Fuensalida was despatched on a special mission to England to see whether there was any truth in the rumour of another marriage, and instructed to keep a close watch on de Puebla, who was said to be entirely under Henry's influence.   De Puebla was brimming over with self-satisfaction at achieving " a masterpiece of diplomacy," when making the final arrangements for the marriage, and gave a variety of reasons for his delay — " the absence of the Prince of Wales, the Great Seal being kept at Westminster, the absence of the king and queen in Calais, the fact that the Latin secretary was suffering from ague, that the third son of the king had died, and that he himself was suffering great pain." [1]   Fuensalida's report was not reassuring. He certainly thought the match was in some danger, and repeated de Puebla's remark that, " judging by the national character, it was quite likely that the English had changed their minds." [2]

All this seems to have been a cobweb spun from the suspicious brains of the Spaniards.   Preparations for the marriage, then expected in August, were going on all over England, and Henry was spending large sums on jewels and so forth.   But Ferdinand could not get rid of his suspicions.   Various excuses were made to delay Katherine's departure, and Ferdinand announced that he wished the marriage ceremony, already twice performed, to be repeated as soon as the prince had completed his fourteenth year.[3]   Henry thought the third repetition of the

[1] Berg., *Spanish Cal.*, No. 268.   The allusion is to the death of Prince Edmund in the summer.   [2] *Ibid.*, pp. 235–8.

[3] Arthur's birthday was 22nd September, so this stipulation meant a delay until the following spring.

ceremony unnecessary, but gave way to de Puebla's representations, and the marriage took place at Ludlow Castle, the Prince of Wales's seat, on 22nd November, the Bishop of Worcester officiating. De Puebla, as proxy of the princess, was placed at table above the Prince of Wales on his right hand. More respect was paid to him than he had ever before received in his life—he told his master. Disputes about the size of Katherine's Spanish household followed. The list had been drawn up on a generous scale, as it was anticipated that Henry would pay the salaries,[1] but the council were violently opposed to her bringing so many Spanish gentlemen and menservants with her, and specially " abhorred " the idea of the Majordomo or Lord Steward. Henry declared that the number was unnecessarily large. " The princess," he wrote, " will be better and more respectfully attended by English ladies and gentlemen than ever princess has been served before." De Puebla reported that the king and queen wished very much that the ladies who were to accompany the Princess of Wales should be " of gentle birth and beautiful, or at least that none of them should be ugly." The Spanish ambassador was still oppressed by the " nightmare " of trying to induce Henry to accept 35,000 crowns worth of the plate and jewels the princess was bringing with her as the first instal-

[1] The household was to include four ladies-in-waiting and their servants, six maids of honour, and two slaves to attend them, a majordomo, a master of the ceremonies, a cupbearer, a " master of the hall," a secretary, a confessor, an almoner, two chaplains, six pages, a chief butler, marshal, and warden of the chapel, three gentlemen-in-waiting, four equerries, two squires, a laundress, housemaids and fourteen other servants. Doña Elvira Manuel (who later played an important part in Katherine's story) was at the head of the household. Berg., *Spanish Cal.*, No. 288.

ment of the marriage portion, an interpretation of
the treaty which Henry was not disposed to accept.
There is a very interesting letter from Isabella to
Henry, written on 23rd March 1500-1, expressing her
gratification at hearing of the splendid preparations
that were being made for her daughter's reception.
Though she delighted in them as signs of the magnificent grandeur of her brother Henry,[1] she ardently
implored him that her daughter should not be the
cause of expense but of happiness to England, and
that the substantial part of the festival should be
Henry's love for his true daughter.[2]

Henry's suggestion that the princess should land
at Gravesend was not favoured by Isabella, who preferred Southampton or Bristol, as safer harbours.
In spite of the 100,000 nobles spent in vain preparations the year before, still greater efforts were being
made. Tournaments and meetings of the Knights
of the Round Table were arranged, and distinguished
foreigners were invited over to witness the celebrations.[3] The young Duke of York went to Southampton to superintend preparations for her reception.
At last, on 21st May, after further delay caused by
another rising of the Moors and a low fever from
which she was only just recovering, Katherine left
Granada. Owing to the heat, she travelled by
very slow stages, and did not reach Corunna until
the middle of July. On August 25 she embarked,
but was driven back by storms and hurricanes. She
disembarked at Laredo, waiting for more favourable

---

[1] Henry had been pressing for the use of this style.

[2] Berg., *Spanish Cal.*, i. No. 293.

[3] *L. and P. Hen. VII.*, i. 404-17, ii. 103-5; *Hardwicke Papers*,
i. 1-20.

weather. On Monday, 27th September, the fleet
again sailed. Henry, hearing of her unfortunate experience, had sent one of his ablest captains to look
out for the princess and convoy her to England.
The princess, however, was still pursued by ill-luck,
and on the voyage met with furious winds and
thunderstorms. On Saturday, 2nd October, at three
o'clock in the afternoon, she reached Plymouth harbour. The nobility and gentry of the neighbourhood
had flocked into the town. One of her attendants
wrote to Isabella that " She could not have been
received with greater rejoicings if she had been the
Saviour of the world." [1]

A month went by before Henry set out to meet
her, though he wrote her a letter of welcome,[2] and
sent a number of English ladies, headed by the
Duchess of Norfolk, to form her suite. He met
Katherine at Dogmersfield on 6th November, and
there they were joined by the Prince of Wales.
Ferdinand's instructions that the princess was not to
meet her husband or father-in-law before the wedding
day had been overruled by Henry, who announced
that he became Katherine's guardian as soon as she
set foot on English soil. There was music by Katherine's minstrels, and the prince and princess danced
together. Henry wrote to Ferdinand later telling
him how much he admired Katherine's beauty as
well as her agreeable and dignified manners.

It had been arranged that Katherine should make
her public entry into London alone, the king and
royal family viewing the procession from a platform
in Cheapside, and on November 12th, at about two

[1] Berg., *Spanish Cal.*, i., No. 305.
[2] *L. and P. Hen. VII.*, i. 126–8.

o'clock in the afternoon, Katherine rode from Lambeth over London Bridge into the city, followed by a great train of nobles and gentlemen. It was a scene of extraordinary gaiety and splendour. The procession passed through crowds of rejoicing citizens. The streets were lavishly decorated; pageant followed pageant at different points of the city. At London Bridge she was met by a pageant which included St. Katherine and St. Ursula, both of whom recited very long poems, which, however, were a mere prelude to the eloquence which "Polycy," "Noblesse," "Vertue," "the Archangel Raphael," and others lavished on her at later stages of the route. The final pageant represented the heavens with seven golden candlesticks, and "a man goodliche apparailed representyng the ffader of heven." "Goodly ballades, swete armony, musicall instrumentes sounded with heavenly noyes on euery side of the strete." Katherine was lodged in the bishop's palace near St. Paul's, where she was visited by the king and queen and the Countess of Richmond soon after her arrival. On the following Sunday (14th November), Arthur and Katherine were married in St. Paul's Cathedral by the Archbishop of Canterbury and fifteen other prelates. The stately ceremony took place on a raised platform, the bride and bridegroom being dressed in white satin. Standing before the high altar, the Prince of Wales endowed his bride with one-third of the revenues of Wales, Cornwall, and Chester. The banquet that followed was a scene of great splendour, and an opportunity for the display of the king's magnificent plate.[1]

---

[1] For Katherine's reception and marriage, see *City Chron.*, pp. 234–50; Leland, *Collectanea*, v. 352–73; Hall, 493–4. Hall gives certain details as to the wedding night, which are not apparently

The ten days that followed were given up to rejoicings—pageants, banqueting, and " disguisings,"
jousting in the open space in front of Westminster
Hall, and dancing within the Hall.   Katherine danced
in Spanish dress, and the young Prince Henry, we
are told, " perceiving himself to be accombred with
his Clothes, sodainly cast off his Goune and daunced
in his Jackett," greatly to the delight of the king
and queen.   The nobles vied with one another in
" pleasant devices " to vary the monotony of the
disguisings, and a " Lanthorne " in which there were
more than a hundred great lights and twelve goodly
ladies, roused the Herald to even more than his
usual enthusiasm.[1] The chef-d'œuvre apparently was
the device of two mountains, " subtelly convayed and
drawne upon Wheeles," linked by a golden chain,
which represented England and Spain, one green and
planted full of trees, and realistically complete with
"rocks, marveylous Beastes and a goodly young
Ladye in her Haire pleasantly besene," the other like
a rock scorched and burnt with the sun, out of whose
sides " grewe and eboyled " various metals and
precious stones.   The knights and ladies who in-
habited the mountains made music so sweetly that
the Herald is moved to remark that in his mind " it
was the first such pleasant Myrth and Property that
ever was heard in England of long season."   Sunday
afternoon was spent in the gardens at Richmond
playing chess, dice, cards, and bowls, shooting at

derived from contemporary sources, but seemed to have been
inserted later when Henry's attempt to obtain a divorce made
the question of the consummation of Katherine's marriage with
Arthur of great importance.

[1] Leland, *Collectanea*, v., *loc. cit.*

the butts, and watching a Spanish juggler do many "wondrous and delicious Points of Tumbling, Dauncing, and other Sleights."

Henry wrote a very sympathetic letter to Katherine's father and mother. He begged them to dismiss sadness from their minds. Though they could not now see the gentle face of their beloved daughter, they might be sure that she had found a second father, who would ever watch over her happiness, and never permit her to want anything that he could procure for her. Arthur himself wrote that he had never felt so much joy in his life as when he beheld the sweet face of his bride. He and Katherine retired to Ludlow Castle soon after the wedding.

These rejoicings symbolised the triumph of one of Henry's dearest ambitions. The new Tudor dynasty was now united in marriage with one of the proudest royal houses in Europe. At the same moment he was arranging an alliance which was to prove far more important in the future. An embassy from Scotland arrived in London on 20th November with powers to settle the terms of the long proposed Scotch marriage. Since the treaty of December 1497, negotiations for the marriage had been dragging on, their uneventful course being occasionally broken by unpleasant incidents on the Border. Henry's strong desire for peace is visible all through.

Margaret, the bride-elect, was a delicate, backward child about eleven years old; the proposed bridegroom was a man of twenty-eight, notorious for his adventures with women, who at the time of the negotiations had a liaison with the beautiful Lady Margaret Drummond.[1] But scruples as to

---

[1] See Berg., *Spanish Cal.*, pp. 169, 170, 176.

suitability were unfashionable, and the mysterious death of Lady Margaret removed one awkward difficulty.[1] The negotiations ended in a treaty drawn up on 24th January 1501-2. It was agreed that a proxy marriage should take place at once, and that the young bride should be handed over to her husband not later than September 1, 1503. Important clauses arranged for free commercial intercourse and for the peace and security of the Border. Thus a close offensive and defensive alliance was inaugurated. The suggestion of some doubter that the alliance might lead to the subjection of England was met by Henry's confident answer that " the greater would draw the less." [2]

As usual, Henry's hour of success was embittered by a secret source of anxiety. The Earl of Suffolk had lent himself to another desperate plot, and had fled from England for the second time in July or August 1501. After negotiations conducted through Sir Robert Curzon, formerly governor of Hammes,[3] he put himself and his claims under the protection of the King of the Romans. About the time when

[1] Henry had spoken of the objections felt by him and the queen on account of their daughter's youth, but probably only with the view of making the Scotch keener on the match. Henry also hinted at a possible marriage between Margaret and the heir to the throne of Denmark, again with the same object in view.

[2] Rymer, xii. 787–803; *City Chron.*, pp. 253–5; Hall, 494; Pol. Verg., 610; Busch, p. 356, criticising Gairdner, *Henry VII.*, p. 187. The proxy marriage took place at Richmond on the day after the signing of the treaty, the Earl of Bothwell, lately Henry's jackal, acting as proxy for James IV. Leland, *Collect.*, iv. 258–64; *Excerpta Historica*, 127.

[3] Curzon's attitude has been much debated, but the view that he was all the time acting, in Henry's interests, as a spy upon Suffolk seems the most probable. For a full discussion of the point by Dr. Gairdner and Dr. Busch, see Busch, *op., cit.* pp. 364–5, 441–5.

Katherine landed in England there was a meeting
at Imst in the Tyrol between Maximilian and the
English refugees. Maximilian hailed this new opportunity of getting hold of another of Henry's rebels,
but as usual he was lavish of nothing except promises. He welcomed Suffolk as his " very dear and
well-beloved cousin," and suggested that he should
take up his abode at Aix-la-Chapelle, where he remained for years waiting upon fortune. Policy as
well as poverty bridled Maximilian's hostility, and
the treaty of May 1499 was very valuable to Henry
at this crisis. A suggestion that the King of England
might advance 15,000 crowns to Maximilian for his
Turkish war was dangled as a tempting bait before
his eyes, and Philip was using all his influence to improve the relations between the two princes. It was a
struggle of policy against the antagonism of mutually
repellent personalities, and in the end Maximilian put
off Suffolk with promises and began to consider the
terms of the treaty offered by Henry.

Somerset and Warham were despatched as the
English plenipotentiaries, with instructions, dated 28th
September 1501, to demand the immediate surrender
of Suffolk and the other rebels, and, if this were
agreed upon, to offer 50,000 crowns as a present, not
a loan. The instructions are an illustration of Henry's
diplomatic skill, and of his care for the honour of
England. The money was not to be given on any
terms which could suggest that he offered it as the
price of peace, which he and his progenitors, Kings of
England, had never done, " for it coude not so stand
with their honour." Over these terms the English
and Burgundian envoys haggled for months at
Antwerp. Maximilian tried hard to get " oon of the

myghtyest prynces of alle the Crystyn faithe" to
promise a larger sum; he suggested a marriage between Prince Henry and his granddaughter Eleanor,
but was either too chivalrous, or too deeply committed to Suffolk, to surrender him.

Meanwhile in England Henry had taken prompt
measures. On November 7th, Suffolk was proclaimed
a traitor at St. Paul's. His property was confiscated,
and his relatives and adherents were arrested. His
brother, Lord William de la Pole, and his cousin, Lord
William Courtenay, were imprisoned in the Tower, and
later sent across to Calais, where they remained till
the end of the reign. One brother, Sir Richard de
la Pole, however, "so craftely conveyed and so
wisely ordered hym selfe in this stormy tempest that
he was not attrapped eyther with net or snare."
Other conspirators, however, were less fortunate.[1]
Sir John Wyndham, and Sir James Tyrell—the
murderer of the Yorkist princes—and many others
were arrested and executed in the following May.

The subsidy Maximilian angled for was to be used
against the Turks, whose rapid advance westwards
was a very real danger. By 1500 they had overrun
Greece, and their fleets scoured the Mediterranean.
If the Christian faith was not to lose more ground
their advance must be checked. The cry of "the
Cross against the Crescent" should have roused the
sympathies of Europe. But neither the pressing
danger, nor the glamour of a new Crusade, availed
to unite the princes of Europe. It was a materialistic

[1] Bacon's story that Henry obtained the surrender of Guisnes
Castle, of which Tyrell was in command, by an act of the blackest
treachery, rests only on the authority of a letter written by Suffolk,
who naturally took the most unfavourable view of Henry's actions.
See *L. and P. Hen. VII.*, i. 181.

age, uninfluenced by great ideals. The theory of the
unity of Christendom had given way to the stern
fact of bitter rivalry between the princes. The Pope
and Emperor remained as symbols of the vanished
unity, but the then holders of both offices were not
the men to arouse the loyalty or obtain the submission of Europe. Maximilian's authority was
set at nought by even the princes of the Empire,
Alexander VI. was a corrupt sybarite to whose cove-
tous fingers the gold of Christendom would have clung.
Alexander, however, as the obvious champion of
Christendom, issued his appeal to the princes of Europe.

It met with little response. Louis of France was
absorbed in ambitious schemes. He had met with some
success in Italy, and by the end of 1499 was master of
Milan and Naples. A friendly understanding as to the
partition of the latter duchy united him and Ferdinand for the moment, and made them deaf to the
Pope's appeal. Henry's attitude is interesting, and
more sympathetic than might have been expected.
The Venetian envoy reported his " excellent disposition towards the Christian expedition," and he was
urged to attack the " rabid and potent enemy of
Christendom " in the following spring. He answered
the Pope's appeal in a masterly letter. The terms of
politeness reveal, as they were meant to do, Henry's
real distrust. He expressed his admiration for the
Pope's published intention of leading the war against
the infidel in person, and regretted that the distance
of England from the scene of combat—a seven months'
journey from Venice—prevented him from giving any
help.[1]

But this evasive answer did not mean that Henry
was indifferent to the peril of Europe. On the con-

---

[1] Ellis, *Letters*, I. (1), 50–59.

trary, it appears that he was one of the few princes of Europe who had any serious intentions with regard to the Crusade. Though he had persuaded Alexander that the tax of one-tenth imposed by him upon the clergy was " contrary to the liberties of the kingdom " and therefore could not be collected, he himself obtained the grant of a similar sum from Convocation, £4000 of which he presented to the Pope.[1] None of the other princes of Europe did as much as this, though some of them collected Crusade taxes, which they converted to their own uses. Henry's action is the usual blend of generosity and carefulness. Though unwilling to place his English gold in corrupt hands, he was quite prepared to give handsome subsidies to more dependable champions of Christendom. Contemporaries quite appreciated the sincerity of his attitude. Cardinal Hadrian records that Henry not only promised pecuniary support, but also that he would himself go in person to the war against the Turks in defence of the Christian faith. Empty boasting was alien to Henry's character. We are bound to believe, as contemporaries did, that the offer was genuine, as well as the offer made some years later when Julius II. sat in Alexander's place.[2]

In the spring of 1502 there happened " a lamentable chaunce to the kynge, queene and all the people." On the 2nd of April the Prince of Wales died at Ludlow Castle. A life full of promise ended prematurely, to the deep grief of the king and queen. After lying in state at Ludlow the prince's body was

---

[1] *Memorials*, p. 413; Wilkins, *Concilia*, iii. 646. The Pope supplemented Henry's gift by issuing bulls for the sale of indulgences in England in 1501. *L. and P. Hen. VII.*, i. 93–100.

[2] See below, pp. 361–2.

taken in a mournful and stately procession, illumined
by the glare of torches, to Worcester. There in the
cathedral the prince was buried with great pomp.
The bier was draped with a " rich Cloth of Majestie,"
and surrounded by tapers and by banners bearing the
arms of England, of Spain, Wales, Cornwall, Chester,
Normandy and Guienne, and Poitou, and the arms of
Cadwallader, the British ancestor of his house.   " Then
the Corpe with Weeping and sore Lamentation was
laid in the Grave. . . . He had a hard heart that
wept not," wrote the chronicler. . . . " Then God
have Mercye on good Prince Arthur's Soule." [1]

The death of the Prince of Wales was a public
calamity as well as a private grief.   One boy's life
alone stood between the nation and a renewal of civil
strife, and all the hopes of the Tudor dynasty centred
in him.   Suffolk's exulting letters bring out the danger
of the position.   King Henry, he wrote, could not live
much longer, and if Prince Henry died he would at once
succeed.   Prince Henry, however, was a gallant, high-
spirited boy, whose brilliant health seemed to mock
at Suffolk's hopes.[2]   Round him the king, with his
tireless patience, began to re-weave the subtle web of
his diplomacy.   The Spanish alliance, the fruit of
tedious years, had lost its chief security by Arthur's
death, but Ferdinand was even more anxious than
Henry for the alliance to be maintained.   In the
earlier negotiations, Ferdinand had appeared to yield
reluctantly to Henry's importunity; he was now prepared to make overtures for the marriage.   On the
10th of May 1502, as soon as he heard the news of

---

[1] Leland, *Collectanea*, v. 373–81 ; Pol. Verg., 612 ; Hall, 497 ;
City Chron., p. 255.

[2] A month after Prince Arthur's death he was created Prince of
Wales. Hall, 497.

Arthur's death, he despatched the Duke of Estrada
with powers to conclude a marriage between Katherine and Prince Henry. He was ordered to keep
these powers secret until he had asked that the
princess should be sent back to Spain with her dowry
as soon as possible, taking great pains to impress
Henry with the sincerity of their anxiety for their
daughter's return.

With the beginning of these negotiations we are
plunged anew into the familiar atmosphere of suspicion
and chicanery. Ferdinand soon began to suspect that
Henry might try to avoid the responsibility of providing for Katherine. A letter of 29th May breathes alarm,
in spite of his attempts to reassure himself and his envoy
by declaring that "it was impossible to suppose that
such a prince as the King of England could break his
word at any time." His suspicions gathered strength
as time went on, and in addition he had heard rumours
that a marriage between Prince Henry and a French
princess was contemplated. In July he wrote very
urgently to Estrada, ordering him to have a marriage
contract drawn up with all possible speed, but " not
to show so much eagerness that it may cause the
English to cool." Even the old idea of an English
war for the recovery of Guienne and Normandy was
dragged out again, and Spanish help was to be offered
to Henry for this preposterous adventure. Many
very anxious letters written by Isabella to Estrada
in July and August remain. He was to disguise his
sovereign's eagerness for the match by pressing for
Katherine's instant return. " They could not endure
that their beloved daughter should be so far from
them when she was in affliction." A rumour had
already reached Isabella that Henry contemplated
retaining the marriage portion, and she wrote at once

to express her disbelief in the report.   She could not
believe that Henry, " being as he is so virtuous a
Prince, so truthful, and such a friend to justice and
to reason, and of so honourable a character," would
break his promises.   This testimonial seems, from
the context, not to be a mere flattering remark
destined for transmission, through Estrada, to Henry,
but an expression of Isabella's genuine opinion.   Subsequent negotiations undeceived her as to Henry's
purpose.   Perhaps she was trying to reassure herself
by repeated expressions of her belief in Henry's
integrity, for she certainly felt very anxious on the
question of the marriage portion.

To these advances Henry made little response.   He
held the key of the position.   Katherine was in
England and dependent on him, and 100,000 crowns
of her marriage portion had already been paid to
him.   His position in Europe was so much stronger
that the Spanish alliance became a less glittering lure.
On 19th June 1502 the prolonged negotiations with
Maximilian ended in a commercial treaty at Antwerp,
and on the following day another treaty was drawn
up.   By this Maximilian undertook not to give help
or protection to English rebels and to dismiss them
from his territory.   In return Henry promised to
give Maximilian £10,000, to be used in the war against
the Turks.   The money was paid over on 1st October,
and the treaty was proclaimed in London three weeks
later.[1]   Henry's willingness to pay £10,000 in an
attempt to bind the faithless Maximilian to withdraw his support of Suffolk, proves how much he

---

[1] *L. and P. Hen. VII.*, 152–177 ; *Excerpta Historica*, 129 ; Rymer,
xiii. 3–10, 12–27.   Suffolk and his confederates were again proclaimed as traitors from St. Paul's Cross, and the terrors of a Papal
bull anathematising rebels was added.

feared the refugee's plans. He paid a high price for his fears. The treaty, unsatisfactory in its terms, was interpreted by Maximilian in a spirit which made it almost useless to Henry. He allowed Suffolk to remain at Aix, on the plea that it was a free town of the empire, and that he had no authority to turn him out. The only change was that he no longer supplied the refugee with funds. He remained at Aix, running deeper into debt, surrounded by Henry's spies, and rendered desperate by the confiscation of his estates and the execution of his friends. It appears from a hint contained in a letter of Isabella's that she and Ferdinand, though ostensibly trying to use their influence with Maximilian in Henry's interests, were working for his surrender to Spain, not to Henry. The refugee wrote a series of letters to Maximilian imploring him for help, and announcing that he and King Henry could never be together in England without one of them perishing.

The end of the year (1502) found Henry still postponing a definite agreement with Spain about the marriage, and negotiating with Louis of France, to whom he declared that he would be willing to pay ten or twelve thousand crowns for Suffolk's surrender. In December he despatched Sir Thomas Brandon and Nicholas West to take the Order of the Garter to Maximilian and obtain his oath to the treaty. After a month's delay at Cologne they met Maximilian at Antwerp, and succeeded in getting him to bind himself in a very solemn way. He took the oath in the church of St. Michael, kneeling before the altar with the English envoys, and, with his hand on the Gospels, uttered the word " Juramus " at the moment of the elevation of the Host. As far as forms went the elusive prince was firmly bound. It was not the fault of the envoys that he took his obligations so lightly. The accounts the ambassadors furnished to Henry are rather amusing.[1] While the town was blazing with bonfires, and the windows displaying " brennyng cressentes," Maximilian began to show his usual dexterity in evasion, giving various specious reasons for refusing to be invested with the Garter, and for delaying the proclamation of Suffolk and his adherents through the towns of the empire. The remonstrances of Henry's envoys were treated lightly. Maximilian and his council consulted with " grete laughter." The envoys resented their treatment, but were too stupid and too honest to be a match for Maximilian, who obtained a further delay by despatching an embassy to Henry to settle the disputed points. The embassy arrived in England at the end of March 1503. Then followed a repetition of the proceedings in Antwerp. Henry solemnly swore to the treaty in St. Paul's Cathedral, the city rejoiced with bonfires, and Maximilian's proxy was received into the Order of the Garter at Windsor. But the question of Suffolk was not yet settled.[2]

The year 1503 saw two events of the first importance in the English royal family, the death of the queen and the marriage of the Princess Margaret. On 11th February, her thirty-seventh birthday, Queen Elizabeth died in the Tower, ten days after giving birth to a princess. It is strange that the queen's last confinement should have taken place in the Tower, a place with such dark memories for the people of her house.[3] There is a touching account of

[1] L. and P. Hen., VII., ii. pp. 189–220.
[2] See below, p. 326.
[3] According to the City Chronicle (p. 258) it was a premature confinement — the queen " entended to have been delyvered at Richemount."

the king's grief, and the dead queen was sincerely
mourned by the whole nation. Her body lay in
state in the Tower chapel, near the then unknown
grave of her murdered brothers, and was afterwards
taken in procession through the streets to Westminster, an effigy of the queen in crown and robes of
state being placed above the coffin. The pall bore
the queen's arms and her appropriate motto, "Humble
and reverent." The burial took place in the Abbey.
There, in the centre of the gorgeous chapel of
Henry VII., beneath Torregiano's beautiful monument, rests Elizabeth, the daughter, sister, wife, and
mother of kings.

Margaret's marriage to James IV. took place on
August 8th. The summer had been spent in preparations, and the king seems to have made up his mind
that the first bride of the Tudor house should have
a suitably magnificent outfit. Many embroiderers
were hard at work for the Queen of Scots, perhaps
adorning her garments with the red roses of Lancaster,
which appeared in every possible place, from cushions
to the trappings of palfreys. In June the king was
buying jewels and plate to the value of £16,000 for
the bride. On June 27 Margaret left Richmond on
her way to Scotland. Henry went with her as far as
Collyweston in Northampton—one of his mother's
residences—and from there she went on alone attended
by a gorgeous retinue of nobles. The Herald gives
a detailed account of the whole journey, which includes vivid descriptions of Margaret's meeting with
James, of his graceful manners and accomplishments,
of the wedding in St. Giles' Cathedral, and of the
rejoicings that followed. It appears, however, from
Margaret's later letters, that she was far from
happy in Scotland. She pined for England and

ELIZABETH OF YORK
From the full-length effigy on her tomb in Westminster Abbey

the English court, and the family from which she was exiled. Her pathetic letters to Henry show her as one of the many royal victims of politic marriages.[1]

Death had been busy in the king's household as well as in his family, and the figures conspicuous in the early years are henceforth absent. The death of Morton in 1500 had removed one of Henry's wisest ministers. He had spent his youth in the dangerous atmosphere of the civil wars, and learnt pliability and dexterity therein. When exiled to Flanders he became the brains of Richmond's enterprise, and Henry never forgot the debt. Morton became in 1485 a member of the Council, in 1486 Archbishop of Canterbury, in 1487 Lord Chancellor, and in 1493 a Cardinal. He opened Parliament with his elaborate Latin orations, delivered answers to ambassadors, and so on. Bacon's account of Morton as a man " in his nature harsh and haughty, much accepted by the king but envied by the nobility and hated of the people," is probably less reliable than that of Sir Thomas More, who spent his youth in Morton's household and knew him intimately. " In his face did shine such an amiable reverence as was pleasant to behold, gentle in communication, yet earnest and sage. He had great delight many times with rough speech to his suitors to prove, but without harm, what prompt wit and what bold spirit were in every man. In his speech he was fine, eloquent, and pithy. . . In the law he had profound knowledge, in wit he was incomparable, and in memory wonderful excellent." [2] He was a statesman of a good type, who played his conspicuous part

---

[1] See, for instance, Ellis, *Letters*, I. (1) 41–3.
[2] More, *Utopia* (ed. Lumby), p. 27.

with ability and dignity.[1] Tradition makes him the inventor of " Morton's Fork," but though he became unpopular as the supposed author of Henry's extortions,[2] what evidence there is goes to prove that he tried to restrain the king.   Certainly things became much worse after his death.

Sir Reginald Bray, who died in 1503, had also spent his life in Henry's service, and enjoyed an unusual measure of his confidence.   Bacon states that Bray was " noted to have had with the king the greatest freedom of any counsellor," though he suggests that he used this freedom to flatter the king, but Hall writes—" he was so bold that if any thinge had bene done against good law or equitie, he would, after an humble fassion, plainly reprehende the king. . . . He was a very father of his country, a sage and a grave person, and a fervent lover of justice." [3]   Like Morton he incurred considerable unpopularity in connection with the heavy taxation.

The extent of the influence of men like Morton and Bray over Henry must remain a secret, but the scanty evidence that remains affords no proof that they pursued any original policy, except Morton perhaps with regard to ecclesiastical affairs,[4] but the loss of men who had shared his exile and won his hardly given confidence must have added to the lone-

[1] He had a magnificent taste in building, and relics of his work may be seen at Wisbech and in St. Mary's Church at Oxford. When Bishop of Ely he drained the fens round Peterborough, and " Morton's Dyke " still runs seaward through the marshes.

[2] See *City Chron.*, p. 232.

[3] Hall, *Chron.*, 497. Like Morton he was a lover of splendid buildings. The design for the rebuilding of St. George's Chapel, Windsor, and that of the chape of Henry VII. at Westminster, are supposed to have been his, and he laid the first stone of the latter on 24th January 1502–3.

[4] See below, p. 309.

liness of a king surrounded by men whom he could
command but could not trust. A fine influence was
removed from the king's court, and men of a baser
stamp, who had proved themselves willing and unscrupulous, became Henry's servants if not his advisers. To ascribe to the death of Bray and Morton,
however, the deterioration in the character of Henry's
policy in his later years that has often been noticed,
is to allow too much weight to their influence. No
adviser ever had power to mould Henry's policy, and
the change in its nature was due to the inevitable
hardening of an ungentle character with advancing
years. Carefulness degenerated into avarice, paternal
despotism into tyranny, caution into cunning.

But already by 1503 Henry had completed most
of his enduring work, the alliance with Spain and
Scotland, the re-establishment of England among the
powers of Europe, and—by far the most important—
the establishment of the Tudor despotism in England.
On the financial and legislative work which gave
Henry the right to be considered the founder of that
despotism, little has yet been said.

CHAPTER VII

LEGISLATION AND FINANCE : THE FOUNDATION OF THE TUDOR DESPOTISM

IN contrast with his diplomatic activity, painfully intricate and only partially successful, Henry's work in England has the attraction that comes from boldness and success. He found in England a sphere in which all his first-rate abilities were exercised, in which all the strength of his strong, unlovely personality was exerted. His struggle with the forces of disorder and reaction, his unvindictive triumph, the patient accumulation of power and wealth that raised the Crown far above all forces in the State, and made it the mainspring of history in the following century, can claim the interest that comes from an achievement of first-rate importance. The dynasty he founded bore the stamp of his personality. He settled its character, chose its armour and weapons, and his spirit animated it to the end. He can claim to have introduced a new idea into English politics —that apparent contradiction in terms, a popular despotism.

Where did Henry go for his political ideal ? Considerable stress has been laid by at least one modern writer on the supposedly foreign origin of Henry's constitutional policy,[1] but beyond Ayala's words,

---

[1] " It must have been in France that Henry formed those theories of personal government that he tried to introduce into the English constitution." Busch, *op. cit.*, p. 294.

" He would like to govern England in the French fashion but he cannot do it," there is no evidence to support this. In some comparatively unimportant details, French and foreign influences appeared. His exile abroad had certainly familiarised him with the continental theories of kingship, but his own native talent taught him what pitfalls to avoid. The idea which gives the Tudor despotism its peculiar character and secured its permanence, that of despotic power based on popular approval and maintained by an alliance of the Crown and the middle classes against the nobles, was certainly alien to the spirit of French despotism. It was Henry's own contribution to political theory; it was evolved from a study of contemporary conditions and strengthened by the Tudor instinct for popularity. The path of popular despotism upon which Henry and his successors trod had a different direction to that which led from the Louvre through Versailles to the Bastille.

The rule of Edward IV. furnished Henry with a recent example of English despotism, but surface similarities do not conceal the fundamental contrast between his work and that of his predecessors. A new spirit transformed the old methods. Henry's power was based on an alliance with the people, Edward's led to a reign of terror, when even the first excuse of absolutism, strong government, failed. He even failed to secure his own dynasty, and with the disappearance of Edward V. and his brother the era of violence and hopeless anarchy seemed to have returned. Things were different from the beginning with Henry VII., and he won his way to the only possible solution for the difficulties of the time, when with care and patience he set up a popular despotism.

The disorderly weakness of England at his accession cried out for strong rule. Parliamentary government had been a lamentable failure, and the people, who had proved themselves unripe for power, were ready to sacrifice the theory of freedom for the fact of peace.   The failure of this premature attempt had been followed by a riot of aristocratic faction. The memory of Lancastrian anarchy fought for the Tudors; occasional arbitrary conduct seemed a smaller evil than lack of governance. Tyranny was as discredited as Parliamentary government. The exhausted country had submitted to the rule of Edward IV. and Richard III., but their bloodstained sceptres failed to maintain order, and a reaction had brought about the triumph of Henry VII. He it was who succeeded in finding a new basis for despotism, and built up a new type of monarchy which suited both the genius of his people and the temper of his house.

In the Tudor despot the demagogue was but thinly veiled. The vast power the king wielded was drawn from the people's will, and with a flash of insight Henry VII. realised the promise of this new alliance. " It was the definite aim of the Tudors to pose as social reformers," we have been told,[1] and though the first Tudor is not haloed with the modern aureole of social service, he was none the less the saviour of society in England.

Even from the beginning the drift towards despotism is visible. Long before he had made his throne secure, long before popular sentiment had gathered round the new monarchy, we find him taking the first steps in this direction.   Before

[1] *Social England* (ed. Traill), ii. p. 626 ; Pollard, *Factors in Modern History*, p. 71.

Parliament met or his title was confirmed he was
exercising all the rights of an absolute king. The
first and obvious duty of restoring order was taken
in hand at once, with a judicious mixture of firmness
and lenience.   No wholesale convictions of defeated
foes revolted popular sentiment.   Violence and
robbery were put down with a strong hand. Confidence in the stability of the government and in its
power to protect the individual revived, and popular
opinion—that great security for peace—began to
range itself on the side of a dynasty that had a
hereditary title as well as the force of arms behind it.
As the knowledge that the king was about to marry
Elizabeth of York spread through England, men
began to hope for a peaceful compromise of a question
that had devastated England for two generations.
The Yorkist disturbances of the early years of the
reign hide from view the extent of popular acquiescence, and before the princes of Europe realised that
the Tudor dynasty was firmly established, some sentiment of loyalty was already attached to it in
England.

Henry attached to his sceptre national feeling
as well as national interests.   It has often been
pointed out that the growth of international rivalry
in Europe is a feature of the age in which Henry VII.
lived.   In England, owing to its island position and
the long wars with France, a feeling of national unity
had appeared early.   The peculiar character of
English feudalism and of English municipalities made
decentralising forces less strong than abroad, and it
was easier for national to replace local ambition.
These facts gain a new significance in connection
with the foundation of the Tudor despotism, and
were responsible for much of its success.   National

self-consciousness was growing restive. "An appeal
to Magna Carta would have left a Tudor audience
untouched," but it could be roused to enthusiasm
by a hint of national pride or an allusion to the
splendid heritage which Englishmen were beginning
to realise. It was this growing pride in nationality
that the Tudor sovereigns fostered, represented,
and profited by. Like the rest of his dynasty,
Henry was perfectly in touch with contemporary
feeling. The floating atoms of thought and opinion
held in suspense among the mass of the people were
crystallised in the action of its sovereign. In the
king the aims of the people found expression, in his
policy they took effect, and this intimacy with
national sentiment became the mark of the dynasty
he founded.

It is characteristic of the practical turn of Henry's
genius that he was able to translate this harmony of
feeling between the king and the nation into a regular
alliance between the Crown and the middle classes,
acting through their representatives in the House of
Commons. He drew his strength from the loyalty of
the dwellers in field and city, not from the towers
and walls of medieval castles or the leadership of
feudal hosts. The influence of capital was fast
changing the basis of society. Personal relations between lord and man were being superseded by the
complex, impersonal relationships of commerce and
industry, of employer and employed. From the
decay of a feudally organised society the middle class
emerged. Rich citizens began to compete with feudal
lords, and became richer with the revival of trade.
The class which had thus obtained wealth found the
path to political power opening before them, and,
owing to certain peculiar features of English society

—the absence of rigid social castes and the union of the knights of the shires with the burgesses in the House of Commons—their representatives in the House of Commons had the strength that came from the union of the landed gentry with the wealthy townsmen. In an era of transition, therefore, Henry VII. enlisted the support of the class which was rising while he levelled the last outstanding feudal figures to whom the past belonged. The forces that combined in his support represented all the progressive and hopeful elements of society. As one conspiracy after another was formed and failed, the hopelessness of their aims, the threat involved in their success, was stamped upon the popular mind. They were empty of any promise except the return of anarchy, they represented the party of faction and reaction that had everything to gain and nothing to lose by disorder.   The days of civil war were still near enough to throw their dark shadow, and the trading classes, feverishly absorbed in money-making, realised that everything depended on the king's protection. A successful conspiracy would have engulfed their newly earned wealth in the returning waves of anarchy, hence their steady loyalty to Henry VII. The king's occasionally heavy taxation and his unconstitutional borrowings they seem to have regarded in the light of an insurance against the risks of renewed civil war, and isolated acts of tyranny were obscured by the general justice of the king's rule under which the poor and weak found protection and the prosperous citizen found peace.

Over the nobles, discredited by their proved incapacity for rule, weakened and impoverished by the Wars of the Roses, Henry won his first triumph. They had no leader ; the men with personality or ambition had fallen on the field of battle or by the axe, and they were divided by memories of civil strife. Against them was a resolute man, bent on reducing them to obedience, who struck one hammer stroke after another at the overgrown power which was the root of disorder. There is little wonder that he prevailed.

In his first Parliament they had to take an unpalatable oath against maintenance and livery.[1] This first blow attacked the root of their political power and the outward signs of their aristocratic dignity. The armed bands who, swaggering under feudal badges, had overawed the countryside, intimidated sheriffs, and bullied juries, felt that their days were numbered. Private war, once a necessity, became a prohibited and almost unattainable luxury. But the effect of this first step must not be exaggerated. The practice of keeping bands of armed retainers was too much part of the life of an English nobleman to be abandoned at once. The tigers needed careful watching even after their teeth were drawn. One statute after another repeated the tenor of the oath, adding penalties. The " feedmen " of the Duke of Northumberland, the " great Host " of the Lord Strange, the retainers of the Duke of Buckingham, of the Nevilles, and other nobles [2]— though not as familiar as the retinue of the Earl of Oxford, that has won an anecdotic immortality— existed late in Henry's reign to show how much stronger custom still was than law. The unsuccessful rebellions, the sharp justice of the Star Chamber, the obscuring of the spirit of faction by years of peace,

---

[1] This was drawn up on the lines of an oath taken in 1433, when the lords had sworn not to maintain felons. *Rot. Parl.*, vi. 344*a*.

[2] Leland, *Collectanea*, iv. 213.

completed the work that legislation had begun. By the
end of the reign the typical English nobleman had
found other occupations than the medieval ones of
riot and civil war.[1] He was a much more peaceful
character, who was beginning to appreciate the refine-
ments of Renaissance culture and a gentler civilisation.

Henry was too politic to take their traditional
occupation from his nobles without giving them some
new interest to take its place. His attitude to the
old nobility is an interesting example of his skill.
By his unrevengeful policy he conciliated all except
the irreconcilables, and the great names of the feudal
aristocracy became conspicuous among the men who
adorned his court. The Duke of Buckingham and
his brother nobles were splendid figures at jousts,
revels, and " disguisings," and remained at court
under the king's eye planning further displays of
glittering magnificence instead of in the distant provinces keeping up almost royal state and meditating
treason. Though none of the older nobility, except
the king's immediate relatives and the Earls of
Oxford and Surrey, obtained important employment
in the State, the king's tact kept them satisfied with
their ornamental rôle. Though they were occasionally employed as dignified ambassadors on diplomatic
missions which called for no special ability, their
real mission in life was to shine in the brilliant con-
stellation revolving round the throne. It was a
definite part of the king's policy to keep them about
the court, and it appears that their absence attracted
his notice and made him suspicious.[2] Henry's

[1] The *Italian Relation* (p. 39) is very clear on this point. " In
former times . . . the nobles kept retainers. . . . Of these there
are few left, and those diminish daily."

[2] André, *Annales*, p. 125.

example was followed by his successors, who inherited from him an ineradicable and perhaps excusable jealousy of the great aristocrats. At no period of English history were the nobles more conspicuous at court, yet at no period had they less real power in the State.

This ornamental nobility was balanced by a new official class. Merchant blood ran in the veins of the Tudors themselves, and gave them sympathy with men of non-noble birth. The important offices of State were given to men of comparatively obscure birth, who owed everything to the king and had no traditions of aristocratic independence behind them. Men like Morton, Fox, and Warham obtained the dignity necessary for their exalted office by holding high ecclesiastical rank, and their success encouraged talented men of humble birth to hope for similar careers. Bray, Empson, Dudley, and Wolsey were all men of the non-noble class who found their way to office under Henry VII. His choice of middle-class ministers was imitated by his successors, and though he personally created few new peerages, a patent of nobility was often the reward of service to the State in the later Tudor period. The new nobility, as it has been called, owes its origin to the policy of Henry VII.[1]

As Henry amassed wealth and set on foot splendid traditions, the gulf between royalty and the aristocracy widened. This process of exalting the royal dignity continued. His children did not marry among the English nobles, as had been the unfortunate tradition, but among the other royal houses

[1] See list of Henry's creations, *Forty-seventh Report of Deputy Keeper*, App. 79–83.

RICHARD FOX, BISHOP OF WINCHESTER
1448—1528
From the National Portrait Gallery copy of the picture by Joannes Corvus at
Corpus Christi College, Oxford

of Europe. After Warwick had been executed, little of the blood royal flowed in the veins of subjects. The Crown withdrew to a position of splendid isolation, and its strength was unchallengeable by any noble or group of nobles.

Even the Church, with all its great traditions behind it, became a support of despotism, not a bulwark of freedom. Though the hierarchy was as strong as ever in wealth and estates, the Church was rapidly losing its power with the people. The advent of the critical spirit of the Renaissance, the revival of insular hostility to a body under the control of Rome, the secularisation of the Church, the decline of the monastic ideal, and the scandals of sanctuary and benefit of the clergy, deprived the Church of influence and involved her in unpopularity. By the humiliation of the baronage and the weakness of the Papacy the Church had lost its former allies, its natural leaders had become the king's servants, and it sank into dependence on the Crown, bringing to it all the dead weight of its vast possessions.

The position of the Crown gained strength from the intellectual revival. The Renaissance brought with it the revived study of the Roman civil law with its imperial language and absolutist sentiment. " What is pleasing to the prince has the force of law," [1] became a familiar maxim, and a growing band of scholars looked to the king for patronage and reward. The ideas of Macchiavelli's *Il Principe* and the rule of the Italian despots had familiarised Europe with the sight of the autocrat whose sceptre was adorned with the graces of art and literature.

The power of a monarchy that thus represented

[1] Ulpian.

the popular will early gathered round it national
sentiment. " No one but a Tudor poet," it has been
said,[1] " would have thought of the ' Divinity that doth
hedge a king' or have written :

> "Not all the water in the rough rude sea
> Can wash the balm from an anointed king.
> The breath of worldly men cannot depose
> The deputy elected by the Lord."

Under the dynasty founded by Henry the people
had the opportunity of looking at the best and
strongest side of the theory of kingship, and it is not
by accident that Shakespeare and the rest of the
Elizabethan dramatists are silent about the elected
representatives of the people while they idealise and
dignify the monarch. It is curious to notice how the
reverence for and awe of the Crown deepened as the
reign went on. Henry deliberately fostered this by
his personal dignity and aloofness from the common
people, and by the growth of splendour and ceremonial at his court. It is not for nothing that the
word " Majesty " appears first in this reign. The king
deliberately set himself to hedge his throne by all
outward forms and observances. " He had nothing
in him of vainglory," wrote Bacon, " but yet kept
state and majesty to the height, being sensible that
majesty maketh the people bow."

Henry's relations with Parliament introduce the
most characteristic feature of the despotism he
founded. A series of pliant Parliaments gave a legal
colour to the methods of Tudor government, and
enforced the royal will through their legislation.
Though in Henry's time the system of legalising
absolutism did not reach its climax, it was he who

[1] Pollard, *Factors in Modern History*, p. 75.

established the tradition. The king succeeded in making Parliament subservient without resorting to clumsy methods of corruption. His dealings with the legislature were not according to any of the former models. His Lancastrian descent and immediate summons of Parliament may have raised hopes that the king was going to tread in the way of his Lancastrian ancestors, and that the age of Parliamentary government had returned. But the king's scheme was very different. He chose a middle way between the too great dependence on a popular assembly associated with the weak rule of Henry VI. and the hatred or contempt for Parliament shown by Edward IV. and Richard III. He originated a method which, while it preserved the time-honoured forms of Parliamentary liberty, secured the practical predominance of the royal will.

It is Henry's success in using the power he had acquired over Parliament to secure a legal basis for his despotism and arm it with still further powers that is the most novel feature of his rule. Men were familiar with tyranny, and familiar with Parliamentary government, but the blend of the forms of liberty and the fact of absolutism was new. At the beginning, at all events, everything was done under legal forms. It was not until the king had furnished himself with new weapons forged for him by Parliament, and had hedged round his dynasty with every legislative sanction his ingenuity could devise, that he abandoned his Parliamentary ally, and resorted to the more obvious and usual methods of absolutism.

How was this subservience of Parliament obtained ? Not in the main by any underhand juggling with the electorate, or any political wire-pulling, but by that practical coincidence between the will of the king and the wishes of the people's representatives to which allusion has before been made. Satisfied of their unity of aim, Henry's complaisant Parliaments put into his hands powerful weapons against their common foes, and their trust in him made them sanction some of his most arbitrary actions. On most points the identity of interests was obvious, and with consummate tact the king avoided collision on the points where harmony between Crown and people was not complete.[1] Finance was almost the only question upon which difficulty arose, and it was the king's reluctance to arouse the opposition of Parliament and the people by asking for large supplies that drove him to the questionable financial expedients of the later part of the reign.

The king, it may be noticed, was not without many sources of influence which he could have used to restore harmony, if any hint of popular opposition were revealed. In this connection the Lower House is the more important. The Upper House reflected in its political nullity the practical weakness of the nobility. Never had the House of Lords been more dependent on the Crown and less a feature of the constitution. This was not due to the extermination of the baronage, a picturesque view of the result of the battles of the Roses that has long been abandoned. Though only eighteen temporal peers sat in Henry's first Parliament, the number afterwards rose to the usual level of about forty.[2] They were, however,

---

[1] The theory of Hobbes that " in monarchy the private interest is the same with the public. The riches, power, and honour of a monarch arise only from the riches, strength, and reputation of his subjects," coincides for once exactly with the facts of the case. Hobbes, *Leviathan*, chapters xix., xx.

[2] Many peers were absent owing to unreversed attainders barring them from sitting. One curious feature is that several of the northern

outnumbered by the spiritual peers, who were more than usually dependent on the Crown, and the House of Lords became a negligible factor in the constitutional situation.

Many of the sources of influence over the Commons discovered by Henry VII. were little used by him, owing to his success in avoiding causes of conflict with Parliament, but they are interesting as anticipations of later methods. The appointment of the Speaker was practically in Henry's hands, though theoretically he was elected by the Commons. The list of Speakers for the reign, Lovell, Mordaunt, Sir Thomas Fitz-William, Empson, Robert Drury, Thomas Inglefield, and finally Dudley, at the height of his unpopularity —all men who were devoted to the king's interests —proves how strong Henry's hold over Parliament was. The fact that the Speaker then managed the whole business of the House, very much in the way that the modern leader of the House does, but in the interests of the Crown not of a party, gave the king considerable influence over proceedings in the Commons. There is little evidence of attempts to control elections either directly, by the use of royal influence, or indirectly, through putting pressure on local magnates. Neither is there any evidence of the creation of new boroughs on royal estates, a favourite method with Henry's successors. The king's policy gave him a position independent of such devices. There is evidence, however, of influence in another direction. Nearly all the new charters granted to boroughs during the reign restricted the electoral

lords, whose loyalty was not suspected, did not receive their writs of summons until late in the reign, or early in that of Henry VIII. This has not yet been explained. See on this point Stubbs, *Seventeen Lectures on Med. and Mod. Hist.*, pp. 407-8.

bodies in the towns. The case of Leicester, where
the change introduced by charter was confirmed by
Parliament,[1] is a fair example. There the elective body
which chose the town officials and the members of
Parliament was reduced to forty-eight, on the plea
that "through the 'exclamacions and hedinesse of
persons of lytel substance' the elections had been
scenes of riot and disorder."[2] This action, taken on
the king's own personal responsibility, is one of the
first cases of the tampering with borough franchises,
which was elaborated in the later Tudor period when
popular independence was reviving.

Owing to the infrequent and brief sessions of
Parliament, most members of the House of Commons
lacked initiative, and had no familiarity with Parliamentary business. They had no leaders, no discipline
or party organisation, no ground of common action,
no burning grievances to rouse them to resist a king
who had a reputation for wisdom and the monopoly
of administrative experience. As a result the House
as a whole took little interest in politics. The question
of peace or war might arouse some enthusiasm, as in
the session of 1491, the demand for large supplies
might and did arouse discussion. But with regard
to general legislation Parliament was apathetic, and
at the same time trusted the king completely. The
interests of both appeared identical, and there is
no record of opposition even to the measures which
invested the king with almost despotic powers.

---

[1] *Rot. Parl.*, vi. 431–3; Campbell, *Materials*, ii. 456–7; Bateson,
Borough of Leicester, pp. 308–14, 319, 324.

[2] On the visit to Exeter, when he enriched the city with the gift
of the hat and sword (still preserved there), Henry modified the
constitution of the city, making it more oligarchic. *Court of Requests* (Selden Soc.), p. 4.

From the first Henry found Parliament a willing tool.
The brief Act recognising the king's title gave an idea
of the kind of thing that was to follow. His right to
reign was acknowledged not bestowed by Parliament.
The voice of Parliament was Henry's voice, the petitions he graciously granted he had himself inspired.
The lead given by this first Parliament was followed
by its successors. The various Acts of Attainder by
which the king made the representatives of the people
share the responsibility for the punishment of his
foes,[1] the Acts of Resumption, and the Star Chamber
Act led up to the legislation of the Parliament of 1495
(called by one writer " the obedient Parliament ")—
legislation which affords very strong proof of the
extraordinary advance in the power of the Crown
since the beginning of the reign. The Act legalising
benevolences placed an arbitrary exaction of the
king's on the same footing as a tax imposed by the
strictest constitutional forms, the Act setting up the
informer system, which will be discussed below, gave
the king an opportunity of making a profit out of the
judicial administration of which he at once took full
advantage. This Parliament, strongly monarchical
in tendency, is the forerunner of the servile Parliaments of Henry VIII. The last Parliament of the
reign, called after a long interval during which the
king's despotic power had grown through years of
non-resistance, went further still. The Act of 1504
gave the king the power of reversing attainders
by letters patent.[2] By this extraordinary statute,
the unopposed passing of which is a measure of
Parliamentary confidence in, as well as obedience to,

---

[1] On this subject see Pollard, *op. cit.*, p. 86.

[2] 19 Hen. VII., cap. 28 ; *Rot. Parl.*, vi. 526 ; *Stat.*, ii. 669. In
1523 Henry VIII. was given the same powers for life.

the king, Henry found himself able to perform the highest act of sovereignty and annul at his pleasure an Act of Parliament passed with all proper formalities.

All this Henry had accomplished without doing any injury to the forms of the constitution. His new plant of Parliamentary despotism had taken root. "He did much to maintain and countenance his laws," writes Bacon, "which (nevertheless) was no impediment to him to work his will." The writers who have credited him with the desire to set up in England a despotism of the continental type appear to miss the very features which made the Tudor monarchy a success. The bodyguard, the spy system, and so on were accidents rather than attributes of his despotism.

Only the outstanding features of the legislation passed by Henry through his complaisant Parliaments can be dealt with here. Legislation aimed at political disturbances and social disorder takes up many pages of the statute-book. The oath against livery and maintenance, already noticed,[1] was followed by legislation which gives a picture of serious disorder. The Act " against unlawful hunting in forests and parks " [2] refers to the facts that " Divers persons in grete nombre som with paynted faces som with Visors and otherwise disguised to thentent they shuld not be knowen riotously and in manner of Werre arraied " had hunted by night as well as by day in the forests and parks, especially in Kent, Surrey, and Sussex, and the result had been " rebelleons, insurrections, riots, robberies, murders, and other inconveniences." It was enacted that offenders

---

[1] See above, p. 49.   [2] 1 Hen. VII., cap. 7

should be brought before any member of the king's
council, or any justice of the peace, night hunting
being made a felony.[1] An "Acte against Murderers "[2]
recited the neglect of the law " and how murders and
the slaying of the king's subjects daily increase in
the land," and enacted that murderers should be
proceeded against at the king's suit within the year,
and that there should no longer be the delay of a
year and a day—the time allotted for an appeal by the
relatives of the slain. Townships were to be amerced
for the escape of murderers ; coroners were given a
fee of 13s. 4d. for every inquest they held, a penalty
of 100s. being imposed upon them for neglect to hold
an inquest. The last provisions were directed against
the notorious slackness of the coroners, which had
resulted in much crime going unpunished.

By another Act single justices of the peace were deprived of the power of allowing bail to prisoners, which
had been much abused in favour of powerful offenders,
" wherby many murdrers and felons eschaped to
the greate displeasure of the king." Two justices
had to agree to allow bail, and the fact had to be
certified at the next sessions or gaol delivery. This
Act and others like it amount practically to a restate-
ment of the ordinary duties of local officials, but the
heavy fines which punished culpable neglect of duty
were novelties. The disturbed state of society is
further illustrated by the necessity for an Act of
Parliament which made the violent abduction and
marriage of women of property a felony.[3]

The abuses of benefit of clergy and of sanctuary—

---

[1] This was an anticipation of Star Chamber methods.
[2] 3 Hen. VII., cap. 2 ; *Stat.* ii. 510.
[3] See also *Star Chamber Cases* (Selden Soc.). Act against Thomas
Keneston, 3 Hen. VII., cap. 32.

another grave danger—were limited.   Benefit of clergy then extended to all who could read, and thus exempted a horde of criminals from the sterner justice of the secular courts.   An Act of 1490 only allowed benefit of clergy once to any offender who was not actually in orders, and provided that if his offence were murder or felony he was to be branded on his left thumb with the letters M or T.   If subsequently indicted he was to lose his benefit of clergy. By later statutes soldiers who deserted from the army, or servants who killed their masters, were entirely deprived of benefit of clergy.   Contemporary opinion declared that the king had been led to pass these Acts owing to the much more satisfactory state of affairs in France.[1]

The right of sanctuary was a similar menace to good government.   Any church could shelter an offender from his pursuers for forty days, and certain specially privileged places could give sanctuary for an unlimited period.   In 1487 an Act of Parliament was passed to prevent the privilege of sanctuary being abused by debtors in order to defraud their creditors.   The opinion of the judicial bench, as well as popular feeling, was hostile to these dangerous privileges, and in the case of Humphrey Stafford (1487) the judges decided that sanctuary could not protect an offender accused of high treason.[2]   This put a powerful weapon into the king's hands, and his position was strengthened by the bulls which his cordial relations with the Papacy enabled him to

---

[1] 4 Hen. VII., cap. 13 ; 7 Hen. VII., cap. 1 ; 12 Hen. VII., cap. 7 ; *Stat.*, ii. 538, 549, 639 ; Pol. Verg., 609 ; *Ital. Rel.*, p. 35. See above, p. 26.

[2] 3 Hen. VII., cap. 5 ; *Stat.*, ii. 513 ; *Year Book*, 3 Hen. VII., fo. 12, pt. 6 ; More, *Utopia*, p. 44 ; Reeves, ed. Finlason.

obtain from three Popes in succession. A bull issued
by Innocent VIII., and confirmed by Alexander VI.
in 1493, deprived a robber or murderer who left
sanctuary and committed a second offence of its
benefits, and authorised the king's officers to take
him out of sanctuary. At the same time the bull
contained a provision, very important from Henry's
point of view, that in the case of a fugitive suspected of high treason taking sanctuary, his place of
refuge might be surrounded by guards to prevent his
escape. In 1504 another bull forbade the reception
of criminals who had left sanctuary into any other
refuge, and provided that all criminals might be
watched by royal guards when in sanctuary.

The bitter fruit of years of tumult and disorder
could not be destroyed at once by Act of Parliament.
Henry's task of restoring order seemed an endless
one. Quite late in the reign native as well as foreign
observers were commenting on the prevalence of
crime and violence. Though the sight of twenty
thieves hanging on one gallows was not unique, theft
was " ryffe and rancke " everywhere.

The streets of London were thronged with beggars
and with idle gentlemen who, said More, " carrye
about with them at their tails a great flock or train
of idle and loytering serving men . . . who jette
through the street with a bragging look and think
themselves too good to be any man's mate." Such
men when they lost their masters had no trade but
theft.[1]

Much of the disorder was caused by the lack of
employment due to the increase of sheep-farming,

---

[1] More's *Utopia* gives a vivid picture of England about the time
of the Cornish rebellion.

the disbanding of the liveried retainers, and by the
spread of luxury and ostentation, " the strange and
proude newefanglenes in apparel, prodigall riot and
sumptuous fare . . . the many noughtie, lewde, and
unlawfull games that send the haunters of them
streyghte a stealynge when theyr money is gone." [1]

Further, a host of vexatious law-suits, the legacy of
civil war, had cropped up to harass the landlord.   No
one felt his title secure, but much was done to restore
a feeling of confidence by the Statute of Fines.[2]   The
fine, which under the original Act of Edward I. had
been an unchallengeable way of conveying land,[3]
had by a later statute (*noun chaque*) lost this ter-
minative effect.   The former efficacy of the fine was
restored by Henry's statute, with increased precautions against fraud.   The theory that this statute
was an instance of Henry's craft and foresight, that
it beguiled the nobility into impoverishing themselves
by making alienations easy, was the product of
Bacon's fancy, and though often repeated is now
abandoned.   As a matter of fact the Act is only a
re-enactment of an earlier Act of Richard III., and
its ostensible purpose of providing a method of
securing a doubtful title to land was its real one.
Its later use by lawyers as a convenient method of
alienating entailed land could hardly have been fore-
seen by Henry, and was of little importance until
considerably later.[4]

Of all the statutes which aimed at restoring order
to the distracted country, the famous Star Chamber

---

[1] More, *Utopia* (ed. *Lumby*), p. 35.   [2] 4 Hen. VII., cap. 24.
[3] 27 Edw. I., s. 1, cap. 1.
[4] The fine had to be proclaimed in Court four times in each of the
three terms following the conveyance, and at the end of the year,
being unchallenged at twelve separate publications, became absolute
and a bar to all further suits.

Act of 1487 is the most important.[1] The preamble gives a vivid picture of the evils the statute proposed to remedy. " The Kyng oure sovereygn Lord remembreth howe by onlawfull mayntenance gevyng of lyveres signes and tokyns and reteyndres by endentur promyses othes writyng or otherwise, embracieries of his subgettes ontrue demeanynges of Shrevys in makyng of panelles and other ontrewe retournes by takyng of money by jurryes by greate riotts and unlawfull assemblez the polacye and good rule of this realme is almost subdued . . . wherby the lawes of the lond in execution may take litell effecte, to the encres of murdres, robberies, perjuries and unsuerties of all men lyvyng and losses of their londes and goodes."

By this Act the Lord Chancellor, the Lord Treasurer, and the Lord Privy Seal, or any two of them, were empowered to summon a bishop and a temporal lord of the king's council with the chief justices of the king's bench and of the common pleas, or in their absence two other judges, and form a court to consider any bill or information laid against any one for misbehaviour of the kind stated in the preamble. They were given authority to summon the offenders to appear before them by writ or privy seal, to examine and punish them as if they had been convicted by one of the ordinary courts of law. At the same time the justices of the peace were to order inquiries to be made by special juries with a 40s. qualification as to the concealment of offences by other inquests.

By later Acts, as will be seen below, the sphere of this court (which, though not designated by the name of the Star Chamber in the Act of 1487, may, for the sake of convenience, be called by that name) was

[1] 3 Hen. VII., cap. 1.

considerably enlarged. Acts of 1495 provided that
" heinous riots " were to be reported to the Star
Chamber by justices of the peace, that cases of perjury
were to come before it, and that appeals could be
brought to it in criminal cases. In 1504 a new Act
against retainers mentioned the Star Chamber. It
gradually attracted business of a very varied character. Quarrels between the Merchant Adventurers
and the Staplers, gild disputes, cases of usury and
forgery, and disputes over enclosures were brought
before it, and thus a court of the king's servants had
in its hands the commercial and industrial interests
of the people.[1] The vast increase in the power of the
king, who by a court set up outside the ordinary
jurisdiction could thus control the daily lives of his
subjects, can hardly be exaggerated.

This Act is another of the cases in which originality
of device cannot be claimed. It has been pointed
out that it derived its " statutory pedigree " from an
Act of 1453, which empowered the Chancellor to summon rioters before the Council,[2] and further the Act of
1487 only adapted for particular cases powers derived
from a much older source, the authority exercised
by the king's Council in its judicial capacity. But
though it did not set up the " Star Chamber," nor
introduce any startling novelty in administrative
machinery, the Act was of first-rate importance for
practical purposes. It converted a temporary and
abandoned experiment into part of the permanent
machinery of government. The process sketched out
in the reign of Henry VI. was hardened and defined.
The Act increased the number of offences with which

---

[1] Leadam, *Star Chamber Cases* (Selden Soc.) ; *Somerset Star
Chamber Cases* (Somerset Rec. Soc.). See also Appendix III.,
p. 423, below.   [2] Leadam, *op. cit.*, Intro., lxiv. *seq.*

the Council had the clear authority of Parliament to deal, legalised the issue of writs of privy seal, long a subject of contention between king and Parliament, and extended to a number of specified offences the partly abandoned power of the Council to examine defendants on oath. Like other engines of Tudor absolutism, the court of Star Chamber was a despotic excrescence growing out of constitutional usage, and sacrificing the forms of justice in particular cases to the good of the State. There is little doubt that its action in the early days of the Tudors was almost uniformly beneficent. It touched a class of offenders against whom the ordinary courts were powerless, rescued weak suitors from the tyranny of juries bribed or coerced by the local magnates, and substituted for the decision of a venal official, or the verdict of a corrupt or coerced jury, the judgment of uninterested and highly-placed statesmen. Rapid and effective action took the place of the delays by which legal process had often been made a denial of justice. The simplicity of its procedure swept away technicalities, anomalies, and injustice. "It was a law unto itself, with hands free to invent new remedies for every new disease of the body politic." [1] The enthusiasm of Lambarde, who wrote of the Star Chamber as "this most noble and praiseworthy court, the beams of whose bright justice do blaze and spread themselves as far as the realme is wide," is a sufficient contrast to the wholesale denunciations of it current in the seventeenth century. But the points that made for its usefulness in the reign of Henry VII., led to the defects that produced its condemnation later. The temporary supersession of the jury system, the condemnation of

[1] Maitland, Eng. Law, 1307–1600 (*Social Eng.* (ed. Traill), ii. 657).

the accused on written evidence, without the opportunity of being confronted with witnesses, its rapid methods, the growing practice of examining the defendant in secret and subjecting him to torture under a licence obtained from the Privy Council, all these things were liable to become weapons of arbitrary tyranny. Its very freedom from formalism and reluctance to consider itself bound by its own precedents, the elasticity that had made the court valuable in the early period, were twisted into arbitrariness and illegality. The court that had been the safeguard of the weak and a security for order in unquiet times, degenerated in less able hands and more peaceful times into the weapon of weak cruelty, and it finally perished in well-earned ignominy.

The legislation of the Parliament summoned in the autumn of 1495, after Warbeck's raid on the shores of Kent, reflects the critical character of the situation. The Act which promised security to those who supported the king *de facto* is important as a measure of the king's uneasiness, rather than for its effect in reassuring his subjects.[1] Other Acts were more important. There was a great dread of violence, of some upheaval within the kingdom that would drive the king from his throne.[2] During the late disorders local officials had proved themselves incapable. The jury system was under a cloud; sheriffs and justices of the peace were corrupt and careless. If the king's throne was to survive external dangers, the internal administration must be

[1] 11 Hen. VII., cap. 1; *Stat.*, ii. 568. Dr. Busch sees in it, however, one of Henry's "most important and fair measures to remove the evil of insecurity in matters of law." Busch, *op. cit.*, p. 271. The Act was of some importance in the constitutional disputes of the seventeenth century.

[2] *Paston Letters*, iv. 894.

reformed. Very important legislation was passed
through Parliament which still further increased the
control of the Crown over local institutions. The
Star Chamber Act had already provided for the trial
of sheriffs who had neglected their duty, but this
Parliament went further, and a new statute imposed
heavy fines on such offenders. The Act also provided a check upon the justices of the peace, by
ordering that complaints against them were to be
taken to the justices on assize or to the king and
chancellor — that is, to the Star Chamber. The
preamble of the Act stated the king's wish " that
his subjects should live at peace under his laws and
increase in riches and well-being," but the Act was
not repealed when the danger was over.[1]

Other statutes, as we have seen, extended the
jurisdiction of the Star Chamber to perjury, in cases
touching the king,[2] and re-affirmed its powers in connection with " heinous riots." [3] Another Act, evidently
passed with a view of diminishing the number of
vagrants, who became a grave political danger in this
year of crisis, provided that all beggars incapable of
work should be returned to their own hundreds. The
severe penalties imposed by an Act of Richard III.
were abrogated, and the vagrant was to be set in the
stocks for three days on the first offence and for six
days on the second offence. Scholars, soldiers, and
sailors who begged were required to show a licence
from the governing body of their university or
from their commanding officers.[4] This statute, which
seems to anticipate the later distinctions between
able and impotent beggars, was evidently successful.

[1] 11 Hen. VII., cap. 15, cap. 24 § 6, cap. 25 § 2; Stat., ii. 579, 589, 590.
[2] 11 Hen. VII., cap. 25; Stat., ii. 589–90.
[3] 11 Hen. VII., cap. 7; Stat., ii. 573.
[4] 11 Hen. VII., cap. 2; Stat., ii. 569.

Perkin Warbeck found no crew of vagabonds and out-of-works to support him, and in 1504 it was found possible to reduce the penalties upon vagrancy to a day and a night in the stocks.[1]

The Star Chamber statute had not completed the reform of the jury system, and still more drastic treatment was required. An Act of 1495 set up machinery by which appeal might be made from the verdict of a jury. In civil cases the appeal lay to a special jury of twenty-four summoned to hear the appeal, and if the verdict of the original jury was reversed each member of it was fined £20. In criminal cases appeal lay to the Star Chamber, which thus obtained control of the whole criminal administration of the country.[2] In 1504 this legislation, which had been passed for a term of years only, was renewed as to civil appeals but not as to criminal appeals.[3] It has been suggested that Henry had the settled purpose of destroying the jury system—that typically English institution that was so much misunderstood by contemporary foreign observers [4]—but as usual the evidence of sinister design is absent. In civil cases he arranged for appeal from one jury to another, and the legislation as to criminal appeals was not renewed during the reign. As a matter of

---

[1] 19 Hen. VII., cap. 12; *Stat.*, ii. 656.

[2] 11 Hen. VII., cap. 24; 11 Hen. VII., cap. 25; *Stat.*, ii. 588–90. There had been a difficulty in obtaining a sufficient panel, met by reducing the qualification of jurors. Later in the reign the qualification was doubled, which suggests a marked improvement in social conditions. 19 Hen. VII., cap. 13; *Stat.*, ii. 657–8.

[3] 19 Hen. VII., cap. 3; *Stat.*, ii. 649.

[4] The Italian observer wrote of the jury system in the reign of Henry VII. as a bad custom, and declared that those who could not bear the discomfort of being shut up "without food, fire, or means of sitting down" had to agree to the verdict of their more Spartan comrades. *Ital. Rel.*, p. 33.

fact, however, it appears that criminal appeals were still occasionally taken to the Star Chamber in spite of the lapse of the legal authorisation. In 1504 the laws against livery and maintenance were strengthened by a statute which imposed fines for breaches of the earlier Act, and gave a certain inquisitorial power to justices of the peace, who were ordered to summon before them any they should " thynke to be suspect of any reteynour."

The effect of these centralising statutes can hardly be exaggerated. They introduced the efficient local administration which became one of the features of Tudor rule. The king enlisted in his service all the political capacity he could find, placing much reliance on the minor country gentry who became the props of the Tudor throne, and, though his government was high-handed, it was strong and dependable. The excesses of the local tyrants, the cramping fetters of the exclusive corporations, gave way before the power of the king. Many despots had given place to one— a despot enlightened by practice in ruling, and broadened by considering the nation as a whole.

Side by side with the Star Chamber, Henry set up, or rather established on a permanent footing, a court which is less well known. The Court of Requests, the " poor man's court of equity," aimed at providing a summary tribunal for the adjustment of civil cases under the rules of equity. Like the Star Chamber, it is an offshoot of the Council, but it bears clear marks of the theory that made the king the fountain of justice, in the fact that for a long time it followed the king on his progresses through the kingdom. This practice was gradually given up, though an isolated instance has been found as late as 1544, and the legal element grew stronger as time went on. The court

seems to have been popular as well as effective, and
its reorganisation is a proof of the king's tenderness
for his poorer subjects.[1]

The volume and importance of all this legislation
supports the familiar paradox that the Tudor despotism saved the essence of Parliamentary government.[2] Henry VII. roused Parliament from a state
of impotence. In the reign of Edward IV. Parliament " seemed to have nothing better to do than to
regulate the manufacture of cloth. . . . If for a
moment it can raise its soul above defective barrels
of fish and fraudulent gutter tiles this will be in order
to prohibit ' cloish, kayles, half bowl ' " and other
unlawful games.[3] Henry brought Parliament back
from the contemplation of particular and local interests to the great affairs of the nation. It is true
that Parliament only entered upon its new and important work under the heavy hand of a master ; but
experience in dealing by legislation with great
national questions would have been cheaply purchased by the sacrifice of independent powers of
regulating the " making of worsteds " or the herring
trade. But even this sacrifice Parliament did not
have to make. The new work of becoming the instrument of despotism thrust upon the national assembly
by Henry VII. did not absorb all its energies. Its
activity in the regulation of special trades continued.
The Statute Rolls of Henry VII. make curious reading. Legislation making great constitutional changes
comes side by side with Acts prescribing punishments
for those who stuffed beds with " improper feathers,"

[1] *Cases in Court of Requests* (ed. Leadam), Selden Soc. It is
suggested that the name of the court was taken from that of a
French court of a similar nature.

[2] Maitland, Eng. Law, 1307-1600 (*Social England*, ii. p. 647).

[3] *Ibid.*, p. 647.

restraining the evil practices of itinerant pewterers, or ordering the repair of Bristol pavements.[1] The share in government (or at all events in legalising the Acts of government) was given to Parliament by Henry VII. for his own personal convenience, but it brought about results of the highest importance. The king brought Parliament back to the old line of development interrupted by two generations of anarchy.   He started it on a course which made it a natural development for Parliament to alter the national religion, become supreme in finance, and ultimately, by changing the succession, to obtain control of the executive government.   The system of the first Tudor despot contained in it the essence of Parliamentary monarchy.

Henry's financial policy invites both admiration and criticism.   The latter it has obtained in abundant measure ; the sensational faults of the later have obscured the patient, meritorious work of the earlier years.   In some respects Henry's treatment of finance was the most difficult—though perhaps the most successful—of all the work he did for England.   He found the country exhausted, the exchequer empty, even the crown jewels in pawn.   He maintained a precarious throne against foreign and domestic foes, kept up a splendid court, and yet left a fabulous treasure to his son.   His extraordinary success was not due to the accident of a general economic recovery in England, or to the brilliant and original devices of a financial genius.   Neither was it the result of the painful accumulations of a throned miser ; [2] the king's personal expenditure was lavish, his court was magni-

---

[1] *Rot. Parl.*, vi. 388.

[2] On this point Bacon has been blindly followed in spite of the weight of contrary evidence.   See Berg., *Spanish Cal.*, p. 206; Brown, *Ven. Cal.*, No. 870.

ficent, his rewards to followers generous, his prefer-
ence of public policy to private gain constant.   He
was a generous host and a liberal ally.[1]   His success
was the result of improved management, careful
account-keeping, constant attention to detail, and
judicious economy.

In his reorganisation of the ordinary sources of
revenue, Henry showed the skill of a born financier.
Of these sources the Crown lands were the most
important.

Though the vast estates of York and Lancaster
had been added to the Crown lands, the ruinous
wars, and the extravagance of both Lancastrian and
Yorkist kings had led to great alienations of territory.
Heavy mortgages encumbered many estates, and land
and buildings were neglected and ruinous.   In the
very first month of his reign, Henry showed his characteristic grasp of the detail of finance, and before he
met his first Parliament he had the management of
the Crown lands at his fingers' ends.   In September,
when he had been only a week or two in his capital,
he was arranging for the repair of royal castles in
Chester and Flint, and appointing loyal followers
as keepers of other strongholds.   New stewards and
bailiffs of royal manors were appointed, new parkers
and masters of the game in the royal forests.   From
Berwick to Cornwall we find evidence of the king's
activity.[2]   Revenues from Crown lands, hitherto
paid into the Exchequer, were transferred to the
control of special commissioners in order to avoid
delay.   The leases under which Crown lands were

---

[1] In 1502-3 he spent £90,327 from the privy purse in entertaining
foreign guests.   Privy Purse Expenses, *Excerpta Historica*, pp. 126-
131.

[2] *Materials*, passim; and Bateson, *Records of Leicester*, pp. 308-373.

GREAT SEAL of HENRY VII (¾)

held were reviewed, and nearly all the new leases provided for the payment of " improved rents " in addition to the former rents.[1] Repairs were undertaken at Windsor, Westminster, and the Tower of London; order was brought out of chaos, and waste and neglect restored. The Crown lands were constantly augmented during the reign by the forfeitures of traitors and rebels, though the harsh action of these confiscations was mitigated by limitations in favour of widows and heirs.[2] The first Parliament of the reign passed an Act of Resumption restoring to the Crown all lands alienated since 2nd October 1455. Other Acts followed later, and finally the " obedient Parliament " displayed its subservience by restoring to the Crown property alienated as far back as the reigns of Edward III. and Richard II.[3]

The result was that Henry had in his hands an accumulation of landed property far greater in extent than any king before him, which, besides increasing his income, added to his already vast power. These great lands supported a small army of servants and officials, disciplined and devoted to the king's service, and provided lucrative posts with which the king augmented the scanty salaries of ambassadors and other State officials.[4] There are not sufficient data for an exact statement of the revenue received by Henry from the Crown lands, but the well-informed

---

[1] In 1495 this policy was pushed to extremes on the lands appropriated to the Prince of Wales. Leases of land from which a larger rent could be expected were simply annulled, the land being let on new terms.

[2] See *Rot. Parl.*, vi. 398–400.

[3] This Act does not seem to have been acted upon to any great extent. It was a threat rather than a reality. *Rot. Parl.*, vi. 336–84, 459–62, 465–9.

[4] See *Materials*, and *L. and P. Hen. VIII.*, vol. i., Intro.

Italian observer was not very far out when he estimated it at 547,000 crowns (£109,000).[1]

The profitable incidents of a dying feudalism,
wardships, marriages and reliefs, formed a considerable
but diminishing item of the royal revenue.   In addition Henry expected freeholders owning land worth
£40 to take up the honours and burdens of knight-
hood, and towards the end of the reign Empson's
notorious activity was displayed in searching out and
fining defaulters.   The later years of the reign, fertile
in financial expedients, produced also a revival of
the royal claim for aids on the knighting of the king's
eldest son and the marriage of his eldest daughter.
In 1504 Henry claimed both these aids, though Prince
Arthur was dead and Princess Margaret had been
married for some years.   There was considerable
opposition in Parliament, led, it is said, by Thomas
More.[2]   With characteristic tact Henry disarmed
opposition, and contented himself with a smaller
sum than that offered by the Commons.[3]

A third source of revenue was the customs duties.
Henry's first Parliament showed itself generous in
this matter, and, following the precedent set in the
reign of Richard III., granted tonnage and poundage
to the king for life.[4]   The king's far-sighted and
disinterested commercial policy was rewarded by a
steady increase in the customs duties, which by the
end of the reign had reached a total of over £40,000,
a rise of twenty-eight per cent.[5]

[1] *Ital. Rel.*, pp. 47–9.
[2] Dr. Stubbs suggests that this legend is doubtful.   Stubbs,
Lectures on Med. and Mod. Hist., p. 418.
[3] The Commons offered £40,000, and the king took £30,000.
[4] *Rot. Parl.*, vi. 268–70.
[5] This estimate is taken from Dr. Busch, p. 283, on the authority
of Schanz, *Englische Handelspolitik*, &c.   Cf. *Ital. Rel.*, p. 50, which
gives the average at £40,000.

But these sources of revenue were barely adequate. The old maxim " that the king should live on his own " could only be translated into practice by the most careful management in time of peace. The constitutional method of obtaining the money required for imminent or actual war or for any extraordinary expenses was by Parliamentary grant. There are records of only five such grants during the reign, and it is obvious, from the tone of the preambles, that these grants were still regarded as exceptional provisions for a national emergency, rather than as an ordinary part of the revenue of the Crown. The usual form of the levy was that of a tax of a tenth and fifteenth, which, though originally arranged as an income tax on inhabitants of corporate towns and of rural districts—roughly corresponding to a tax upon personal and real estate— had been fixed since 1332 on the basis of that year's levy, and consequently produced a sum of about £38,000. This form of tax was open to grave objections. The changes in the centres of population and the decay of once flourishing towns necessitated very large remissions in the contributions assessed upon certain places. The levy therefore could not be collected in its entirety, and as the new towns were not separately assessed, it certainly did not represent the taxable capacity of the people. In his first Parliament Henry VII. made an experiment of some importance, and tried to supersede the antiquated assessment by a new levy. It took the form of a grant of the tenth part of each man's annual income from land, with 1s. 8d. from every ten marks of personal property.[1] This attempt to supersede the

[1] A similar experiment had been made by Edward IV. in 1472. Parliament, however, with a short memory, declared that no such

old fixed levy proved a complete failure, probably through the absence of any suitable system of valuation and assessment, and the king, instead of the estimated £75,000, obtained only about £25,000. In the following year the old system was restored, a fifteenth and a tenth being voted to make up the deficit. In 1491 two-fifteenths and tenths were granted, and were followed by a rising in Yorkshire ; in 1495 Parliament was not asked for a new vote, but the crisis of 1497 produced two separate grants of two-fifteenths and tenths—about £120,000. This exceptionally heavy tax led to the march of the Cornishmen on the capital. The king found that the limit of Parliamentary taxation had been reached. Only once again in the remaining years of his reign did Henry ask Parliament for a grant, and this took the form of the feudal aids above mentioned.[1] Henry found that his power of imposing his will upon Parliament had its limits, and he discovered easier ways of raising money that fostered instead of irritating his despotic temper.

Some of these were innocent enough. He devised his own very successful methods of making wars and rumours of wars a source of profit. The greater part of the large vote obtained from Parliament for the French campaign was saved by the Treaty of Etaples, which itself added a punctually paid French pension

grant had ever before been made. Lincoln, Great Yarmouth, New Horsham, and Cambridge were specially exempted. A subsidy upon aliens was granted at the same time, at the rate of 6s. 8d. from every alien craftsman, 40s. from every alien merchant, and so on.

[1] *Rot. Parl.*, vi. 532–4. Each of these grants was supplemented by a vote from Convocation, which in 1502 also voted a tenth for an expedition against the Turks.

to the king's income.   The Scotch invasion was used
in the same way.[1]   Another irregular but not
illegal device was that of granting new privileges to
cities and trading companies in return for a money
grant.   London bought new privileges for £5000 in
1478, but in 1505 had to pay 5000 marks for a confirmation of them.

The king was not too proud to embark in more
obviously commercial speculations on his own account,
and various notes of the profits obtained by royal
trading in wine, wool, and tin have been preserved.[2]

In emergencies the king asked for and obtained
loans from his subjects, from great cities, and from
private individuals.   He obtained loans from the city
of London four or five times—amounting in 1487–8 to
£6000—but these loans were always repaid.[3]

After the critical period of the reign was over,
financial methods gradually degenerated.   Arbitrary
and novel financial expedients were substituted for
the routine of Parliamentary grants.   The king had
the common-sense gift of adapting his methods to his
circumstances.   He walked softly in the early days
of insecurity, but, his throne once secured, the autocratic bias of his race appeared.   He became impatient
of the constitutional methods that with small results
brought bitter hostility.   In finance as elsewhere the
years 1495–8 are the turning-point, and the evils
increased as the reign went on.   Even in the time of
Morton and Bray, however, financial methods were

---

[1] More alludes to the " counterfayte wars " and peace made with
" holy ceremonies to blind the eyes of the common people."
Utopia (ed. Lumby), p. 52.

[2] *Excerpta Historica*, pp. 98, 108, 111, 124.

[3] *City Chron.*, pp. 193, 194, 212, 213; *Hist. MSS. Com. Rep. III*,
App. 240.

not above suspicion. The benevolence taken in 1491 in anticipation of the French war had the quasi-legal sanction of a Great Council. Private individuals who were reputed to be wealthy were approached by specially appointed royal commissioners, and asked to contribute to the king's necessities definite sums fixed with reference to their supposed property. It is in connection with these benevolences that the Chancellor won unenviable fame as the supposed inventor of the profitable dilemma of " Morton's fork." The assumption of a free-will gift barely veiled the true nature of these demands, but a few years later, in 1495, Parliament gave a legal basis to the tax and empowered the king to collect arrears.[1] It was a fatally easy way of raising money, produced large sums with the minimum of general discontent, and kept in check men whose wealth might have made them formidable.[2]

Benevolences, though strictly speaking illegal, were not glaringly so, and they had the sanction of custom. But in later years Henry's methods became more and more questionable.

The darker side of the financial history of the reign gathers round the names of Empson and Dudley, described by Hall as " two ravenynge wolves " with a " garde of false perjured persons apperteignynge to them." Dudley was a lawyer of a good Sussex family, who had been made a member of the Privy Council soon after the king's accession. He was a

---

[1] 11 Hen. VII., cap. 10.

[2] The scandalous proceedings against Capell, the London alderman, fall well within the earlier period. A case brought into the Court of Requests throws new light on Capell's character. He was bold enough to deny that the king had unlimited authority in the city of London. *Court of Requests* (Selden Soc.), p. 8.

man of great ability. In his book the *Tree of the Commonwealth*, written in 1509, he warns the young king against the very evils with which his name is associated, denouncing them with the eloquence for which he was famous. Empson, though of humble birth—he was the son of a sieve-maker—had been chosen as Speaker of the Parliament of 1491. As early as 1496 a proclamation of Warbeck's had pilloried him as responsible with Fox for the exactions.

From the poverty of the people in general the large fortunes of merchants and others were beginning to emerge. These accumulations of capital were reached by the notorious activities of Empson and Dudley. The evil spread like a canker, and by 1500 they had reduced their practices to a system and were all-powerful in finance. The unscrupulous devices hitherto occasionally adopted grew into habitual extortions. Together they " turned law and justice into wormwood and rapine " ; they were " the king's horse-leeches and shearers, bold men and careless of fame, and that took toll of their master's grist." This vivid phrase is illustrated by many a dark story of oppression and wrong. Brutality and chicanery, espionage and blackmail, were the instruments of their ingenious wickedness ; they terrorised the rich and trampled on law and justice. The possession of wealth was punished as if it were a crime. They drew over England a net which few men of position or substance escaped. The estates of the wards of the Crown were crippled by the exactions of huge fines at their coming of age ; many manors were unjustly claimed as held in chief of the Crown, and owing to the years of civil war, proof to the contrary, if dared, was difficult. The worst feature of the whole sordid business was the perversion of law and justice

by the infliction of enormous fines for the breach of old
statutes that mouldered forgotten, and it is probable
that Empson and Dudley were themselves the origi-
nators of this policy of extortion under cover of the
law that they carried to such shameful lengths.   The
worst features appeared after 1495, when an Act was
passed allowing judges to initiate proceedings for
minor offences on the information of private individuals.   As a result a vile mob of informers sprang
up to drag innocent offenders against a forgotten
code into the clutches of their money-making machine.
Upon these "dishonest, cunningly-devised, and false
accusations" huge fines were imposed.[1]   The perse-
cution of William Capell, of Thomas Kneysworth,
the Lord Mayor, and the ruin brought upon Sir
Robert Plumpton, of which we have details,[2] gives
us an idea of the treatment of a host of forgotten
men who suffered from a similar abuse of the king's
office as the foundation of justice.   The necessary
verdicts were obtained from juries by a system of
mingled terrorism and bribery.   Letters came down
to sheriffs directing them in the way they should go,
obstinate jurors were fined and imprisoned, and the
Privy Council dictated verdicts to the judges.   The
inventors of these corrupt devices were themselves
corrupt—"They preyed upon the people both like
tame hawks for their master and like wild hawks for
themselves," and the victim who got caught in the
new fiscal machinery could sometimes obtain his
release by bribing one of the presiding mechanics.
"Noble men grudged, meane men kycked, poore men

[1] The Earl of Northumberland was fined £10,000.
[2] See *Plumpton Corresp.*, cvi.-cxiv., 147, 151–4, 161–2, 167–70, 183–86; *City Chron.*, pp. 195, 199, 205, 261, 262; André, *Vita*, 108, 126; *Year Book*, 10 Hen. VII., fo. 7.

lamented, preachers openly at Paules Crosse and other places exclamed, rebuked and detested, but yet they would never amende." In spite of the popular hatred of the king's jackals, the system was continued to the end of the reign.

The fact that it was hugely profitable would perhaps have been sufficient for Henry, but even contemporaries could see in the king's methods something more than wholesale robbery. Polydor Vergil noticed that the king singled out the very wealthy for his attentions, more with a view of keeping them humble than from covetousness; and Ayala that the king feared that riches would make his subjects insolent.[1] Henry had to the full the Tudor jealousy of subjects who had great wealth or a great position. A phrase of More's sums up the king's attitude: "No abundance of gold can be sufficient for a prince . . . whereas on the other part neade and povertie doth holde and keep under stowte courages, and maketh them patient perforce, takynge from them bolde and rebellynge stomakes." He wished to see them all suitably humble, sensible of their dependence on royal favour and unable to compete with the magnificence of the Crown. It seems, however, to be pushing the defence of his hateful methods too far to view them from the standpoint of a struggle with capital.[2] Though we may agree that the heavy fines which crushed possible opponents were not due to personal avarice, nothing can palliate the abuses which poisoned the stream of justice at its source.

The king's genuine financial reforms come as a

---

[1] Pol. Verg., 613, 616 ; Berg., *Spanish Cal.*, p. 177.
[2] Busch, *op. cit.*, 298.

relief after the story of his extortions. When it came to a question of expending his ill-gotten gain, he dropped the character of a highway robber and found himself at home in that of a comfortable, thrifty merchant.

A considerable reform was carried out in Henry's first Parliament, which provided that £14,000 yearly derived from Crown lands and customs duties should be appropriated to the support of the royal household, and a sum of £2105, 19s. to the expenses of the king's wardrobe.[1] The change was very popular. It removed the old grievances about excessive purveyance for the necessities of the court when on its travels, and did away with the peculations of court officials who had made very inadequate payments for the goods and provisions they took from the people. This system of appropriating fixed sources of revenue to definite expenses was carried further. The customs of the Staple were assigned to the maintenance of Calais, and a fixed revenue was allotted for the upkeep of the border forts of Berwick and Carlisle.[2]

This strict dealing with money was carried through all the spending departments. Accounts were minutely and rigidly kept, and the strictness required from officials bound the king himself. The " Privy Purse Expenses " are an example of his account-keeping, though Bacon's story of the king laboriously jotting down accounts in a note-book he kept at his side, is a caricature of his carefulness.

---

[1] *Rot. Parl.*, vi. 299–304. See also 11 Hen. VII., cap. 62 ; *Stat.*, ii. 627–30 ; *Rot. Parl.*, 497–502. Edward IV. had made a similar experiment (*Rot. Parl.*, vi. 198), but the change introduced by Henry VII. was permanent.

[2] *Rot. Parl.*, vi. 394 ; 11 Hen. VII., cap. 16.

As a result of savings and exactions, reforms and malpractices, Henry succeeded in his aim of accumulating a great treasure. Long before his death his reputation for wealth had spread through Europe. According to one report he had accumulated so much gold that he was supposed "to have more than well nigh all the kings of Christendom";[1] and yet at his death he left a huge hoard of treasure, as well as magnificent plate and jewels, to his son.[2]

In the later years of his reign there was a considerable change in Henry's constitutional methods. In spite of the control he had obtained over Parliament, he showed a tendency to govern without even such nominal check. Parliament was only summoned once during the last thirteen years of the reign, and when it met, in 1504, Henry announced that he did not mean to call Parliament together again without " great necessity and urgent cause." The reason may perhaps be found in his irregular but lucrative financial methods, and in the impatience of opposition that came from advancing age and familiarity with supreme power. Henry no longer needed Parliament as a subservient ally to give support to an usurping dynasty, and he shirked a conflict over finance as an unnecessary irritation to a powerful monarch whose rule was undisputed and undisturbed. The prestige of the Crown grew with every year that went by

---

[1] Brown, *Ven. Cal.*, i. p. 346.

[2] Bacon's estimate of the treasure at £1,800,000 has been followed by later historians, though the source of it is not apparent. It was certainly not too high an estimate. In 1497 the Milanese envoy estimated Henry's savings at £1,350,000, to which he added £112,500 yearly (Brown, No. 751, 795, 942). In 1509 he was described as " the wisest and richest lord now known to the world."

without a meeting of the people's representatives. Parliament met so seldom that it took on the appearance of an exceptional and occasional part of the State machinery, the Crown representing the permanent and vital part of it.

The king's personal taste for autocratic government came to the front. By the increasing use of letters patent and proclamations he extended the sphere of his personal action. By proclamation he prohibited commercial intercourse with the Netherlands, and by proclamation allowed its renewal.[1] Every year he grasped more power.

His provision for the defence of his throne and kingdom was thorough and effective. In naval affairs he did his usual pioneer work. At his accession there were apparently only four ships owned by the Crown, there was no reserve of naval stores, and pirates roved the Channel unchecked. His reign is a very significant one in the history of the navy. He adopted the policy of building ships for use as men-of-war only, in order to have a nucleus to strengthen the hastily armed ships hired from the merchants. He added to the royal navy the two finest men-of-war ever seen in England, the *Henry Grace à Dieu* (afterwards known as the *Regent*) and the *Sovereign*. Both were built in England under the superintendence of Bray and Guildford, and were launched in 1488 and 1489.[2] The first dry dock in England was built

---

[1] He not infrequently enlarged the scope of Acts of Parliament by proclamation, *e.g.* Proclamations dealt with the coinage, regulated trade, ordered the taking up of knighthoods, &c. *e.g. City Chron.*, p. 212.

[2] In 1497 two smaller ships, the *Sweepstake* and the *Mary Fortune*, followed. The *Margaret* was captured from Scotland, and the *Carvel of Eu* and the *King's Bark* were purchased. The new ships built by Henry were the first to be fitted with portholes.

by Henry at Portsmouth in 1496.[1] With characteristic economy the king adopted a policy of hiring out
his men-of-war to merchants when they were not
required for the royal service, and the *Sovereign* once
took a trading voyage to the Levant. The effect of
the Navigation Laws on the development of the
merchant fleet has already been noticed.[2] Further,
he inaugurated the bounty system, a bonus of about
5s. a ton being given to shipbuilders who constructed
suitable vessels,[3] began a naval storehouse at Greenwich, and started the manufacture of heavy guns in
England, usually attributed to Henry VIII.[4]

The navy under Henry VII. became a weapon of
offence, not a mere means of transport for troops.
In the blockade of Sluys in 1492, and in the height of
the Perkin Warbeck difficulty, it did valuable work.
But the important point is not the actual exploits of
the fleet—though they were creditable enough—but
the beginning of the naval development, which, followed up by Henry VIII. and triumphing under
Elizabeth, left to seventeenth and eighteenth century
England the ambition for the command of the seas.[5]

Henry's unambitious land policy made the development of the army less necessary, and therefore less
striking, than that of the navy. Fortune as usual
fought for the king. A great change in the art of
war was going on. The increasing use of gunpowder
reduced the glittering army of feudalism to im-

---

[1] The interesting question as to where Henry got his idea of a
dry dock from cannot be settled. There were no such docks in
France or Spain. Oppenheim, *Naval Accounts*, xxxiv.–xxxvii.

[2] See above, p. 164.

[3] This policy was pursued by Henry VIII. and Elizabeth. Oppenheim, *Naval Accounts*, xxix., xxx.

[4] Oppenheim, *op. cit.*, xxx., xxxiii., 84 *n.*

[5] Clowes, *Royal Navy.*

potence, and diminished the chances and therefore the frequency of rebellions. The strict watch and ward kept at Calais, Berwick, and the Tower of London—the gates and the key of the kingdom— did not escape foreign observers. In the Tower the king kept a great store of the heavy artillery that decided the fate of thrones, and the gloomy fortress on the river played a great part all through the Tudor period. The Italian observer reported that Henry meant to keep his hold on the realm he had won ; he had shown in the crises of his reign " that if worsted in the open field he would defend himself in the fortresses. . . . He did not mean to wager the Crown on the issue of a single battle." [1] By crushing the power of the great nobles, and by suppressing livery and maintenance, he secured control of the ordinary militia and left it without a rival. Thus he was able to put into the field a force which, with the help of a train of artillery, was sufficient to crush the various rebellions. The institution of the yeomen of the guard, the small company of " proved archers, strong, valiant, and bold men," that added dignity to the king's person, attracted considerable notice at the time,[2] and was later the nucleus of the standing army. There are a few expressions to be found in contemporary historians which hint at the employment of German mercenaries. Thus medieval traditions and modern methods went hand in hand.[3]

But Henry's military and naval arrangements were not the key to the situation. His was not a bloodstained military despotism ; but a rule that, depending

[1] *Ital. Rel.*, pp. 45, 46.   [2] *Ibid.*, p. 39. See above, p. 42.
[3] André, *Annales*, 127 ; Pol. Verg., 567 ; *Ital. Rel.*, 45, 47 ; Brown, No. 751. See Fortescue, *Hist. of British Army*, 1, 77-8, 108-14, for a full account of the changes introduced by Henry VII.

upon statecraft and the balancing of opposing forces, governing by persuasion and insinuation, brought the king into very intimate relations with his subjects, and only at the end showed the bold hand of tyranny. There are many glimpses of the way in which the king's compelling, if not agreeable, personality swayed events. Royal letters, comparatively few as they are, show how intimate the king's relations with his subjects were. Those who helped him at critical moments received graciously worded letters thanking them for their good and agreeable service.[1] Henry's influence over those with whom he came personally into contact seems to have been very strong. The king evidently realised the extent of his persuasive power, and was anxious to subject to it men as diverse in character as James of Scotland, the Earl of Kildare, and the Archduke Philip. All the really responsible posts in the kingdom were held by men who constantly came into contact with the king. "He was affable and both well and fair spoken," writes Bacon, "and would use strange sweetness and blandishments where he desired to effect or persuade anything he took to heart."

But the king's personal influence was used to coerce as well as to cajole. The true Tudor note, imperious, high-handed, threatening, is often struck in Henry's letters. Sir William Say, who thought of overawing the next sessions by an "unlawful assembly and conventicle," received a peremptory letter from his sovereign, ordering him to come to the king "to hear his mind in the matter."[2] The bailiffs of Lancaster who had "taken lyveries and conysaunces to

---

[1] e.g. see *Plumpton Corresp.*, Intro., xcviii.
[2] Ellis, *Orig. Letters*, I. (i.), 40.

the great damage of the town " were terrified by a
sharp letter from the king ; the men of Leicester
who " of their obstinacie and frowardnes " presumed
to use their own stalls, shambles, and ovens instead
of those " bilded for their ease " (and for the king's
profit !) were roundly rebuked.[1] The whole history
of the king's relations with the great and disaffected
city of York are a splendid instance of his autocratic
methods.[2] He did not hesitate to interfere with
municipal elections, even in the capital itself, where
in 1505 a properly elected sheriff was set aside, **and**
the return of the king's nominee at a new election
ordered and secured.

The deterioration in the method and spirit of
Henry's government in his later years has already been
mentioned. It seems as if the king's character, which
shone in adversity, was warped by success. The
harsh methods, excusable in danger, became harsher
when obedience invited a milder rule. To this period
belong the things which have been blots on the
king's fame, the detestable financial methods, the spy
system, and the base activity of the informers.

The power of the Crown threatened the liberties it
had formerly guarded. A statute of 1495, passed by
the Parliament which has so many valuable laws to
its credit,[3] had introduced the odious system of the informers, which was certainly foreign to English juris-
prudence. The Act which was passed to provide
against the corruption of jurors, authorised any individual to lay information before any justice of the
peace, or assize judge, who could institute proceedings
in his own court against the alleged offender, and try

---

[1] Campbell, *Mat.*, ii. 275, 369-70, 461-2, 476-7.
[2] *Gent. Mag.*, N. S., vol. xxxvi., p. 460.
[3] It passed 65 statutes, a very large number for the time.

the case without a jury. The only safeguard against malicious prosecution was that the informer had to pay the costs of the person wrongfully accused, if he failed to make good his charge,[1] and it appears that this safeguard was often evaded.[2] By the statute of 1504, inflicting further penalties on maintenance, the same informer system was set in motion. Here we have the first appearance of the sinister machinery of espionage and paid informers which is frequently characteristic of despotism, and the first glimpse of the process by which the court of Star Chamber degenerated into the hated weapon of weak tyranny.

This system of " secret spials," the king's " flies and familiars," has earned well-merited obloquy as an excrescence of foreign origin, alien to the English character, foisted by Henry on his people. This system of espionage, which grew out of the dangerous circumstances of the early years, when treason and rebellion were bred in rumour and whisper, suited the darker side of the king's temper, and was continued long after the dangers that might have partially excused it were over. There are many evidences of its prevalence; Henry's agents varied from the Scotch nobles, whose repulsive dealings with him have already been noticed, down to the " monk with a berde," whose investigations in Ireland met with their inextravagant reward. Even the courts of foreign princes harboured Henry's spies, and the actions of the English refugees were watched and reported on.[3] The man who spoke seditiously of the Crown—" against our majesty royal " is the sig-

---

[1] 11 Hen. VII., cap. 3 ; *Stat.*, ii. 570.   [2] *Ital. Rel.*, pp. 333-4.
[3] These underground methods are illustrated by an intrigue which took place in 1503. The story is more than usually fantastic ; it is difficult to be sure who was traitor and who spy. See *Hist. Soc. Trans.* (N. S.), xvi. 133–151, xviii. 157–195.

nificant phrase used—sat in the pillory and lost his ears.[1] Municipalities were ordered to put down "contrivers of forged news," the Bishop of Durham is ordered to search "the caskettes, males, and tronkkes" of suspected persons in his franchise.[2]

And yet such was the strength of his position, that his increasingly despotic rule became increasingly popular. His policy spared the common people and pressed hardly on wealthy individuals, depressed the great nobles and favoured the "faithful commons," preserved the constitutional forms of popular freedom, while in individual cases the weight of despotism wrested these forms to the king's own ends. Working through the venerable forms of the constitution, the king allied himself with the most stable and at the same time the most progressive elements of society. Commerce and capitalism, the forces that have been conspicuous in the modern world, were enlisted under Henry's standard. Every gift of nature and fortune marked him out for kingship, and every nerve was strained by this bold, self-willed, dominating man to secure his grip on the kingdom he had won. He never lost sight of this object. His diplomatic successes, his zeal for peace and chain of marriage alliances, his firm treatment of Ireland, and successful commercial policy, all added prestige and security to his despotism. Every success he gained abroad made him more formidable at home. When he died, the great work he had undertaken was done. He altered the balance of the English constitution for more than a century, and left to his successors the fabric of a despotism touched with the Tudor characteristics of popularity and success.

[1] *Gent. Mag.*, loc. cit., 460, 462; *City Chronicle*, 256.
[2] *L. and P. Hen. VII.*, i. 98–100.

CHAPTER VIII

IRELAND : THE RENAISSANCE : VOYAGES OF DISCOVERY

IRELAND at the accession of Henry VII. reproduced
in an exaggerated form all the evils of anarchy and
violence that were to be found in England. The central
government, too weak to check disorder even in
England, was powerless to repress outrage in distant
Ireland. There tribal war flourished; the yoke of
England lay lightly upon the people. The patriarchal
system of clan government still remained among the
Celtic tribes. The authority of the nominal government was non-existent outside the English Pale, a
strip of territory about thirty miles wide stretching
from Dublin to Dundalk along the coast nearest to
England. Where the Norman conquerors had landed
and first settled, their descendants, the Anglo-Irish
nobility, still lived, maintaining their grip upon even
this little fraction by building a chain of castles.
But Irish influences had leapt the barrier, and the
Anglo-Irish lords of the Pale became year by year less
English in their habits and sympathies and less alien
from the wild Irish who howled outside the Pale.
The strife within the ring of castles was bitterer and
more constant than the tribal wars without. The
two great ruling families—the Butlers and the Geraldines—had quarrelled with more or less violence for
centuries, and the Wars of the Roses had added fuel to

the flame.[1] They, of course, took different sides, and attached themselves fanatically to the parties of the red and the white rose, whose fortunes cannot have affected them very deeply.

The power of the English Crown was shadowy enough. English kings had borne the title of Lords of Ireland for hundreds of years; they had taken up the burden of responsibility without power, a burden, it must be confessed, they bore very negligently. It was the custom to delegate the power of the king to a Viceroy or Lord-Lieutenant, who was usually a member of the royal family. The Lord-Lieutenant, however, was but the shadow of a shade. The real power lay with another official. The plan had long been adopted of making the Irish govern themselves by appointing one of the Anglo-Irish lords as Lord-Deputy. It was the holder of this office who exercised the only authority that was recognised in Ireland, but the sword of justice in the hand of the Lord-Deputy did not reach beyond the English Pale. Even within the Pale it was the weapon of a faction rather than the arm of the law, and was quite as likely to be used against as for the far-off English king. Authority of a kind, however, the Lord-Deputy certainly had, and the office was therefore a bone of contention among the rival parties. André did no injustice to Ireland when he described it as " a country of savages, a den of thieves and murderers, where there is neither peace, love, nor concord, but only treason and the foulest deeds." [2]

Thus Henry VII. when he had secured his hold upon England, was faced by an Irish problem as acute

[1] For an account of the feuds, see *Book of Howth*, i. 177.

[2] André, Les douze triomphes de Henry VII., *Memorials* (ed. Gairdner), 147.

as any of its endless line has been. The state of Ireland was a menace to his scarcely established throne. If he were to be safe in England, he must make good his hold upon a country of which he was nominally lord, but where men of his race were safe only on the edge of the country, and where even within this strip the supreme authority was in the hands of the hereditary foes of his house.

Ownership of broad lands in Ireland had given the house of York some influence there. Richard Duke of York's period of office as Viceroy was a brilliant memory. He had declared for an independent Irish Parliament; his son, the Duke of Clarence, had adopted a similar policy of conciliation, and tradition associated the Yorkists with the dream of Irish independence. The Geraldines, who supported the Yorkist party, were the most powerful family in Ireland. One Earl of Kildare had been Lord-Deputy under Edward IV., and his son had held the office under Richard III. Their rivals, the Lancastrian Butlers, had been disgraced and attainted, and the head of the family, Thomas, Earl of Ormond, was living in England.

The king did not make any changes at first. The Duke of Bedford was given the empty title of Lord-Lieutenant,[1] and the outlawed Butlers were restored to their estates. The Earl of Ormond, who resided in England, became a member of the Council, was appointed chamberlain to the queen, and received a pension and other marks of royal favour. His bastard cousin, Sir James Ormond (who is often called Earl of Ormond by Irish writers), was practically

[1] Campbell, *Materials*, i. 384. He was to hold office for two years, but all appointments and promotions in Ireland were reserved for the Crown. In 1488 his appointment was renewed. *Ibid.*, ii. 351.

the head of the clan in Ireland, and represented the absent earl.[1]

Though the hostility of the Geraldines to a Lancastrian king was unpleasantly certain, Henry dared not interfere with them. He confirmed the Earl of Kildare in his title of Lord-Deputy; his brother, Thomas Fitzgerald, remained Chancellor of Ireland. Thus the Yorkist party, defeated in England, were still supreme in Ireland, and ready to take any opportunity of thwarting the king. Lambert Simnel's appearance was an opportunity, and Irish enthusiasm crowned him king in Dublin, and carried him over to make his ill-fated attempt on England.[2]

One or two towns, the most important of which was Waterford,[3] had held aloof from the pretender, but the rest of the country had flaunted its disloyalty. Every one of note, from the Lord-Deputy and the archbishop downwards, had dabbled in the plot. Henry obviously could not punish the whole country as rebels; clemency was the only possible attitude. Again he ignored what he could not punish, and the Irish rebels were not included in the attainders of the English Parliament.[4] Even after the battle of Stoke had disposed of Lambert Simnel, the Geraldines in Ireland remained in revolt, and Dublin itself was in their hands. The loyal town of Waterford was rewarded by a letter from Henry himself, giving them permission to capture the Geraldine rebels and seize all their goods bound for Dublin.[5]

[1] Campbell, *Materials*, i. 130, 295, 528.   [2] See above, p. 63.
[3] It had given shelter to the Butlers and other loyalists. Feeling rose so high that Kildare dared not trust his herald within the walls of the town.
[4] *Rot. Parl.*, vi. 397; *L. and P. Hen VII.*, i. 383–4; *Book of Howth* (Carew Misc. Papers.), pp. 388, 472, 473.
[5] *Carew Papers*, p. 467.

In May 1488 the king made his first cautious move towards asserting his authority in Ireland. He entrusted to Sir Richard Edgecombe, who seems to have been chosen for many delicate negotiations, the difficult task of trying to obtain some security for the future good behaviour of the Anglo-Irish lords. He was directed to receive and pardon those Irish who would submit and take a new oath of allegiance, and to proceed against rebels and traitors. He was also if possible—and this was given a very important place in the detailed instructions he received from the king—to induce the Earl of Kildare by the offer of a safe conduct to come over to England to visit the king. But Kildare excused himself, and Henry's hope of trying the effect of his personal influence upon the rebellious earl was disappointed. Edgecombe's mission was fairly successful. The mayors and corporations of Waterford, Kinsale, Drogheda, Trim, and even Dublin took the oath of allegiance, but he had a hard task with Kildare and his followers. The earl kept him waiting in Dublin over a week. When he at last arrived, Edgecombe received him without ceremony, " and made not reverence and courtesy to him or his followers." After " many fayned and unreasonable delays," the earl and his men, receiving promise of pardon, made their submission. In spite of Edgecombe's " right fell and angry words," they refused to give surety for their good behaviour. " They would rather become Irish every one of them," they said, and Henry's envoy had to content himself with drawing up a strictly worded oath. This did not please Kildare, and had to be modified. The earl, on 21st June 1488, having been " shriven and assoiled from the curse that he stood in by virtue of the Pope's Bull," swore allegiance to Henry, holding his right hand over the host. His followers and the bishops did the same, and a general pardon was proclaimed.[1] A solemn *Te Deum* was sung, the church bells rang, and the earl wore a collar of the king's livery round his neck as he rode through the streets of Dublin When Edgecombe sailed for England at the beginning of August, the widespread disaffection in Ireland was masked under a decent veil of submission and obedience.[2]

Kildare, emboldened by impunity, set up a reign of terror in Ireland. The Archbishop of Armagh, who, according to his own account, had remained loyal to Henry throughout the Lambert Simnel episode, wrote a letter of complaint bringing serious charges against the earl, and suggesting as a solution of the difficulty that he, the bishop, should be appointed as chancellor to keep the earl in check.[3] At the same time Kildare had petitioned Henry for confirmation in his office of Lord-Deputy for a period of nine or ten years, with a salary of £1000. Negotiating through John Estrete, receiver of taxes in Dublin, Henry promised him a safe conduct and favourable consideration of his petition, on condition that he appeared at Henry's court before the 1st of August 1491.[4]

[1] Edgecombe had taken with him powers for a general pardon. Campbell, *Materials*, ii. 315–317.

[2] A full account of Edgecombe's mission is given in Harris, *Hibernica*, pp. 59–77, where Edgecombe's detailed report is printed.

[3] *L. and P. Hen. VII.*, i. 383–384.

[4] *L. and P. Hen. VII.*, i. 91–3. There has been considerable difficulty in assigning an exact date to these undated instructions, but Dr. Busch has shown, I think conclusively, that the dates usually given (1486 or earlier still) are wrong. The undated letters from Kildare and his followers printed by Gairdner, *L. and P. Hen. VII.*, evidently refer to these instructions, and the latter, on the evidence brought forward by Dr. Busch (*England under the Tudors*, chap. i. note 11), may be placed in July 1490.

Nearly a year went by before Kildare wrote, excusing himself for his non-appearance in very dutiful language, on the plea that his presence in Ireland was necessary to settle the feuds between his cousins the Earl of Desmond and the Lord Bourke. He made many protestations of loyalty. " I beseech humbley your noble grace to be my gracious lord, for I am and shal be durynge my lywe your true knight and never shal be proved otherwise," and so on. Letters signed by other Irish lords supported his plea, and enlarged on his loyalty and on the fact that the north of Ireland would be destroyed by the king's Irish enemies in his absence.[1] But almost at the very moment when these dutiful letters were being sent to Henry, Kildare and Desmond were involving themselves in further treachery. The support given by Kildare to Perkin Warbeck, when he appeared in Ireland in the autumn of 1491, has already been noticed.[2] The king at last felt himself strong enough to punish Kildare's treachery, and on 11th June 1492, Walter, Archbishop of Dublin, was made Deputy in Kildare's place. Sir James Ormond, who had been the leader of the army sent in the previous December against the Irish rebels, was made Treasurer, and Alexander Plunkett Chancellor of Ireland.[3] All the Kildares were therefore deprived; Henry refused to receive Kildare's messengers, and the disgraced earl had to intercede with his old rival, the Earl of Ormond, to use his influence with the king. He denied that he had " aided, comforted, or supported the French lad," and tried to excite Ormond's jealousy about the favour shown by Henry to his " base cousin." [4] Henry remained firm, but Ormond

---

[1] *L. and. P. Hen. VII.*, i. 380-4.   [2] See above, pp. 113-5.
[3] *L. and P. Hen. VII.*, ii. 372-4   [4] *Ibid.*, ii. 53-6.

was not strong enough to keep order. The old feud
again blazed fiercely. Butlers and Geraldines wasted
each other's lands and rioted in the streets of Dublin.[1]
A meeting of the leaders held in the cathedral ended
in a free fight. Sir James Ormond took refuge in
the chapter-house, and refused to leave his refuge
until terms of agreement had been settled, and even
then a hole had to be cut in the door through which
Kildare and Ormond shook hands.

It was clear that there could be no peace in Ireland
while Ormond was in authority and Kildare in disgrace. The earl again sued for a pardon, which he
received conditionally on 22nd March 1493, promising to present himself in England before the 1st of
October. A few days later the forfeiture of Kildare's
lands was annulled, on condition that he sent his
eldest son to England within six months. This
policy of subjecting the Irish lords to the influence
of an English education was imitated and carried to
much greater lengths by Henry VIII.

In May or June 1493, Kildare and several other
Irish lords, including the Lord of Howth (to whose
lively pen we owe an account of some of their meetings with Henry) arrived at the English court. He
records a remark made by one of them, who, trembling
with fear, was walking with some English lords in a
procession. " Sir," he said to the Lord of Howth,
" there shall be no butchery done upon none of us
this time, praise be to God, for the face of the axe
is turned from us." Henry was in no mood for
executions, but he treated his late rebels to a touch
of his ironic humour when he provided as their cup-
bearer " their new king, Lambarte Simnel." " None
would have taken the cup out of his hands, but bade

[1] *Book of Howth*, p. 176.   [2] *Ibid.*

the great Devil of Hell him take before that ever he saw him." " Bring me the cup if the wine be good," said the Lord of Howth, being a merry gentleman, " and I shall drink it off for the wine's sake and mine own sake also, and for thee, as thou art, so I leave thee, a poor innocent." [1] The other Irish lords had not the assurance that came from Howth's loyalty (he had warned the king of Simnel's " mad dance " and of Perkin Warbeck's schemes), and they felt the sting of Henry's mocking words, " My masters of Ireland, you will crown apes at length." [2]

Though Kildare received a full pardon (22nd June 1493), he was not restored to the office of deputy, which was given to Lord Gormaston, one of the lords who had accompanied Kildare to London, while Ormond was given an annuity of £100 and the constableship of Limerick Castle.[3] Kildare again visited England in November in the hope of being reinstated, but in this he was disappointed.[4] Henry had resolved on trying another experiment. He abandoned the tradition of choosing the deputy from among the Irish lords, and resolved to appoint an Englishman of ability and tried loyalty, who would not be hampered in his treatment of Irish affairs by alliance with either of the rival houses.

On 12th September 1494, Prince Henry became Lord-Lieutenant of Ireland in place of the Duke of Bedford, and Sir Edward Poynings, who had already distinguished himself in Henry's service, was appointed Lord-Deputy.[5] Two other distinguished Englishmen, the Bishop of Bangor and Sir Hugh

[1] *Book of Howth*, p. 190.   [2] *Ibid.*
[3] *L. and P. Hen. VII.*, ii. 374.
[4] Dr. Busch (*Henry VII.*, p. 341) gives reasons for doubting the dates assigned by Dr. Gairdner and Bagwell to these visits.
[5] *L. and P. Hen. VII.*, ii. 374 ; Rymer, xii. 558–62.

Conway, were given the offices of chancellor and
treasurer, and new chief justices were appointed.
On 13th October 1494, Poynings landed at Howth
with a force of 1000 men,[1] and at once marched
against the rebels who had supported Perkin Warbeck in Ulster. Both Geraldines and Butlers marched
under his banner. This strange unanimity was not
to last long. Before the campaign was well begun
Kildare fell under suspicion. It was alleged that he
and the Earl of Desmond were plotting with the
King of Scotland against Henry, and the conduct
of James Fitzgerald, who seized the castle of Carlow
and defended it obstinately against Poynings, gave
some colour to the charge. The divisions in his own
ranks made Poynings give up his punitive expedition.
After the capture of Carlow, he retired to Drogheda
and summoned the Parliament which met on 1st
December 1494, and passed the famous Poynings' Acts.[2]
One statute provided that no Parliament should be
summoned in Ireland until the cause of summons
and the proposed legislation had been submitted to
and approved by the king in council, and the Irish
Parliament was then to be summoned under the great
seal of England. The second statute provided that
all Acts, "late made within the said realm of
England," should be in force in Ireland.[3] These
statutes were of permanent importance, and governed
the legislative relations of England and Ireland for
three hundred years. The Irish Parliament became

---

[1] For Poynings' commission, see *Patent Rolls*, 12 September, 10
Hen. VII., m. 18.

[2] *Irish Statutes*, p. 3 ; *Carew Papers*, pp. 456, 483–4.

[3] Disputes arose later as to the meaning of this Act, the decision
being that all statutes of the English Parliament made prior to
1495 should be in force in Ireland. Maitland, *Const. Hist.*

an echo of the king in council in England. Henry
achieved in Ireland a legal foundation for the system
of personal government, which lasted long after his
work in England had been swept away.

Less attention has been given to the other legislation of the Parliament of Drogheda, which, however, read in connection with Henry's establishment
of despotism in England, is curiously interesting.
It struck at all the forces of disruption and disorder.
Kildare was attainted for his recent treason, arrested,
and sent to England.[1] An Act was passed providing
that judges and other officials were to hold office
at the king's pleasure, not for life. Livery and
maintenance were forbidden, family war-cries were
prohibited, and licences to carry firearms had to
be obtained from the deputy. Some of the provisions of the Statutes of Kilkenny, which had
attempted to promote the spread of English customs by legislation, were re-enacted. Another
enactment shows the king's anxiety to mark off
the boundaries of the " English Pale." Every in-
habitant of the marches of Dublin, Meath, Kildare,
and Louth were to make a double ditch of six feet
above ground on the side " which meareth next unto
Irishmen." Further, an Act provided that no man
who was not born in England could be constable of
any of the eight castles of the Pale. The necessity
for these provisions proves the weakness of the
English colony in Ireland, and illustrates the cautious
character of the king's methods, which succeeded
where a more ambitious policy would have failed.[2]

Henry had also attempted to deal with the financial

---

[1] *Carew Papers*, pp. 483–4.
[2] At the same time Henry was making strict inquiry as to the
Irishmen resident in England. *City Chron.*, p. 207.

problem. The royal revenue had greatly declined and Ireland did not even pay for the expenses of government. In 1495, William Hattcliffe, one of the clerks of account in the royal household, who had gained experience of the king's methods, was sent over to Ireland, nominally as under-treasurer, but with very wide powers. He practically overhauled the whole system of expenditure, investigated the returns of sheriffs, and audited the lord treasurer's accounts. His accounts, which are minute and curious,[1] deal with varied items of expenditure—the payment of English troops in Ireland, subsidies to Irish allies and the general expenses of government. Many payments to spies, who were generally priests or monks, are entered. One visited the marches of the Pale to report on the habits of the people there; another went to Munster to spy upon Earl Desmond, Perkin Warbeck, and other rebels, and so on.[2] The accounts include Hattcliffe's personal expenses and detailed items like the price of the key of the Dublin customs house. In spite of Hattcliffe's care, the revenue obtained from Ireland, though possibly adequate in time of peace, was insufficient in time of war or rebellion.

In July 1495, Perkin Warbeck was again in Ireland, and the country was in arms in his support. Poynings himself marched against him, but the joint attack of Warbeck and Desmond on Waterford was beaten off by the mayor and inhabitants before the king's troops arrived.[3] Reinforcements and supplies of money were sent over to Ireland, and Hattcliffe's accounts

---

[1] An extract is printed in Gairdner, *L. and P. Hen. VII.*, ii. 297–318. Instructions for this financial inquiry are printed pp. 64–67, and are typical of the king's careful methods.

[2] *L. and P. Hen. VII.*, ii. 298, 299.   [3] See above, p. 130.

showthat the expenditure largely exceeded the revenue. Even when the pretender had gone, peace was not restored. The practice of employing Irish chiefs to fight against their rebellious fellow-countrymen made a state of war profitable to many. Sir James Ormond, that " deep and far-reaching man," lies under the suspicion of being at the bottom of many of the later disturbances. He found his profit in stirring up sedition, which he was later employed to put down.[1]

The Geraldines also, incensed at Kildare's detention, were making raids on the English district and keeping the whole country in an uproar. The king found that the earl's people gave him more trouble when he was in England than ever before, and it seemed politic to give him another chance of proving his loyalty. The personal equation may have counted for something. The *Book of Howth* gives several stories of Kildare's stay in England. We are told that he was " but half an innocent man without great knowledge or learning, but rudely brought up according to the usages of his country." His blunt speech and unpolished manner—" oft in his talk he thou'd the king and the rest of his council "—seem to have amused the king. He was called upon to answer various charges brought against him by the Bishop of Meath, one of them being a riot when the earl chased him into a church and, finding him kneeling bare-headed in the chancel, " By Saint Bride," said the earl, " were it not that I know that my prince would be offended with me, I could find it in my heart to lay my sword upon your

[1] *L. and P. Hen. VII.*, ii. Intro. xl. As Dr. Gairdner has pointed out, it would seem that just when Kildare grew loyal, Ormond became seditious.

shaven crown," and so took the bishop. To charges
of this kind the earl protested he could find no ready
answer ; " the bishop was learned and so was not he,
and those matters was long agone out of his mind,
though he had done them, and so forgotten." He
took the opportunity to tell three " good tales of
this vicious prelate;" whereupon the king and his
lords " could not hold their laughter, but the earl
never changed countenance." The king advised him
to choose a wise counsellor; and his answer introduces
the story, which, though well known, must be repeated
as one of the few which give a glimpse of Henry in
his lighter moods. " 'Shall I choose now,' said the
earl. ' If you so think good,' answered the king.
' Well, I can see no better man than you, and by
Saint Bride ! I will choose none other.' ' Well,'
said the king, ' by Saint Bride it was well requisite
for you to choose so, for I thought your tale could
not well excuse your doings unless you had well
chosen.' ' Do you think that I am a fool ? ' said
the earl. ' No,' said he, ' I am a man in deed both
in the field and in the town.' The king laughed
and made sport; and said, ' A wiser man might have
chosen worse.' ' Well,' said the bishop, ' he is as
you see, for all Ireland cannot rule yonder gentleman.'
' No,' said the king, ' then he is meet to rule all
Ireland,' and so made the earl Deputy of Ireland
during his life, and so sent him to the country with
great gifts." [1]

Henry had the tact and instinct for judging men
possessed by all the Tudors. Though tenacious of his
dignity, he appreciated plain speaking from a bold
man, and found a way of profiting by the daring
that made Kildare formidable in opposition. Kil-

[1] *Book of Howth*, pp. 180–1.

dare's attainder was reversed, he was restored to his titles and dignities and his appointment as Lord Deputy.[1] He had evidently fallen much under the king's influence. He had married as his second wife Elizabeth St. John, Henry's first cousin, and he left his son Gerald as a hostage at court. Henceforward he does not seem to have wavered in his allegiance.

Hattcliffe's accounts prove that the work of reducing Ireland to order was going on. A subsidy was collected at double the old rates, but there were still heavy expenses in maintaining the English troops and subsidiary Irish levies.[2]

The best evidence of the success of Henry's Irish policy is the lack of support obtained by Perkin Warbeck when he reappeared before the city of Cork on 20th July 1497. In this most critical moment of a difficult reign, great issues hung on the fate of the adventurer's last bid for fortune. The hope of Irish support was a vital point in his plans. That support, however, he failed to get. His former friends had been won over by Henry, and even Desmond failed him. The city of Waterford once more proved its loyalty, and fitted out four ships to give chase to Perkin. It was obvious that Ireland was no longer a happy hunting ground for traitors and pretenders. The city of Waterford received a letter of thanks from the king, a cap of maintenance, and the proud title of *Urbs intacta*.[3]

For the rest of the reign; affairs in Ireland did not call for Henry's interference. There were the usual

[1] 6th August 1496 ; *Rot. Parl.*, vi. 481–2 ; *Stat.*, ii. 612–3 ; *Excerpta Hist.*, 109.

[2] *L. and P. Hen. VII.*, ii. pp. 316–7.

[3] Smith, *Waterford*, printing the king's letter. See above, pp. 155–6.

tribal wars, but Kildare managed his country without
appealing to the king. Henry reaped the reward
of having put in authority a man who did not shirk
responsibility.   There is evidence that the king's
influence and authority over the deputy remained
untouched, and Kildare carried out his policy of
extending Anglo-Irish influences and of depressing
the natives.   His work was made easier by the death
of his old rival, Sir James Ormond, in July 1497 ; this
brought the end of the feud.

The king's policy of Anglicising Ireland was pushed
on rapidly.   Cork was visited and garrisoned by Kildare, and the citizens were forced to take the oath of
allegiance to Henry.   A Parliament held by Kildare
in 1498, after punishing the Irish who had supported
Perkin Warbeck, passed Acts discouraging the use
of Irish weapons.   Dwellers within the Pale were
to wear English dress and use English weapons, the
native darts and spears being forbidden.[1]

In 1503 Kildare again visited England at Henry's
order.   The king was evidently convinced that his
authority over Kildare was too well established to
require a hostage for his good faith, and he allowed
the earl's eldest son Gerald, with his English wife,
to return with him to Ireland.   The wearisome story
of the wars waged by Kildare in Ulster and Con-
naught against a rebellious grandson can fortunately
be omitted.   The only point of importance is the
increasing use of field artillery, which gave a great
advantage to the troops of the deputy and made
it easier to put down rebellion.   In these wars
Kildare's side was the English side, and his victories
meant the further spread of English influence.   In
the battle of Knoctoe, 1504, the deputy opposed

---

[1] Bagwell, *op. cit.*, i. 118 ; Gilbert, *Irish MSS.*, vol. iii.

to a wild Irish horde a small but comparatively disciplined force in which the representatives of peaceful civilisation—churchmen and lawyers—were too numerous for the tastes of many of his supporters.[1] Kildare gained a signal victory—" The Irish durst not fight a battle never after with the English Pale," [2] we are told—and his good service was rewarded by Henry. Kildare became a Knight of the Garter and his son Lord Treasurer of Ireland. A few years later, in 1508, he held a Parliament which granted a subsidy,[3] and at Henry's death his deputy's authority was unchallenged in the Anglo-Irish district, which he is credited with having greatly enlarged. According to the Irish chronicler, " Peace, golden peace, descended upon the country." Even Ireland, "the standing failure of English sovereigns, had been handled by Henry not wholly without success." [4] For the first time submission paid better than rebellion. The king had left his mark on Ireland.

There is an obvious danger of exaggerating the influence of the Renaissance on contemporary England, of throwing back to its first beginnings our knowledge of its effect in its later stages. In the beginning it was destructive, not constructive. It put men out of conceit with their traditional studies, habits, and ideals, without at first giving them anything in their place. Intellectual chaos was added to social upheaval without any one being consciously the gainer. There was an absolute revolt against medieval mysticism. The Papacy and Empire lost the support

---

[1] *Book of Howth*, pp. 181–5. Kildare's speech before the battle reminded his men that they fought for the honour of their prince.
[2] *Ibid.*
[3] *Irish Stat.*, 24 Hen. VII.; *L. and P. Hen. VII.*, ii. App. 380.
[4] *Social Eng.* (ed. Traill), ii. p. 613.

of uncritical reverence for their age-long claims to universal dominion. Viewed in the light of religious speculation, ecclesiastical sloth appeared more blatant, but found no cure. The effect on the choicer spirits of the age was disturbing, the effect on the mass of the people was practically *nil*. It was not until long after the death of Henry VII., that the results of the Renaissance on English society could be seen. Yet the first movements of the new spirit are none the less interesting for being obscure.

From Italy, the Mecca of scholasticism, came the impulse for the emancipation of learning. Duke Humphrey of Gloucester, the princely patron of Italian scholars, the benefactor of university libraries, had been the pioneer of the new learning in England. He was followed by a band of churchmen and scholars who went abroad to study the revived classical learning. Next came William Selling, and his disciples Linacre, Grocyn, Lily, and Latimer, who laid the foundations of the new learning in England. The beginning of the new reign and the first harvest of the Renaissance in England were almost simultaneous. Linacre and Grocyn returned to England about 1490, and established the study of Greek at Oxford. A revival of learning and of activity at both the universities followed. New foundations became fashionable. The king's mother founded two colleges at Cambridge—St. John's and Christ's. The Bishop of Ely founded Jesus College ; the king himself gave large sums for the completion of King's College, founded by his pious uncle, and endowed scholarships in the university. At Oxford, Brazenose was founded by the Bishop of Lincoln, and Corpus Christi by the Bishop of Winchester. Grocyn was followed in his humanist study of the Scriptures by

Colet, who is described by Vergil as distinguished by the virtue of his soul and mind and by the purity of his life and manners. He was honoured, he says, among the English almost like a second St. Paul the Apostle.[1] Thus it is in this reign that theological criticism made the first breach in the wall of medieval theology through which poured all the changes of the Reformation.

The critical spirit found a sphere of destructive action in the practice as well as in the theory of the Church. It was an age of great secularisation. From the bishops, Morton, Fox, and Warham, who were the king's ministers, down to the humblest monks in the abbey of St. Albans, there is evidence that the churchmen of the late fifteenth century were escaping from the restrictions of the contemplative life. There had been no religious movement in England since the days of Wycliff. Learning was dead in the Church; the average churchman who had intellectual gifts employed them in the intricacies of a barren scholasticism, and the rank and file found an outlet for their energies in the ordinary pursuits of laymen. The ambitious man heaped up wealth; bishoprics were sold, pluralities were common, and he found it easy to buy his steps upwards. Men whose ambition took another form joined in the scramble for land which is a feature of the early Tudor period. Parsons quarrelled with their parishioners, and lawsuits between the great abbots and their lay neighbours were frequent. Churchmen won an unenviable notoriety by their high-handed methods of dealing with commons and wastes, enclosing lands for their parks. Like his neighbour the squire, the abbot

[1] Pol. Verg., op. cit., 618. He mentions Colet's foundation of St. Paul's School and the appointment of William Lily as master.

occupied himself hunting and hawking, and rode
abroad attended by troops of servants wearing his
livery.[1] The life of the average churchman was not
worse, but it was not conspicuously better, than that
of the laymen he mixed with. Many of the lower ranks
of the clergy wasted their time and brought their calling
into disrepute. The sermons preached by the friars at
St. Paul's Cross attacked the clergy for wearing lay
dress, carrying swords and daggers, and frequenting
taverns, and drunkenness and brawling were common.
The Convocation of Canterbury in 1486 had to deal
with the matter openly.[2] The language of the Act of
1485, which gave the bishops power to commit clerks
to prison for immorality, suggests the prevalence of
grosser evils.[3]

There was a constant complaint that church buildings were allowed to fall into decay, that hospitality
was neglected, that scholarship was dead, and that,
owing to the decay of the universities, there were
no longer any scholars to teach divinity or preach
in cathedrals and monasteries. Venality spread like
a canker through the Church. The popes, who sold
bulls, benefices, indulgences, licences for non-residence
—a crying scandal— and traded away their spiritual
power for pence, found apt imitators on a smaller
scale. Henry VII. rewarded his faithful ministers
with bishoprics. He even thought of a bishopric for
the rascally Spanish ambassador—and his nobles
found Church preferment for their servants. Boys
of ten or twelve who had obtained a master's degree
after a year's study at Oxford or Cambridge became
venerable archdeacons before they knew how to sing
matins. " Benefices," writes Dudley in his *Tree of the*

---

[1] *Star Chamber Cases*, ed. Leadam (Selden Soc.).
[2] Wilkins, *Concilia*, iii. 618, 619, 620.   [3] *Stat.*, ii. 500-1.

Commonwealth, " are given not to the virtuous or the learned, but to such as can be good and profitable stewards of houses and clerks of your kitchens . . . and to such as can surely and wisely be receivers of your rents and revenues, and rather than fail will boldly distrain a poor man's cattle and drive them to pound till they starve from hunger."

But the corruption of the Church attracted the notice of these Renaissance scholars. Colet and Erasmus poured out a flood of destructive criticism. The follies and self-seeking of the clergy came under the lash of biting irony that had not spared the occupants of St. Peter's chair. Dean Colet's sermons at St. Paul's were an outspoken attack against the corrupt lives of the clergy, and upon certain doctrines of the Church, which drew down upon him the censure of the Bishop of London. Colet was, however, saved from prosecution as a heretic by a powerful protector—Archbishop Warham. It was obvious that the new spirit was in the ascendant at Henry's court, and its ultimate triumph was foreshadowed.

The new reforming spirit found another outlet in the visitation of the monasteries. Archbishop Morton had been one of the first Oxford scholars affected by Italian influences, and being impressed by the need for monastic reform, obtained from Pope Innocent a bull for a visitation. A terrible indictment was brought against the Abbey of St. Albans. Morton charged the abbot with having " laid aside the pleasant yoke of contemplation and all regular observances, hospitality, alms, and other offices of piety. . . The ancient rule of your order is deserted," he wrote, " not a few of your fellow monks giving themselves over to a reprobate life. . . ." He accused the abbot of having appointed as prioress of the neighbouring and dependent nunnery a woman who had already been married, and who lived in adultery with the monks. All the worst charges brought by anti-Catholics against the monastic system were made in the case of this monastery. The abbot was said to have sold the common property of the abbey, cut down and sold the woods, taken away the jewels, and so on; and the Archbishop's letter stated that "the brethren of the abbey live with harlots and mistresses publicly and continuously within the precincts of the monastery." [1] Similar scandals were revealed by the visitation of the diocese of Norwich. Incidental notices prove that similar disorders were rife up and down the country. The famous priory of Walsingham, which was much favoured by Henry VII., shared in the general demoralisation. The Prior of Bath swaggered about followed by eighteen men wearing his livery, while his neglected church fell into ruin and decay. The Abbot of Malmesbury brutally ill-treated his dependents, the Prior of Sheen was foully murdered by one of his monks. Though serious vice was less common than secularisation, it was evident that the vital spirit of monasticism had fled. [2] The rapidity with which the Reformation took root in England and the violence of the reaction against the faith of centuries are explained.

As the Church let its high standard slip, its influence declined. It had lost its spiritual and intellectual

---

[1] Wilkins, *Concilia*, iii. 632-4. There has been much discussion about the case of St. Albans. See *Eng. Hist. Rev.*, xxii. 365-6, xxiv. 91-6, 319-21.

[2] *Visitation of Norwich, Visitation of Southwell* (Camden Soc., 1888, 1890); *Bath Chartul.* (Somers Sec. Roc.), Intro. lxvii., lxviii.; *Star Chamber Cases* (Selden Soc.), Intro. xxii.; *City Chron.*, 259.

leadership, and England was ready for the seed sown by Renaissance scholars, the growth from which forced its way through the thickets of medieval scholasticism, and challenged the system of ecclesiastical dominion that had made learning the monopoly of one class.

But as usual in this reign of contrasts, old traditions flourished side by side with the new thought. While there might be toleration for new forms of inquiry, there was none for old forms of heresy. The Church that had abandoned her great ideals still claimed empire over the intellect. Heretics were ferreted out and set in the pillory, those who refused to recant being burnt at the stake. In 1494, a woman over eighty years of age was burnt at Smithfield for nine articles of heresy. In one case it appears that a priest convicted of heresy was converted by the exhortations of the king himself, " whereof his grace had great honour," but the stake still claimed its victim.[1] In many other places, Canterbury, Norwich, and Salisbury, and at Amersham in Buckingham, Lollardry seems to have flourished. Thus fires were burning at Smithfield, a few hundred yards from the spot where Dean Colet's eloquence was stirring up a much more formidable revolt against Church doctrines.

Thus the influence of the Renaissance had spread from Oxford to the Church. The new monarchy was to prove a powerful agent in spreading the new ideas among the nobles and gentry, and ultimately among the middle classes. The Italian influences at court were considerable. The king employed many Italians

[1] *City Chron.*, 200, 208, 222, 226. A few heretics were pardoned on condition that, for the rest of their lives, they wore gowns embroidered with a cross and a faggot in red.

in his service. Giovanni Gigli, sent to England as
a papal collector, became Henry's diplomatic agent
at Rome, and was rewarded with the bishopric of
Worcester. He it was who celebrated the king's
marriage with Elizabeth of York in an elaborate
Latin poem. Silvestro Gigli, his nephew, was Henry's
Master of the Ceremonies, and later was resident
ambassador at Rome, He was a man of letters,
and corresponded with Erasmus. Peter Carmeliano,
besides being Latin secretary and one of the king's
chaplains, seems to have been a court poet as well.
He was followed as Latin secretary by Ammonio
and Peter Vannes, both of whom were Italians.
Adrian de Castello, the collector of Peter's Pence
in England, also passed into Henry's service, became his agent at Rome, and later ambassador to
Alexander the Sixth. Of all the Italians employed
by Henry VII., the most famous was the historian
Polydor Vergil, who came to England in 1501 as
sub-collector of Peter's Pence. He was taken into
the king's favour, became Archdeacon of Wells, and
resided at court. His famous *Anglicæ Historiæ Libri*,
a book which marks a very great advance in English
historical work, being carried out on a large scale and
in a critical spirit, was begun in Henry's lifetime
and with his encouragement.

It was design, not chance, which led Henry to
employ all these Italians. He found they understood
and sympathised with his aims, as his backward
subjects could not do, and they had had a diplomatic
training of a kind unknown in England. Meanwhile
the king reproduced—on a very modest scale, it is
true—the patronage of literature characteristic of the
Italian princes. Those few of his own subjects who
reached any eminence in literature enjoyed court

favour. The foremost of these was John Skelton, who wrote various poems on the royal children and became the tutor of Prince Henry, for whom he wrote the *Speculum Principis*, a treatise which is now lost. His courtly poems gave little promise of the satiric power which he displayed later, in the reign of his pupil. Henry was ready to encourage any talent that displayed itself. Bernard André was retained to sing the king's praises in pompous Latin, but his turgid rhetoric cannot be taken very seriously as literature. Distinguished men like Erasmus were welcomed at court.[1] The king spent considerable sums on buying books. He added a fair number of books to the royal library, paying as much as £25 to one Frenchman, and gave rewards to encourage the new art of printing.

The education of the royal children represented the triumphs of Renaissance ideals of culture at Henry's court. Prince Henry—the young Octavius of England as he was called—was unusually accomplished.   In his boyhood he was a type of the brilliant figures of the Renaissance period. He had great personal beauty, was extremely musical, a graceful dancer, a fine sportsman, no mean Latinist, and a very fair poet, without a touch of the intellectual torpor and lack of physical grace supposedly characteristic of the barbarous English.

The magnificence of the first of the Tudors was displayed after Italian fashions. The king bought Italian furniture, sent to Italy for cloth of gold and damask. Gorgeous church vestments were made and embroidered for him in Florence. Even the royal tomb was entrusted to an Italian, Pietro Torregiano,

---

[1] Erasmus, however, was disappointed at not receiving more tangible proofs of royal favour.

and its appearance in a chapel which is a masterpiece of English perpendicular work, is typical of the conflict between medieval and Renaissance influences.

The same influences also reached England through the king's diplomatic relations with Italian princes. Though there had been official communications on commercial matters between England and the State of Venice for a long time, the first formal embassy from Venice was sent to London in 1497. Henry was on very friendly terms with the Dukes of Milan, Ferrara, and Urbino. The last was honoured with the Order of the Garter. He occasionally exchanged presents with the King of England, Henry receiving on one occasion a painting by Raphael, which must have been one of the first examples of the Italian masters ever seen in England, where painting, except in the form of illuminations, was almost unknown.

Henry VII. was the first English sovereign since Henry III. who cared in the slightest degree for art. With his reign the long barren period ended, and a new era began.[1] He is believed to have invited the Flemish artist Jan Grossaert or Mabuse to England, though the portrait often ascribed to him, which is said to be that of Henry's three children, is probably not by his hand. He certainly obtained the king's patronage, and several pictures of the Flemish school, notably the portraits of Lady Margaret and the "Marriage of Henry VII. with Elizabeth of York," were painted by Flemish artists in London during Henry's reign.

But it is from his interest in building and architecture that Henry's ambition to be a patron of art is best realised. A beautiful palace arose at Richmond out of the ashes of the royal residence (itself built by

[1] *Social England*, ii. 680-3.

Henry) at Sheen.   New York was done at St. George's Chapel, Windsor, and Baynard's Castle was rebuilt. The noblest monument of all, the Chapel of Henry VII. at Westminster, which still holds the dust of the Tudor despots, is a glorious example of Gothic architecture, and its stately splendour is beyond all verbal tribute.

The king's example was followed by his subjects; from his ministers Bray and Morton down to the citizens of provincial towns like Bristol, every one of wealth and importance built largely and splendidly.[1]

Thus the light hitherto held by a small band of University men began to spread through England, and the motive power of this diffusion was the new monarchy.   Henry VII. focussed the forces that during his reign transformed England from medievalism to modernism.   The despotism he established made the Crown the centre of society.   His court became the spring of national activity, and gave a definite lead to society.   The great princes of feudalism had been replaced by smaller men, above whom the king reigned in lonely splendour.   The descendant of the feudal baron left his isolated castle to enter the king's service.   The social influences radiating from the king's court reached the provinces, and the households of the nobles employed about the king echoed the ideas of the court.

" From the prince," wrote Sir Thomas More, " as from a perpetual well-spring cometh among the people the flood of all that is good or evil." [2] Henry VII. was the source of power, the creator of employment, the dispenser of office.   The court led as a stepping stone to the great careers of arms,

[1] *City Chron.*, pp. 226, 234 ; *Social England*, ii. 637-8, 676-8.
[2] More, *Utopia* (ed. Lumby), 25.

diplomacy, and administrative employment; and thus Italian influences at court found an ever widening sphere of influence. Even those who had no special leanings to scholarship, found the very fabric of their lives, their habits, customs, tastes and occupations, the houses they lived in, and the clothes they wore, being imperceptibly but permanently changed by the influence of new ideas imported from the Continent.

In addition to the direct influence and imitation of the court, another force led to the spread of a liberal education. Posts in the king's service were thrown open to men of the class hitherto shut out by birth from any hope of official employment. Diplomatic posts hitherto monopolised by foreigners were given by Henry to his subjects, and foreign diplomacy became more important during Henry's reign than it had ever been before. Permanent embassies brought England more closely in touch with the Continent, and afforded opportunity of distinction to the ambitious. Stile, Savage, Wingfield, and above all Wolsey, were the front rank in the army of English diplomatists who have represented their country in the courts of Europe ever since, acting as a centre of cosmopolitan influences on their return.[1]

It is no inconsiderable change that the statecraft of the new monarchy brought about. Military skill was no longer the only vital part of a gentleman's training; if he was to succeed, he must be educated as well. The standard had been exceptionally low. The

[1] Erasmus found England much less insular than might have been expected; foreign influences were strong, and there was a thirst for knowledge like that on the Continent. Froude suggests that the Englishman of the reign of Henry VII. was more in touch with the feeling of the Continent than he is at the present day. Men of birth spoke one universal language, and the barrier of religious differences had not arisen.

average nobleman read little, wrote indifferently, and
spelt vilely ;[1] even a merchant carrying on a considerable business could only just make himself
intelligible;[2] the mass of the country gentry could
neither read nor write. By throwing open a career
to men of talent, Henry set on foot a movement,
which by the reign of Elizabeth had filled England
with the " Italianate Englishman," and had given
even the middle classes some interest in literature.

Another great influence for popularising learning
had been introduced eight years before the accession
of Henry VII. Caxton had set up his printing-press
in Westminster, and by the date of his death (1491),
about 95 books had been printed. Caxton was
followed by Wynkyn de Worde, and between 1477
and 1500 about 400 books were printed in England.[3]
The introduction of printing, though it had little
influence at the time, is important of course as
perhaps one of the strongest forces that has ever
moulded the mind of the nation.

The reign of Henry VII. saw the beginning of
mighty changes. The critical spirit was thrusting
itself into all the dark places of medieval thought,
questioning the foundations of accepted beliefs.
Under this new influence medieval priestcraft and king-
craft gave way to a new theology and a new monarchy.
Feudalism and manorialism were replaced by the
new divisions of capital and labour, and from the decay
of communism sprang the triumph of individualism.

The voyages of discovery that took place in the
reign of Henry VII. are interesting rather as the
first chapter in the story of maritime adventure

---

[1] The Earl of Suffolk's letters are an example of this.
[2] *Cely Papers.*   [3] *Social England,* ii. 726, 732.

which carried the English trade and flag all over the
world than for their intrinsic importance. Great
daring and enterprise met with little practical result.
It has often been said that Henry discouraged the
adventurers, and, by his short-sighted greed, let slip a
golden opportunity. But this seems to be a deduction
from the theory of the conduct that could be expected
from a man of avaricious temper rather than to be
founded on fact. Henry certainly missed his first
chance. He lacked imagination, and, sated with
adventures in his youth, was disinclined to embark
in speculation; but the Spanish success was a turning-
point, and all the evidence goes to prove that he
helped the later attempts generously as long as they
had any reasonable prospect of success. Their failure
was due, not to the king's apathy, but to the chimera
of the North-west Passage.

When Bartholomew Columbus appeared at the
English court to try and enlist the king's sympathy for
his brother's schemes, Henry had only been a few years
on the throne, and all his resources were taxed by
his difficult position. The idea of trying to find a
new trade route to the East was sufficiently attractive
for the king to promise help in an indefinite way.
But Henry's pre-occupations spelt delay, and in the
meantime Christopher Columbus convinced Ferdinand,
made his great voyage, and discovered the New World
for the King of Spain. Henry learnt the result of
Columbus's voyage in 1493, and from that moment
his attitude changed; he had found out that the

---

[1] The question as to how far Henry had committed himself to
Bartholomew Columbus is a difficult one. It is discussed by Dr.
Busch (p. 360), who comes to the conclusion that the king probably
promised help. The main point, however, that Henry's promise
came too late, is indisputable.

visionary scheme had resulted in profit to his rival, the King of Spain.

Meanwhile Henry's own subjects had taken up the idea of finding a new route to the East.   Trade with India had been cut off by the conquests of the Turks, and Englishmen were fired with the hope of discovering a North-west Passage, which would bring them again into touch with the riches of the East. It was this will-of-the-wisp which led the English adventurers to waste their strength in vain on the inhospitable shores of North-East America.

Brazil, the fabled isle of gold and spices, was another goal of their hopes.   Bristol was the centre of the maritime spirit.   If we reject as doubtful the story that Christopher Columbus sailed from Bristol to the North-west in 1477, we are on firm ground with the voyage of Thomas Lloyd from the same city in 1480, in search of Brazil.   Ayala, writing in 1498, said, " The people of Bristol have for the last six or seven years sent out every year, two, three, or four light ships in search of the island of Brazil and the seven cities." [1] The moving spirit in these adventures was John Cabot, a Genoese, who was therefore a man of some experience when he applied to Henry for help in 1495.[2] Henry was by this time aware of the importance of the Spanish discovery,[3] and gave Cabot a much more encouraging reception than Columbus.   On March 5, 1496, the king issued letters patent to his well-beloved John Cabot, citizen of Venice, and his sons, giving him

---

[1] Berg., *Spanish Cal.*, i. p. 177.

[2] *Ibid.*, p. 89.   The King of Spain wished his ambassador to dissuade Henry from these " uncertain enterprises," which " could not be executed without prejudice to them and the King of Portugal."

[3] *Excerpta Hist.*, p. 92, contains a notice of the reception of a Spaniard who gave the king a present of spices.

power and authority to sail east, west, and north,
with five ships under the royal standards and the
flag of England, to discover any islands or territories
hitherto unknown to Christendom. He was empowered in the king's name to take possession of and
subdue any country he found, and rule it and its castles,
towns, and villages, as Henry's " vassal and governor,
locum tenens, and deputy." All this the Cabot
family were to do at their own expense. The profits
they might retain for themselves with the exception
of one-fifth, which was to be paid to the king, who
graciously exempted them from customs duties on
any merchandise they might bring back with them
from the newly discovered lands.[1] Henry, however,
was rather more generous than the terms of the
letters patent suggest, and, " at the besy request
and supplicacion of Cabot," he manned and pro-
visioned one ship in the expedition,[2] which sailed
from Bristol in May 1497.[3] The results, however,
did not come up to the sanguine hopes of the voyagers.
On 24th June, they touched the mainland of North
America, probably on the coasts of Labrador. On
these frozen shores they discovered no " castles,
cities, or villages " to be occupied in the king's name,
nor did they return rich with gold and spices. They
sailed first south and then north-west without coming
across any trace of human occupation except snares set
to catch game and a needle for making nets. They
were able to report, however, the existence of rich
fishing grounds which would make England inde-

---

[1] The patent is printed in full, Rymer, *Fœdera*, xii. 595–6.

[2] This is founded on a statement in the *City Chronicle*, p. 224.

[3] The date of this voyage was formerly in dispute, 1494 being
assigned to it by some writers, but the correct date 1497 has long
been ascertained. Harrisse, *Jean et Sébastien Cabot*, 52–60 ; Biddle,
Memoir of Sebastian Cabot, 71–9 ; Busch., *op. cit., p.* 361.

pendent of Iceland.[1] The reward of £10 paid on
10th August " to hyme that founde the new Isle " is
not the measure of Henry's satisfaction, for Cabot
received a grant of £20 a year to be paid from the
customs of Bristol.[2] Cabot was styled the " Great
Admiral." He was the man of the hour. " These
English run after him like mad people," was the
comment of a Venetian visitor.

Preparations were now made for an adventure on
a much larger scale, which roused Ayala to protest
to Henry that the land he was in search of was
already in the possession of the King of Spain, " But
though I gave him my reasons," he wrote, " he
did not like them." [3] Ayala and Puebla speak of
the whole expedition as equipped by Henry, and
recent research has supported this view.[4] The king
realised that great issues were at stake, and proved
it by giving his support during these very critical
years.

Cabot's second expedition of five ships sailed in
the spring of 1498, with the object of revisiting the
recently discovered land, and attempting to open up

[1] Harrisse, *op. cit.*
[2] *Excerpta Historica*, p. 113; *Pat.*, Dec., 1497.
[3] Berg., *Spanish Cal.*, i. p. 177.
[4] Busch, p. 361; *Excerpta Hist.*, 116, 117; Stow, *Annales*, 482;
Berg., 177; Harrisse quoting Puebla, pp. 328–9; Brown, No. 750.
Harrisse, *op. cit.* (p. 102), Cunningham, *op. cit.* (pp. 419, 444), and
Thorold Rogers, *Hist. of Agriculture*, iv., Pref. ix., xii., take the view
that Henry gave little help, "which view," says Dr. Busch, "really
has nothing in its favour except its antiquity." Busch, p. 361.
Harrisse's words are a frank acknowledgment of his reason for
rejecting the evidence of Puebla, Ayala, and the *City Chronicle* :
" Aussi ne croyons-nous pas, malgré l'expression employée par
Puebla et Ayala, que les cinq navires furent expédiés aux frais de
Henry VII., dont l'avarice était notoire." The tradition of Henry's
blind avarice has grown into a myth which some writers prefer to
any evidence they may find contradicting it.

trade with it.[1]   John Cabot seems to have died during
the voyage, and one ship damaged by storm had to
put back into an Irish port.   The voyage cannot have
been a great success.   No reference to the adventurers'
return has been found, though we know that the
squadron was expected back in September 1498,
and that Sebastian Cabot returned in safety.   He is
never heard of again, however, in Henry's employment.[2]
The king had lost interest in voyages of discovery;
the results of his attempts to share with Spain the
riches of the New World had been disappointing.
He gave no support to the subsequent voyages
made by Bristol citizens,[3] which all being directed
to the north-west failed to find the " Spice Islands."
They opened up the Newfoundland fishery, however,
and this attracted the king's notice.   In 1501 he
granted a patent to three Portuguese merchants
residing in Bristol to sail on voyages of discovery
under the royal flag.[4]   The language of the patent
suggests a revival of the king's hopes.   They were
empowered to take possession of any land they found,
to carry English subjects to settle there, to govern
the new lands, appointing deputies to govern towns
and cities, and make and execute laws.   The patentees
were to enjoy the office of King's Admiral, were to
have exclusive rights of trading for ten years, and of
importing gold, silver, and precious stones.   Further,
they were empowered to punish any one who visited

[1] The letters patent authorising the expedition were dated
Feb. 3, 1498. They have been printed by Biddle, *Mem. of S. Cabot,*
pp. 76–7, and by Harrisse, pp. 327–8.

[2] There is a period in Cabot's life of which practically nothing is
known. Biddle, *op. cit.*, pp. 91–3.

[3] It is curious that none of these voyages are referred to in Ricart's
Calendar, ed. L. Toulmin Smith.

[4] 19th March 1501; printed by Biddle, App. 312–20.

the new land without permission. This expedition
must have reached America or Newfoundland, for
in the following year there were in London three
men found by the Bristol merchants in an " Iland
ferre beyonde Irelond ; the which were clothid in
Beestes Skynnes, and ete Raw fflessh, and Rude in
their demeanure as Beestes." [1] Their wildness, however must have yielded to the civilising influences of
fifteenth-century London with some rapidity, for two
years later two of them, who were kept by Henry
at Westminster, were " clothed like Englishmen and
could not be discerned from Englishmen." [2]   In
September 1502, the Bristol merchants " that have
bene in the New founde Launde " were granted £20
from the king's privy purse.[3] Some members of the
expedition obtained another patent in December
1502, similar to the first, but with an extension of the
time of exclusive trading to forty years, and the
voyages continued till the end of the reign.

As we have seen, they were only partially successful.   In spirit and object they were worthy of the
voyages of the Elizabethan period ; they hoped to
plant English settlers beyond the sea,[4] and acquire
new land for the English Crown, but the contrast of
actual achievement with these high hopes is pathetic.
The explorers found no territory suitable for commerce
or colonisation, though the fact that such a development was contemplated is very interesting. A few
rare animals, Newfoundland hawks, " wild cattes,"
and " popyngays " presented to the king, and the

[1] *City Chron.*, p. 258.   [2] Stow, *Annales*, p. 485.
[3] *Excerpta Historica*, 129.   In January of this year " the men
who found Thisle " had received £5.   *Ibid.*, p. 126.
[4] Priests sailed in the ships that the Christian faith might follow
the English flag.

unhappy " wilde men " who dragged out their existence in Westminster, these were the only tangible
results of the voyages of the reign. They had,
however, a certain importance. To have reached
the mainland of America before Columbus was no
slight achievement. The experience learnt from the
disappointments of these early voyages made the
deeds of the Elizabethan seamen possible. John
and Sebastian Cabot were the pioneers of a great
host of mariners who led England to find her destiny
on the seas and to found the first among " all the
British dominions beyond the seas."

It is easy to undervalue the effect of these early
voyages upon the thought as well as upon the practice
of the succeeding generation of Englishmen. Added
to the revelations of the scientists, they annihilated
men's preconceived ideas of the universe. Astrono-
mers and geographers taught that the earth " far from
being the centre of the universe was itself swept
round in the motion of one of the least of its countless
systems." [1] Much that men had believed to be true
was proved to be false. The cloud that from the
beginning of things had hung thick and dark round
the borders of civilisation was suddenly lifted.

[1] Bryce, *Holy Roman Empire*, p. 313 ; *cf.* Froude, *Short Studies*,
i. 404.

CHAPTER IX

LAST YEARS : 1503-1509

AT the end of 1503 Henry felt at last secure. " The king's estate was very prosperous ; secured by the amity of Scotland, strengthened by that of Spain, cherished by that of Burgundy ; all domestic troubles quenched, and all noise of war (like a thunder afar off) going upon Italy." [1] Henceforward the story of the king's reign loses dramatic interest. The struggle for the throne was over. England was safe and growing in prosperity ; the House of Tudor was despotic in England, and a power abroad. Meaner ambitions filled the king's last years. The history of the reign is no longer filled with " roughe and sharpe battailes, pernicious seditions, strife, tumulte, and the deathe of many noble and meane persons," but with " the contencion of familiar thinges, the gnawinge at the hartes and the freatinge of myndes and vowes " [2] —in short, with all the intricate manœuvres of a restless and elaborate diplomacy.

In the beginning of 1504 Henry's fifth Parliament met. It was probably summoned by Henry in order to strengthen his hand in dealing with Suffolk. On January 25 it was opened by a speech from Archbishop Warham, who had followed Morton as Chancellor. Acts of attainder were passed against Suffolk and his friends, and the measure by which concessions were made to the Hanse merchants [3] was probably

---

[1] Bacon, *op. cit.*, p. 217. [2] Hall, *Chronicle*, p. 499.
[3] See above, p. 176.

designed to procure Suffolk's surrender. Though the
Act had no very important consequences, being
ignored as soon as Suffolk's departure from Aix in
April 1504 made the alliance of the Hanse merchants
useless, it is a striking proof that Henry anticipated
grave danger from the earl's manœuvres.

The exile's recent adventures made the king uneasy.
He had remained a long time at Aix, eating his heart
out in inactivity, overwhelmed by debt, and harassed
by his creditors. Maximilian only gave him just
enough help to keep his head above water. Early
in 1504 there was a change in his position. Attracted
by the specious promises of Duke George of Saxony,
who hoped to use the exile in negotiating an alliance
with Henry, Suffolk fled from Aix in April 1504,
leaving his brother Richard behind him as a hostage
for the payment of his debts. Misfortune still pursued
him. On his way through Gueldres with a safe
conduct he was seized by Duke Charles of Gueldres
and kept in close confinement in Hatten.[1] Duke
Charles was at this time struggling to throw off the
overlordship of the Duke of Burgundy, and, like the
Duke of Saxony, he hoped that the possession of
Suffolk might win him the English alliance. Henry
was certainly desperately anxious to get hold of
Suffolk. In the light of after events, it appears that
the king overrated the danger, but he was no prophet,
and the head of Perkin Warbeck, who had shaken
his throne, still mouldered on London Bridge. In
the autumn of 1504 there were rumours that Henry
intended to pay the Duke of Gueldres a large sum
for Suffolk's surrender, and he urged that Spanish

[1] On this subject see Dr. Busch, *op. cit.*, p. 368, note 9, referring
to extracts from the Dresden State Archives; also *L. and P.
Hen. VII.*, i. 260–2.

influence should be used to obtain it, " thus enabling
him to make an example of him to his kingdom."
Henry's relations with Philip were becoming difficult.
Philip was annoyed at the suggestion that Henry should
pay the Duke of Gueldres for Suffolk's surrender, as
he knew the money would be used against him. New
duties had been imposed by Philip upon English merchants.[1]   Henry retaliated, and there was bitter feeling
on both sides. Suffolk meanwhile remained at Hatten.

Meanwhile negotiations for the Spanish marriage
were dragging on as usual.   In April 1503, a horrible
rumour had reached Isabella, that a marriage between
the king and his daughter-in-law had been mentioned
in England.   Isabella expressed her disgust in round
terms.   " It would be a very evil thing," she wrote,
" the mere mention of which offends the ear; we would
not for anything in the world that it should take
place. Speak of it as a thing not to be endured."
The report originated with the garrulous de Puebla,
and seems to have been founded on gossip alone,
and even then his story was that a marriage between Henry and Katherine was much " talked of in
England," not that Henry contemplated such a step.[2]
One historian, however, accepts de Puebla's words as
a proof that Henry contemplated marrying Katherine,
and uses some strong words about the " monstrous
proposal—an outrage upon nature."   In the absence of
any confirmatory evidence, and in view of de Puebla's
spiteful knack of making baseless charges, Henry's
innocence of this intention can be presumed.[3]

Katherine's position in England waiting for the
delayed betrothal was not very dignified.   Isabella was

[1] This is a difficult point which has already been discussed. See
above, p. 169.   [2] Berg., *Spanish Cal.*, p. 295.
[3] Gairdner, *Henry VII.*, p. 190 ; Busch, *op. cit.*, pp. 207, 378.

anxious to extricate her from it. The preparations
for her departure—a feint before—were to be pushed
on in earnest.[1] Isabella also rather quaintly proposed
to dispose of Henry's rumoured intentions with regard
to Katherine by suggesting another lady as the object
of his attentions in the person of her niece the Queen
of Naples. By the summer the difficulties had been
adjusted for the moment, and a marriage treaty,
already drafted in September 1502, was ratified by
Henry (June 23, 1503).[2]

Ferdinand, Isabella, and Henry bound themselves
to use their influence at the court of Rome to obtain
a papal dispensation for the marriage between Henry
and Katherine, who had become related in the first
degree of affinity through the previous marriage
between the latter and the late Prince Arthur. The
question as to the consummation of the marriage,
now raised for the first time, derives considerable
importance from later events. The inquiries made by
Ferdinand and Isabella in England led them to
believe that the marriage had not been consummated,
and Ferdinand announced this to his ambassador in
Rome, explaining, however, that the terms of dispensation must be made to cover the possibility of
an actual union having taken place, in order to avoid
any objection on the part of the English, " who are
much disposed to cavil." [3] The other provisions

[1] Isabella, however, condemned Henry's attempt to keep the
dowry in round terms as a " barbarous and dishonest proposal,
not consonant with reason or with right human or divine." The
opinion of the lawyers she consulted on the point was much more
guarded, though on the whole favourable to her point of view. See
Berg., *Spanish Cal.*, pp. 304, 305.

[2] Rymer, xiii. 76–86 ; Berg., *Spanish Cal.*, pp. 306–8.

[3] Dr. Busch discusses the whole question of the various papal
bulls and briefs, with their bearing on the divorce proceedings.
Op. cit., pp. 376–8.

followed the precedent of the treaty for the marriage
of Katherine and Arthur, the instalments of the
dowry already received being taken in part payment
of the dowry due for the second marriage.[1] The
betrothal ceremony followed two days later. The
treaty was confirmed by Ferdinand and Isabella in
September, and by Henry in the following March.[2]

Ferdinand's formal ratification contains eulogistic
words about Henry: " He possesses all and every
virtue of a great king ; his faithfulness especially is
so great that he would prefer to die rather than break
his word." His private letters to his ambassador
show that he was genuinely pleased at the treaty,
and, though he thought its terms rather unfavourable
to Spain, the value of the English alliance outweighed
these disadvantages. The King of France had made
an attack upon Rousillon, and Ferdinand hoped that
Henry would help him in accordance with the treaty.
He appealed for 2000 English infantry, and revived
the old lure of the conquest of Guienne and Normandy.
Isabella's letters breathe the same spirit of satisfaction. She spoke of the great love she had always
borne Henry, and urged her ambassador to spread
abroad reports that Henry was going to send a
considerable body of troops to Spain, " because as
you will see such tidings and rumours will inspire
France, and will produce a favourable impression in
Italy." Henry's letters of the same date are very
different in tone.

At the risk of labouring the point unduly, the
complete change in the relative positions of England
and Spain must be noticed. The situation from 1485

---

[1] On the same 23rd June a commercial treaty was signed, for which
see above, p. 182.
[2] Berg., *Spanish Cal.*, Nos. 372-8, 380. Rymer, xiii. 76-9.

to 1497 is reversed, and in 1503 it is the prestige of
the English alliance that is considered worth some
sacrifice by Ferdinand and Isabella.   It becomes the
normal thing for them vehemently to urge Henry to
assist them, and for the latter to adopt an attitude
of irritating indifference.   Many of the delays were
deliberately introduced by Henry.   The key to his
difficult policy in this matter was his desire not to
lose his strong position.   As long as the marriage was
put off and Katherine remained dependent upon him,
he had the whip hand of Ferdinand and Isabella.

There was considerable delay in obtaining the papal
dispensation.   For this Henry was not responsible.
Two Popes, Alexander VI. and Pius III., had died in
rapid succession, and on 1st November 1503 Julius II.
had been installed as Pope.   Time went on, and in
spite of the urgent representations of the Spanish
ambassador, the dispensation was still delayed.   The
new Pope consented to send an informal brief to comfort the dying Queen of Spain in her last days, but the
formal bull was still withheld.   He excused himself
to Henry, who with flattering haste had despatched
an embassy to congratulate him on his elevation, and
give him his " filial and Catholic homage," on the plea
that the case needed full investigation.[1]

It is a mistake to suppose that Prince Arthur's
death was the end of Katherine's brief happiness,
and that henceforward she was made miserable by
Henry's cruelty.   The exact opposite was the case
for some years.   Henry continued to treat Katherine
in the spirit of his promise to her parents.   In July
he was providing money for her household at the
rate of £100 per month, and ordering that if any

[1] Berg., *Spanish Cal.*, i. pp. 309, 314, 326, 328, 330; *L. and P.*,
ii. 112–125. See Busch, *op. cit.*, p. 376, note 3.

surplus remained it was to be given to the princess
to spend as she liked. A little later, when Katherine
had an attack of ague, Henry took her with him to
Richmond and then spent a fortnight with her, at
Windsor, " hunting deer in the forest nearly every
day." When she had another and more serious attack,
Henry wrote a very affectionate letter to her from
Sheppy Island, asking anxiously for news of her,
assuring her that he loved her as his own daughter,
and was ready to do anything for her that might
give her some pleasure.

The Spanish ambassador Estrada wrote telling
Ferdinand and Isabella of Henry's kindness to
Katherine. In the same letter he gives an interesting
reference to the king's method of training his heir.
" It is quite wonderful how much the king likes
the Prince of Wales. He has good reason to do so,
for the prince deserves all love. But it is not only
from love that the king takes the prince with him ;
he wishes to improve him. Certainly there could be
no school in the world better than the society of such
a father as Henry VII. He is so wise and attentive
to everything, nothing escapes his attention. . . . If
he lives ten years longer, he will leave the prince
furnished with good habits, and with immense riches,
and in as happy circumstances as man can be." [1]

A little later Katherine wrote asking Henry to settle
the quarrels between various members of her household ; but he excused himself from the task, saying
that, as Spanish subjects, they were not under his
jurisdiction. Yet in spite of this disclaimer, he
secretly settled the matter, Donna Elvira's control
over the household being confirmed. The king was
anxious that Katherine should not know of the part

[1] Berg., *Spanish Cal.*, pp. 329, 330, 331-5, 338.

he had taken in it; " he did not wish to cause dissatisfaction to the princess in anything." Donna Elvira was the proud recipient of a present from the king—a St. Peter in gold to be used in a head-dress— a special mark of favour hitherto given by Henry only to royal ladies. Every scrap of evidence that remains proves that Henry was kind and considerate to Katherine. De Puebla's gossiping letters give a vivid picture of the king's attitude at this date. The question of his marriage was again brought up. Henry professed that he had not made up his mind to take another wife, but he asked "such very particular questions " about the Queen of Naples, that de Puebla wrote requesting that a picture of the said Queen, " portraying her figure and the features of her face, should be made as quickly as possible and sent over to England." [1]

The king and his council seemed pleased at the suggestion of the marriage with the Queen of Naples, and de Puebla wrote: " He lauded your highnesses above the cherubim." Henry, however, declared he was not going further without obtaining more particulars about his proposed bride, " for your Highnesses must know," wrote de Puebla, " that if she were ugly and not beautiful, the King of England would not have her for all the treasures in the world, nor would he dare to take her, the English thinking so much as they do about personal appearance." Henry was anxious to send an embassy to Valencia to make a personal report on the lady. De Puebla opposed this, explaining his action when writing to Ferdinand thus, " I have never seen an ambassador who has gone hence to Spain, and who has not come back disgusted with the country, owing to the inconvenience of travelling,

[1] Berg., *Spanish Cal.*, pp. 303, 324, 327, 333–4, 338.

which in England is like going from one wedding
to another."

The air was full of marriage rumours. Henry had
begun to think about another possible bride, the
recently widowed Duchess of Savoy. A match between the Princess Mary and the eldest son of the
Archduke Philip had been proposed, and—what was
very disquieting to Ferdinand and Isabella—a French
ambassador had been sent to England to propose a
marriage between the Prince of Wales and Margaret of
Angoulême.[1] All this made Ferdinand very uneasy,
and he surpassed himself in attempts to gain from
Henry the closer alliance to which he was unwilling to
commit himself. A letter of his dated November 24,
1504, just after Estrada returned to Spain, abounds
with flattering expressions of his regard for Henry.[2]
He enclosed a copy of the papal dispensation, and
a decree allowing English ships the same rights and
privileges of freighting in Spanish ports as Spanish
ships, this concession being made " on account of the
very great love and the bond of indissoluble alliance
and friendship which exists between us." [3] Two days
later Ferdinand's whole position had been changed.

On November 26, 1504, on the very day that her
daughter Katherine was writing an anxious letter
saying that she could not be satisfied or cheerful
until she heard from her mother, Isabella of Castile
died. The effect of her death illustrates Bacon's
description of her as " the corner-stone of the greatness
of Spain that hath followed." It brought another

---

[1] *Ibid.*, Nos. 427, 460, 467–8 ; *L. and P. Hen. VII.*, ii. 125–46,
340–62.

[2] *L. and P. Hen. VII.*, i. 241–3.

[3] In the following spring Henry issued orders to the same effect.
Berg., *Spanish Cal.*, Nos. 438, 439, 442 ; Rymer, xii. 114–16.

change in the shifting quicksands of European politics.
Henceforward Ferdinand and his son-in-law Philip
struggled for the possession of Castile, which, as
it passed by descent to Isabella's daughter Juana,
Philip claimed to rule in her right. He took the
title of King of Castile, and prepared to set out with
Juana for their kingdom. Ferdinand, however, under
the terms of Isabella's will, had been appointed regent
during Juana's absence, and he hoped to retain the
chief authority there.

The threatened separation of Castile and Aragon
had a considerable effect on the tortuous policy of
Henry's later years. He gradually drifted away
from the alliance with Spain, which had been the
keynote of his former diplomacy. Ferdinand was
now a much weaker ally, and there were ominous
signs of a coalition against him. Henry had no wish
to find himself " left to the poor amity of Aragon,"
and feared that "whereas he had been heretofore a
kind of arbiter of Europe, he should now go less and
be overtopped by so great a conjunction." [1] Henry
had never really trusted Ferdinand ; they had known
each other too well for mutual confidence, but since
the marriage of Katherine and Arthur their diplomatic relations had been marked by great surface
cordiality. From the date of Isabella's death this
disappears, and Henry's attitude to Ferdinand varies
with the security of the latter's hold upon Aragon.
Their altered relations reacted in a very unfortunate
way on the position of the Princess Katherine.
Henry's mind was filled with much more glittering
schemes, and she had become the pledge of an alliance
that had ceased to attract. She became a pawn in
the very ugly game played by Henry and Ferdi-

[1] Bacon, *op. cit.*, p. 226.

nand, and her happiness was sacrificed to their
knavish intrigues. The removal of Isabella's personal influence over Ferdinand had almost as bad
an effect on Katherine's position as the material loss
of the kingdom she had ruled. Ferdinand, who
seems to have cared little for his children, added to
his daughter's difficulties by withholding the later
instalments of the marriage portion, and by leaving
her without money. Neither of the kings wished to
undertake to provide for her. Henry would acknow-
ledge no responsibility for her support as long as the
marriage portion was withheld. She was between
the upper and the nether millstones. Kindness,
however, prompted Henry to go beyond his denial
of legal obligation, and he provided for the princess's necessities to some extent. A man of more
generous temper would, no doubt, have done this
without haggling about the marriage portion. But
Henry was not a man of generous temper, and
Katherine's necessities became a lever to extort
from Ferdinand the later instalments to which he
was bound.

For some time after Isabella's death both the
competitors for Castile were bidding for Henry's
friendship, and he hoped to gain Philip's friendship
without abandoning the alliance with Ferdinand. He
was still thinking of the bride proposed for him by
Ferdinand and Isabella. In the summer of 1505
Henry's envoys, John Stile and two others, were in
Spain visiting Valencia to report on the lady's charms.
The " curious and exquisite enquiries " they were
directed to make remain on record,[1] and their answers
suggest that they were impressed with the serious
nature of their embassy and quite devoid of any sense

[1] *Memorials*, pp. 223-239.

of humour.   Henry's minute inquiries they answered
with equal minuteness.   With scrupulous honesty
they refrained from crediting the royal lady with
any charms which had not been revealed to their
inquiring eyes.   They would not commit themselves to any opinion as to her height, because she
sat on a cushion, and because of the height of her
slippers.   Their report, which reads like a police
description, stated that she was not painted but had
a very fair and clear skin, a somewhat round and
fat face, " the countenance cheerful not frowning,
and steadfast not light."   The envoys felt justified
in assuming, from the ends of the queen's hair that
were to be seen under her kerchief, that the rest
was brown in colour.   Her eyes were " brown, somewhat greyish, her nose arched in the middle. . . .
She is much like nosed unto the queen her mother."
The king's long list of questions left nothing uncata-
logued—forehead, lips, teeth, arms, hands, neck,
fingers, and so on.   Henry was told how much she
ate and what she drank, that she understood French
and Latin, but could not speak either language, and
that she was not known to have any personal blemish
or deformity.   A careful picture was to be painted
by a competent artist, and if the painter found that
he had omitted " any feature or circumstance " of
the lady's visage, he was to alter the picture to a
perfect likeness.   It is interesting to notice that
Henry, in spite of his reputation for austerity and
avarice, drew up twenty-three questions dealing
with the lady's personal charms, and only one as
to her worldly possessions.   The answer to the last
cannot have been considered very satisfactory.   The
jointures of the queen and her mother in the kingdom of Naples had been confiscated, and they were

dependent upon an allowance of fifteen or sixteen thousand ducats made to them by Ferdinand.

The same ambassadors who made this confidential report were directed to go on to Ferdinand's court and make careful inquiries as to the state of affairs in Spain, Ferdinand's position and prospects, and the attitude of the nobles towards him. They were instructed to say that Henry was in good health, that he was " right joyous and merry, his realm in good peace and tranquillity, and his subjects in due obeisance and wealthy condition, established in peace, quiet, and restfulness with all outward princes," and were to be lavish in assurances of Henry's loving attitude, and of the " firm band of amity and kindness that had connected their wills." They reached Ferdinand's camp in Segovia on July 14th, and proceeded to collect information for the twenty-two articles of their report. The questions set down for them to answer are an interesting example of Henry's diplomatic methods, and of his anxiety to be posted up with first-hand information. The gist of their long and valuable report was that Castile could only be secured through Juana, whose authority as heiress of the kingdom was reverenced more than Ferdinand's. As to Henry's reputation in Spain, his envoys were able to assure him that he was regarded by many of the nobles as one of the wisest and mightiest princes of the time, but frankly added that many of the nobles and gentlemen had " no knowliche of yowr grace nor of yowr reame, the whiche thynke that ther ys no land butt Spayne." Henry had inquired about the personal appearance and habits of the brother sovereign with whom he communicated so often but had never seen, and was told that Ferdinand was a finely built man, very

strong for his age (about fifty-six), with a fresh
complexion and a smiling countenance. He had lost
a tooth in front which made him lisp, and he had a
slight cast in his left eye when speaking or smiling.
There were rumours about his marriage, but the
envoys had been told by one of the king's chaplains
that he had been advised by his physician not to
marry because of " a certeyn diseas the whiche he
hathe under his syde." He was the master of a
great treasure, which he kept in a strong castle.[1]

Before Henry received the report of these envoys,
he had gone a little further in the direction of the
alliance with Philip, and was weighing in his mind
the attractions it offered. But before throwing in
his lot with Maximilian and Philip he was anxious
for trustworthy information about their real attitude.
He instructed one of his envoys, John Savage, to
make careful inquiry as to whether Maximilian
sincerely offered his daughter to him, or whether
he was playing the hypocrite.[2]

About the same time (June 27, 1505) there was a
curious little scene at Richmond. Young Prince
Henry, on the eve of his fifteenth birthday, made a
solemn declaration before Fox, Bishop of Winchester,
that he had been contracted during his minority to
the Princess Katherine, and that, being now near
the age of puberty, he refused to ratify the marriage
contract, and denounced it as null and void. This
declaration was signed by Prince Henry and by six
witnesses. It seems certain that it was not a personal protest on the part of Prince Henry, but a
political move of the king's, who wished to postpone
the wedding owing to Ferdinand's altered position

[1] *Mem. of Hen. VII.* (Rolls Ser.), pp. 240–281.
[2] Berg., *Spanish Cal.*, No. 429.

and the other alliances proposed for his son.[1] At
that very time French ambassadors were in England
negotiating for Prince Henry's marriage with Margaret of Angoulême,[2] which had been discussed at
intervals since 1502. Henry professed himself anxious
to be related by marriage to Louis, " the prince he
loved most in the world " ; but he proposed himself,
not Prince Henry, as bridegroom for Margaret of
Angoulême, who was then about thirteen. Louis
seems to have been quite content with the substitu-
tion. He promised to give his niece a dowry of
100,000 crowns—more than the sum given to a
daughter of France—and gave assurances that he
would use his influence to obtain the surrender
of Suffolk.[3] In October rumours of a French match
were abroad in England. It was said that Henry
thought of marrying Louise of Savoy, Margaret's
mother, and that he had also been offered a French
and a Spanish bride. In addition, the king was said
to be secretly discussing two marriages for Prince
Henry—one with Eleanor, the daughter of Philip,
and the other with the daughter of the King of
Portugal. The Portuguese ambassador reported that
it was likely that the marriage with Katherine would
be undone, as it weighed much upon the king's conscience.[4] This anticipates the appearance of the royal

[1] Brewer, *L. and P. Hen. VIII.*, iv. 3, 2588 ; Herbert, *Life of
Hen. VIII.*, pp. 387–9 ; Berg., *Spanish Cal.*, No. 435.

[2] It is interesting to notice that Sir Charles Somerset—afterwards
Lord Herbert—one of the witnesses who signed Prince Henry's
declaration—was the ambassador who was sent to France in August
to discuss these proposals. *Excerpta Hist.*, p. 133.

[3] *L. and P. Hen. VII.*, ii. 125–46.

[4] *Ibid.*, ii. 145–6. The idea of the match with the Queen of
Naples had by this time been given up. Little is heard of it after
the return of Henry's envoys. He probably shelved it in favour
of more brilliant prospects.

conscience that played such an important part in the next reign.

Thus half the crowned heads of Europe were involved one way or another in negotiations for an alliance with Henry. " He will make his choice where best he may," wrote the Portuguese ambassador. Other observers doubted whether he was in earnest in many of these plans, and whether he was not deceiving the kings of France and Spain for his own purposes, especially with a view to obtaining the surrender of Suffolk. His desire to obtain the hand of Margaret of Savoy seems to have been genuine enough, but the lady had no liking for the proposed match. Negotiations, however, were continued. Maximilian sent ambassadors to England in August, bringing with them two portraits of Margaret and the news that Suffolk was in the hands of the Archduke Philip.

Relations with Spain were not improved by commercial difficulties. Some English merchants trading to Seville had been refused permission to export goods thence in their own ships in spite of Ferdinand's recent decree, and eight hundred English sailors had appeared before the king at Richmond, " all ruined and lost." According to de Puebla, Henry fell into a great rage, and reproached him bitterly. " The words which came from his mouth were vipers, and he indulged in every kind of passion." In a few days however, Henry had recovered his temper and sent de Puebla a present of a buck.[1]

De Puebla seems to have flattered himself that the negotiations with the archduke would come to nothing owing to his unpopularity in England. He tells a curious story of how he checkmated Katherine, who had been quite won over by Maximilian's am-

---

[1] Berg., Nos. 438, 439, 442 ; *Mem. of Hen. VII.*, p. 436.

bassadors, and who wrote a secret letter to try and
induce Henry to agree to meet the archduke and the
Queen of Castile at Calais on their way to Spain.
De Puebla declared to Katherine, " with tears running down his cheeks," that this suggestion of an
interview was due to the machinations of Don Manuel
(the treacherous brother of her mistress of the robes,
Donna Elvira), who wished to injure Ferdinand.
Katherine was persuaded to write another letter to
Henry contradicting the first, which de Puebla rushed
off to deliver personally.

By the end of the year Ferdinand and Henry had
drifted still further apart. Ferdinand had made
peace with France,[1] and was on the eve of marrying
Germaine de Foix, niece of Louis XII., who renounced in her favour his claims to the kingdom of
Naples. Thus the great cause of dispute between
France and Spain was removed, and Ferdinand's
smooth announcement that he and the King of
France had named Henry as the " guardian of the
treaty " could not conceal the widening breach.
Henry on his side was gravitating towards the archduke, and rumour declared that a league between
Henry, Maximilian, Philip, James of Scotland, and
perhaps the Pope had been formed.

Suffolk's claims were still causing Henry intense
irritation. The Venetian envoy wrote that he was
a great thorn in Henry's side, " for he knows that the
people of England love and long for him, and one
day or other he might do the King of England much
mischief." He had passed into Philip's power by
the capture of Hatten in July 1505, and the sub-

[1] Treaty of Blois, 12 Oct. 1505. André's suggestion that Henry
brought about this friendship between France and Spain is very
wide of the mark. André, *Annales*, pp. 88–89.

mission of the Duke of Gueldres. There was great
excitement in the Netherlands, where the feeling
against England was very strong owing to renewed
commercial difficulties. Philip's subjects hoped " to
put a curb into the mouth of the King of England,"
but their master's attitude was a disappointment.
His relations with Henry were becoming cordial.
The negotiations for the hand of Margaret were
continued, and twice during 1505, in April and
September, Henry lent large sums of money to Philip
for the purpose of his voyage to Spain.[1] The probable explanation is that Henry was anxious to see
the King of Castile in Spain acting as a check upon
Ferdinand, whose recent marriage with Germaine
de Foix threatened a Franco-Spanish *entente*. The
rumoured coalition mentioned by the Venetian ambassador was beginning to take shape. Henry was
ranging himself with Burgundy, Castile, and the
Empire against Aragon and France.

Meanwhile the unhappy Suffolk had another change
of gaolers. Philip, unwilling to offend Henry by
keeping his rebel, had returned him to Duke Charles.
He remained for some months in prison in Gelderland, where he was already heavily in debt. He wrote
many pitiful letters to Philip in his extraordinary
spelling, asking Philip to order his release. " Ef I
vare the fardes yend of the vord I veld be at ys
comand ment to fovel fele ys plessor," &c.[2] In the
autumn of 1505 he was again handed over to Philip

---

[1] *Excerpta Historica*, pp. 132, 133. Dr. Busch thinks the large sums
set down in the Privy Purse accounts (£108,000 and £30,000) are
a mistake. Busch, p. 186, note 2. Philip had been detained in
Flanders by the war in Gelderland.

[2] *L. and P. Hen. VII.*, i. 253–7, 263–5, ii. 142, 381–2 ; Ellis,
Letters, iii. (i.) 123–34.

and kept in strict captivity in Namur.[1] At last, in
the beginning of 1506, Suffolk, wearied with vain
promises and disappointed hopes, beset with creditors
on all sides, made up his mind to try and settle the
matter with Henry himself. He did not abandon
his lofty claims. His communication took the form
not of an appeal for pardon, but of negotiation for
a treaty. Envoys from " the Duke of Suffolk of
England " were sent to treat with duly authorised
persons to be appointed by Henry as to the settlement of the troubles in England which arose from
the disagreement between him and the king. He
asked for restoration to his estates and to the dukedom
of Suffolk, and for help to recover his liberty. There
was a provision that the agreement should be signed
by Henry and the Prince of Wales and confirmed
by Parliament.[2] But on the very day that Suffolk
drew up these precious instructions (January 28,
1505-6) his fate was settled by an arrangement
between Philip and Henry.

A fortunate accident had thrown an opportunity
of meeting Philip and Juana in Henry's way. After
waiting long for a favourable wind, they had sailed
on the 10th of January, " with great pomp passing
the narrow seas," but after four days in the Channel
the high winds increased to a " terrible hurricane,"
the same " hidyous wind " that blew the golden
eagle from the vane of St. Paul's. The guns and
everything movable were thrown overboard, the

---

[1] The explanation of these changes seems obscure. It may have
been a manœuvre to deceive Henry. The second loan had already
been paid over to Philip, who had nothing more to gain for the
moment. The question is difficult and not perhaps of great importance. See Busch, pp. 190, 371.

[2] *L. and P. Hen. VII.*, i. 278–285 ; Ellis, *Letters*, iii. (i.) 140, 141.

ship heeled over, Philip narrowly escaped being
swept overboard.   Fire broke out three times on the
ship, which, driven before the gale, at last reached
land at Portland.   The other ships of the fleet were
scattered.   The one on which the Venetian ambassador sailed put in at Falmouth, which he described
as " a wild spot where no human being ever comes
save the few boors who inhabit it."   He reported
that the Cornishmen were a barbarous race, speaking
a language so different from that of Londoners that
the latter could not understand them any better than
the Venetians.[1]

Philip at once sent to inform Henry of his arrival,
" calling him father," and suggesting, in spite of the
advice of his suite, that he should take the opportunity of visiting him.   Henry welcomed the
suggestion.   It was one of the occasions upon which
he loved to dazzle all eyes by his magnificent
court and win fair opinions by the display of princely
generosity.   The neighbouring gentry were ordered
to attend and entertain the royal guests.   Servants,
palfreys, and litters were sent to Portland, and on
January 31st Henry received Philip at Windsor
Castle.   He rode out to meet him, and the two
princes saluted and embraced each other bareheaded.
Henry treated his guest with splendid courtesy.   A
week of stately ceremonial and lavish entertainment
followed.   There were several private interviews
between the two kings, who vied with each other
in their courtesies, conveying and reconveying each
other to their lodgings with much polite show.   The
King of Castile was introduced to Princess Katherine
and to Princess Mary.   Katherine danced in Spanish
array ; Princess Mary also danced, and played upon

[1] Brown, *Ven. Cal.*, Nos. 862–865.

the lute and the clavegalles, to every one's great admiration.   The week passed pleasantly, hunting deer
in the forest, playing tennis, " horse-baiting," hawking,
and wrestling between Englishmen and Spaniards.
On the 9th of February Philip was invested with
the Order of the Garter.   After the ceremony the
treaty of alliance, binding both parties to mutual
defence and to a surrender of rebels, was signed by
Henry and Philip, who swore to it on the gospels
and the sacrament.[1]   Prince Henry then received
the Order of the Golden Fleece.[2]

Philip visited Richmond and London before he
left.   He parted from Henry on Monday, 1st March,
and made his way to Falmouth to join the queen and
his suite.   The visit had been a great success.[3]   There
does not seem to be much proof of the story that
Henry made capital out of Philip's misfortunes and
wrung concessions from an unwilling guest, though
his host's personal influence, calculated splendour,
and generous treatment [4] may have induced Philip to
make arrangements which he afterwards regretted.[5]

A treaty for the marriage of Henry and Margaret
of Savoy, signed by Philip on March 20, 1506, was
very favourable to Henry.   Philip's sister was to

[1] Rymer, xiii. 123–7 ; Berg., No. 451.
[2] Queen Juana had arrived at Windsor on Feb. 10, but unfortunately, in view of her later history, there is no account of her
appearance or behaviour.
[3] For accounts of the visit see *Mem. of Hen. VII.*, pp. 282–303 ;
Berg., *Spanish Cal.*, No. 451 ; Brown, *Ven. Cal.*, Nos. 862–869 ;
Paston Letters, iii. 403–6.
[4] Philip said that Henry could not have done more for him had
he been his own father.   He had paid him every honour and defrayed
his expenses and those of his retinue on their journey.
[5] The tone of his language does not support the theory that he
felt that he had been victimised, though Bacon suggests that the
King of Castile was " willing to seem to be enforced."

have a dowry of 300,000 crowns, and to receive from
Philip yearly the sums of 18,850 crowns and of 12,000
crowns in satisfaction of her jointure from her two
previous marriages.   Maximilian and Philip were to
use all their influence to induce Margaret to consent
to the marriage.   The treaty also provided for a
strict alliance between the two princes, and that all
rebels and fugitives should be given up by both
monarchs.   Philip signed the treaty on behalf of
Maximilian also, and promised that he would confirm
it within four months.[1]   The commercial treaty
(April 30), which accompanied it was even more
favourable to England, and in fact contained so
many concessions that Philip was reluctant to
ratify it.[2]

Neither treaty contains any provision as to the
treatment of the Earl of Suffolk.   There are
several conflicting accounts on this point.   Bacon
gives a vivid story of Henry's private conversations
with Philip on the subject of " that same harebrain
wild fellow my subject, the Earl of Suffolk," but
unfortunately his report seems to be imaginative.
There is also no authority for the statement of an
eye-witness who described Philip's reception that
" unaxed the King of Castile proferred the king to
yield Edward Rebell."   According to another account,
Henry gave a " solemn promise in writing sealed with
his seal " that Suffolk should receive a full pardon
for all his offences.   The Venetian ambassador relates
that Henry had given a promise and public oath to
pardon Suffolk and restore him to his estates.   Hall,
following Vergil, also states that Henry " promised
faithfully of hys awne offre to pardon Edmund de la

---

[1] Berg., *Spanish Cal.*, No. 460, 463–6, 483.
[2] Rymer, xiii. 132–142. See above, p. 170.

Poole of all paynes and execucions of death." The truth lies somewhere between these different reports.[1]

Philip sent one of his suite to conduct Suffolk to England. He was handed over to the English garrison at Calais on March 16th, arrived in England on 24th March—nearly a month before Philip sailed —and was at once lodged in the Tower. His life was spared as Henry had promised, but he remained in prison until the end of the reign.[2]

The treaties signed by Philip were valueless until they were ratified. The confirmation of the marriage treaty, though anxiously expected by Henry, was not made until 2nd September, and there was obviously no intention of ratifying the commercial treaty. In spite of this, Henry had been doing his best to fulfil his obligations to Philip, and in the summer of 1506 wrote offering to help his ally against the Duke of Gueldres, who had again rebelled.[3] Maximilian, however, had to give Henry the unwelcome news that he had failed to persuade his daughter Margaret to agree to the marriage. He had written personal letters and sent ambassadors. The duchess said that, "though an obedient daughter, she would never consent to so unreasonable a marriage"; but he thought her reluctance was due to the machinations of the French foxes, and promised Henry that he would not give up until he had ob-

---

[1] *Mem. of Hen. VII.*, pp. 282–303; Letter from A. de Croy to Maximilian, Berg., *Spanish Cal.*, i. pp. 379, 385; Brown, *Ven. Cal.*, No. 870; Hall, *Chronicle*, p. 501.

[2] *Chron. of Calais*, pp. 5, 6; Brown, *Ven. Cal.*, Nos. 869, 872, 874.

[3] He offered a thousand archers for three months, or a loan of 20,000 gold crowns to pay other troops. He seems to have helped Philip effectively by dissuading Louis of France from supporting the rebellious Duke. *L. and P. Hen. VII.*, i. 289–300, ii. 164–7; Berg., *Spanish Cal.*, No. 491.

tained her consent, and that he would pay her a personal visit for that purpose. Henry wrote rather coldly in reply that he was sorry that Madame Margaret made so many difficulties about the treaty of marriage, hinting that he might accept " one of the great and honourable matches that were daily offered to him on all sides." [1]

Meanwhile the situation in Spain needed careful watching. Philip had reached Castile safely, but found himself opposed at every point by Ferdinand. It was the ambition of each to govern Castile in right of Juana. Her character was another difficulty. Already before she left Flanders there were sinister rumours that she was mentally unsound. The reports about her became more and more unfavourable. The Venetian ambassador, who in September 1506 had reported that she bore herself " like a sensible and discreet woman," and, in January 1506-7, that she showed great bravery during the storm at sea, wrote in March that her " intellects were not sufficiently sound for the burden of government." [2] From this time all the reports harp on the same string, and it is impossible not to suspect that Philip took the worst possible view of his wife's malady owing to her constant quarrels with him and her expressed determination to rule Castile herself. Unprejudiced observers like the Venetian envoy, who saw Juana while she was at Falmouth, used language which hints at a dark conspiracy between Ferdinand and Philip to deprive Juana of the government on the ground of her incapacity. The ambassador wrote in April 1506 that Philip and Ferdinand had arranged " to circulate a report before she arrived

[1] Berg., *Spanish Cal.*, No. 491.
[2] Brown, *Ven. Cal.*, Nos. 854, 865, 872.

in Spain that she was unfit to govern," with a view
to preventing the Castilian nobles, who were devotedly attached to her, from insisting on the queen
governing them in person.   It was notorious that
Philip and Juana got on badly together, and the
theory of a plot between husband and father-in-law
seems probable enough on the face of it.[1]   In June
Philip was thinking of shutting her up in a strong
fortress, a measure from which Ferdinand dissuaded
him.   Philip and Ferdinand certainly made friends
in the summer of 1506, the basis of their agreement
being that they were to govern Castile jointly, Juana
being excluded on the ground of incapacity.[2]

In September the whole situation was changed by
Philip's death at the age of thirty.   The prospect
that Ferdinand would attempt to exclude Prince
Charles from Castile roused all the latent hostilities
of Europe.   It was rumoured that the King of France
would support Ferdinand's action, and Maximilian
wrote to Henry in great alarm, begging for his help
and for a loan of 100,000 crowns to defend the young
archduke's dominions.   Henry saw that the un-
ratified treaties he had made with Philip were so
much waste paper after his death, but, while he
hastened to disclaim any further interest in the war
in Gelderland, he showed an inclination to cling
to his friendship with Maximilian in hope of the
marriage with Margaret.   A new commercial treaty
was also considered.   The other side also made a
bid for his alliance.   French ambassadors hastened
to England to offer the daughter of the Duke of
Angoulême to Henry in marriage, but Henry refused
this offer, not having given up hope of the Duchess

[1] *Ibid.*, No. 873.
[2] Berg., *Spanish Cal.*, i. *Suppl.*, Intro. xxiv.–lxxx.

Margaret.   There is ample evidence of Henry's
estrangement from Ferdinand.   The usual recriminations about the marriage portion had taken on
a very bitter tone, and Ferdinand excused himself
on the plea that the remaining part of the portion
was in the hands of the late Queen Isabella's trustees,
that he was absent in Italy, and that Juana was
unable, through her " unspeakable affliction " at the
death of her husband, to sign an order.

The Princess Katherine was the unfortunate
scapegoat of their hostility.   In December 1505 she
had appealed to Ferdinand for money in vain, and
she declared that she and her servants had not a
single *maravedi* except for food.   She complained
bitterly that de Puebla's letters were " full of calumny
and lies," and that he was the cause of all her suffer-
ings.   In the spring and summer of 1506, she had
several severe attacks of fever.[1]   In April she wrote
that she was in debt for food, and that Henry, owing
to the non-payment of the marriage portion, refused
to pay her debts, though she asked him with tears.
Her people were ready to beg, and she herself had
for six months been near death.

It is difficult to reconcile these bitter complaints
with the friendly tone of Katherine's letters to
Henry and his to her.   Henry wrote in October
putting a house at Fulham at her disposal, as she
thinks it will improve her health to be so near him.
If she prefers any other house, she has only to say
so and it will be kept for her.   Next year her position was improved by a new marriage scheme, which
promised to add another link to the weakened chain
of the Anglo-Spanish alliance.   It is from one of
Ferdinand's letters to Katherine, written in March

[1] Everett Green, *Letters of Royal Ladies*, 131-154.

1507, that Henry's proposal that he should marry
Philip's widow, Juana, is first mentioned.[1] The
golden crown of Castile outweighed the attractions of
the proposed marriage with Margaret, and although
negotiations for that marriage were continued,
Henry's chief efforts between 1507 and 1508 were
secretly directed to the new scheme.

Henry's attitude in this matter has been made the
subject of many hard words. He has been represented as a monster who was willing to marry a
maniac in order to snatch at a crown, but a review
of the evidence disposes of the most revolting part
of the story.[2] Until Henry received a letter from
Ferdinand early in 1508, he had no reason, as far
as we know, to think that Juana was mad. Before
the date of that letter he had been told of nothing
except the infirmity alluded to by de Puebla. Henry
was certainly guilty of a lack of delicacy in being
anxious to marry a woman who was rumoured to
be weak-minded, but the very fact that Juana, with
a kingdom for her dower, was incapable of ruling
tempted Henry shrewdly to try and marry her and
rule Castile in her right. His attitude was no outrage upon contemporary feeling in the matter of royal
marriages or upon the standards of a coarse age.
When Ferdinand forwarded the darker details of
Juana's state of mind—the story of her insane devotion to her husband's unburied corpse, and so on—
the negotiations were allowed to drop.[3] Another aspect
of the affair seems to be evidence of Henry's declining
powers. It was strange if he believed that Fer-

[1] Berg., *Spanish Cal.*, p. 405.
[2] See below, Appendix iv.
[3] Berg., *Spanish Cal.*, Nos. 522–4, 526–7, 541, 545, 548, 551–3,
575, 577, 588, and pp. 405, 409, 413, 415.

dinand was sincere in the proposal for the marriage.
He must have known that Ferdinand, after his experience with Philip, would do anything to prevent
his daughter marrying another prince who would
try to exalt Juana's authority at his expense.
Was Ferdinand likely to neutralise the union of
Castile and Aragon ?   The insincere diplomacy of the
period makes it difficult to know what Henry really
believed ; but though it is conceivable that he was
playing with this, like other marriage schemes, in order
to strengthen his diplomatic position, the simpler
explanation that he was in earnest about the match
is the more probable.   He certainly was not sufficiently sanguine about it to make it his only scheme.
As usual, he had two strings to his bow.   As his
hopes of the Castile marriage faded, his suit for the
hand of Margaret of Savoy became keener.   He was
certainly sincere in his efforts for this match, which
harmonised with the drift of his later policy, steadily
setting away from Spain.

Just before Easter in 1507, Henry had had a severe
attack of quinsy, which for six days prevented him
from eating and drinking, and weakened him so
much that his life was despaired of, but he had
made a rapid recovery.   Within a fortnight he was
receiving ambassadors and discussing some of his
many marriage schemes, and by the late summer
he was quite restored to health.[1]   De Puebla wrote
on 5th October 1507 that the king spent every day
hunting and hawking, that since he recovered from
his illness he had been better and stronger than
ever before, and was even growing stout.   The same

---

[1] Berg., *Spanish Cal.*, Nos. 511, 543 ; André, *Annales*, 108 ; Brown,
Ven. Cal., No. 896.   See also *L. and P. Hen. VII.*, i. 233, for an
earlier illness of the king's.

letter describes Prince Henry as " already taller
than his father, with limbs of gigantic size. There
was not a finer youth in the world." [1]

At the same time the scheme for a marriage
between Henry's daughter Mary, and Philip's son
Charles, which had been mooted during Philip's
stay in England, began to take definite shape. Fear
of France made Henry's alliance very desirable to
Maximilian, and throughout the autumn of 1506 ambassadors discussed the three points of the alliance—
the confirmation of the unwelcome commercial treaty,
the marriage of Mary and Charles, and the marriage
of Henry and Margaret.

By the spring an agreement had been reached,
and in May 1507 a treaty was made which was considerably less favourable to England than the un-
ratified treaty. The fact that Henry was prepared
to accept this proves that he appreciated the value
of the proposed match between Charles and Mary.[2]
In September 1507 the complicated nature of the
situation is illustrated by the fact that envoys from
France, Flanders, Denmark, Scotland, the Pope,
the King of the Romans, as well as the Spanish
ambassador were with Henry at Woodstock. France
had declared war upon Burgundy, and all the powers
were anxious to make Henry take sides definitely.
Both marriage projects were under discussion ; and
though the king wrote a letter to the Duchess Margaret
promising to use his influence to prevent France
from attacking Burgundy, and sent her a present
of six horses and some greyhounds, he continued

---

[1] Berg., *Spanish Cal.*, No. 552.

[2] In 1499 the Duke of Milan had asked for her hand, she being then
three years old, for his son, but had been refused. Brown, *Ven. Cal.*,
No. 790.

the secret negotiations for the marriage with Juana.[1]
A propos of these presents to Margaret, de Puebla
suggested to his master that Henry would much
appreciate a gift of black and chestnut Spanish
mules, and would probably present Ferdinand with
some English and Irish hackneys in return. A
little later the confusion of open and secret schemes
for marriage alliances was increased by the reopen-
ing of negotiations for a French marriage, the proposal being that Prince Henry should marry the
sister of the Duke of Angoulême. Nothing came of
this, but it was utilised by Henry, who, by practice, had gained a conjuror's dexterity in keeping
half-a-dozen things in the air at the same time,
to put pressure on Ferdinand, who began to think
that, after all the years of waiting, the marriage
between Katherine and Henry might never take
place.

In September 1508 Henry's hopes of a marriage
with Margaret received a severe check. Maximilian
had written to her in September 1507 begging her
" to amuse Henry with false hopes and prevent him
allying himself with France and Spain." Margaret
had evidently suggested that she might consider the
Prince of Wales as a suitor, but Maximilian told
her that they would never consent to that, and he
tried to win her over to consider Henry's suit favourably by suggesting that she might remain ruler of
the Netherlands, and spend three or four months
of the year there. Accordingly in October, Margaret sent a " very loving letter " to Henry, which
he at once read to de Puebla.[2] But when Henry

---

[1] Berg., *Spanish Cal.*, No. 543.
[2] *Ibid.*, Nos. 463–8, 483, 547 ; *L. and P. Hen. VII.*, ii. 153–160 ;
Brown, *Ven. Cal.*, Nos. 883, 885–6.

pressed his suit, Margaret's real decision had to come
out.   In vain Maximilian painted the advantages of
the English match in glowing terms, and referred
to Henry as " a pattern of all the virtues " ;[1] Margaret
made her refusal very plain, though she tried to
soften it by saying that she was fully aware of
Henry's noble qualities, and would never marry any
one but him.   She pointed out, however, that she
had already been married three times, and that she
feared she would never have any children, and
would therefore displease the King of England.   She
also referred to the marriage portion suggested by
her suitor as exorbitant.   It was obvious that she
had made up her mind, yet Henry did not give up
hope.[2]

In the other scheme for uniting the royal houses
of Austria and England he was more fortunate.
On 21st of December 1507 the treaty for the marriage of Prince Charles and Princess Mary was signed,
and was accompanied by a treaty of mutual alliance
between Henry and Charles.   The Princess Mary
was to receive a dowry of 250,000 crowns.   The
betrothal was to take place before Easter 1508, the
marriage was to follow within forty days of the
prince's fourteenth birthday, and three months later
the princess was to be sent to join her husband.[3]
The match was celebrated by great rejoicings in
the capital, and by tournaments.   André wrote a
song in honour of Madame Marie to celebrate the
occasion.

Henry was delighted at his success.   His diplo-

---

[1] See *L. and P. Hen. VII.*, i. 305, 324, ii. 153–5.

[2] *Ibid.*, i. 301–3, 323–7 ; Berg., *Spanish Cal.*, No. 558.

[3] Rymer, xiii. 171–88; *Mem. of Hen. VII.*, 95, 96 ; André,
Annales, 95–6.

macy had gained a great triumph. An heiress of
the house of Tudor was to marry one of the most
powerful princes in Europe. He wrote that his
realm was now " environed, and in manner closed
in every side with such mighty princes, our good
sons, friends, confederates, and allies," that it was
perpetually established in wealth, peace, and prosperity.[1] A comparison with the state of England
at his accession some twenty years earlier is a striking
comment on the king's rare words of exultation.
But the alliance was very irritating to Ferdinand.
A treaty which profoundly affected his interests had
been signed by Henry without consulting him. It
was too late to interfere, but he did not conceal his
annoyance. The tone of his letters was very bitter.
Yet, much as he would have liked to, he could not
afford to quarrel with Henry. The match was still
in danger. The Prince of Wales was not much inclined for it, and the king's indifference was obvious.
He spoke of the King of Aragon as a " stout Frenchman," and dropped hints of some scheme by which
the Emperor might rule Castile, apparently as regent
for Juana and Prince Charles, and deprive Ferdinand
of his influence there.

In the face of this danger Ferdinand had to try
and conceal his resentment at the match between
Charles and Mary, and push on the marriage between Henry and Katherine by every means in his
power. He wrote to his ambassador about the
scheme for an Anglo-French match, and said that
if Henry broke faith with him he would make a worse
war upon the King of England than on the Turks.
These threats, though not for publication, show the

[1] Halliwell, *Letters*, i. 194–6.

feeling of exasperation which filled Ferdinand at
Henry's growing independence and indifference.
On August 7, referring to Henry's very rigid attitude about the marriage portion—he had demanded
payment in cash, and refused to accept a valuation
of the princess's plate and jewels—Ferdinand alluded to his extreme covetousness, and said that
he would break entirely with him were it not for the
Princess of Wales. He feared being cheated. In
dealing with people of " no honour and of indifferent character," it was necessary to take great
precautions ; Henry's demands were against all right
and charity. He even hinted that Katherine might
be poisoned in order to get hold of her marriage
portion ! Arrangements for its repayment were to
be made that Henry might be freed from the temptation of killing Katherine. The whole tone of the
letter is bitterly hostile, and the strangest contrast
to the former flatteries.

The recall of de Puebla and his replacement by
Fuensalida (now governor of Membrilla), who had
arrived in England early in 1508, had added to the
friction. Membrilla irritated Henry by adopting an
independent attitude very different from the pliancy
of de Puebla. Henry actually announced that as the
dowry had not yet been paid the marriage should not
take place. He refused to give Membrilla an audience,
and the palace guard refused him admittance.[1] Both
sides seemed to be drifting towards war.

The position of Princess Katherine at this moment
was extremely painful. Her letters are filled with
pathetic complaints of the humiliations she was
forced to endure.[2] She wrote that she was abso-

[1] André, *Annales*, pp. 109, 110 ; Berg., *Spanish Cal.*, Nos. 586,
588, 590.   [2] See Berg., *Spanish Cal.*, Nos. 545-6, 603, 604.

lutely penniless, that she had been obliged to sell
her property, and that she was dependent upon
the king's charity. Revolting as Henry's conduct
appears, something can be said in extenuation of it.
Ferdinand must share the responsibility for his
daughter's unhappy plight. He refused either to
contribute to her support, or to pay the remainder of
the marriage portion. Henry felt that he was being
cheated, and what he gave to Katherine he gave
grudgingly. In justice to Henry, and without any
attempt at special pleading, it must be noticed that
there were scandals in Katherine's household which
throw some doubt upon her complaints of dire poverty.

When Membrilla arrived as ambassador he found
a state of affairs in the princess's household which
reflected little credit upon Katherine and much upon
Henry's forbearance.

In 1506 the princess had appointed as her confessor a certain friar, Diego Fernandez, who rapidly
obtained an influence over her that was very injuri-
ous to her reputation. She made him her chancellor,
distinguished him by many marks of favour, and
admitted him to an extraordinary intimacy. The
whole court was seething with scandal about her
imprudent conduct, and Membrilla felt bound to
communicate the affair to his master. He wrote
that the whole of the princess's household was
governed by this young friar, who led her into many
errors.[1] He described the friar as "young, light,
haughty, and scandalous in an extreme manner."[2]
Henry himself had been obliged to remonstrate
sharply with Katherine. Slander already connected
the name of the princess with the friar, "who had

[1] Berg., *Spanish Cal.*, Supp. to vols. i. and ii., p. 13.
[2] *Ibid.*, pp. 14–22.

neither learning, appearance, manners, competency, or
credit."   " The King of England and all the English,"
wrote Membrilla, " abhor to see such a friar continually in the palace and amongst the women."   It
is curious to notice that within five days of the
date of Membrilla's report Katherine wrote bewailing her miserable position.   She complained that
Henry had treated her differently ever since Ferdinand's alliance had lost its importance to him.
She had been obliged to sell her household goods
to provide herself with money.   Henry had told her
that he was not bound to provide either for Katherine or her servants, but that the love he bore her
would not allow him to do otherwise.   Katherine was
anxious to pay some of her servants who annoyed
her and send them away, but her greatest affliction was not having the means adequately to
maintain her confessor, the best that ever a woman
in her position had, and so on.   She complained that
the ambassador had quarrelled with the friar, and
the latter's threat to leave her reduced Katherine
to a pitiable state of distress.[1]   She implored her
father to order the confessor to stay with her, and
to write asking Henry to have the confessor " very
well treated and honoured." [2]   It is difficult to discover the truth when the only reports we have come
from interested parties, one bent on condemning,
the other on eulogising the friar.   But, apart from
the inherent improbability of the ambassador daring
to write absolutely untrue reports to his master, the
friar's own letters show him to have been a man of
great coarseness even in a lax age, and he himself reported facts proving that the princess confided in him
to an extraordinary and very unbecoming extent.[3]

[1] *Ibid.*, p. 21.   [2] *Ibid.*   [3] *Ibid.*, pp. 34, 43, 44.

Further, the unsuitability of the friar for his position
in the princess's household is proved by the fact
that he was in later years (1515) convicted of immorality.[1] It is difficult, therefore, not to concur
in the ambassador's rather than in the princess's
estimate of the confessor. His influence over Katherine did not improve her relations with Henry,
but we find the latter acting with considerable forbearance. We have on record a striking instance
of the friar's influence. In defiance of the king's
express wish, and obeying the friar's commands,
the princess refused to go to Richmond to meet
the king. The English gentlemen who had come
to escort her had to go to Richmond without her,
leaving her alone with the friar and her servants.
On the following day she made her appearance at
Richmond, accompanied only by three of her women,
the friar, and two servants. Henry was not un-
naturally displeased at conduct which was undig-
nified, if nothing worse, and for three weeks he
took no notice of Katherine, and did not send to
inquire for her when she fell ill. The ambassador
himself paid a tribute to Henry's forbearance, and
admitted that he had blamed the king unfairly,
that he wondered not at what he had done but at
what he refrained from doing, especially as he was
not of the temper readily to allow disobedience.
Further, the ambassador's letters let fall a hint that
gives another explanation than Katherine's of the
necessity that forced her to sell her plate. The
princess, he wrote, was with difficulty prevented
from selling a piece of plate every day to satisfy the
follies of the friar. Within a fortnight the princess
had sold gold plate for two hundred ducats, and had

[1] Berg., *Spanish Cal.*, Supp. to i. and ii., p. 45.

nothing to show for it. It had all gone in books
and in the friar's expenses. The case against the
friar is strengthened by the fact that the next
Spanish ambassador corroborates Membrilla's view
of the situation. He speaks of the friar as the worst
man he had ever known. It is obvious that in the
unfortunate differences between Henry and Katherine
the fault was not entirely his.[1]

Meanwhile the Pope was again pressing the claims
of a crusade against the Turks. Henry, as we have
seen, had preserved a sympathetic but judiciously
non-committal attitude to the question. He had
been lavish in expressions of interest, and had even
helped the cause by a handsome contribution, but
his cautious temperament had prevented him from
throwing himself heartily into the Papal schemes.[2]
But as Henry neared the end of his life, his real piety
triumphed over his caution.

The steady advance of the Turks filled Eastern
Christendom with dread. In 1506 Henry had been
chosen by the Knights of Rhodes, who were the
vanguard of resistance to the Turks, as their "protector, champion, patron, and defender throughout
the whole Christian world and in his own famous
kingdoms." [3] In the following year, urged perhaps by
his sharp attack of quinsy, Henry showed signs of
justifying this complimentary title by definite action.

In a letter written from Greenwich on 15th May
1507,[4] to the Pope, Henry explains that ever since
his accession he had been intent on the universal
peace of Christendom. He had never cherished

---

[1] *Ibid.*, p. 37.   [2] See above, p. 230.
[3] *L. and P. Hen. VII.*, i. 287-8.
[4] Two copies of this letter, differing slightly, remain. See Berg.,
Spanish Cal., i. No. 519 ; Brown, *Ven. Cal.*, No. 893.

dreams of foreign conquest, not through lack of military resources, treasure, and power, but because he was averse by nature to the shedding of Christian blood. He was now bound to nearly all the princes of Christendom by treaties of alliance and ties of blood. He begged the Pope to restore peace to Christendom, and, that being done, to proclaim a crusade against the infidels, and invite the Christian princes to send ambassadors to Rome to settle the practical details of the proposed joint campaign. The Holy Father, who was wise and strong in body and mind and obeyed by the princes of Christendom, would earn eternal glory if he avenged the humiliation of centuries on the detestable infidels. In July the Pope wrote in reply complimenting Henry on his letter (which he had read ten times himself and then read to the Cardinals), but throwing cold water on the suggestion of an assembly of ambassadors at Rome, as previous experience of such assemblies had shown that the Christian powers always failed to agree as to who should command, what places to attack first, and so on. He suggested that help might be sent to those Christian princes who were already fighting against the infidels.[1] Henry took the Pope's hint, and suggested to Ferdinand that he might send an army of the renowned English bowmen to help him against the Moors. A joint expedition from Spain, Portugal, and England might do wonders; and it was believed that a force of English bowmen could in a few years conquer the whole of Africa. Ferdinand's reply was not enthusiastic. He put off the proposed war in Africa " till his other affairs should have been arranged." Henry's new-found zeal was not dashed, and in September he

[1] *L. and P. Hen. VII.*, ii. 170–174.

wrote another long letter to the Pope, urging the
joint expedition upon him in the strongest terms.
He suggested that " a trinity of kings from the west "
might lead the advance eastwards towards the Holy
Sepulchre, and promised, with every appearance of
sincerity, that even if no other prince was forth-
coming, he, Henry, would undertake the war in his
own person.[1] Nothing came of this appeal, however,
the Pope being occupied with more mundane cares
until April in the last year of the king's life, when
Julius II wrote again to revive the scheme for an
attack upon the Turks. The appeal came too late;
the dying king was unable to accede to the Pope's
request. During the stormy zenith of his career
Henry had felt an impulse to take up the burden of
a Christian prince in defence of Christendom against
the Turks, but except for his pecuniary contributions it remained an impulse only. The defence of
his kingdom and the settlement of his dynasty absorbed all his attention until late in life, when
success brought him leisure, and illness reminded
him of the claims of religion—too late.

In the same year there was friction between England and Scotland. The marriage between James
and Margaret had been a great success from the
political point of view, though the bride herself seems
to have been miserable enough. Henry had been
able to count upon Scotch neutrality and sometimes on
Scotch sympathy in his relations with foreign powers.
James, for instance, had adopted a very correct
policy in the question of the Earl of Suffolk,[2] and
in 1505 he had agreed not to revive the old alliance

[1] *Ibid.*, 174–9, Woodstock, 18th Sept.
[2] See *L. and P. Hen. VII.*, ii. 207–210, 211, 213 ; *Epis. Reg.
Scot.*, i. 6–9, 30–34.

between Scotland and France.[1] In spite of this, however, French influence was still strong in Scotland, and in later years, the traditional policy of stirring up strife with England was revived. James IV. was led to take up the cause of Duke Charles of Gueldres, and even wrote to Henry (8th January 1507) threatening to abandon his alliance with England if Henry supported the Duke's enemies. Further, James had interfered in Ireland, in support of O'Donell. The growing unfriendliness was emphasised in January 1508, when Henry arrested the Earl of Arran, who was travelling through England without a passport on his way back from France. There had been many complaints before of this practice of Scotchmen travelling in disguise through England, but James strongly resented Arran's detention.[2]

The dispute gave Thomas Wolsey, one of Henry's chaplains, his first diplomatic employment. He was sent to Scotland on January 23, 1507–8, and Arran was allowed to leave England. The great difficulty was the attitude of the Scotch nobles. James seems to have been loyal to the English alliance, but the traditional friendship with France was much more popular in Scotland. Wolsey's diplomacy, however, succeeded in reconciling Henry and James, and the friendship between England and Scotland was not broken until the next reign.[3]

In the summer of 1508, it was rumoured that Maximilian was thinking of one of his sudden changes of policy, and, lured by the hope of alliance with

[1] See Ayloffe, *Cat. of Anct. Charters*, p. 316; André, *Annales*, pp. 105–7.

[2] *L. and P. Hen. VII.*, ii. 207–10, 211–13, 237–42 ; *Epis. Reg. Scot.*, i. 6–9, 30–34.

[3] See Wolsey's report. Pinkerton, *Hist. of Scotland*, ii. 445–450 ; *L. and P. Hen. VII.*, Pref. lxi. ; *Eng. Hist. Rev.*, iii. 471–7.

France, contemplated abandoning the lately arranged marriage between Charles and Mary, in order that the former might marry the Princess Claude of France, to whom he had once been betrothed. Henry had again been seriously ill in February 1508, and it was rumoured that he was in the last stages of consumption. He did not intend, however, to let slip the threads of his policy, and, though reluctant to break with France, hoped to hasten the postponed betrothal ceremony between Mary and Charles.[1] It was these conflicting aims that gave Wolsey a second opportunity of distinguishing himself. In August 1508 he was sent into Flanders by Henry. Of the details of this mission we have no account, but Wolsey evidently succeeded in overcoming for the moment Maximilian's inclination to France. In October he was again in the Netherlands discussing the inevitable difficulties about the Princess Mary's dowry, and trying to stir up opposition to Ferdinand's government of Castile.[2] Henry's letters to Wolsey prove that even in November 1508 he still clung to the hope of a marriage with Margaret. On 7th November he wrote to his " dear and beloved cousin " an affectionate letter, and told his envoy that if he married the duchess he would be quite contented to make his abode in Burgundy for a good space every year, and that if the government was not entrusted to him and Margaret jointly, he, Henry, would be quite willing to let her go there to stay whenever convenient.[3]

[1] *L. and P. Hen. VII.*, ii. 342–9 ; Brown, *Ven. Cal.*, No. 906.

[2] His report gives an account of the reception of the English embassy at Antwerp (*L. and P. Hen. VII.*, i. 425–7), and the " sweet words " of the emperor on the subject of the English alliance (*ibid.*, i. pp. 372–4).

[3] *Ibid.*, i. 449–52.

At last, after a long delay, which was very annoy-
ing to Henry, Maximilian's envoys arrived in England, and a proxy marriage between Charles and
Mary took place at Greenwich on 17th December.[1]
The ceremony was followed by arrangements as
to the repayment by Maximilian of the loan from
Henry.[2]

Strangely enough, the last few months of Henry's
life saw a reversal of the whole diplomatic situation.
The isolation of Ferdinand and the coalition against
him, upon which Henry prided himself, gave way,
and the king's triumph was shattered.   Events in
Italy gave a new direction to the ambitions of the
princes of Europe.   Ferdinand had secured his hold
upon Naples, and by a successful campaign in 1507
Louis XII. had regained his influence in North Italy.
Maximilian chose this moment to renew his claims
to imperial dominion in Italy, and found himself resisted in his design by France, Spain, and Venice.
But while he pursued these shadowy schemes, the
revolt of the Duke of Gueldres, assisted by France,
was endangering the substance of his hold upon
Burgundy.   At this crisis the alliance with England,
concluded in December 1507, was very valuable.[3]

All Maximilian's plans failed, however.   He failed
in Italy, and he failed in Gelderland.   Louis XII.
also had ambitious designs in Italy, which were
thwarted by the opposition of Venice.   Common
interests drew Louis and Maximilian together, and
after a great deal of secret negotiation, the two

[1] Rymer, xiii. 236–9.
[2] Certain jewels were left in pledge by Maximilian, the jewel
known as " le riche Fleur de Lys " being pledged for 50,000 crowns.
L. and P. Hen. VII., i. 440 ; Rymer, xiii. 234, 239, 242.
[3] The treaty was confirmed by Maximilian early in 1508.

princes agreed to abandon their mutual hostilities
in favour of an attack on Venice. The change was
fatal to Henry's schemes.

The diplomacy of Europe centred round the conference at Cambrai between Margaret of Savoy and
the Cardinal d'Amboise, representing Maximilian
and Louis. Though English envoys attended the
conference at the special invitation of Margaret,
they were only concerned with the state of affairs
on the surface and knew nothing of the secret negotiations which were transforming the diplomacy of
Europe. The question of Gelderland, the ostensible reason of the conference, was indeed settled
by the appointment of the Kings of England, France,
and Scotland as arbitrators. Henry's instructions
to Wingfield, based on the situation as known to him,
were quite beside the point. The absorbing interest
of the conference was the settlement of the Italian
question, in which England was not concerned.

Wingfield was urged to press for the dissolution
of the alliance between the King of France and
Ferdinand, to try and deprive the latter of the
regency of Castile, and obtain his exclusion from
the treaties at Cambrai. He was to declare Henry's
willingness to accept an alliance with France, to be
strengthened by a marriage with a French princess.[1]
Henry was obviously out of touch with the situation.[2] On December 10, 1508, the formation of the
League of Cambrai joined France and Maximilian
in common hostility to Venice, and a little later the
Pope and Ferdinand were also admitted into the
League. It was a bitter disappointment to Henry ;

---

[1] The probable date of these instructions was Nov. 1508.

[2] *L. and P. Hen. VII.*, i. 426–52, ii. 365–7 ; Berg., *Spanish Cal.*,
No. 600.

instead of being a member of a coalition designed
to attack Ferdinand, he found himself almost the
only power not included in the League.

But Henry was not the man to acquiesce in even
momentary exclusion and isolation. In spite of his
increasing physical weakness, the king patiently set to
work to rearrange the threads of his policy. Fortunately there was no disposition to exclude him
from the League. He received an invitation to join
it, but the prospect of dismembering the republic of
Venice, which had led the powers of Europe to drop
mutual animosities, had no lure for him.

The threatened republic appealed urgently to him
for help. In January 1508–9, they had found out
about the League of Cambrai. Their consul in London was directed to approach Pietro Carmelianus,
Henry's Latin secretary, and try and avail himself
of his favour with the king, "who had always loved
the state as his special friends." In this crisis of
their fortunes no effort was to be spared to attach
Henry to their side. The envoy was to point out
that France meditated the ruin of Italy, hoped to
obtain the imperial crown for Louis, and the chair
of St. Peter for the Cardinal of Rouen. They were
persuaded that Henry would interfere to save them,
"both of his goodness and because of the safety of
the whole Christian world." On 30th January an
ambassador was sent to England charged with the
duty of informing Henry of the "deep rooted and
detestable greediness" of the King of France, and
of his ambition to become "monarch of the universe"
and of his other "unbecoming and immoderate
cravings." Henry and Venice both realised that
the only hopeful line of policy was an attempt to
detach Maximilian from his recent alliance with

France.   Maximilian's conduct had been thoroughly characteristic.   His recent alliance with Henry and a three years' truce with Venice he had broken without scruple, to pursue one of those ambitious dreams which had been the bane of his life.

By the time the Venetian ambassador reached London in March, Henry was too ill to give him an audience, though he expressed his good intentions towards the republic.   He had already written to Maximilian to try and adjust his quarrel with Venice. A short time afterwards the King of France declared war against Venice, and the French and Papal forces attacked its territory, but Henry died before this news reached him.[1]

Henry's final communications with Ferdinand in the last months of his life remain to be noticed. After the failure of his attempt to isolate Spain, there was a return to the friendly tone characteristic of their former relations.

In January and February 1509 Henry wrote to John Stile, his envoy in Spain, directing him to inform Ferdinand that the long-delayed marriage should soon take place, and Ferdinand replied that he would send an ambassador with powers to settle the question of the dowry.   Stile reported that great efforts were being made, however, to detach the King of Spain from the English alliance. Ayala said that he used all his influence in favour of England, and that he was not carried away by the anti-English party in Spain.   Stile, however, admitted frankly enough that the Spaniards were " wondrous close, subtle, and crafty far passing his understanding," and evidently distrusted Ayala. Stile's position seems to have been very uncomfortable,

[1] Brown, *Ven. Cal.*, i. Nos. 929, 936, 939, 940.

and he wrote that he would have had as good cheer
and company as ambassador to the Turks or to
Barbary as he had there. The upshot of it all was
that Ferdinand agreed to forget his displeasure at
the betrothal of the Prince of Castile without his
consent on condition the marriage between Henry
and Katherine was immediately concluded. He
declared that he and the King of England had been
and were now great brothers and friends. This
last despatch, which Henry never lived to read,
dealt as usual with the time-worn topics of the dowry
and the marriage portion. The long negotiations
between Henry and Ferdinand ended on a familiar
note.[1]

Rumours of Henry's illness had been carried all
over Europe in the spring of 1509. His malady,
which was a form of consumption, took a turn for
the worse in March. " Perceiving that death was
not far off tarrying," a general pardon was proclaimed
to all who had offended against the king's laws,
thieves and murderers alone being excepted.[2] By
the end of the month the king was in great danger.
On the 14th of April he was reported to be *in extremis*,
and on the 21st of April, " so consumed with his long
malady, that nature could no longer systeyne his
lyfe," Henry VII. died at Richmond in the fifty-
third year of his age.[3]

His will, which was dated March 30, 1509, is of
considerable interest. It breathes the spirit of a
genuine and simple piety. He expressed his wish

---

[1] *Mem. of Hen. VII.* (Rolls Ser.), pp. 431–448.

[2] Fisher, *Sermon on Death of Hen. VII.* (Early Eng. Text Soc.,
xxvii.), 271-2.

[3] Fisher gives an account of the king's last painful days, when
" for the space of xxvii houres . . . he laye continually abiding the
sharpe assautes of deth."

to be buried in Westminster Abbey, " the common
sepulchre of the kings of this realm," in the chapel
that he had begun to build anew, where daily masses
were to be said for his soul and the souls of his wife
and ancestors.　He left £5000 to finish the chapel
and provide for the carving of the royal arms and
badges on windows, walls, doors, arches, and vaults.
He directed that his funeral should be carried out
" with special respect and consideration to the
laude and praising of God, the welthe of our Soule
and somewhat to our dignitie Royal, eviting alwaies
dampnable pompe and oteragious superfluities."
Money was left to provide for ten thousand masses
to be said for the king's soul within one month after
his death.　£2000 was to be distributed to the poor,
the sick, and to the prisoners, who were to be asked
to offer prayers for the king's soul, " so that oure
Soule may fele that as thei loved us in our life, soo
thei may remember us after our deceasse."　Provision was made for payment of the king's debts
and for the satisfaction of wrongs done by the king
or by his order.[1]　Bequests were made for founding
chantries and almshouses, hospitals at York and
Coventry, for the repair of highways and bridges,
and for various " dedes of merite, almose, pitie, and
charite."　The king's signature was dated the 10th
of April, ten days before his death.[2]

[1] The names of Empson and Dudley appear in the list of those
who were to give satisfaction with the Archbishop of Canterbury,
the bishops of London, Winchester, and Gloucester, and other
members of the king's council.

[2] Will of Henry VII. (ed. Astle).　The indentures between the
king and the Abbot of Westminster are in a book bound in crimson
velvet in the Harleian Library, No. 1498.　See description of
binding (Astle, Will, Appendix I.).　There are five seals with the
king's arms, illuminated portraits, &c.

The pomp and ceremony with which the king had surrounded his state appearances lent dignity to his funeral.[1] On Tuesday, May 8th, the king's body was brought from Richmond to London, and in the evening a stately procession, lit with torches innumerable, passed slowly through the streets of the capital to St. Paul's. The king's coffin lay under a golden canopy on a chariot drawn by seven horses, their black velvet trappings emblazoned with the arms of England. The coffin was covered by an effigy of the late king, crowned and in Parliament robes, and bearing the sceptre and orb; at the head and foot sat two mourners. The king's courser, led by Sir Thomas Brandon, followed his dead master. "A noble knight, the mourner," bore the king's standard behind the coffin. Then followed the Duke of Buckingham, the temporal lords and barons and the abbots and bishops on horseback, judges in their robes, and a long procession of monks and friars, singing dirges as they walked. The king's steel helmet with its golden crown was borne by a Welsh knight. Sir Edward Howard wore his armour and bore his battle-axe reversed, and the caps and swords sent by three Popes were borne by esquires. When the cathedral was reached, the coffin was borne up through the nave by fourteen men of the king's guard, " because of its great weight," and lay that night before the high altar of the cathedral under " a goodlie curious Light of Nine Branches." On the following morning, after three masses and a sermon by John Fisher, Bishop of Rochester,[2] the king's body was taken in procession to Westminster.

[1] A full account is given by the Herald. Leland, *Collectanea*, iv. 303–9. See also *L. and P. Hen. VIII.*, i. App., No. 5735.
[2] *Early English Text Society*, xxvii., 1876, pp. 268–88.

Emery Walker, Photo

KING HENRY VII
From the full-length effigy on his tomb in Westminster Abbey

That night the dead king lay there in state, the
gloom of the abbey being pierced by a space of
light round the coffin, near which stood " the most
costly and curious light possibly to be made by
man's hand, which was of twelve principal standards."
On the morrow (Thursday, 10th May) the late king's
armour, his helmet, shield, and sword were given
as offerings.   Even his courser was ridden up through
the abbey and offered at the altar.   The Duke of
Buckingham and the other nobles laid palls on the
bier, "in token of their homage, which they of dutie
ought to do unto the king."   When the effigy and
the palls were removed, the wooden shell was revealed covered with black velvet adorned with a
huge white cross.   Within was a leaden coffin bearing the inscription, " Hic jacet Rex Henricus Sep-
timus."   The coffin was laid in the vault by the side
of the queen's.   The absolution was pronounced,
earth was thrown upon the coffin by the archbishop ;
the lord treasurer, lord steward, and other officers
of state broke their staves and threw them into the
vault, the heralds took off their tabards, " cryinge
lamentably in French, ' The noble King Henry the
Seaventh is deade. ' "   A moment later the shouts
of the heralds acclaimed his successor, " God send
the noble King Henry the Eighth long life."   There,
in the centre of the gorgeous chapel that is a monument to the dignity and splendour of his proud race,
lies the dust of the founder of the Tudor dynasty,
" a king who lived all his tyme in the favour of
fortune, in high honour, riches, and glory, and for
his noble actes and prudent pollecies worthy to be
registered in the booke of fame."

CHAPTER X

PERSONAL : IMPORTANCE OF THE REIGN

" A DREARY life and a dreary reign." That is the
summary of a modern sketch of King Henry.[1] It
is a strange comment on a life of which the strange
vicissitudes recall the fabled adventures of heroes of
romance, and on a reign that, beginning with the
achievement of a crown from the hawthorn bush on
Bosworth field, saw the first voyages into the New
World, and gathered the first harvest of the Renaissance. Yet the comment is not a novel one. It
follows the general tradition that clothes the reign
with a pall of impenetrable dulness. The cry is
that the reign lacks dramatic interest, that it is
a bleak interlude between the death struggles of
feudalism and the great political and social convul-
sions that followed. Historians one after another
dwell on the importance of the period and bewail
its dulness ; [2] it is the one thing apparently that
may legitimately inspire their eloquence. The reign
certainly suffers from the fact that it came between
two periods of violent catastrophe. It was a time
of experiment not yet confirmed, of discovery not
yet verified ; and when the curtain falls on Henry
VII. there is a feeling that it is but a prelude to a

[1] A. D. Innes, *Twelve Tudor Statesmen.*

[2] Bishop Stubbs, for instance, who in a few vivid sentences has
summed up the great developments of the reign, goes on to comment
on its failure to be interesting. Stubbs, *Lectures on Mediæval and
Modern History*, pp. 384–9.

much more stirring play. But the reign does not lack the interest of a gallant and successful struggle against odds that at first seemed overwhelming. It is rich, too, in the promise of great beginnings, the end of which still lies out of sight. The reproach of dulness ought not to cloud the reign that made the glories of Elizabethan England possible.

Yet, after all, it is easy to explain this lack of interest. There is a strange absence of detailed contemporary evidence.[1] The half-seen figures of Henry and his ministers seem to struggle dimly in a twilight world of their own, and to be separated by more than a generation from the robust figures of their descendants, who play their parts on a well-lighted stage. Even the fact that Henry had Bacon for his biographer does not entirely atone for the lack of the intimate, revealing details of the king's character. A grey mist still lies between him and us ; form but not colour has come down to us. What we know, too, of the people of the period is not arresting. The picture lacks those gallant and heroic figures that loom larger than life on the canvas of history. No amount of special pleading can make Henry VII. a hero of romance ; his ministers were all prosaic figures. Practical common sense seems to be their dominant characteristic. Morton, Fox, and Bray were men of sound ability, but there was no brilliance, no flash of genius, to relieve their humdrum usefulness. With Empson and Dudley we get a note of more striking colour, but their villainy took the unromantic form of sordid chicanery, base alike in method and motive. Even the one great

---

[1] The invention of the printing press may have had some influence on this, and the age of monkish chroniclers was past. Stubbs, *op. cit.*, p. 386.

crime of the reign—the execution of Warwick—is
not of a character to arouse strong feeling, and lacks
the sinister interest of a personal motive. Even the
romantic career of the " White Rose " is touched
with the prevalent absence of heroism. Perkin
Warbeck's gallant figure was the mask of an ignoble
spirit, tainted with the baseness of personal cow-
ardice. Neither the king's mother nor the queen are
particularly interesting.[1] The ability of the former
was directed in uninteresting channels, and the queen
had beauty, grace, and piety, but little character.

In spite of the tradition of repellent hardness that
clings round it, the study of Henry's strange complex character is curiously interesting. The portrait
that Bacon drew still holds the field,[2] and no attempt
to sketch the king's character can stand without
borrowing from his nobly worded study of this
" Solomon of England," a study " which nothing
extenuates but sets down naught in malice," of a
man who, whether he was great or small, was at all
events the mainspring and origin of the whole policy
of the reign. It is the picture of the politic king that
Bacon draws for us with his master hand—remote
from human feelings, guiltless of love or hatred,
without pity and without resentment, without passion and without weakness. No one can deny that
it is a striking figure, grey, relentless, and inhuman,
that looms across the intervening centuries. But at
the risk of blurring this clear outline, the evidence
inaccessible to Bacon must be remembered. The
lines of his splendid sketch must be modified. The
king was more human than he has been portrayed,
less aloof, less mysterious, less impressive, perhaps.
It is like an attempt to replace a magnificent paint-

1 See below, pp. 385–8.   2 Bacon, *op cit.*, pp. 237–45.

ing by a faithful photograph, a sacrifice of art to
truth.

The dark, stern, secret figure Bacon has made us
familiar with had a less sinister side which is revealed to us by contemporaries. Many of the
qualities for which they praised the king, and which
seem most alien to Bacon's account, have the support
of hard fact. He was neither harsh nor unkind.
Considering how few are the original records that
survive, the amount of evidence that exists to
prove this is remarkable. Royal letters, letters
patent, and royal accounts bring before us unques-
tionable proof of his generosity and benevolence.
In gratitude to those who had helped him or any
of his house he is never wanting; [1] he was com-
passionate to victims of accident, redeemed debtors
from prison, undertook the support of poor children.
He paid the debts of traitors, and pensioned those
dependent on them. He raised a tomb to King
Richard's memory and supported the widows of Lord
Fitz Walter and of Perkin Warbeck. Bacon's theory
that he had an ineradicable hatred of the House of
York is disproved by his generous treatment of
Northumberland, Surrey, and a crowd of lesser men.
The old picture of the harsh and sinister despot gives
way to that of a king who was both kindly and considerate. He admitted his subjects to intimate personal relations, and gave ear to their petitions. To
take at random from a month of his life : he dealt
with the woes of a disappointed lover, deceived by
the " nygromancer," who had promised to help him
to the woman he desired, he gave his protection

[1] See *Materials,* passim. Lord Nevill's young son was brought
up at court. His horse, bridle, and saddle, and a " Kendall cote for
littell Nevil " were paid for out of the Privy Purse. *Excerpta
Historica,* p. 122.

to the wife of a lunatic, and interfered to protect a
nun who had suffered ill-usage.[1]   He did not forget his
schoolmaster or the son of his old nurse. We find him
giving £1 "to one that had his hand smyten off," 6s. 8d.
" to one that was hurt with a gunne," and so forth.

He was not difficult to approach, and as he jour-
neyed through his kingdom came into contact with
many of his poorer subjects.   Thus we hear of him
drinking ale in a farmer's house, stopping to watch
the reapers in a field and giving them a tip of 2s.,
giving 3s. 4d. to a woman who approached him as
he rode to Canterbury to give him " a neste of
leverets."   It is a homely picture which shows the
king in a less forbidding light.   It was also his custom
and that of the queen to accept graciously a variety
of small offerings brought to them by their subjects,
giving them small rewards.   The poor woman who
brought a present of " butter and chekins," and the
girl who brought almond butter (for use on Good
Friday, when ordinary butter was forbidden), received
small gratuities.   " A fool for bringing a carp "
was paid 12d., and a woman who brought two glasses
of water to the king on one of his rides was given
five shillings.   Among the innumerable offerings
were apples and oranges, cherries and strawberries,
" posies of flowers," venison, rabbits, quails, wood-
cocks, cock-pheasants, tripe, " puddinges," " aqua
vite," malmsey wine, a fresh sturgeon, a nightingale,
a pomander box, a pair of clavicords, rose-water, and
cocks for fighting at Shrove tide.[2]

Again, the tradition of the king's ascetic aloofness

---

[1] Campbell, *Materials for Reigns of Rich. III. and Henry VII.*, i.
251, 310.

[2] *Excerpta Historica*, passim ; *Privy Purse Expenses of Elizabeth
of York* (ed. Nicolas).

has to give way before the records of his court. Contemporary descriptions have been preserved of many
of the great ceremonies of the reign, the king's coronation, the coronation of Elizabeth, the christening
of Prince Arthur, the marriages of Arthur and Margaret, the creation of Prince Henry as Duke of York,
the funerals of Arthur and Elizabeth, and of the
king himself.[1] From them all we get the same impression of great splendour and dignity, of stately
symbolism and ecclesiastical ritual. The Tower of
London was the royal palace on many of these
ceremonial occasions. Westminster Abbey was the
scene of coronations, and St. Paul's of national
thanksgiving when the king appeared in triumph
to give thanks for victory. The Thames plays its
part in many of the pageants; with its barges
furnished with " baners and stremers of silk richly
besene " and its thousands of swans.[2]

The king's private account book, Elizabeth's privy
purse expenses, and the Roll of the Great Wardrobe take us behind the scenes and show us the
material upon which the king relied for his effects.
The king himself made a magnificent figure at all the
great ceremonies of the reign, and seems to have had
a pronounced taste for gorgeous clothing, and above
all for jewels, on which, between 1491 and 1505, he
spent over £100,000.[3] Even on comparatively in-

[1] *Rutland MSS.;* Leland, *Collectanea.*
[2] *Italian Relation.* The background of it all was the capital,
built of brick and timber, which impressed foreign observers with
its wealth, abounding with "every article of luxury and with a
great quantity of wrought silver." There were fifty-two goldsmiths'
shops in the Strand alone. *Ibid.,* pp. 42–4.
[3] On January 4, 1504, the sum of £30,000 was paid out of the
Privy Purse "for divers precious stones from beyond the see"
purchased by the king. *Excerpta Historica,* p. 131.

formal occasions Henry was richly dressed. The
Venetian ambassador found him at Woodstock
dressed in a violet gown lined with cloth of gold, his
collar enriched with many jewels, and his cap with
" a large diamond and a most beautiful pearl." [1]
He led his army into France in a magnificent suit of
armour, the helmet gleaming with pearls and jewels
bought specially for it from the Lombard merchants.
The nobles aped the king's tastes, and glittered
with goldsmith's work and with "goodly chaines of
fine gold." On one occasion the Duke of Buckingham wore a gown of needlework set upon cloth of
tissue and furred with sable, valued at £1500, and
the gold trimming alone of Sir Nicholas Vaux's
gown was worth £1000. [2] The king encouraged all
this, and often gave pieces of rich silk or velvet to
his nobles, such as " forty-one yards of riche satin
to make the Earl of Oxford a gowne," [3] and honoured
with his presence the weddings of many members
of his court. [4]

The *Ordinances of the Household* (1494) reveal
the ordinary surroundings of Henry's daily life. [5]
The ceremonial of the court was designed to set
the king in a niche apart, invested with every circumstance of pomp and dignity. The directions

[1] Brown, *Cal. of Venetian Papers*, i., No. 754. The privy purse
accounts contain amusing references to the details of Henry's
costumes.   Thus, "an estrych (? ostrich) skynne for a stomacher "
(*Excerpta Historica*, p. 95), pynne cases 8s., the king's hatt bande
of silke 4s., to a barber that did shave the king 4s.

[2] *Italian Rel.*, Note, p. 73; Stow, *Annales*, 484. Sir Thomas
Brandon wore at Katherine's wedding a chain valued at £1400.

[3] *Excerpta Historica;* Roll of Great Wardrobe, *Materials*, ii. 1-29,
175-6.

[4] A list of the weddings which Henry attended can be found in
Coll. Top. and Gen., i. 21, 22.

[5] *Soc. of Antiquaries Proc.*

are much more minute than those for the household of
Edward IV., and it is not fanciful to see in the increasing strictness of etiquette evidence of studied design.[1]
The king made his public appearances with great
pomp and under a cloth of estate. The furniture
and decoration of the royal palaces became increasingly luxurious. The descriptions of the hangings of
rich tapestry and cloth of gold, of carpets and cushions
embroidered with Tudor devices, of cupboards of
rich gold plate, and of the elaborate furnishing of the
royal bedchambers show a marked advance.[2] The
king kept a splendid table, at which seven or eight
hundred people dined daily.[3] The menu at the
state banquets usually included certain popular dishes,
shields of brawn in armour, venison, pheasants,
swans, peacocks (appearing in the glory of feathers
and tail), capons, " crane with cretney," " lamprey
in galantine," " pike in Latymer sauce," " perche in
jellie dipt," snipes, quails, larks, partridges, and
" conies of high grece." The sweets included cus-
tards, " marchpayne royal, and tarte poleyne." Each
course was finished by a Sotelte, an elaborate device
in pastry representing allegorical figures.[4]

The splendour of Henry's court had more than
a personal significance. It was designed to invest

[1] Exact rules, for instance, are laid down as to the method of
" serving the king with spice (gingerbread, cakes, dried fruit, &c.,
practically dessert) and wine. They were handed by the nobleman
of the highest rank present, while the Archbishop stood on the
king's right hand and took spice and wine in his turn " when the
king made him a becke." The regulations for making the king's
bed were equally minute.

[2] See the account of Queen Elizabeth's elaborate bed-chamber.
Leland, *Collectanea*.

[3] " His Majesty," wrote the Italian visitor, " himself spends
£14,000 annually upon his table." *Italian Relation*, p. 47.

[4] *Rutland Papers*, p. 119.

the new dynasty with the glamour of royal state and dignity, to catch the eye of Europe and suggest the strength of vast wealth. It was no accident when a newly-arrived ambassador or envoy found the court in full dress, everything marvellously well ordered and served, and the queen jewelled and surrounded by magnificently apparelled ladies.[1] Henry fully realised the effect of the trappings of royalty on the popular mind, and took care not to destroy his growing prestige by impromptu appearances in public. His state appearances were calculated to impress the minds of spectators, and be magnified by rumour in the country. His long progresses through the disturbed parts of England had the same end in view.[2]

Henry set the example of royal magnificence that became characteristic of the Tudor sovereigns, reigning at a period when royalty reached its climax in England. This outward pomp did much to foster the growing reverence for royalty, to set it on a pinnacle far above the subject, to create the atmosphere of devoted loyalty to the throne that found its expression in the Elizabethan period.

To harmonise with the gloomy colours he has chosen, Bacon denies to Henry any relaxations. "For his pleasures," he says, "there is no news of them," and, while admitting that the court was enlivened by "triumphs of justs and tourneys and balls and masks,"[3] suggests that Henry was "rather a princely and gentle spectator than seemed to be

[1] Leland, *Collectanea*, iv. 242.

[2] Though he usually travelled in the summer, the roads often had to be repaired before the royal retinue could proceed.

[3] For a vivid account of the tournaments to celebrate the creation of Prince Henry as Duke of York, see *L. and P. Hen. VII.*, i. 388–404; *City Chron.*, p. 202.

much delighted." According to Bacon he spent his leisure time making " notes and memorials of his own hand, especially touching persons, as whom to employ, whom to reward, whom to inquire of, whom to beware of, what were the dependencies, what the factions, and the like, keeping, as it were, a journal of his own thoughts," but though this fits in aptly with Bacon's view of Henry's character, there are other accounts of the way in which the king spent his leisure which are a great contrast to this theory of gloomy seclusion.

Henry was an ardent sportsman, and took every opportunity of getting away from the cares of state for a few weeks' hunting in the royal forests. He hunted in the New Forest, at Enfield, Waltham, and Woodstock, as well as at Windsor.[1] He jousted, shot at the butts, played tennis, dice, cards,[2] and " chequer board," was interested in bull-baiting, bear-baiting, and cock-fighting. Besides splendid tournaments, banquets, and " goodly disguisings," we hear of " plays in the White Hall," Twelfth Night processions, and the good sport provided by the " Abbot of Misrule," when special efforts were made " to cause the king to laugh." Morrice dancers and tumblers, conjurers, little dancing girls, and rope walkers vied with " a Spaniard that played the fool " (and received £2 !) and " a felow who distinguished himself by eating of coales." His idle hours were enlivened by the wit of one or another of a troop of court jesters, Scot and Dick " the master fools," Peche the fool, Dego the Spanish jester, the " foolyshe

pastimes

---

[1] One autumn a train of ambassadors had to follow him about from one forest to another.

[2] The Privy Purse expenses give the record of his losses. " My Lord of York " played dice in his very early years.

Duc of Lancastre," and others.[1] Henry certainly had a considerable sense of humour and a ready wit, sardonic and ironical though it may have been. Monstrosities of one kind or another seem to have had a special interest for the king—" the grete Walshe child," " the littell Scottisman," the " grete woman of Flanders," and so on. The king also had a collection of wild animals to which he occasionally added. The famous lions and leopards were kept at the Tower.[2]

Like most Celts, Henry was very musical, and never travelled without taking in his train some of his minstrels, trumpeters, harpists, or pipers. The queen and the princesses also kept their bands of musicians. On all his progresses Henry was received with music, and had many opportunities of enjoying and paying for " incidental music " of the most varied kind. On one occasion the king gave £1 " for a child that plays upon the recorders "; another time " the Waytes " received 10s., William Newark was given £1 for making a song, and children singing in the garden at Canterbury received 3s. 4d. Harpists, hornists, violinists, organists, and trumpeters all received gratuities. The royal children were all musical, and there are many entries of sums spent on instruments for them.

Henry was not without a touch of Celtic romance and imagination. He was proud of his Welsh ancestry and his mythical descent from the old kings of Britain. The red dragon of Cadwallader flaunted on the royal banner. His first-born son was given

---

[1] *Excerpta Historica*, passim. A jester even went with the king on his journey to France.

[2] One accident is recorded, a man dying from the bite of one of the king's lions.

the name of the traditional hero of Britain, and was born in the ancient city of Winchester, the scene of some of Arthur's exploits. Celtic clanship made the king mindful of the Ap Thomases and Ap Rhyses who had supported him, reward the Welsh rhymers, remember St. David's day, and so on Many details of the king's surroundings reveal his fondness for symbolism. The Tudor colours of white and green appeared everywhere, the Tudor arms and the red and white Tudor rose on everything from altar vestments to cushions and the king's portraits. The Tudor device of a crown in a hawthorn bush recalled the coronation on Bosworth Field.

Too little has often been said on the king's attempt to spread an air of culture and refinement about his court.[1] He gave his patronage to literature and the arts, rewarded poets and ballad-makers, bought rare books, encouraged printing, and raised for himself a lasting monument of stone. He shared the spirit of adventure and discovery, kept an alchemist at work within the Tower, and rewarded a man who made gunpowder.[2] Thus the records prove that the old idea of Henry as the penurious and ascetic king must be abandoned. He was no sinister, savage despot, with no mind above the tortuous tricks of a suspicious tyranny, but a gracious, liberal-minded monarch, with a marked taste for splendour and pageantry, a more or less conscious imitator of the methods of the Italian despots.

Henry's relations with his family have given rise to some discussion, and here, too, Bacon's view must be qualified. "The domestic history of his more famous son is not more thoroughly repulsive," writes

[1] See above, pp. 311–316.   [2] *Excerpta Historica*, passim.

one great authority.[1] The theory to which Bacon has
lent the support of his great name, that Henry treated
his wife badly and her mother worse, long held the
field,[2] but is now so discredited that it is hardly
worth dwelling on. The evidence of documents and
of contemporary historians contradicts the absurd
and untrue statements that have been made. Henry
restored Elizabeth's mother " to her fame as a
woman and her dignity as a queen." [3] She was
Prince Arthur's only godmother, and was sometimes
present at court on state occasions.[4] The other
story—about Henry's unkindness to his wife—has
been disposed of in the same way. There is no shadow
of support for the theory that Henry was jealous of
her position as heiress of the House of York. Elizabeth received every possible mark of honour and
favour. All her public appearances were surrounded
with great state, the Yorkist colours of murrey and
blue were displayed in the liveries of her attendants,
and the white rose of York was emblazoned on the
trappings of her palfreys.[5] On the day of her coronation, which was unusually gorgeous, the queen was
allowed the monopoly of public attention, Henry

[1] Dr. Gairdner, *L. and P. Hen. VII.*, ii., Intro. xxvii. In his
Henry VII., however, Dr. Gairdner takes a gentler view. See
p. 179.

[2] Hume speaks of the king's " disgust towards his spouse,"
Heywood of her lifetime rendered miserable by the dislike in which
the king held her.

[3] *Privy Purse Expenses of Eliz. of York* (ed. Nicolas), Intro. lxxvii.–
xciii. He also restored her lands to her. Campbell, *Materials*, ii.
265–271.

[4] Leland, *Collectanea*, iv. 249. Her will has been quoted as a
proof that she was reduced to destitution by Henry's knavery, but
as she had only a life interest in her property, she had naturally
little to leave.

[5] Leland, *Collectanea*, iv. 239–241.

being an unseen spectator of the scene.   The king's
fair wife was the central figure of all the ceremonies
of his court and shared in all its amusements.[1]   There
is evidence that the royal pair were on thoroughly
good terms with each other.   Their letters were
affectionate, they were constantly together, and
Henry treated her very generously in money matters.
They often gave each other little presents, and the
queen with her own hands adorned Henry's helmet
with jewels, and embroidered his Garter mantle.[2]
No one can read the simple, touching story given
by the herald of the grief of the royal pair at the
death of Prince Arthur, and continue to believe in
the old story of Henry's hatred of his Yorkist queen.
" When the king understood that sorrowful heavy
tidings he sent for the queen, saying that he and his
queen would take their painful sorrows together.
After that she was come, and saw the king, her lord,
and that natural and painful sorrow, she with full
great and constant comfortable words besought his
grace that he would first after God remember the
weal of his own noble person, the comfort of his
realm and of her. . . .   Then the king thanked her
of her good comfort.   After that she was departed
and come to her own chamber, natural and motherly
remembrance of that great loss smote her so sorrowful to the heart, that those that were about her
were fain to send for the king to comfort her.   Then
his grace, of true, faithful, and gentle love in good

---

[1] The queen occasionally went hunting.   Like Henry she enjoyed
dancing, cards, and dice, and kept a fool, and sometimes took part
in the " disguisings."   *Privy Purse Expenses of Eliz. of York*,
pp. 21 *seq.*   She was specially interested in gardening.

[2] *Excerpta Historica*, pp. 89, 91, 96, 112, 129; *Privy Purse Exp.
Eliz. of York*, p. 8.

haste came and relieved her, and showed her how
wise counsel she had given him before, and he for
his part would thank God for his son, and would
she should do in like wise." [1]   Henry's ability and
energy left Elizabeth no scope for political action
(for which she was unfitted by character and circumstance), but as daughter, wife, and mother she
seems to have been all that is tender and womanly. [2]
Erasmus describes her as brilliant, witty, and pious.
According to André she was deeply religious and
widely charitable, and generous to all who had
served her. [3]   Some of her habits showed a very
frugal mind.   Her gowns were often mended, re-
lined and retrimmed, but in spite of these economies,
owing to her generosity, she was constantly in debt
and had to be helped by Henry. [4]   On her early death
the king ordered that this most gracious and best
beloved princess should be buried with great pomp,
and then " privily departed to a solitary place to
pass his sorrow, and would no man should resort
unto him." [5]   John de Giglis' rhapsody about "the
illustrious maid of York, most beautiful in form,
whose matchless face, adorned with most enchant-
ing sweetness shines," seems to have been more *à
propos* than many courtly effusions.

Henry's mother was a really able woman, " strict
and stately, a woman of great experience and of many

---

[1] Leland, *Collectanea*, iv. 373.

[2] See *Privy Purse Exp. of Eliz. of York*, lxv.–civ.   She was very
generous to her portionless and dependent sisters, and to Princess
Katherine.   *Ibid.*, pp. 9, 79, 94, 99, &c.

[3] André, *Vita*, p. 37.

[4] *Excerpta Historica*, pp. 107, 111, 127.

[5] *Antiquarian Repertory*, iv. 654; *Privy Purse Expenses of Eliz.
of York*, xcvii.–ci.

MARGARET BEAUFORT, COUNTESS OF RICHMOND AND DERBY
1441—1509
From the painting, by an unknown artist, in the National Portrait Gallery

husbands," [1] but her activity found little scope in politics after Henry's accession. She employed her talents on matters of court ceremonial, became a patron of literature, and founded a professorship at Oxford and a college at Cambridge. Fisher dwells much on her piety and asceticism.[2] Ayala thought she had considerable influence with Henry, more than pleased the queen, who, though popular, was powerless. Bacon's account is that " his mother he reverenced much, heard little " ; but in the absence of further evidence all theories about the extent of her influence over Henry are equally admissible, and may be equally wrong. All we know is that Henry repaid her devotion by the gift of his rare affection.[3] Erasmus has left a charming picture of the life of the royal family at their favourite palace of Richmond. All Henry's children were well educated, most of them were accomplished and musical. The young Prince Henry, a handsome boy, already showing signs of a high spirit, strong will, and haughty temper, had been well educated, and treated Erasmus to a Latin speech, to which the mortified scholar, taken unawares, could make no apt reply.[4]

Henry's treatment of Katherine has already been discussed,[5] and it appears that, though there were faults on both sides, Henry's natural kindliness was warped to some extent by a desire to get the better of Ferdinand and by Katherine's own imprudence. The king's relations with his family, therefore, bear

[1] Stubbs, *Lectures on Med. and Mod. Hist.*, 397.

[2] Fisher, *Month's Mind of Lady Marg.* (ed. Mayor), 259–310.

[3] Their letters are very intimate and tender. See, for instance, Halliwell, *Letters*, 188; Ellis, *Letters*, I. (1), 42–8; Everett Green, *Letters of Royal Ladies*, pp. 118–9.

[4] *Letters of Erasmus*, ed. Froude.

[5] See above, pp. 334–5, 357–360.

scrutiny better than is common in royal houses, but
he does not seem to have cared much for any one
outside his family.

He was constitutionally indifferent to women. No
records of his gallantries have come down to us.
Yet he was a keen critic of feminine beauty. His
curiously minute inquiries into the physical charms
of many of the fair and royal ladies of Europe (his
ambassadors had to satisfy him on more than twenty
points) are in piquant contrast to what we know of
the " grave and reverend churchmanlike king." A
solid dower would not satisfy the elderly widower
on the look-out for a rich young wife; the heiress
must be a beauty as well. Henry is really amusing
for once, even if unconsciously so. But he was a
man of contrasts, and the story of his pursuit of Juana
of Castile, though shorn of its most revolting aspect,
reveals much more than his usual indifference. It
shows us Henry in one of his most inhuman moments,
almost brutally absorbed in his " politic " schemes.

But all these details of Henry's private life, which
seem so much at variance with Bacon's grey-toned
study, do not detract from its essential truth.
Though sharing in the amusements of a splendid
court, he remained intellectually alone. His great
aim was kingship, his passion was statecraft. It is
not strange, therefore, that history has dwelt little
on the gentler features of Henry's character. They
were no addition to the driving power that made and
kept him king. The history of a reign chequered
by privy conspiracy and rebellion was little affected
by the fact that the king had genial manners, a
lively humour, and a deep affection for his few
intimates.

The contrast between medievalism and modernism

characteristic of the period appears in the character of the king himself.   In external characteristics,
like much of the England of his day, he was medieval,
a strict and pious churchman, a mighty hunter, and
a founder of religious houses.[1]   Henry's piety was
undoubtedly sincere.   Vergil states that the king
gave generously to religious objects, and never let
business or lack of time prevent him from hearing
two or three masses daily ;   that he gave alms in
secret, following the Christian precept, maintained
an almoner in his household, and secretly gave large
sums of money to provide masses for his soul and
for the welfare of the whole realm.[2]   He prayed much,
we are told, and on Church festivals especially recited the canonical hours, and in the hour of triumph
he never forgot to give thanks ; his religion went
beyond mere outward observance.   He founded
many religious houses and chantries,[3] and went on
pilgrimages to the famous shrines of the kingdom.[4]
In his will Henry directed that a kneeling figure of
himself in golden armour, holding in its hands the
crown of England, should be given to each of these
shrines ; and a golden figure of St. George, weighing

[1] He was specially interested in the Franciscans, and founded
six religious houses for that order.   See Pol. Verg., *op. cit.*, p. 617.

[2] *Ibid. ;* Fisher, *op. cit.*, 268–288.

[3] Three chantry priests, for instance, were maintained at the
king's expense in Westminster Abbey, and the Grey Friars sang
daily in Carmarthen church for the souls of the king's father and
many anniversaries and obits, " orisons, prayers and suffrages,"
were maintained (MSS. Harl. 1498, fo. 916).   The king's will left
money for tapers and lights to burn about his tomb, " continually
and perpetually while the world shall endure."

[4] It is interesting to notice that Sir Richard Guildford, one of the
king's intimate friends, went on a pilgrimage to the Holy Land and
died there.   *Pilgrimage of Sir Richard Guildford* (Camden Society).
See also *Privy Purse Expenses, Excerpta Historica*, p. 88.

140 ounces, set with diamonds, rubies, pearls, and
sapphires, to St. George's Chapel, Windsor.   Among
his most cherished relics were a piece of the Holy Cross
brought from Greece, the leg of St. George captured by
Louis of France at the siege of Milan, both of which
the king left in his will to the altar within the railings
of his tomb at Westminster.   The king never forgot
what he called "the seven works of Mercy, Pitie,
and Charitie."   He endowed almshouses, and to provide for the care of the poor, the sick, and the dying
he founded Savoy Hospital, "because there be fewe
or noon suche like commone Hospitallis within this
our Reame, and that for lack of theim infinite nombre
of pouer nedie people miserably dailly die, no man
putting hande of helpe or remedie."¹   Henry was an
obedient son of his Holy Father the Pope, and received from three Popes in succession the conse-
crated cap and sword which distinguished him as a
prince of the Church militant.   His minister, Morton,
was made a cardinal, but he failed to obtain the
canonisation of his late uncle, Henry VI., for which
he had been very anxious.   In the midst of rebellion
at home and threatening intrigue abroad, he had
made considerable sacrifices of money for the
Crusades.²

All the more sinister by contrast appear his dark
medieval traits, the secretiveness, superstition, and
suspicion that increased with advancing age.   He
trusted few men, suspected many.   He had been
plunged too early into the bitter waters of adversity,

¹ *Will of Henry VII.*, ed. J. Astle, p. 15.   The king also contemplated the foundation of two similar hospitals in Coventry and
York, and left £40,000 by his will for their endowment, but this
bequest was not carried out by his executors.   He also founded almshouses in Westminster.

² See above, p. 230.

and as a fugitive exile, eating the bread of dependence at the courts of France and Burgundy, had
learnt to watch and school himself until repression
had killed all spontaneity. He was " a dark prince
and infinitely suspicious." Yet the system of
espionage he introduced into England had the excuse
of political necessity, " he had such moles perpetually working and casting to undermine him," and
nothing is heard of any attempts to entrap men like
the contemporary activity of the Inquisition in Spain
or of the Medici family. The king gave no personal
countenance to informers,[1] and his spies only worked
where treason was known to be in the air.[2] But the
character that had been moulded and hardened by
adversity was warped by this continual suspicion in
the day of triumph. " His continual vigilance," we
are told, " did sometimes suck in causeless suspicions
which few else knew." Superstition, too, had a
strong hold on the king's mind. Priests and astro-
nomers often appeared at court armed with " prognostications " and prophecies of approaching doom.[3]
At times the ghosts of his dead past seemed to peer
and beckon over the king's shoulder; the execution
of Warwick was a sacrifice of the king's hatred of
bloodshed to his panic-stricken dread of a prophesied
danger.

But these were defects of his later years; in his
prime he showed a very modern and tolerant spirit.
He had the faculty of looking at men and events with

[1] See the story told at the time of the Buckingham conspiracy.

[2] See the *Paston Letters*, iii. 323, for the watch kept over the
Earl of Surrey's household.

[3] One of these " prognostications," brought to Henry on 8th Jan.
1492 (*Excerpta Historica*, p. 85), has been preserved. See *Report on
MSS. of Lord Middleton* (Hist. MSS. Com. Rep. 1911), pp. 263–6,
and App. p. 613.

a half-humorous detachment.   No catastrophe could
disturb him.   Rebel subjects threatening the capital,
a Scotch army crossing the border, a pretender on
the high seas bent on invasion, failed to rob the king
of his presence of mind.   No succession of dangerous
plots unnerved him, no ingratitude incensed him, no
sudden gust of anger obscured his statecraft.   He
was patient in adversity and in victory unrevengeful.
Bacon speaks of Henry as " a merciful prince," and
notices his aversion to bloodshed.   " His pardons
went both before and after his sword," he writes ;
and Hall also alludes to his " merceful pitie."   But
there is much more to be said of a tenderness for
human life that is startling in view of the contemporary tradition of brutality.   Henry's attitude to
rebellion was really original.   He shook himself free
of the cruelty that had stained the civil wars, when
victory for one side had meant death and confiscation for the other.   He abandoned the proscriptions
hitherto associated with tyranny.   The axe of the
headsman and the dungeons of the Tower were rarely
employed in comparison with former reigns.   Political impostors met a scornful clemency that emphasised their ignominy.   The executions of his reign
were so much measures of political necessity that
they seemed to Bacon but slight blots on the king's
fame.   Warwick, Stanley, and Audley were the only
important victims sacrificed by a king who had
taken up the blood-stained sceptre of Richard III.
Henry had a short memory for the former deeds of
men who gave him their support, and thus he won
over the nobler spirits to his side.   The king denied
to the Yorkist cause the strength that comes from
martyrdoms.   The battle of Stoke was the last great
baronial conflict on English soil, and Warbeck's im-

posture, though it had the dangerous support of foreign princes, brought no outburst of Yorkist enthusiasm in England. In all this Henry showed a spirit that would be called generosity in another king. But again the strange contrasts in the king's nature obscure his nobler qualities. He did not demand blood as the price of rebellion, but cash. A swarm of collectors of fines and compositions settled down like flies on rebellious counties, and the appreciation of princely clemency is obscured by a memory of his unroyal bartering of pardons for pence. Again, the success of this unrevengeful habit of the king's as a measure of policy obscures the fact that it arose not from calculation but from a mind averse to bloodshed, a kindly temper that abhorred severity, and a lofty magnanimity that would not stoop to revenge. And yet this tolerance, this modern judicial spirit, had its unfortunate side. It marked out the king's intellectual loneliness. The times were those of intense partisanship, bitterness had accumulated in the faction fights of the Roses, and the king's cold tolerance was alien to the contemporary spirit.

Vergil, who seems to have been a very acute observer, notices Henry's sensitiveness to public opinion—a very modern trait. He was anxious to make a good impression ; " he did not forget that his life was watched by the eyes of many." But the fervid loyalty that Henry schemed and contrived for eluded him. His total lack of enthusiasm made his character non-magnetic. He was too cautious, too calculating, too cold. There was no flash of daring to beat upon men's minds and fire enthusiasm. His appeal was to the head, not to the heart. Though he gained the confidence and support of his people, he did not win their love. He was a patient, secret, very lonely man, with a strength of will and character that won him success, not sympathy. He had no favourites, hardly any friends. There is no record of a strong personal attachment.

He had all the Tudor self-will and impatience of being ruled ; his ministers were servants first and counsellors afterwards. As Bacon put it : " He was of an high mind, and loved his own will and his own way, as one that revered himself and would reign indeed. Had he been a private man he would have been termed proud, but in a wise prince it was but keeping of distance, which, indeed, he did towards all, not admitting any full or near approach to his power or to his secrets. For indeed he was governed by none. . . . He had nothing in him of vainglory, but yet kept state and majesty to the height." [1]

He was too strong to fear ability in others, and could employ as his servants the ablest men in the kingdom, being confident of his own power of keeping them as tools. " Neither did he care how cunning they were that he did employ, for he thought himself to have the master reach." This self-confidence was not misplaced. Of all his counsellors, only one, Sir William Stanley, fell from loyalty to treason. Henry's faithfulness to his servants is noticed by Bacon.[2] No minister of his became the scapegoat of an unpopular or abandoned policy.

Another of the modern traits in Henry's character was his freedom from insularity. This was appreciated by foreign observers. Ayala wrote that the king, not being a pure Englishman, desired to

---

[1] Bacon, *op. cit.*, p. 240. " No one," wrote Vergil, " had so much power with the king as to be able to dare or do anything of his own authority . . . he willed to rule not to be ruled by others."

[2] Bacon, *op. cit.*, pp. 242-3.

employ foreigners in his service, which was checked by the diabolical and unequalled jealousy of his English subjects. His exile had familiarised him with the continental spirit, and he knew how much England missed by lack of intercourse with the world beyond the Channel. Therefore, as we have seen, he welcomed foreign influences at his court, and, most important of all, began the practice of keeping resident ambassadors at the European courts.

On the much discussed question of Henry's avarice, Bacon has a few words that anticipate the modern verdict. He paints for us no vulgar miser, but a wise prince intent at first only on escaping the poverty that crippled contemporary rulers, and in later years carrying carefulness about money to excess through " nature, age, peace, and a mind fixed upon no other ambition or pursuit." Contemporary opinion acquitted him of " gredy desire of riches or hunger of money." As we have seen, he could spend magnificently. His heavy exactions were dictated by policy, not greed. Ayala had heard from the king's own mouth that " he intended to keep his subjects low, because riches would only make them haughty," and politic motives encouraged the recovery of those he had shorn. As Vergil put it, he wished to see their plumes grow again. " He mervellously enriched his realme and himselfe, and yet left his subjects in high wealth and prosperity."

Many of the qualities that made Henry a good king have made him an unpopular man. He was too businesslike for his kingly office. Thrift is the most repellent of all the virtues, and thrift on the throne seems stationed too high. This may have something to do with the feeling of cold dislike that has gathered round King Henry. His good deeds are unheroic, his bad deeds were not great crimes, but sordid actions for which some politic extenuation can be found. It is impossible to become enthusiastic in praise or blame, it is even difficult to allot either without reservation. The king was neither virtuous nor vicious, but lived an average life in a moderate way. It was not until premature old age had gripped the king that the darker shades in his character became prominent.

One great historian even compares him unfavourably with Maximilian, and asserts that while morally Henry was far the superior, every one likes Maximilian better.[1] But is this so ? Can we honestly prefer the glittering pinchbeck of the proudly styled King of the Romans to the stern figure of the founder of the most characteristic dynasty that ever wore the crown of England, the maker of modern England, the forerunner of our naval greatness ? If we do, it is strange indeed.

But in the region of intellect much bolder language can be used. The king's ability was marvellous.

There is no doubt of the reputation that Henry won for himself. If we leave out of account the panegyrics of courtly historians, it is clear that he left behind him " a name which was the admiration of the succeeding age."[2] To Bacon he was the Solomon of England ; to Burleigh he was a storehouse of all heroical virtues ; to Stow " a prince of marvellous wisdom, policy, justice, temperance, and gravity."[3]

[1] Stubbs, *Lectures on Mediœval and Modern History*, p. 387. " All the balance of real goodness, what measure there is of politic honesty, purity of life, reality of character, straight-forwardness in religion, intelligent appreciation of his people's needs, every moral consideration, is in favour of Henry Tudor: yet we like Maximilian better."

[2] *L. and P. Hen. VII.*, ii., Intro. xxviii.

[3] See also Fabyan, *Chronicle*, p. 690.

Hall, following Vergil, gives the contemporary opinion with no uncertain voice. He was " of wyt in all thynges quycke and prompte, of a pryncely stomacke and haute courage. In great perels, doubtfull affaires, and matters of weighty importaunce, supernaturall and in maner devyne. . . . He was sobre, moderate, honest, affable, courteous, bounteous, so muche abhorring pride and arrogancy, that he was ever sharpe and quicke to them which were noted or spotted with that crime."

Bernard André, in his usual style of tedious panegyric, compares the king's difficulties to the twelve labours of Hercules, and finds a parallel in each case. Richard III. is the Erymanthian boar, Margaret of Burgundy the Amazons, Perkin Warbeck in Ireland is Cacus hiding in a cave, the factions of the red and white rose are the Hydra, and so on. The fact that a court poet was capable of imaginative glorification of his patron is not specially significant, but even the most captious critic can find some meaning in the parallel. It is not an empty flattery, but a rendering, in the taste of the time, of a very real tribute to the king's success.

Fisher's eulogy on the king's personal gifts—his quick and ready wit, his retentive memory, wide experience, and gracious speech—contains another eloquent summary of his successes. " Leagues and confederacies he had with all Christian princes ; his mighty power was dread everywhere, not only within his realm, but without also ; his people were to him in as humble subjection as ever they were to king, his land many a day in peace and tranquillity." [1]

His reputation abroad was, as Bacon points out,

[1] Fisher, *Sermon on Death of King Henry* (Early Eng. Text Soc., xxvii.).

even higher than it was at home. " Foreigners noted that he was ever in strife and ever aloft." In his later years the reports of foreign ambassadors are uniformly couched in the same tone of admiration for the king's wisdom and belief in the strength of his position. The Spanish envoy reported that the king was rich, had established good order in England, and kept the people in such subjection as had never been the case before. " His good fortune," wrote the Italian visitor, " has been equal to his spirit, for he has never lost a battle. From the time of William the Conqueror no king has reigned more peaceably than he has, his great prudence causing him to be universally feared." [1]

He came to the throne with a reputation for wisdom, and the years spread round him the glamour of success. This valuable growth of prestige Henry fostered by bringing into play his personal influence, by no means a negligible factor, dazzling the eyes of ambassadors and envoys by a display of wealth and splendour, winning them over by his gracious bearing. " He put them into admiration," writes Bacon, " to find his universal insight into the affairs of the world. . . . So that they did ever write to their superiors in high terms concerning his wisdom and art of rule." [2]

Henry loses nothing by comparison with his foreign contemporaries Ferdinand, Louis, Charles, Maximilian, and Philip. He was by far the ablest of them all. His task was harder, and he accomplished more than

---

[1] *Italian Relation*, p. 46.

[2] As we have seen, de Puebla came under Henry's influence to such an extent that he forgot his duty to Ferdinand and Isabella. The Venetian ambassador, after a long audience, reported that the king was gracious, grave, and dignified. He knighted the ambassador, gave him a collar worth 500 ducats and a fine horse from the royal stables. Brown, *Ven. Cal.*, i. Nos. 754, 764, 765.

any of them. Whether we regard methods, morals, or achievements, the balance must be in favour of the Tudor.

Was Henry a great king ? The answers to this question have been very different. Bacon seems rather to under-estimate than over-estimate the king's ability. He regards him as an opportunist, dexterous in evading danger rather than provident in preventing the cause of it, near sighted rather than long sighted ; and to this psychological weakness more than to the pressure of circumstances Bacon attributes the constant perils and dangers which menaced him. " The perpetual troubles of his fortunes (there being no more matter out of which they grew) could not have been without some great defects and main errors in his nature, customs, and proceedings." [1] But, with all deference, it seems unfair to burden the king's character with responsibility for the troubles which made care and watchfulness a necessity. Further, he declared that Henry lacked lofty aims, and that his achievements were inconsiderable when viewed in connection with the manner in which he was endowed by nature and fortune. An opportunist he certainly may have been, with the gift of snatching gain from circumstances, but it is idle to deny that he had one great aim to which all else was subordinated—that of founding in England a dynasty that could claim and enforce obedience, gain and use power ; and this aim, though it lacks the glamour of a disinterested ideal, has certainly the dignity of practical utility. Bacon's complaint is really a reading of the reign in the light of the political theories current in his own time.

Another great historian, after asking the question

[1] Bacon, *op. cit.*, p. 244.

whether Henry was a great king, returns a doubtful
answer. He finds in him none of the " self-denying
devotion which gives itself for the people "—no
impulsive well-doing.[1] And yet these things, though
perhaps the qualities we might look for in a good
man, would have been defects in a great king placed
in Henry's position. It was not " impulsive well-
doing " that England needed, but the conduct based
on coldly reasoned foresight that Henry gave her.
Self-denying devotion would not have been as useful
to England as the heavy hand of a determined
despot. When Henry came to the throne, weakness
and disorder were arresting facts that made a practical
aim faithfully pursued more valuable than the most
enlightened theories. No weak hand could have led
the divided and distracted nation, but Henry VII.
was the strongest of all the heavy-handed Tudors.
Not swayed by sudden personal caprice like Henry
VIII., not subject to moods of irresolution and inde-
cision like Elizabeth, his strength of will and purpose seemed superhuman. When the chance he had
waited for long came at last, it found him prepared,
and he fortified his position with all the arts and all
the dogged grip of a successful adventurer. What
he once grasped, he held for always ; he never lost
ground, but inch by inch pushed forward.

The eloquent sentences in which Bishop Stubbs
qualifies Henry's greatness seem to prove it. He
cannot be denied the title of a great king ; whether
he was a good man is a matter of opinion, whether
he was an attractive one is generally negatived. He
had none of the arts of the demagogue, but all the
qualities of the despot. He was a statesman first of
all, and as a statesman he must be judged.

[1] Stubbs, *op. cit.* p. 425.

" What he minded, he compassed," and success crowned his fine struggle to bring order out of anarchy. He found England weak, he left it strong ; he found it divided, he left it united. He founded a dynasty, and left to his son the example of successful despotism, a strong title, a great treasure, a subservient nobility, a dependent Church, a submissive Parliament, and a popular policy. From the bloodstained horrors of dynastic strife there emerged an England of fair promise.

Unfortunately, while a master mind has emphasized the grey tones of Henry's character, chance has made us familiar with a very sombre portrait of the king's person. Most of the existing pictures show a grey, wasted face with set, harsh features furrowed by suspicion and anxiety, a steely grey eye, and a pinched, forbidding mouth. But all these pictures have the same original, the cast taken after death for his monument. Of the king in his prime we have no picture, and the contemporary accounts of Henry's beauty, his golden hair and brilliant complexion, seem almost unbelievable. Yet they all agree in essentials. Hall, following Vergil, whose authority as a contemporary is unchallengeable, wrote of Henry as a man " of body but leane and spare,[1] albeit mighty and stronge therwith, of personage and stature somewhat hygher then the meane sorte of men be, of a wonderfull beutye and fayre complexion, of countenaunce mery and smylyng, especially in his communication." [2]

---

[1] This is a curious rendering of the word " gracile," which appears in Vergil's account.

[2] Hall, *Chron.*, p. 504 ; Pol. Verg., p. 616. Others speak of the king's sweet, well-favoured face, his goodly and amiable person, his natural complexion of the fairest mixture, and so on.

But the familiar portraits of the king, painted when time and his " sorrowful life " had set their mark upon him, are full of character. It is a strong, bold, hard face, the face of a man acute and penetrative, cold and determined, of a leader of men not of a popular hero, a man to be obeyed and feared, not loved. Strength not sympathy, watchfulness not generosity, are written in the much-lined face.

Even if there be a difference of opinion about Henry's personal character, there can be none about the importance of the reign. It is a historical commonplace that the end of the fifteenth century marks the line between medieval and modern Europe. Though obviously no such line of demarcation can be scientifically accurate, the history of the reign of Henry VII. reveals the constant contact and conflict of things new and old, both in fact and theory. A Crusade and a voyage in search of the North-West Passage come together; a law forbidding usury, and an enormous expansion of the credit system; an invasion of France by the king in person, reviving the memory of the triumphs of Crecy and Agincourt, and an anticipation of the modern attempt to secure peace by maintaining a balance of power in Europe.

It is almost impossible to read the reign in the contemporary spirit. It is easy to exaggerate the immediate effect of events which later proved to be of immense importance ; there is a constant temptation to read too much of the future into the events of the time. To us the reign appears a time of beginnings, of fresh starts in nearly every branch of human activity ; but the points which contemporaries —not being prophets—dwell upon are the details of conspiracy and the incidents of diplomacy. The germs in which the history of modern Europe was hidden escaped them. Dying medievalism and aspiring modernism were in contact, but the friction produced only a spark here and there, no illuminating flash to make its mark on the contemporary imagination. We have not, therefore, on anything but the king's personal character the verdict of the men of his own day.

There is an irrational but irresistible feeling of disappointment that no dramatic events ushered in these great beginnings. Their effect during the reign was insignificant, and occasionally—as in the case of the printing press, which at first almost smothered creative literature—bad. Mighty changes of principle were introduced, but the principle long lay buried under a series of empirical experiments. The Cabot voyages set the ships of England on the course which was to found the world empire of a great naval power, but for practical purposes they were little more than unsuccessful commercial speculations. The New World of the West was discovered by accident in an attempt to find a new route to the old trading grounds of the East, and the failure of that attempt appeared more significant in the reign of Henry VII. than the continent discovered by chance. The same point is to be noticed about the Renaissance : the spirit of modern Europe was there, but it was at first inarticulate. The visible links with the past attracted eyes which could not see, as we do, the links leading on to a mighty future. In another aspect the reign began a period which ended only with the Napoleonic wars, a period dominated by the territorial ambitions of rival European states. Europe was in the throes of a great separatist movement. The old bonds of the

Papacy and the Empire were giving way, and the separate states of Europe were pushing their opposing way in a world which had lost its old boundaries by the geographical discoveries. The admitted tendency of modern writers to exaggerate the effect of national character on history need not obscure one of the most interesting points in the reign—the emergence of a self-conscious national spirit with keen ambitions. In England, national replaced local patriotism, and hardened rapidly within natural frontiers.

The political rise of the middle class, whose influence on history before the age of great revolutions is a purely English phenomenon, is another new feature. The strength of the English House of Commons during the centuries that followed the death of Henry VII. was an exception to the usual position of the third estates in other European countries. This development, which has been an ingredient giving a marked flavour to the development of national character, was due in great measure to the Parliamentary despotism of Henry VII. and his descendants.

Sixteenth-century English history is the era of triumphant personality. The sovereigns of the Tudor line drove their personality deep into history, and the stamp of those bold, strong figures is printed deeply for all time. Personal character became a potent force, but the period of its triumph was the result of the work done by the uninspiring founder of the mighty dynasty. The slow, secret, patient work of Henry VII. laid the foundation upon which his successors reared the glittering fabric of their dominating personalities.[1] He was the ancestor in char-

[1] Henry VII. and his famous son now face each other across the entrance to the lobby of the House of Commons, and these modern

acter as well as in fact of that curiously individual family. In his complex nature we find most of the characteristics of his descendants—the ruthless strength of his son as well as the literary interests of his grandson, the narrow piety of Mary and the common sense and commercial spirit of Elizabeth—and from him they inherited the delicate tact and instinct for popularity common to them all.

In spite of the lack of contemporary recognition, it is hardly an over-statement to say that every force—political, social, religious, and intellectual—which moulded the history of England for some four hundred years appeared first in the reign of Henry VII. We have seen the founding of the Tudor despotism, the creation of a royal navy, the revival of learning, the introduction of the printing press, the beginning of modern diplomacy, the appearance of national self-consciousness ; we have seen the anticipation of the mercantile system, of the idea of the balance of power, of the rise of the middle class, and of the dissolution of the monasteries. Finally, the voyages of discovery heralded the dawn of a new age, in which the Atlantic replaced the Mediterranean and England became the central fortress of civilisation instead of its last outpost on the edge of the unknown.

wall paintings happily reveal the essential contrast between them. It is a contrast between mind and matter, between the frail tenement of a mighty spirit and triumphant materialism, between the man who fought for and him who inherited, success.

APPENDICES

I

ITINERARY OF HENRY VII

Note.—*The Charter, Patent, and Close Rolls of the reign furnish the greater part of the Itinerary. Additions from other sources, such as the collections of royal letters, and the privy purse expenses, are distinguished by the reference numbers.*

1485. *Aug.* 22, Bosworth Field ; 27, London.[1] *Sept.* 1–3, Westminster ; 3, Guildford ; 5, Westminster ; 6–7, Guildford ;[2] 8–19, Westminster. *Oct.* 30, Westminster (Coronation in Abbey). *Nov.* 7, Westminster (Opening of Parliament) ; 8–19, Westminster.[2] *Dec.* 1–9, Westminster ;[2] 10, Westminster (Prorogation of Parliament) ; 17, Greenwich.[2]

1486. *Jan.* 18, Westminster (Marriage with Elizabeth of York); 21, Westminster.[2] *Feb.* 24, Westminster.[2] *Mar.* 10, Ware, Royston ; 11, 12, Canterbury ; 16, Peterborough, Stamford ; 17, Stamford ; 22–28, Ely. *April* 1–5, Lincoln ; 7–15, Nottingham ; 21–28, York ; 29, 30, Doncaster. *May* 2–5, Nottingham ; 8–12, Birmingham ; 10–15, Worcester ; 20, Gloucester ; 21, Bristol; 22, Gloucester ; 23–26, Bristol ; 28, Abingdon ; 30, Westminster. *Aug.* 30, Somersham (co. Huntingdon). *Sept.* 1–6, Winchester ; 7, Salisbury ;[2] 9, East Dereham ;[2] 10, Brandon Ferry (co. Suffolk); 12–16, Downham ; 14, Greenwich,[2] Christchurch Monastery (in Southwark); 17–27, Winchester. *Oct.* 2, Malling Abbey ; 4, Winchester ; 9, Greenwich ;[2] 13–24, Winchester.[2] *Nov.* 1, Greenwich ;[2] 6–11, Westminster ;[2] 13–22, Greenwich ; 22–*Jan.* 13, 1487, Greenwich.[2]

1487. *Jan.* 1–13, Greenwich ;[2] 21–24, Windsor ; 22, Canterbury ; 25, Moor ;[3] 27–31, Sheen.[2] *Feb.* 1–*March* 11, Sheen.[2] *Mar.* 19, Chertsey Monastery ;[2] 20, Westminster ; 22, Croydon,

---

[1] *City Chronicle* (ed. Kingsford).
[2] *Materials for Reign of Henry VII.* (Rolls Ser.).
[3] This, the " royal manor of Moore," is probably Moor in Essex.

Sheen ; 25, 26, Chertsey ;[1] 28, Fulham ; 30, Hevingham Castle, *April* 1–2, Colchester ;[1] 4–8, Bury St. Edmunds Abbey ;[1] 10, Colchester, East Harling ;[1] 11–13, 17, Norwich ; 17, Walsingham ;[1] 18–19, Cambridge ; 22, York ; 22–30, Coventry.[1] *May* 1–8, 9–14, 17, 22–27, 31, Kenilworth Castle.[2] *June* 1–5, Kenilworth Castle ; 16, Battle of Stoke ; 24, Leicester ; 27, Kenilworth Castle ; 29, Pontefract ; 30, Kenilworth. *July* 1–18, Kenilworth ; 20, Raby ;[3] 21–22, Kenilworth ; 25–26, Nottingham ; 29, Pontefract ; 30–31, York. *Aug.* 1–6, York ;[1] 8, 11, 13, Durham ; 9, Croft ;[4] 14–18, Newcastle-on-Tyne ;[1] 19–20, Durham ; 22, Richmond (co. York) ; 23–24, Ripon ; 25–27, Pontefract Castle ; 28, Newark, Chesterford ; 29, Stamford ; 30, Huntingdon. *Sept.* 1–3, Warwick ;[1] 8–10, Leicester Abbey ;[1] 11, Warwick ;[1] 11–12, Rockingham Castle ;[1] 17–26, Warwick. *Nov.* 2, St. Alban's Abbey ; 4, City of London ;[5] 9, Westminster (Opening of Second Parliament) ; 17–30, Westminster ; 20, Greenwich ; 23, Tower of London ; 25, Westminster Abbey (Coronation of Queen). *Dec.* 1–5, Greenwich ; 11–18, Westminster ; 19–22, 25–31, Greenwich.[6]

1488. *Jan.* 10, Rochester,[1] Esher ;[7] 13–23, Greenwich ; 29–*Feb.* 1, Westminster.[1] *Feb.* 2–6, Greenwich.[1] *Mar.* 5, Sheen ;[1] 6, Westminster ;[1] 8–17, Sheen ; 18–20, Canterbury ; 21–22, Sandwich ;[1] 23–24, Dover ;[1] 25–31, Canterbury. *April* 1, 2, 5, 8, Canterbury ; 8–11, Windsor ;[1] 14, Southampton ;[8] 16, Maidstone ; 17–18, Chichester ;[1] 19 (Easter Day), Windsor ; 20–28, Windsor. *May* 1, Sheen ; 3–21, Westminster ; 25–28, Windsor ; 29–30, Croydon.[9] *June* 1–2, Croydon ; 2, Sheen ; 4–14, Windsor ; 8, Maidstone ; 18–20, Westminster ; 28–*July* 14, Kenilworth Castle.[1] *July* 1–14, Kenilworth Castle ;[1] 16, Abingdon Abbey ;[1] 19, Wood-

---

[1] *Materials* (Rolls Ser.).

[2] Ellis, *Letters* I., 1.

[3] This was the Durham seat of the Nevill family.

[4] This is probably a hamlet in Yorkshire on the Durham side of the Tees.

[5] *City Chronicle* (ed. Kingsford).

[6] Leland, *Collectanea,* iv.

[7] Esher was the site of a royal manor or palace.

[8] Leland, *Collectanea,* iv. The king visits and inspects Venetian galleys.

[9] When at Croydon the king was entertained at the Archbishop's palace.

stock manor ;[1] 23, Kenilworth ;[1] Tame ;[1] 26, Abingdon ;[1] 27–
Aug. 4, 8–12, Windsor ;[1] 13, Horsham ; 15, Lewes ; 16, Charing ;[2]
17, Battle ; 20, Raby ; 23, Lewes ; 27, Arundel ; 29, Slindon.
Sept. 3–9, Windsor ;[1] 10–11, Knole ; 16, Ashford ; 19, 22, Can-
terbury. *Nov.* 1–2, Windsor ; 4, Sheen ; 10–30, Westminster.
Dec. 1–18, Westminster ; 23, Maidstone ; 25–27, Sheen.

1489. *Jan.* 3, Maidstone ; 11–13, Westminster (Opening of
Third Parliament) ; 14, Windsor ; 15–28, Westminster ; 29, Sheen.
Feb. 1–23, Westminster ; 23, Westminster (Parliament prorogued).
April 4, Windsor ; 8–*May* 12, Hertford Castle.[1] *May* 1–12,
Hertford Castle ;[1] 27–*June* 3, York ; 4, Pontefract ; 10, Notting-
ham ; 11, Harborough, Leicester ; 12, Northampton ; 14, St.
Albans ; 18, Woodstock ;[1] 21, Northampton ;[1] 20–*July* 13,
Windsor.[3] *Aug.* 4, Sonning ;[4] 4–*Sept.* 19, Windsor. *Oct.* 4,
Westminster (Second Session of Third Parliament opens). *Nov.*
1–30, Westminster. *Dec.* 4, Westminster (Third Parliament pro-
rogued).

1490. *Jan.* 24, Westminster (Third Session of Third Parliament
opens). *April* 10–11, Canterbury. *July* 11–28, Westminster.[5]
Aug. 14, Windsor ; 15, Eltham.[6] *Sept.* 10–15, Manor of Woking ;
17, Woking ; 19, Ewelme Manor (co. Oxford) ; 22, Windsor ;[1] 28,
Westminster ; 30, Ewelme Manor. *Oct.* 16, Ewelme ; 21, 24, Mortlake. *Nov.* 15–18, 21–26, Windsor ; 29–30, Westminster.[7] *Dec.*
1–3, 7–19, Windsor ; 21, Greenwich ; 23, Maidstone ; 26–28, Westminster.

1491. *Jan.* 2–8, Maidstone. *Mar.* 31, Canterbury. *April* 3
(Easter Day), Canterbury ; 4–8, Canterbury. *June,* Greenwich (*June* 22, Birth of Prince Henry). *July* 11, Greenwich ;[8]
19–20, 22, Colchester ; 28, Norwich. *Aug.* 4, Bury St. Edmunds ;
5 Ely ; 10, Northampton ; 14, Leicester ; 31, Tewkesbury. *Sept.*

---

[1] *Materials* (Rolls Ser.).

[2] The Archbishops of Canterbury had another palace here.

[3] During July and August the king was hunting in Windsor
Forest and Enfield Chase. Leland, *Collectanea.*

[4] The king had a hunting lodge at Sonning.

[5] *L. and P. Hen. VII.*

[6] There was a royal manor at Eltham.

[7] On these dates Prince Arthur was created Prince of Wales and
Princess Margaret was christened. Leland, *Collectanea.*

[8] Ellis, *Letters,* II. (i.), 170–3.

2–6, Gloucester ; 8, Kingswood ; 10–14, Bristol ;[1] 19, Wells ; 29, Shaftesbury ; 30, Salisbury. *Oct.* 1, Salisbury ; 5, Marlborough ; 14, Westminster[2] (Meeting of Third Parliament) ; 15–30, Westminster. *Nov.* 4, Westminster[2] (Fourth Parliament prorogued).

1492. *Jan.* 8, Isleworth ;[3] 18, Windsor ;[3] 23, Sheen ;[3] 24, Westminster (Second Session of Fourth Parliament) ; 25, Tower of London.[3] *Mar.* 5, Westminster (Fourth Parliament dissolved). *April* 5, Canterbury ; 6, Sheen ;[3] 15, Windsor ; 19, Sheen ; 22–24, Canterbury. *May* 1, Mayfield[4] (co. Sussex) ; 7, Sheen. *July* 19, Windsor ;[3] 22, Greenwich ;[3] 30, St. Mary Cray,[3] Maidstone ;[3] 31, Sittingbourne. *Aug.* 1–12, Canterbury ; 13, Sittingbourne ; 14, 15, Maidstone ; 16, Dartford ; 17, Greenwich ;[3] 27, Windsor. *Sept.* 4, Dartford ;[3] 7, Maidstone ;[3] 9, Sittingbourne ; 10–24, Canterbury ; 24, Sandwich ; 24–30, Canterbury. *Oct.* 2, Dover (King sails for France) ; 2–16, Calais ; 18–30, Boulogne. *Nov.* 1–4, Boulogne. *Dec.* 7–11, Calais ;[3] 17, Dover ; 19, Greenwich ; 22, City of London (State visit) ; 25, Westminster.

1493. *Jan.* 1, Westminster.[5] *Feb.* 14, Lambeth ;[5] 19, Westminster.[6] *Mar.* 2, Westminster ;[5] 30, Canterbury. *April* 2–10, Canterbury ; 15, Windsor ;[6] 21, "At Richard Lees" ;[6] 22, Buckingham ;[6] 25, Banbury, Warwick ;[6] 30, Coventry.[6] *May* 13, Northampton.[6] *June* 5, Coventry.[6] *Aug.* 22, Saltwood ; 27, Maidstone. *Oct.* 2, Colly Weston ;[6] 17, "Moorhende " (? Moor Place, Surrey) ; 20, "At Richard Lees " ;[6] 22, Windsor.[6] *Dec.* 22–26, Maidstone.

1494. *Jan.* 4, Maidstone ; 7, Windsor ;[6] 12, Winchcombe ;[6] 15, Fowlers ;[7] 17, Woodstock ;[6] 18, Minster Lovell ;[6] 19, Oxford ;[6] 22, Woodstock ;[6] 23, Fowlers ;[6] 24, Wycombe ;[1] 25, Windsor ;[6] 26, Isleworth ; 31, Westminster. *Feb.* 23, Sheen. *Mar.* 13, Uxbridge ; 20–30, Canterbury. *April* 2, Greenwich ;[6] 5, Dartford ;[6] 8, Rochester,[6] Canterbury ; 9–14, Canterbury ;[6] 15, Sandwich ;[6] 19, Dover ;[6] 26, Dartford ;[6] 30, Greenwich.[6] *June* 1, Sheen.[6] *Aug.* 2–10, Sheen ;[6] 12, Syon Abbey ;[6] 14, Windsor ; 19, Reading ; 20, Ewelme ; 23, Abingdon.[6] *Sept.* 1, Woodstock ;[6] 4,

---

[1] *Ricart's Calendar of Bristol,* 45–47.

[2] *Rot. Parl.* (Rolls Ser.), vi. 440.

[3] *Privy Purse Expenses, Excerpta Historica* (ed. Bentley).

[4] The Archbishop of Canterbury had a palace there.

[5] Stow, *Annales.*

[6] *Privy Purse Expenses ; L. and P. Henry VII.*

[7] Near Cranbrook in Kent.

Langley ; 12–16, Canterbury. *Oct.* 1, Westminster ; 26, Sheen ; 27, Westminster. *Nov.* 1, Westminster (Prince Henry created Duke of York[1]) ; 2–14, Westminster. *Dec.* 22, Knole ; 23, Greenwich ; 26–29, Tower of London.

1495. *Jan.* 30, Westminster ; 31, Greenwich.[2] *Mar.* 2, Sheen. *April* 1, Sheen ;[2] 18–27, Canterbury ; 28, Westminster. *May* 7, Eltham ;[2] 15, Sheen.[2] *June* 21, Wycombe ;[2] 22, Notley[2] (co. Bucks) ; 23, Woodstock.[2] *July* 1, Chipping Norton ;[2] 2, Evesham ;[2] 3, Tewkesbury ;[2] 4, Worcester ;[2] 10, Bewdley ;[2] 12, Ludlow ;[2] 15, Shrewsbury ;[2] 16, Combermere Abbey ; 17, Holt Castle[2] (co. Worcs. or co. Denbigh) ; 18, Chester ;[2] 20, Kenilworth Castle ;[2] 27, Vale Royal Abbey ; 28, Alnwick ; 30, Latham.[4] *Aug.* 3, Knowsley ;[2] 4, Warrington ;[2] 5, Manchester ;[2] 6, Mayfield (co. Staffs.) ; 8, Newcastle ;[2] 10, Stafford ;[2] 11, Lichfield ;[2] 12, Burton ;[2] 13, Derby ; 28, Loughborough ; 29, Leigh (? co. Salop). *Sept.* 1, Wollaston ; 4, Colly Weston ;[2] 11, Rockingham ; 12, Northampton ; 16, Banbury ; 19, Woodstock ;[2] 29, Ewelme ;[5] 30, Bisham. *Oct.* 1, Windsor ;[2] 3, Sheen ;[2] 14, Westminster (Meeting of Fifth Parliament) ; 16, Westminster.[2] *Nov.* 16, Ely Place.[6] *Dec.* 21, Westminster.

1496. *Feb.* 26, Sheen.[2] *Mar.* 24–*April* 4, Canterbury. *April* 5, Westminster ; 15, Maidstone ; 16, Sheen.[2] *May* 12, Sheen ;[2] 15, Westminster ;[2] 17, Sheen.[2] *June* 12–21, Sheen ;[2] 23, Merton Abbey ; 25, Chertsey Abbey ; 26, Guildford. *July* 2, Faversham Abbey ; 3, "Alfford" ; 5, Waltham[2] (Bishops' Waltham held by the Bishops of Winchester) ; 10, Porchester ;[2] 14, Southampton ;[2] 20, Bewley ;[2] 21, Isle of Wight ;[2] 23, Bewley ;[2] 25, Christchurch ; 26, Poole ;[2] 27, Corfe Castle.[2] *Aug.* 5, Salisbury ;[2] 10, Haytesbury ;[2] 11, Broke[2] (co. Wilts) ; 12, Bath ; 13, Bristol ;[7] 19, Acton Turville ; 21, Malmesbury Abbey ; 25, Cirencester Abbey ;[2] 30, Woodstock.[2] *Sept.* 9, Wycombe ;[2] 10, Windsor ; 21, Windsor. *Oct.* 24–*Nov.* 5, Westminster (Great Council) ; 30, St. Paul's Cathedral (State Visit).[2] *Nov.* 1–5, Westminster. *Dec.* 25, Greenwich.

---

[1] *L. and P. Henry VII.*

[2] *Privy Purse Expenses.*

[3] Ellis, *Letters,* I. (i.), No. xi.

[4] This was one of the seats of the Earl of Derby.

[5] This was the seat of Edmund de la Pole, Earl of Suffolk.

[6] King and queen dine with the serjeants (*City Chronicle*).

[7] *Ricart's Calendar of Bristol.*

1497. *Jan.* 16, Westminster (Meeting of Sixth Parliament) ;
Feb. 17, Sheen.[1] *Mar.* 13, Westminster,[2] (Sixth Parliament
dissolved); 17, Sheen; 18, Maidstone;[1] 25–26, Canterbury. *April*
17, London;[1] 21, Greenwich.[1] *June* 5, Aylesbury;[1] 11, Buckingham;[1] 12, Banbury;[1] 13, Woodstock;[1] 14, Abingdon;[1] 15,
Wallingford;[1] 16, Reading, Windsor,[1] Kingston, Lambeth;[1] 18,
St. George's-in-the-Field,[1] Blackheath, St. Paul's;[1] 18–23, Tower
of London.[1] *July* 1, Sheen;[1] 29, Netley Abbey (co. Hants) ; 30,
Woodstock. *Aug.* 1–19, Woodstock;[3] 19, Cornbury (co. Oxford) ;
21, Minster Lovell;[1] 22, Woodstock.[4] *Sept.* 1–13, Woodstock ;[1]
17, Cirencester ;[1] 28, Malmesbury Abbey ;[1] 29, Bath ;[1] 30, Wells.[1]
Oct. 2, Glastonbury ;[1] 3, Bridgwater ; 4–5, Taunton ;[1] 6, Tiverton ;[1]
7, Exeter.[1] *Nov.* 18, Sheen; 23, Westminster. *Dec.* 25, Sheen.

1498. *Feb.* 21, Greenwich (Birth of Prince Edmund). *Mar.* 15,
19–21, Westminster; 23, 24–26, Maidstone ; 28, Charing. *April*
2–17, Canterbury ; 19, Maidstone ;[1] 20, Faversham Abbey,[1] Canterbury ;[1] 26, Sittingbourne;[1] 27, Rochester ;[1] 28, Dartford.[1] *May*
8, Tower of London ; 15, Elsing ; 23, Hertford. *June* 9, Westminster ; 15, Sheen.[4] *Aug.* 1, Havering ; 3, Bordefeld ;[1] 4, Mont-
gomery ;[1] 6–11, Castle Hedingham ;[5] 14, Bury ;[1] 20, Buckenham
Castle[6] (co. Norf.); 21, Norwich ;[1] 22, Blickling (co. Norf.) ;[7]
23, Walsingham ; 24–25, Lynn ; 29, Knole. *Sept.* 5, "At Pet.
Herough's " ; 7, Colly Weston ;[1] 8, Huntingdon ;[1] 12, Harrowden[8]
(co. Northants) ; 13, Northampton ;[1] 16, Edgcote ;[9] 19, Banbury ;[1]
20, Woodstock; 21, 30, Knole. *Oct.* 1, Croydon ; 4, Langley,
Woodstock. *Nov.* 22, Westminster ; 30, City of London (Reception
to Prince of Wales).[1] *Dec.* 28–31, " At my Lord Bath's."[11]

1499. *Jan.* 1–13, " At my Lord Bath's " ;[11] 18, Westminster ; 19,
Greenwich ;[1] 27, Westminster.[11] *Feb.* 2, Sheen ;[1] 6, Greenwich ;
24, Greenwich. *Mar.* 5–21, Greenwich ; 23–31, Canterbury.[12]
April 1–3, Canterbury. *May* 4, Wanstead ; 7, Tower of London.

---

[1] *Privy Purse Expenses.*   [2] *Rot. Parl.*
[3] Ellis, *Letters,* i.   [4] *L. and P. Henry VII.*
[5] Visit to the Earl of Oxford.
[6] This was the home of Sir Thomas Knyvet.
[7] This was the home of Sir Thomas Boleyn.
[8] The residence of Sir Nicholas Vaux.
[9] Visit to Sir Reginald Bray.   [10] *City Chronicle.*
[11] This was a visit to Oliver King, Bishop of Bath and Wells.
[12] Bergenroth, *Spanish Calendar.*

June 15, Sheen ; 25, Langley ; [1] 26–27, Abingdon ; [1] 29, Donning-
ton ; [1] 30, Andover ; [1] 31, Winchester.[1] *Aug.* 2, Southampton ;
3, Beaulieu ; 9, Isle of Wight; 23, Quarr Abbey ; 24, Portchester.
Sept. 2, Bishop's Waltham ; 3–20, Winchester; 23, Frefolk ; 26,
Basingstoke. *Oct.* 9, Windsor; 24–*Dec.* 7, Westminster.[2] *Dec.* 8,
Wanstead ; 14, Elsing.[1]

    1500. *Jan.* 13, Sheen ; [1] 14, Hatfield.[1] *Feb.* 5–10, 24, West-
minster.[3] *April* 7, London ; [4] 21, Canterbury. *May* 2–5, Canterbury ;
3–*June* 9, Calais. *June* 16, Dover, Maidstone ; 20, Canterbury ; [5]
22, Westminster.[6] *July* 24, Greenwich ; [5] 25, Burnham Abbey ; [1]
28, Croydon. *Aug.* 6, Westminster ; [2] *Sept.* 5–25, Woodstock ; 28,
Notley. *Oct.* 1–6, Notley ; 9, Woodstock ; 15–28, Woodstock ;
30, Woodstock. *Nov.* 4, Woodstock.[4] *Dec.* 5–11, Woodstock ;
16, Lanthony Abbey (co. Glouc.) ; 18, Abingdon ; [3] 19–31, Lanthony
Abbey.

    1501. *Jan.* 2, 5, Lanthony Abbey ; 9–13, Woodstock. *Mar.* 21,
Richmond. *April* 10, Eltham ; 24–29, Westminster.[2] *May* 1,
Tower of London ; 9, Westminster ; [3] 29, Lanthony Abbey. *June*
4, Lanthony Abbey. *July* 31, Mile End.[7] *Aug.* 2, Westminster ; [2]
7, 14, 20, 21, Lanthony Abbey ; 23, Martyn Abbey ; 26, Lanthony
Abbey. *Sept.* 25–*Oct.* 4, Richmond. *Nov.* 4–9, Dogmersfield ; [8]
10, Baynard's Castle ; [3] 12, London ; 14, St. Paul's Cathedral
(Marriage of Arthur and Katherine); 15, Westminster ; 16, Baynard's Castle ; 17–26, Westminster; 28–*Dec.* 31, Richmond.[3]

    1502. *Jan.* 14–25, Richmond.[9] *Feb.* 22–*April* 3, *May* 27, West-
minster. *June* 22–28, Westminster.[3] *July* 20, Woodstock.[4] *Aug.*
1–3, Woodstock. *Sept.* 24, Woodstock ; [1] 28–30, Langley.[1] *Oct.* 1,
Woodstock ; 18, 20, Windsor ; 30–*Nov.* 28, Westminster. *Dec.* 21,
St. Alban's.[1]

[1] *Privy Purse Expenses.*
[2] Rymer, *Fœdera.*
[3] Bergenroth, *Spanish Calendar.*
[4] *Venetian Calendar.*
[5] *L. and P. Henry VII.*
[6] Funeral of Prince Edmund.
[7] At Mile End there was a manor house belonging to the Abbots
of St. Osyth.
[8] Meeting with Katherine.
[9] After the burning of Sheen the new palace built on the site was
named Richmond.

1503. *Feb.* 2, Barking;[1] 3–11, Tower of London[2] (Death of Queen Elizabeth). *Mar.* 30, Baynard's Castle.[3] *April* 2, St. Paul's Cathedral ; 8, Baynard's Castle ; 10, Westminster ;[4] Windsor.[5] *May* 4, Westminster. *June* 23, Richmond. *July* 1, Eyton ; 8, Colly Weston ; 13, Westminster. *Sept.* 1; Tutbury; 4, Ashby ;[1] 6, Merivale Abbey ; 7, Astley ; 23, Speen, Banbury, Langley. *Oct.* 2, Minster Lovell, Abingdon ; 17, Cambridge.

1504. *Jan.* 25, Westminster (Opening of Seventh Parliament). *Aug.* 15, Nottingham Castle.[6] *Feb.* 8–*March* 23, Westminster. *April* 23, St. Paul's ;[2] *July* 8, Westminster ; 10, Richmond. *Aug.* 4, Sheppey Island ;[7] 25, Lewes ; 28, Alfold.[1] *Oct.* 1, Farnham Castle ;[8] 11–*Nov.* 1, Richmond.[1] *Nov.* 20–*Dec.* 5, Westminster.

1505. *Jan.* 12–20, Wanstead.[1] *Feb.* 24–28, Croydon ; 10, 15, 26, Canterbury. *April* 12, Chertsey ;[1] 14, Woking ;[1] 20, Chertsey ;[1] 21, Richmond.[7] *May* 1–25, Richmond. *June* 11, Richmond.[7] *July* 28, Otford (co. Kent) ; Windsor. *Aug.* 3, Charing ; 4–28, Knole. *Sept.* 13, Cranbourne ; 26–28, Otford. *Oct.* 15, Reading ; 17, Windsor.

1506. *Jan.* 31–*Feb.* 12, Windsor ;[9] *Feb.* 12–28, Greenwich. *Mar.* 1–2, Windsor.[9] *April* 15, Greenwich ;[10] 30, London.[7] *May* 8, Richmond ; 10–15, Westminster ;[7] 18, Richmond.[4] *June* 9, 12, Otford. *July* 23, Lambeth ; 30, Malshanger. *Aug.* 1, 2, Chichester ; 12, Wanstead ;[7] Greenwich.[7] *Sept.* 16, Guildford.[11] *Oct.* 1–18, Woking ;[7] 28, Windsor.[7] *Nov.* 5–*Dec.* 15, Westminster.[4]

1507. *Jan.* 28, Westminster. *March*, Richmond.[7] *April* 7, Richmond ; 11, Westminster ;[7] 15, Richmond ;[7] 20, Woking.[4] *May* 3, Richmond ;[4] 11, 20, Westminster.[7] *July* 17, Greenwich.[7] *Aug.* 27–*Sept.* 9, Woodstock.[10] *Sept.* 9, 15, Langley ;[12] 16–29,

---

[1] *Privy Purse Expenses.*
[2] *City Chronicle.*   [3] Leland, *Collectanea*, iv. 265.
[4] Rymer, *Fœdera.*
[5] King of Romans installed as Knight of the Garter.
[6] Ellis, *Letters*, III. (1), 117.
[7] Bergenroth, *Spanish Calendar.*
[8] This belonged to the Bishops of Winchester.
[9] Visit of Philip of Burgundy. *Memorials of Henry VII.* (Rolls Ser.), 302 *seq.*
[10] *Venetian Cal.*
[11] *L. and P. Henry VII.*, i. 367
[12] André, *Vita.*

Woodstock.[1] *Oct.* 1–5, Winchester.[1] *Nov.* 1, Richmond ; 11, Westminster ; 23–25, Richmond ; 25-*Dec.* 5, Westminster.[2] *Dec.* 13–18, Tower of London ;[3] 16, Wanstead ; Tower of London ;[2] 21–31, Richmond.[2]

1508. *Jan.* 1–7, Richmond ;[2] 7–10, Lanthony ;[2] 11, Chertsey ; 12, 13, Woking ; 20–31, Richmond. *Feb.* 1-*Mar.* 13, Richmond ; 14, At Bishop of Bath's ; 15-*May* 10, Greenwich. *May* 11–15, Eltham ; 15, Greenwich. *June* 14–29, Greenwich ; 30, "At Bishop of Bath's." *July* 1, Mortlake ; 3, Wandsworth ; 7, Richmond, Langley ; 13, Windsor, Staines, Wandsworth ; 14, Richmond ; 20, Greenwich ; 30, Stratford. *Aug.* 1–4, Wanstead ; 5, Eltham ; 9, Hatfield ; 14, Berking ; 23, Berwick (co. Essex). *Nov.* 5–7, Greenwich. *Dec.* 21, Richmond.

1509. *Feb.* 18, Westminster. *March–April,* Richmond. *April* 21, Richmond (death of the king).

---

[1] Bergenroth, *Spanish Calendar.*   [2] André, *Vita.*

II

THE STORY OF PERKIN WARBECK

BACON'S romantic and circumstantial account of
Perkin Warbeck's conspiracy long held the field, but
within the last twenty years it has been replaced
by a different version based upon Warbeck's public
confession,[1] and supported by other contemporary
evidence which was not available until comparatively
recently. Dr. Gairdner, who was the first to give the
revised account,[2] has been followed by Dr. Busch and
other writers. Bacon's account of the plot suffers
from the fact that it is practically an elaborate
embroidery of an originally doubtful statement. Following Hall, who had enlarged a statement made
by Polydor Vergil,[3] he makes the plot begin with
Margaret of Burgundy, and says that she set up the
pretender in the first place.[4] Perkin Warbeck's confession contradicts this story of the origin of the plot.
It must be admitted that contemporaries thought
Margaret originated the whole conspiracy, and André's
account of the affair supports this view;[5] but the
mistake can easily be accounted for. Margaret was

---

[1] Hall, *Chronicle*, 488–9; *City Chronicle*, ed. Kingsford, pp.
219–21.
  [2] *The Story of Perkin Warbeck* and *Henry VII*.
  [3] Hall, *Chronicle*, 462; Polydor Vergil, *Historiæ Anglicæ*, 588.
  [4] Bacon, *Works*, ed. Spedding, vi. 107.
  [5] André, *Vita*, 65–7, 72.

Warbeck's most prominent supporter in all but the preliminary stages of the plot. It was not until Warbeck reached her court that he became a prominent figure in Europe, and the knowledge of her help in its notorious stages and of the value of her constant championship was converted into a theory that she knew and prompted its obscure beginnings.

The fact that the story popularised by Bacon conflicted with the well-known confession of Perkin Warbeck was explained by two alternative suggestions, the first being that the confession was silent upon Margaret's share in the conspiracy because Henry wished to spare her. But this conflicts with evidence that was not available when it was made. Henry showed no signs of wishing to spare the duchess. On the contrary, he made Warbeck repeat, in the presence of the Spanish ambassador, his assertion of the duchess's later complicity.[1] The second suggestion is that the whole confession was a bogus affair, forged by Henry and circulated for his own motives. This is an absolutely gratuitous suggestion without a shred of evidence to support it, and it is contradicted by the first-rate evidence of the *City Chronicle*. The argument that, as the confession was very useful to Henry, he therefore invented it, is a curious instance of mistrust of the king, throwing suspicion on all his actions. As a matter of fact, the genuineness of the confession has been triumphantly vindicated. A search in the archives of Tournai has brought to light evidence that confirms its accuracy in the most trifling details.[2] Further, its general tenor is supported by two of Perkin's own letters that have survived, one written to his mother, the

---

[1] Bergenroth, *Cal. of Spanish Papers*, pp. 185–7.
[2] Gairdner, *Perkin Warbeck*, 265–9.

other to Isabella of Spain,[1] and by other contemporary evidence.[2]

Bacon's suggestion that Warbeck was an illegitimate son of Edward IV. must also be criticised.[3] It is based upon a misconception, originating with Speed, who misunderstood Bernard André's assertion that Warbeck was brought into England by a converted Jew to whom Edward had been godfather. André further relates that the boy had been brought up at the court of Edward IV. by this Jew, his master, and there learnt how to pose as the young Duke of York. This account is not found elsewhere, is contradicted by Warbeck's confession, conflicts with that given by Vergil and Hall, and is probably unreliable.

[1] Gairdner, *op. cit.*, 329; *Archæologia*, xxvii. 156–8, 199; Bergenroth, No. 85.

[2] *Letters and Papers*, Henry VII. (Rolls Ser.), ii. 294; Halliwell, *Letters*, i. 177.

[3] Bacon, *op. cit.*, 133.

III

THE STAR CHAMBER

THE controversy that long existed as to the origin
of the Star Chamber may now be regarded as settled.
Many points, no doubt, are still obscure, but they
are not of the first importance, and the decision that
most modern historians have arrived at is supported
by evidence obtained from a study of selections of
Star Chamber cases.[1] The view prevalent in the
seventeenth century, when the Star Chamber with
all its sins on its head was abolished by the Long
Parliament, was that the Star Chamber originated
with the Act of 1487, that its authority was derived
from that Act, and its competence limited to cases
named in it. Popular indignation, already strong,
was inflamed by the theory that the court had far
outrun its legal powers. This view has now been
proved to be unhistorical. Like "its twin sister
the Court of Chancery," the Star Chamber was an
expression in a specialised form of the judicial authority of the king in council. Such authority was of
immemorial prescriptive origin, and from the reign
of Edward III. the name Star Chamber was occasionally applied to the council when sitting in its
judicial capacity.[2] The famous Act of Henry VII.

[1] *Star Chamber Cases* (ed. Leadam), Selden Society; (ed. Brad-
ford), Somerset Rec. Soc.
[2] Recent researches have thrown light on the work of the Star
Chamber in 1485 and 1486. The *Liber Intrationum* (Harl. MS.,

therefore set up no new court, and did not touch the judicial powers inherent in the Star Chamber. It simply gave special summary powers to a small committee of the council, reinforced it with outsiders possessing legal experience, and prepared it to deal with a special class of cases that menaced the peace and safety of the kingdom. This committee continued its beneficent work all through the reign of Henry VII. ; its small size and wide powers rendering it specially swift and efficient. The elasticity of the court in its early days was remarkable. The members nominated in 1487 were varied by later statutes,[1] and in practice convenience rather than form dictated the membership. The theory that the chancellor, treasurer, and lord privy seal were the only judges has been replaced by the view that all members of the council present gave sentence as judges, the common law judges acting as their assessors.[2] In the beginning of the reign of Henry VIII. disorder had been stamped out, the work of the special court was done, and, at some unascertained date before the end of the reign, it was merged into the general body of the Star Chamber. The larger body, however, clung to the special powers conferred on its committee by statute, especially the power of examining defendants on oath, though it naturally

No. 305, Art. 2) contains notes of the business transacted in the court during these two years. The king often sat there in person. In 1486 the Star Chamber passed a resolution concerning rioting by the servants of noblemen and gentlemen (Lansdowne MSS., No. 83, Art. 72). See C. L. Scofield, *The Star Chamber*.

[1] By 11 Hen. VII., cap. 25, the clerk of the rolls is added, and the lord privy seal, the bishop, and the temporal lord of the council are omitted.

[2] *Year Book*, 6 Hen. VII., fo. 13. See Leadam, *Star Chamber Cases*, Intro. I. xlvi.–xlvii., for a full discussion of this intricate question.

refused to confine itself to the cases assigned by
Parliament to that committee, insisting on the wide
and indeterminate sphere of jurisdiction of its parent
the council. At the same time, the Privy Council
was exercising similar judicial functions, though the
distinction between it and the Star Chamber, if not
great, was recognisable. To put it briefly, though
the *personnel* of both courts was almost identical,
the Privy Council heard the more definitely political
offences, and the Star Chamber the legal offences ;
the former sat in private and at any time, the latter
in public and in term time only ; the latter had the
help of legal experts, who were not members of the
council.[1] The Star Chamber, therefore, was not of
statutory origin, and the Act of 1487 was only an
episode in its history. It was, however, a very important episode practically, because it gave the court
statutory authority to examine witnesses on oath and
issue summary writs, and historically because it led
to confusion as to the origin of the famous court.

[1] All these differences brought the Star Chamber more into line
with the ordinary law courts.

IV

HENRY VII. AND JUANA OF CASTILE

A series of documents have been discovered by Bergenroth which make it very doubtful whether Juana of Castile ever lost her reason. He suggests that she retained her sanity, even after years of barbarously close imprisonment, and that she was quite sane at the time when Henry was negotiating for a marriage with her. His view is that Ferdinand deliberately circulated accounts of her insanity, himself manufacturing proof of it in order to prevent her from governing Castile. Bergenroth's researches make it clear that Ferdinand did not inform Henry of the alleged nature of Juana's malady until some months after the negotiations were opened, and that as soon as he was informed of it he withdrew his suit. Though Henry is not entirely exonerated, the blackest stain on his character is removed.[1]

The extent of Juana's affliction—if it existed at this early date — was certainly exaggerated by Ferdinand, and Henry may have suspected, when the first sinister rumours reached him, that they were deliberately spread abroad by Ferdinand to prevent Juana from governing Castile. When she visited Henry's court in 1505 she was a very handsome woman, without a trace of the terrible malady which is said to have developed so rapidly

---

[1] Bergenroth, *Cal. of Span. Papers*, Supplementary Volume, pp 41–62.

after her husband's death. When in Flanders she
had shown great patience in a difficult situation.
The Venetian ambassador certainly thought her
husband and father were plotting against her, and
that they spread abroad these rumours because they
had found her very intractable and reluctant to
surrender her rights. In June 1506 Ferdinand and
Philip had signed a treaty pledging themselves to
resist any attempt of Juana's to meddle in the government of Castile. Later Ferdinand protested against
this treaty, using language quite inconsistent with
his daughter's insanity. He spoke of helping Juana
to recover her liberty and prerogatives, and, writing
to Katherine just after Philip's death, he spoke of
Juana's " retirement," not her incapacity, as the reason
for her not sharing in the government.

This was the state of affairs when Henry made
his first proposal for Juana's hand, and Ferdinand
wrote in reply that he did not yet know whether
his daughter was inclined to marry again—not a
word about her alleged madness—but that if she
did he would rather she married Henry than any
prince in Christendom. But on reflection, Ferdinand saw the danger of allowing a marriage between
Juana and Henry, and he seems to have resolved on
reviving for his own purposes the dark stories he and
Philip had spread about before. His letter to de
Puebla has been lost, but on 15th April 1507, the latter
wrote to his master describing an interview he had
had with the king at Richmond. This letter, which
proves that de Puebla had said something to Henry
throwing doubt upon Juana's state of mind, is important as the first evidence of Henry's knowledge
of the hints that Ferdinand was circulating. De
Puebla reported that he told the king that with such

a husband as Henry she would recover sooner than
with any other, and that if her infirmity proved
incurable, it would be no inconvenience if she were
to live in England, " For it seems to me that they
do not much mind her infirmity,[1] since I told them
that it does not prevent her from bearing children."
Nothing is here or elsewhere written to Henry that
the queen was incurably insane. Katherine's letters
to her father, giving messages from Henry, show not
the slightest indication that either of them thought
she was insane. Two letters written by Ferdinand
to Katherine in June do not allude to any infirmity
of Juana's, and expressed Ferdinand's intention of
learning his daughter's wishes and inclination with
regard to the match. He showed strange anxiety
that there should be no negotiations with Juana
directly while he was absent from Castile, but wrote
of the comfort it would be to him to leave his daughter
and all his kingdoms under Henry's care and protection. In September negotiations as to whether
Henry's proposed bride should live in England or
Castile were going on, and in one of de Puebla's
letters there is the often-quoted phrase, " The council
of the King of England desires extremely that this
match should be concluded even if worse things
should be said about the infirmity (*dolencia*) of the
daughter of your highness." (Bergenroth trans-
lates " dolencia " as insanity, which seems to be
unusual.) Katherine's letters to Ferdinand and to
Juana make it incredible that she could have been
informed of her sister's alleged madness, and it would
have been strange if Ferdinand told Henry what
he had concealed from Katherine. She wrote to

---

[1] The words used to describe her state are " enfermedad,"
" dolencia," which are to be translated sickness, infirmity.

Juana in October telling her how much Henry had
been attracted by her when she visited England,
and how reluctant he had been to let her go, until
his council advised him, " as he is a very passionate
king," not to come between husband and wife. She
adds some elaborate praise of Henry : " He is a
prince who is feared and esteemed by the whole of
Christendom on account of his wisdom, vast wealth,
and having at his command a great force of well-
trained troops. Above all he is endowed with the
highest virtues. If Juana marries him she will become the most illustrious and the most powerful
queen in the world." Katherine concludes by calling
God to witness that the letter expressed what she
genuinely wished.

Things were going too far for Ferdinand, who
seems to have made up his mind to forward reports
which would put an end to Henry's suit for the
heiress of Castile. He wrote to de Puebla telling
him that Juana still took about with her the corpse
of her late husband, and would not permit it to be
buried. This report was quite effective; though we
have no actual proof that Ferdinand's story was
communicated to Henry, there is a strong presump-
tion that it was, as the wording of the King of Spain's
letter to de Puebla suggests that he intended it for
transmission to the king. Something certainly occurred
to make Henry give up the idea of a marriage with
Juana about this time. He had sent John Stile
to Castile with letters for Juana in the autumn of
1507—the tenor of Stile's instructions makes it incredible that Henry was knowingly wooing a mad
woman—but nothing more is heard of the proposal.
It was reported in the spring of 1508 that nothing
more would be heard of the match. Henry seems to

have had more scruples than he is commonly credited with.

The unhappy Juana was kept a close prisoner as long as her father lived, and lived her life of misery forgotten by Europe or only remembered as the " mad queen of Castile." Bergenroth's researches seem to prove that she never lost her reason, in spite of shameful brutality and neglect, until just the very end of her life.   Her obstinacy and dislike of religious observance may have seemed like madness to the piety of Spain and of the Inquisition.

V

BIBLIOGRAPHY

I. Records

Unfortunately there is as yet no printed calendar of the
Patent and Close Rolls of the reign. The two volumes of
Materials for the Reign of Henry VII. (ed. Campbell, Rolls
Series) supply this deficiency for the years 1485 to 1488.
The same collection prints extracts from the Roll of the
Great Wardrobe and other Wardrobe Accounts. There is
no calendar of State Papers for the period. The nearest
approach to it is to be found in the two volumes of *Letters
and Papers relating to the Reigns of Richard III. and
Henry VII.* (ed. Gairdner, Rolls Series), in which many of
the king's letters to his ambassadors, to foreign princes, to
the Pope, to his family, servants, and subjects, are printed,
together with many other diplomatic documents. The
Appendix to the second volume contains brief notes from
the Patent Rolls. Other royal letters may be found in the
collections edited by Ellis and by Halliwell, in *Letters of Royal
Ladies* (ed. Everett Green), and in *Christchurch Letters* (Camden Society). The *Calendar of Spanish Papers* (ed. Bergenroth, vol. i. and supplementary volume), and the *Calendar
of Venetian Papers* (ed. Brown, vol. i.), contain a mass of
diplomatic correspondence which is invaluable for the
history of the foreign policy of the reign. Rymer's *Fœdera*
(vols. xii., xiii.) gives the text of treaties and other diplomatic documents. The *Memorials of Henry VII.* (ed.
Gairdner, Rolls Series) contains, in addition to André's
works, accounts by the Richmond Herald of several em-

bassies of which he was a member (including the well-known report on the Queen of Naples), and of the visit of the Archduke Philip, together with a report by John Stile of his mission to Spain, and a series of Spanish despatches.

None of the general accounts of the reign have been printed, and very few have been calendared. The *Privy Purse Expenses*, printed by Bentley in his *Excerpta Historica*, is an extract from, rather than a transcript of, the king's private accounts. Some of the queen's expenditure is revealed in the *Privy Purse Expenses of Elizabeth of York* (ed. Nicholas). Oppenheim's *Naval Accounts*, and the reports of expenditure by Hattcliffe in Ireland (printed in *Letters and Papers of Henry VII.*), are almost the only other books in this class.

Little has been done towards printing the legal proceedings of the reign. The *Year Book of Henry VII.* (ed. 1585), the calendar of the Baga de Secretis (which appears in the Thirty-seventh Report of the Deputy-Keeper of the Public Records), the collections of *Star Chamber Cases*, printed by the Selden Society, the Somerset Record Society, and the Yorks Archæological Society, and the *Select Cases in the Court of Requests* (Selden Society), are the chief sources of information.

For ecclesiastical history, Wilkins' *Concilia* (vol. iii.) prints the records of the proceedings of Convocation, with episcopal letters, and so on. The *Register of Bishop Fox* (Camden Society), the *Visitation of Norwich*, and the *Visitation of Southwell*, are also useful.

The calendars of *Carew Papers* (especially the Book of Howth), and the *Calendar of Documents relating to Scotland*, are the authorities for the king's relations with Ireland and Scotland. The Parliamentary history of the reign is to be found in the *Rotuli Parliamentorum* (Rolls Series, vol. vi.), the *Statutes of the Realm* (vol. ii.), and the *Irish Statutes*. From the mass of published borough records the *Letter Books* (ed. Sharpe), *York Records* (ed. Davies), *Records of the Borough of Leicester* (ed. Bateson), and *Ricart's Calendar of Bristol* (ed. Toulmin Smith), may be mentioned as specially important for this reign. The *Will of Henry VII.*, which has been printed, is also valuable.

II. CHRONICLES AND CONTEMPORARY WRITERS

By far the most important is Polydor Vergil's famous work *Anglicæ Historiæ Libri XXVII.*, the twenty-sixth book of which contains a spirited account of the king's reign, written by an Italian who was in England from 1502 onwards. He made a magnificent use of his opportunities, and the greater part of his work, together with his estimate of the king's character, stands unchallenged. Bernard André's work, the *Vita Henrici Septimi* (*Memorials of Henry VII.*, Rolls Series), is of much less value. Though a contemporary, and, by his position as poet laureate, closely connected with the court, his account is confused, inaccurate, and imaginative, written in an adulatory strain, and interlarded with apocryphal oratory. The earlier part of his *Annales* (the account of the years 1504–5) is the usual rambling panegyric, the latter part (the history of the years 1507–8) is much less ambitious and more useful, containing much valuable information.

Hall's *Chronicle* is practically a translation of Polydor Vergil's book, but contains some additional matter. The *City Chronicle*, printed in *Chronicles of London* (ed. C. L. Kingsford), Stow's *Chronicle*, the *Chronicle of Calais* (Camden Society), the *Grey Friars' Chronicle* (Camden Society) Roger Fabyan's *Chronicle*, and the *Cambrian Register* are all valuable. A very interesting account of England, from the point of view of the foreign observer, appears in the *Italian Relation* (Camden Society). In Leland's *Collectanea* (vols. iv. and v.) are printed contemporary accounts of many of the great ceremonies of the reign. This may be supplemented by the *Rutland Papers*, the *Paston Letters*, the *Trevelyan Papers*, and the *Plumpton Correspondence.* The *Cely Papers* throw light on the wool trade, and the *Utopia* of Sir Thomas More gives a picture of England at the beginning of the new century. The *Pilgrimage of Sir Richard Guyldford* (Camden Society) and the *Hardwicke Papers* are of minor importance.

Contemporary ballads which throw light on popular feeling are the *Song of the Lady Bessy* and the *Ballad of Bosworth Field* (printed among the *Percy MSS.* (ed. Hales and Furnivall), Dunbar's *Thistle and the Rose,* Alexander Barclay's *Ship of Fools.* *Les Douze Triomphes de Henry VII.,* a French poem attributed to Bernard André, is printed in the *Memorials of Henry VII.* John Fisher's *Sermon on the Death of Henry VII.,* and his *Month's Mind of the Lady Margaret* (printed by the Early English Text Society) are valuable

III. LATER WRITERS

Bacon's *Life of Henry VII.* occupies an unique position both for its unrivalled style and for the fact that it gives an account of the reign which was copied by all writers until the nineteenth century.

Other works of importance are :—Dudley, *Tree of the Commonwealth;* Walter Harris, *Hibernica;* Herbert, *Life of Henry VIII.;* Hutton, *Battle of Bosworth Field;* Pinkerton, *History of Scotland;* Speed, *History of England,* 1611 ; Starkey, *Dialogue;* Zurita, *Anales de la Corona de Aragon,* 1610.

IV. MODERN WRITERS

Of modern writers, by far the most important are Dr. Gairdner and Dr. Busch.

Dr. Gairdner in his *Henry VII.* (English Statesmen Series), his *Story of Perkin Warbeck,* and his introductions to the *Memorials of Henry VII.,* and to the *Letters and Papers,* gave the history of the reign in the light of modern research for the first time.

Dr. Busch's *England under the Tudors* (vol. i.) is invaluable for its very full references, notes, and criticisms of authorities. Dr. Stubbs' *Lectures on Medieval and Modern History* contain a brilliant sketch of the reign. Other works of importance are :—Anderson, *Origin of Commerce ;* *Archæologia* (vols. xxvii., lv.) ; Bagwell, *Ireland under the Tudors ;* Biddle, *Memoirs of Sebastian Cabot ;* Bourne, *English Seamen under the Tudors ;* Clowes, *Royal Navy ;* Cooper, *Margaret, Countess of Richmond ;* Cunningham, *Growth of English Industry and Commerce ;* *Dictionary of National Biography ;* *English Historical Review* (vols. iii., vi., viii., xiv., xxii., xxiv.) ; Fisher, *Early Tudors* (Political History of England) ; Fortescue, *History of British Army ;* Froude, *Life and Times of Erasmus ;* Gairdner, *Cambridge Modern History* (vol. i. ch. 24) ; Gasquet, *Eve of the Reformation ;* Gross, *Gild Merchant ;* Halsted, *Life of Margaret Beaufort ;* Hakluyt, *Voyages ;* Hallam, *Constitutional History ;* Hudson, *Star Chamber ;* Innes, *Twelve Tudor Statesmen ;* Ives, *Select Papers ;* Maitland, *Lectures on Constitutional History ;* Molinet, *Chroniques,* 1476–1566 ; Mullinger, *University of Cambridge ;* Nichols, *Epistles of Erasmus ;* Pollard, *Factors in Modern History ;* Reeves, *History of English Law* (ed. Finlason) ; Thorold Rogers, *History of Agriculture and Prices ;* Scofield, *Star Chamber ;* Seebohm, *Oxford Reformers ;* Smith, *History of Waterford ;* Stephen, *History of Criminal Law ;* Stubbs, *Constitutional History ;* Traill, *Social England* (vol. ii.) ; Tytler, *History of Scotland ;* Ware, *Annales.*

INDEX

ABDUCTION of heiresses, 257
Abingdon, 54, 411, 413–4, 416–8
Abingdon, abbey, 412
Abingdon, abbot, 75, 112
Acton Turville, 415
Agriculture, 185–7
Agriculture and Prices, History of, 435
Aids, 272, 274
Ainsworth, Henry, 84
Albany, Duke of, 137
Albret, Lord d', 73, 82, 92, 94, 100
Alcock, John, Bp. of Ely, *see* Ely
Alexander VI., Pope, 125, 127, 229-30, 140-1, 259, 330
Alfonzo, King of Naples, (1494), 126
Aliens, subsidy from, 68
Alnwick, 415
Alresford, 415, 418
Amboise, Cardinal d', 367
America, North, 320, 323–4
Amersham, 311
Anales de la Corona de Aragon, 434
Anderson, Adam, 435
Andover, 417
André, Bernard, 34, 313, 431, 433–4
Angoulême, Margaret of, *see* Margaret
Angus, Earl of, 134, 145
Anne (Nevil, of Warwick), Queen of England, 14
Anne (of Brittany), Queen of

France, 7, 72–3, 77–8, 82–5, 92, 94, 96–7, 99–100, 102–3, 104 *n.*, 203
Anne (of Beaujeu), Regent of France, 13, 72
Antwerp, 105, 118, 165, 168–9, 172, 174, 227, 233–4
Aragon, *see* Spain, *and* Ferdinand (of Aragon), King of Spain
Architecture, 314–5
Armagh, Archbp. of, 294
Army, 43, 283–4 ; bibliography, 435
Arran, Earl of, 364
Art, 314
Arthur, Prince of Wales, birth, 56–7 ; created Prince of Wales, 413 *n.*, death, 230–1, 387 ; marriage, 79–82, 90, 102, 136, 204–9, 211–2, 216–25, 328 ; regent, 106
Artillery, 283–4, 304
Arundel, 413
Ashby, 418
Ashford, 413
Astley, 418
Astwood, ——, 123, 212
Atherstone, 19
Attainders, 47–9, 67–8, 123, 255
Attwater, John, *see* Walter, John
Audley, Jas. Touchet, Lord, 148, 150–51
Ayala, Pedro de, 144–5, 151–2, 154–6, 201, 209, 321, 369
Aylesbury, 416
Aynsworth, ——, 79

437

Exeter, Rich. Fox, Bp. of, 9, 12, 22 *n.*, 36, 41, 43
Eyton, 418

FABYAN, Roger, 433
Factors in Modern History, 435
Falmouth, 344
Farnham, nr. Guildford, 148
Farnham Castle, 418
Faversham Abbey, 415–6
Ferdinand (of Aragon), King of Spain, Breton marriage for Don Juan suggested, 96; Castilian policy, 334–5, 337, 348–9, 351–2, 356, 365, 367; Columbus patronised, 318–9; Crusade suggested to, 362; French alliance, 98 *n.*, 110, 119; Holy League, 125, 128, 135, 204; Juana's affliction exaggerated, 351–2, 426; League of Cambrai, 367; marriage negotiations for Katherine of Aragon, 79–83, 89–91, 102, 119, 135, 199, 201, 204–7, 217–9, 231–2, 328–35, 350, 354, 356–8, 369–70; Milanese policy, 229; personal appearance, 337–8; position after Isabella's death, 334–5, 337; Roussillon attacked, 96; Roussillon and Cerdagne recovered, 110; second marriage, 341–2; Warbeck in relation to, 128, 152, 205, 207
Fernandez, Diego, 358–61
Ferrara, 314
Ferrers, Lord, 22, 49
Finance, account of, 269–82; benevolences, *see* Benevolences; commercial policy in relation to, 162–3, 189–92; crown lands, *see* Crown lands; customs, *see* Customs; fines for Warbeck rebellion, 158; French tribute, 109; grant

by council of 1497, 146; Irish, 300–3; loans, 146–7, 275; Parliamentary grants, 46, 68, 86–9, 97, 102, 147; purveyance, 47, 280; tonnage and poundage, 46, 272; treasure, 189–90
Fines (amercements), 277–8
Fines, statute of, 260
Fisher, John, Bp. of Rochester, *see* Rochester; ——, 435
Fisheries, 167, 187, 320–2
Fitzgerald, Jas., 289; Thomas, 63, 65, 292
Fitzwalter, Lord, 123, 377
FitzWilliam, Sir Thomas, 253
Flammock, Thos., 147, 150
Flanders, 72–3, 78, 92–3, 98, 105, 118, 127, 353; trade with, 118, 165–8, 170, 173, 184
Flint Castle, 270
Florence, 126; trade with, 178
Fœdera (Rymer's), *see* Rymer's *Fœdera*
Foix, Germaine de, *see* Germaine, Queen of Spain
Fontarabia, 94
Foreign affairs, 27, 70–111, 117–21, 125–30, 134–42, 196–239, 326–70
Forests, 37, 256–7
Forgery, 262
Fortescue, ——, 435
Fowlers, 414
Fox, Richard, Bp. of Exeter, *see* Exeter; Bp. of Durham, *see* Durham
France, 72–7, 81–5, 90–111, 119, 121, 125–7, 136–41, 202–4, 218, 341, 353, 366–9; trade with, 180–1
Franciscans, 391 *n.*
Frankfort, treaty of, 94, 98
Frederick III., Emperor, 120
Frefolk, 417
Froude, James Anthony, 435